ecpr PRESS

Decision-Making under Ambiguity and Time Constraints
Assessing the Multiple-Streams Framework

Edited by
Reimut Zohlnhöfer and Friedbert W. Rüb

ecpr PRESS

© Reimut Zohlnhöfer and Friedbert W. Rüb 2016

First published by the ECPR Press in 2016

The ECPR Press is the publishing imprint of the European Consortium for Political Research (ECPR), a scholarly association, which supports and encourages the training, research and cross-national co-operation of political scientists in institutions throughout Europe and beyond.

ECPR Press
Harbour House
Hythe Quay
Colchester
CO2 8JF
United Kingdom

Typeset by Lapiz Digital Services

Printed and bound by Lightning Source

British Library Cataloguing in Publication Data

A catalogue record for this book is available from the British Library

ISBN: 978-1-785521-25-6
PDF ISBN: 978-1-785521-67-6
EPUB ISBN: 978-1785521-68-3
KINDLE ISBN: 978-1-785521-69-0

www.ecpr.eu/ecprpress

ECPR Press Series Editors:
Peter Kennealy (European University Institute)
Ian O'Flynn (Newcastle University)
Alexandra Segerberg (Stockholm University)
Laura Sudulich (University of Kent)

More from the ECPR Press Studies in Political Science series:

Global Tax Governance
ISBN: 9781785521263
Peter Dietsch and Thomas Rixen

New Perspectives on Negative Campaigning
ISBN: 9781785521287
Alessandro Nai and Annemarie Walter

Political Violence in Context
ISBN: 9781785521447
Lorenzo Bosi, Niall Ó Dochartaigh and Daniela Pisoiu

Spreading Protest
ISBN: 9781910259207
Donatella della Porta and Alice Mattoni

**Please visit www.ecpr.eu/ecprpress for up-to-date information about new
and forthcoming publications.**

Table of Contents

List of Figures and Tables

List of Abbreviations

Abbreviation	Long form	Meaning
A		
ACF		Advocacy coalition framework
APE		Actor-promoted event
C		
CBI		Confederation of British Industry
CDU/CSU	Christlich Demokratische Union Deutschlands /Christlich- Soziale Union in Bayern	Christian Democratic Union of Germany / Christian Social Party in Bavaria, German parliamentary group
CEER		Council of European Energy Regulators
CiU	Convergència i Unió	Convergence and Union, Catalan Nationalist Coalition
D		
DEHOGA	Deutscher Hotel- und Gaststättenverband	German Hotel and Restaurant Association
DHS		Department of Homeland Security
E		
EAEC		European Atomic Energy Community
EC		European Commission
EEC		European Economic Community
EITC		Earned Income Tax Credit
ERC	Esquerra Republicana de Catalunya	Republican Left of Catalonia
ERGEG		European Regulators' Group for Electricity and Gas
F		
FAA		Federal Aviation Administration
FDP	Freie Demokratische Partei	Free Democratic Party of Germany
FEMA		Federal Emergency Management Agency
FYROM		Former Yugoslav Republic of Macedonia
G		
GC		Garbage can
GTE		Gas Transmission Europe

H

HI		Historical institutionalism

I

ICS	Institut Català de la Salut	Catalan Health Institute
ICV	Iniciativa per Catalunya Verds	Eco-socialist coalition Initiative for Catalonia Greens
i.e.	*id est*	that is; in other words
IP		Institutional processualism

M

MF		Madrid Forum
MP		Member of Parliament
MSF		Multiple-streams framework

N

NAPE		Non-actor-promoted event
NAF		Narrative policy-analysis framework
NCTU		National Counter-Terrorism Unit
NDYP		New Deal for Young People

O

OPA		Oil Pollution Act

P

PET		Punctuated equilibrium theory
PKK	Partiya Karkerên Kurdistan	Kurdish Labour Party
PP	Partit Popular / Partido Popular	Conservative People's Party of Catalonia / Spain
PSC	Partit dels Socialistes de Catalunya	Party of the Socialists of Catalonia

S

SAP	Sveriges Socialdemokratiska Arbetareparti	Social Democratic Labour Party of Sweden
SPD	Sozialdemokratische Partei Deutschlands	Social Democratic Party of Germany

V

VDA	Verband der Automobilindustrie	German Association of the Automotive Industry
VdC	Verband der Cigarettenindustrie	Association of the Tobacco Industry

Contributors

NICOLÁS BARBIERI is a postdoctoral researcher at the Public Policies and Government Institute and adjunct professor at the Department of Political Science, both at the Universitat Autònoma de Barcelona. He was visiting research fellow at the Université Montpellier I. He has published on policy-change, social and cultural policies and non-profit organisations, in journals such as *International Journal of Cultural Policies*, *Métropoles* and *Pôle Sud*.

THOMAS A. BIRKLAND is the William T. Kretzer Professor of Public Policy in the School of Public and International Affairs at North Carolina State University. His research is on how sudden events like natural disasters and industrial accidents influence the policy-process. He is the author of *After Disaster* (1997) and *Lessons of Disaster* (2006).

RAQUEL GALLEGO is Professor at the Department of Political Science and Public Law and researcher at the Institute of Government and Public Policies both at the Universitat Autònoma de Barcelona. She has published on public administration and management reform, welfare policies and decentralisation, in journals such as *Governance*; *Public Administration*; *Public Management Review*; *International Public Management Journal*; and *Regional and Federal Studies*, as well as in edited books by Routledge and Ashgate.

SHEILA GONZÁLEZ is adjunct professor at the Department of Political Science at the Universitat Autònoma de Barcelona and at the Department of Arts and Humanities at Universitat Oberta de Catalunya. She has been visiting research fellow at Universidad Nacional Autónoma de México, Universität Bremen and Instituto Politécnico Nacional de México. She has published on public-policy analysis, migration and educational policies and participatory processes, in journals such as *Educational Policy* and *Educación XXI*.

DAN HANSÉN, PhD, is associate professor in political science at the Swedish Defence University. His research focuses on various aspects of crisis-management, in particular in relation to the law-enforcement sector, with themes such as organisational learning, policy-reform craft and co-ordination/collaboration in crisis. His work has been published in article/chapter format by the Cambridge University Press and in the *Journal of Public Administration Research and Theory*; *Public Administration*; and the *Journal of Contingencies and Crisis Management*, amongst others.

NICOLE HERWEG is a postdoctoral researcher at the Institute of Political Science at Heidelberg University. Her primary field of interest is comparative public-policy analysis, particularly energy policy. She has authored or co-authored several articles on theoretical refinements or empirical applications of the multiple-streams framework.

MICHAEL HOWLETT is Burnaby Mountain Chair in the Department of Political Science at Simon Fraser University in Burnaby, British Columbia, Canada and Yong Pung How Chair Professor in the Lee Kuan Yew School of Public Policy at the National University of Singapore. He works on public-policy theory, with a special interest in resource and environmental policy. His most recent book is *Canadian Public Policy: Selected studies in process and style* (Toronto: University of Toronto Press, 2013).

CHRISTIAN HUß is a Ph.D. student at the University of Heidelberg, Germany. He holds a diploma in Political Science from the University of Bamberg. His research focuses on energy, environmental and economic policy in Germany and Europe as well as the development of the multiple-streams framework in general. In his dissertation, he analyses the several windows of opportunity for phasing-out nuclear power in Germany, using the multiple-streams framework as a theoretical basis. One of his recent papers on environmental policy in Germany during the Merkel II cabinet is published in the peer-reviewed journal *German Politics*.

ÅSA KNAGGÅRD is senior lecturer at the Department of Political Science at Lund University. She studies the interrelation between science and politics in multiple contexts and is presently involved in a project on scientific outreach. Recent publications by Knaggård include 'What do policy-makers do with scientific uncertainty? The incremental character of Swedish climate change policy-making' (2014) and, together with Håkan Pihl, 'The Green State and the design of self-binding – lessons from monetary policy' (in press). Knaggård is affiliated with LUCID (Lund University Centre of Excellence for Integration of Social and Natural Dimensions of Sustainability).

JOHANNA KUHLMANN is a research assistant at the University of Münster, Germany. Her research focuses on policy analysis, comparative welfare-state research (especially labour-market policy) and integration policy.

ALLAN MCCONNELL is professor in the Department of Government and International Relations, University of Sydney, and visiting professor in the School of Government and Public Policy at the University of Strathclyde. His area of interest is public policy, with a particular specialism in issues of policy success, policy failure and the politics of crisis. A major solo work is *Understanding Policy Success: Rethinking public policy*, Palgrave Macmillan, 2010.

ANTHONY PERL is Professor of Urban Studies and Political Science at Simon Fraser University in Vancouver, British Columbia, Canada. His research crosses disciplinary and national boundaries to explore policy decisions made about transportation, cities and the environment. He has published in dozens of scholarly journals and authored five books, recently including *Studying Public Policy*, with Michael Howlett and M. Ramesh, and *Transport Revolutions: Moving people and freight without oil*, with Richard Gilbert.

IRIS REUS is a PhD student at the Bamberg Graduate School of Social Sciences, University of Bamberg. Her research and publications focus on policy analysis and federalism, with special attention to the German *Länder*.

FRIEDBERT W. RÜB is Professor for Political Sociology and Social Policy at the Department for Social Sciences at Humboldt-Universität zu Berlin. His research focuses on the theory of political decision-making, the development of welfare-state structures and social-policy analysis. Currently, he investigates rapid policy-changes in Germany and the vulnerability of democratic societies.

HARALD SÆTREN is Professor at the Department of Administration and Organisation Theory at the University of Bergen, Norway. His current research interests include policy-design and implementation dynamics, comparative public policy, public-policy theories, organisation theories, organisational change and decision-making. His latest major publications include a special issue on Implementation Research in the Age of Governance, in *Public Policy & Administration* 2014 (co-edited with Peter Hupe), which includes his paper 'Implementing the third generation research paradigm in policy implementation research: an empirical assessment'.

FLORIAN SPOHR is a research associate at the Ruhr University Bochum, Germany (Chair of Comparative Politics). He is currently working on a study of interest-mediation in the German parliament. Recent and forthcoming publications include articles about European constitutional policies, policy analysis and labour-market policies.

MEGAN K. WARNEMENT is a doctoral candidate in the Department of Public Administration in the School of Public and International Affairs at North Carolina State University. Her research interests are in policy change and learning after disasters.

NIKOLAOS ZAHARIADIS is professor of political science at the University of Alabama at Birmingham, USA. He has published widely on issues of comparative public policy and European political economy. His latest edited book, *Frameworks of the European Union's Policy Process: Competition and complementarity across the theoretical divide*, was published by Routledge in 2013.

REIMUT ZOHLNHÖFER is Professor of Political Science at the University of Heidelberg, Germany. His research interests include political economy, theories of the policy process and West European politics. He is author and editor of numerous books and has published in many leading political science journals including *Comparative Political Studies*; *Governance*; *Journal of European Public Policy*; *Journal of European Social Policy*; *Social Policy & Administration* and *West European Politics*.

Preface

This volume grew out of a workshop on 'Decision-Making under Ambiguity and Time Constraints: Assessing the Multiple-Streams Approach' at the ECPR's Joint Sessions of Workshops at Johannes-Gutenberg-University Mainz (Germany) in March 2013. The two workshop directors, who would later also become the editors of this volume, had been interested in the multiple-streams framework for some time but felt that a systematic academic debate about the framework was essentially missing. While apparently more and more researchers employed the framework (or parts thereof) empirically, no discussion about the framework's strengths and weaknesses, its theoretical refinement and empirical applicability was detectable. There certainly were a number of empirical applications and ideas how to refine the framework in the literature; but many of these researchers did not seem to respond to what others were doing. Thus, we felt it was time to take stock of the literature and bring together a group of scholars that would engage in a profound discussion on what the multiple-streams framework was good for and what its limitations were.

At the Mainz workshop, fourteen papers were presented and discussed intensively by a group that brought together promising young scholars and more experienced senior researchers. In general, the debate focused on three topics:

a) Theoretical status and relevance of the multiple-streams framework: are all the categories, terms, and parts of the framework well developed or do they need refinement or re-conceptualisation? Is the theoretical lens a heuristic, a concept, a framework or a theory from which hypotheses can be systematically derived (and if so, what could they be)?

b) Empirical application: can the multiple-streams framework be falsified? How can the key concepts of the approach be operationalised for empirical measurement? Does the framework travel to political systems other than the one it was developed for, like parliamentary or multi-level systems? Does it work for different policy fields? And can it fruitfully be applied to stages of the policy-making process other than agenda-setting?

c) Comparative assessment: how robust is the multiple-streams framework compared to other theoretical frameworks or theories, like the advocacy-coalition framework; the punctuated-equilibrium theory; the various institutionalisms; the veto-players theory; social constructivism and so on? And where can elements of other theories or frameworks be combined with the multiple-streams framework in order to expand its explanatory leverage?

The chapters of this volume are – sometimes substantially – revised versions of these fourteen papers from the ECPR workshop (with one chapter being a synthesis of two papers from the Mainz workshop). They critically discuss various aspects of the approach and can essentially be grouped into three parts. While the chapters of Part One deal with overarching questions, the contributions of Part Two discuss many of the most important elements of the framework. Part Three is devoted to empirical applications of the multiple-streams framework in different political systems, different issue-areas and different stages of the policy cycle. Many of the chapters show the explanatory power of the multiple-streams framework – even when applied to decision-making in political systems other than the US. At the same time, many chapters also point to problems that scholars will have to deal with if the framework is to be applied successfully and with substantial value added. While many authors suggest solutions to some of these problems, other issues seem more complicated and need further discussion – and that is exactly what this volume aims at: to spark a lively debate on the theoretical strengths and weaknesses as well as the empirical applicability of the multiple-streams framework.

The editors would like to thank a number of people who helped in putting the volume together. First and foremost, we would like to thank the participants in the ECPR workshop and the authors of the chapters for the excellent discussions in Mainz and for their willingness to take our comments to the individual chapters into consideration and revise their papers repeatedly in response to these comments. We would also like to thank our ECPR Press editors for their guidance and a very pleasant co-operation. Finally, we are very grateful to Linda Voigt for assistance with the manuscript and Deborah Savage for copy-editing.

Heidelberg/Berlin, October 2014
Reimut Zohlnhöfer and Friedbert W. Rüb

Chapter One

Introduction: Policy-Making under Ambiguity and Time Constraints

Reimut Zohlnhöfer and Friedbert W. Rüb

Introduction

When John W. Kingdon published his seminal book *Agendas, Alternatives, and Public Policy* in 1984, it was essentially a book on a comparatively narrow subject, namely, agenda-setting in the political system of the United States of America. And the empirical basis of that study was even narrower, as Kingdon had only investigated health and transport policy in detail, essentially during the 1970s. Nonetheless, one of the core insights of that book struck a chord in the wider literature – namely that policy-making is not an exercise in rational problem-solving. Rather, participation in many policy-making forums is fluid and most policy-makers do not know what they want (in terms of policy) most of the time and would not know how to attain particular policy goals even if they knew which goals they were after. Therefore, there is no systematic connection between a problem and a solution; decisions rather come about as solutions 'look out for' problems and get 'coupled' to these problems by policy-entrepreneurs.

It is certainly no wonder that Kingdon developed his ideas (which themselves were an adaptation of Cohen, March and Olsen's (1972) 'garbage-can' (GC) model of choice, as Harald Saetren reminds us in his contribution (2016, Chapter Two of this volume)) with the US political system in mind. The American presidential system seemed to approximate the assumptions on which the garbage-can model and Kingdon's ideas rested much more closely than the much more orderly (Zahariadis 2003: 1) parliamentary systems prevalent in Western Europe. Thus, the applicability of Kingdon's work was initially restricted mainly to agenda-setting in the United States and Kingdon himself never made an attempt to formulate a more general framework.

Nevertheless, Kingdon's book did provide the foundation of what later became known as the 'multiple-streams framework' (MSF), a framework that nowadays belongs to the most-cited theoretical approaches in the field of policy analysis (see Zahariadis 2014: 25; Herweg 2016). In a recent literature review, Jones *et al.* (2015) report that they found no less than 311 English-language peer-reviewed journal articles applying the MSF published since the year 2000. Thus, at least quantitatively, the MSF seems to be applied more frequently than other theories of the policy process. Baumgartner *et al.* (2014), for example, in a similar endeavour regarding the punctuated equilibrium theory (PET), came up with only 303 PET-related publications – and that included 63 non-journal publications and covered a longer period, starting in 1991. Similarly, Jenkins-Smith *et al.* (2014: 210) only found 224 publications (including eight books and thirteen book chapters) applying the advocacy coalition framework between 1987 and 2013.

Moreover, application of the multiple streams framework has been widened considerably; it is now applied to very different issue-areas, from the regulation of the sugar market (Ackrill and Kay 2011) to labour-market policy (Zohlnhöfer and Herweg 2014); and from devolution (Münter 2005; Bundgaard and Vrangbæk 2007) to privatisation (Zahariadis 1995), to give just a few examples. Moreover, many of these empirical studies also applied the MSF to political systems that differed substantially from the presidential system of the United States. Thus, scholars applied the framework in the context of parliamentary systems, among others to the United Kingdom (Zahariadis 1995; Münter 2005), Denmark (Bundgaard and Vrangbæk 2007) and Germany (Zohlnhöfer and Herweg 2014); to semi-presidential systems like France (Zahariadis 1995); and even to the European Union (Copeland and James 2014). Finally, and probably most importantly, the multiple-streams framework has been extended to explain decision-making rather than just agenda-setting (*cf.* Zahariadis 1995; Münter 2005; Zohlnhöfer and Herweg 2014).

The success of the multiple-streams framework

The multiple-streams framework's success (in terms of applications and citations) probably depended on at least two conditions. On the one hand, to borrow from the MSF's terminology, an academic entrepreneur was needed to prove the framework's wider applicability. As John Kingdon himself refrained from further elaborating on his book – he even declined Paul Sabatier's invitation to contribute a piece on his framework to the volume *Theories of the Policy Process* (Sabatier 2007b: 9) – someone else had to adopt the project and make its popularisation his pet project. That someone probably was Nikolaos Zahariadis, who, in the 1990s, published a book and a number of journal papers in which he applied Kingdon's ideas to privatisation policy in European countries and adapted the approach accordingly (Zahariadis 1992, 1995, 1996). Thus, he demonstrated that Kingdon's approach could fruitfully be applied empirically even in countries other than the United States, with only limited modification. Later studies on other countries and further extensions of the framework followed (Zahariadis 2003, 2005, 2008, 2014).

The second condition that helps explain the MSF's citation success is that its application in contexts for which it was not developed seems to have become increasingly attractive. This is because the terms under which policy-making takes place in other countries than the US (and in particular in the parliamentary systems of Western Europe) have started more and more to resemble the assumptions upon which the MSF was built. In other words: the conditions under which policies are made have changed substantially in recent years – not least in the allegedly more orderly parliamentary systems of Western Europe. With regard to what the multiple-streams framework conceptualises as the problem stream, issues have grown ever more complex and politically more contestable. In many cases, ranging from nuclear energy to the European debt-crisis, even experts from the scientific community vehemently disagree about feasible policy options. So it is fair to say that governments in all advanced democracies often do not fully understand the problems they have to deal with and they do not know if the policies they choose will solve the problems at hand. Furthermore, depending on the policy issue, problem-production and (national) problem-solving have become disconnected – due to Europeanisation and globalisation. Moreover, even if policies are expected to solve a particular problem, they are very likely to produce unintended (and unwanted) consequences that may very well exacerbate other problems.

What is more, with regard to the MSF's political stream, the role of party ideology has diminished in most parliamentary democracies (Katz and Mair 1995; Häusermann et al. 2013). While ideologies traditionally helped the comparatively cohesive parties in parliamentary systems put together somewhat coherent policy programmes, this is less and less the case as the relevance of ideology diminishes. If ideology cannot guide the policy choices of decision-makers any longer, they indeed increasingly resemble Kingdon's actors holding unclear policy preferences. They might still have a preference for pursuing policies that are popular among the electorate but, as voting behaviour itself is also becoming ever more volatile, it is hard for policy-makers to tell who their voters are and what interests they have. Therefore, the policy preferences of decision-makers are growing ever more unclear, even in parliamentary systems with traditionally strong and programmatically comparatively coherent political parties.

Finally, policy-makers have little time to think through their decisions as the pace of economic and social change has accelerated and media reporting has become continuous and more intrusive. Thus, decision-makers act under severe time-constraints, which limit the number of issues a political system can deal with at any given point in time. This, in turn, means that there are many more problems than political systems can attend to. Thus, for all political systems, the most important question becomes how attention is rationed (Zahariadis 2007: 65).

These conditions, in turn, render models of rational problem-solving highly unconvincing, even in political systems that do not resemble the presidential system of the United States, and this made the MSF attractive to scholars of decision-making in these other systems, too.

Nevertheless, there remain significant differences between the American political system Kingdon had in mind when developing his framework and the parliamentary or semi-presidential systems in other advanced democracies to which the MSF has been applied recently (let alone the political system of the European Union). Moreover, if Kingdon's framework is to be applied to decision-making, and not only to the agenda-setting for which it was originally conceived, further adaptations might become necessary. Zahariadis (1995, 2003) suggested a number of relevant adaptions that modified Kingdon's original approach slightly. Although Zahariadis was not the only author to propose modifications to Kingdon's original framework, most of these other adaptations were *ad hoc* modifications in order to make the approach applicable to the particular cases at hand. Thus, close to no systematic debate on potential theoretical refinements of the multiple-streams framework, its analytic value and its empirical applicability has taken place so far. Rather, the approach or some of its key concepts – such as 'policy-window' or 'window of opportunity', 'policy-entrepreneur' and 'focusing event' – have often been used to guide case studies without much consideration of the theoretical implications such work has for the multiple-streams framework itself (*cf.* Herweg 2016). In the following, we first briefly summarise the main argument of the MSF before we discuss the most prominent criticisms of the framework.

The core concepts of the MSF

One of the main reasons for the multiple-streams framework's attractiveness for scholars of agenda-setting and decision-making is its core argument, namely, that policy-making is not a rational response to clearly defined social or economic problems; rather, the MSF argues that there is no systematic relation between a problem that comes first and a solution which is sought in order to solve that problem. Policy-making can instead be seen as a process in which solutions are looking out for problems to which they can be attached. Thus, according to the MSF, the development of policies is basically unrelated to problems and once a problem gets on the agenda, a solution (that is, a policy that can be regarded as a reasonable response to the problem at hand) must already be available. As discussed above, given the omnipresence of ambiguity and the immense time-constraints under which policy-makers have to decide, this idea does not seem to be too far-fetched in most circumstances.

In terms of theory-development, a logical consequence of the insight that the elaboration of policy proposals is (mostly) unrelated to the problems that are currently being dealt with in the political system is to understand both as distinct processes – or streams – that are (mostly) independent of each other. In addition to the problem and the policy streams, the MSF distinguishes a political stream, which comprises the politics dimension of agenda-setting and decision-making. Each stream is assumed to operate according to its own specific logic and independently from the other two streams.

In the problem stream, conditions are turned into problems that need to be dealt with politically if attention is directed to a condition by indicators that change substantially over short periods of time, by feedback from previous programmes or by focusing events like crises or disasters (see Birkland 1997, 1998). Kingdon's (2003[1984]: 90) main insight with regard to the problem stream, however, is that 'problems are … not entirely self-evident'; rather, conditions need to be interpreted and framed in a certain way to make them problems. In the policy stream, experts in policy subsystems interact in policy communities, contributing to what Kingdon (2003[1984]: 166) figuratively calls 'the policy primeval soup'. Policy proposals are put forward by policy-entrepreneurs; these proposals are discussed, criticised, modified and combined or, as Kingdon calls it, 'softened up'. Proposals that meet the policy community's criteria of survival, namely, technical feasibility, value-acceptability, public acquiescence and financial viability, can become viable alternatives that are ready to be coupled, that is, connected to a particular problem. While the policy stream is located at the subsystem level and the dominant mode of interaction is arguing, things look quite different in the political stream. Powering and negotiations prevail in this stream, which is located at the level of macro-politics, where majorities are sought for getting proposals adopted. Thus, the composition of government and parliament is relevant here, as are interest-group campaigns and public opinion or, as Kingdon prefers to call it, the 'national mood'.

If the three streams flow independently through the political system, they need to be brought together at some point in order to make agenda-change possible. This happens during a 'policy-window' or 'window of opportunity'. As Kingdon (2003[1984]: 165) explains, 'a policy-window is an opportunity for advocates of proposals to push their pet solutions, or to push attention to their specific problems'. These opportunities can arise because of changes either in the problem stream – a problem becomes so important that something needs to be done about it – or in the political stream – for example, as a result of changes in government or parliament.

A policy-window is only a *necessary* condition for agenda-change, however. The three streams also need to be 'ripe'; that is to say, a viable alternative has to be available which can be coupled to a problem that has captured the attention of policy-makers; and policy-makers in the political stream must be receptive to both the problem and the proposal to be attached to the problem. If these conditions hold, that is, a policy-window opens and all three streams are ripe, a policy-entrepreneur can try to couple the three streams and get his pet project on the agenda. According to Kingdon (2003[1984]: 179), policy-entrepreneurs are 'advocates who are willing to invest their resources – time, energy, reputation, money – to promote a position in return for anticipated future gain in the form of material, purposive, or solidary benefits'. The policy-entrepreneur is of primary importance in the MSF. As policy-makers have neither a clear idea of what the relevant problem is nor what an adequate solution might be, policy-entrepreneurs can take advantage of the ambiguity and attach their pet project to a specific problem. It is important, however, to keep in mind that policy-entrepreneurs may fail in their attempt to combine the streams, even if the streams are ripe and a policy-window opens. Thus, the MSF leaves room for contingency and sometimes even 'dumb luck' (Kingdon 2003[1984]: 183).

Apart from the idea that policy-making is not an exercise in rational problem-solving, the MSF has been much cited due to the introduction into the scholarly literature of concepts that are lacking in other theoretical approaches, particularly the terms 'policy-window' or 'window of opportunity', which denotes that, at certain times, circumstances may make it much easier to get a policy adopted than at others. Similarly, the concept of the policy-entrepreneur as an actor pushing for a particular policy has turned out to be influential and has been included in other theoretical frameworks, for example, the punctuated equilibrium theory (Boushey 2013).

A critical discussion of the MSF

Despite its success, the MSF has been criticised for a number of reasons (see Weir 1992; Mucciaroni 1992, 2013; Bendor *et al.* 2001; Sabatier 2007a), which we discuss in this section.

One of the core problems of the MSF, according to some critics, is the lack of testable hypotheses. As Paul Sabatier (2007a: 327) explained: 'the multiple-streams framework has no explicit hypotheses and is so fluid in its structure and operationalization that falsification is difficult'. This criticism has two aspects. On the one hand, critics question whether hypotheses can be derived from the framework at all; on the other hand, they doubt that the framework's core concepts can be operationalised properly, as they lack clear definitions due to Kingdon's figurative language. We will discuss these two points in turn.

While it is true that Kingdon (and to a certain extent also Zahariadis) failed to develop falsifiable hypotheses from the MSF, that is not to say that it is impossible to do so. To the contrary, the main argument of the MSF can easily be transformed into a falsifiable hypothesis, namely that an agenda-change becomes more likely if the streams are ripe, a policy-window opens and a policy-entrepreneur is present to couple the streams. This hypothesis could be falsified by showing that agenda-change has occurred although (at least) one of the streams was not ripe, or there was no policy-window or no policy-entrepreneur pushed for the change. Similarly, one could test whether fulfilling the selection criteria increases a proposal's chances to be coupled or whether coupling is more likely to succeed when a policy-entrepreneur has direct access to key policy-makers. Other authors have also derived more specific hypotheses from the MSF that guided specific research questions (good examples include Blankenau 2001; Boscarino 2009; and Hansén 2016, Chapter Twelve of this volume), while Herweg, Huß and Zohlnhöfer (2016) have developed a set of more general hypotheses.

Moreover, other theoretical lenses of the policy process, for example, the advocacy coalition framework, can also be described as frameworks (Jenkins-Smith *et al.* 2014: 188). A particularly telling example is Fritz Scharpf's (1997) 'actor-centered institutionalism', which deliberately abstains from formulating explicit hypotheses. Therefore, we can conclude that it does not seem to be a necessary condition for useful frameworks in policy analysis to provide explicit hypotheses, nor is it impossible to derive hypotheses from the MSF.

The figurative language of the original formulation of the MSF is a more problematic point, however. Streams, open windows of opportunity, coupling, policy-entrepreneurs, primeval policy soup, *etcetera* are indeed concepts that lack clarity and analytical precision. All five basic categorical concepts – the 'policy', 'problem' and 'political' 'streams'; the 'policy-entrepreneur' and the 'window of opportunity' – are highly metaphorical and have to be reconstructed and operationalised for empirical or comparative research. The same holds true for many sub-components of these concepts. 'Indicators', 'feedback' and 'focusing events' for the problem stream; value-acceptability and technical feasibility for the policy stream; and, above all, the 'national mood' for the political stream:

all are concepts not easily operationalised. Moreover, the very idea of a window of opportunity seems to defy operationalisation; it seems much too contingent and, in many cases, is essentially socially constructed. Nonetheless, as Herweg demonstrates in this volume for policy-communities (2016, Chapter Eight of this volume), it is possible to define the relevant concepts much more rigorously than in Kingdon's original contribution. Similarly, Herweg *et al.* (2016) have provided operational definitions for the 'ripeness' of the streams.

A related criticism is that it is impossible to test the MSF quantitatively. While it is true that there are only very few MSF applications using quantitative methods (for an example see Travis and Zahariadis 2002), it is questionable whether this is a valid criticism of a theoretical framework. Some other theoretical lenses of the policy process also mostly or entirely rely on qualitative evidence and Fritz Scharpf (1997: 22–7) has even questioned the usefulness of quantitative techniques for policy research. It is certainly not necessary to go that far in order to concede that a framework may still be valuable that does not lend itself to quantitative testing.

Another critical point, among others put forward by Kuhlmann (2016, Chapter Three of this volume), is that the MSF lacks a micro-foundation. Many observers point out that the assumption of policy-makers with unclear preferences, who essentially do not know what they want, clashes with the role of policy-entrepreneurs, who pursue their pet projects with determination and persistence. The existence of both types of actors does not necessarily hint at a contradiction in the MSF, however. Rather, one might assume that all actors (including policy-entrepreneurs) do indeed have unclear preferences with regard to almost all policies in almost all issue-areas. At the same time, any actor (including a policy-maker) can become a policy-entrepreneur for a single issue, thus pushing for the adoption of that project. The precise reasons for this advocacy of a particular project may vary but it is unlikely that there is a great amount of rationality involved when it comes to explaining who pushes for the adoption of which policy project; rather, chance may play a significant role here. And while a policy-entrepreneur may (even irrationally) push for her pet project, she may have entirely unclear preferences with regard to all other issue-areas currently being discussed. Similarly, Kingdon (2003[1984]: 183) warns us not to 'paint these entrepreneurs as superhumanly clever', so it is unlikely that they act more rationally than policy-makers.

Nonetheless, Kuhlmann's argument that the MSF lacks a micro-foundation should not easily be dismissed. Whether a combination of the MSF with other lenses, that is, borrowing a micro-foundation, as proposed by Kuhlmann, may prove to be a solution to this particular problem is an open question, however.

Nonetheless, it is quite evident that the major approaches to the study of the policy process have substantial commonalities and some scholars have suggested synthesising them (see John 2003; Real-Dato 2009; for a critical discussion see Cairney and Heikkila 2014: 381–4). The punctuated equilibrium theory (PET) and the multiple-streams framework are particularly close in a number of respects. In its early stages, PET has substantially built upon Kingdon's work. While the more recent PET research has focused on the analysis of huge amounts of data and thus has somewhat moved away from the MSF tradition, the MSF may still be profitably integrated into PET. For example, PET seems to have some difficulty specifying at which point in time positive feedback processes occur – a problem that could be solved by referring to the logic of policy-windows and the availability (or otherwise) of viable alternative policies. *Vice versa*, elements of PET may also be introduced into the MSF, as Herweg, Huß and Zohlnhöfer (2016) have demonstrated with regard to issue attention dynamics. In a similar way, the contributions to this volume of Zahariadis and Spohr (2016, Chapters Nine and Fourteen) show the potential of the MSF to be combined with other theoretical lenses as well.

Spohr's contribution in particular is noteworthy, as he combines the MSF with historical institutionalism, thus introducing path-dependency into the MSF. In this way, Spohr addresses the 'lack of historical causality' (Mucciaroni 2013: 322) that some critics of the MSF have emphasised. Zohlnhöfer and Huß, in their contribution to this volume (2016, Chapter Ten), also integrate path-dependence into the MSF; they, however, simply argue that path-dependence can be considered as one element of the 'criteria for survival' in the policy stream, as policy-experts will not deem proposals technically feasible that do not take the relevant policy-path and the restrictions stemming from path-dependent developments into account.

A second element that critics say is missing from the MSF (apart from path-dependence) is institutions. Indeed, there is ample evidence in the literature that institutions matter for policy-outcomes because they influence the aggregation of preferences, regulate the speed of the policy-process, provide actors with veto-points and balance the power-relations within the political system (Immergut 1990, 1992; Scharpf 1997; Steinmo *et al.* 1992; Tsebelis 2002). And it is true that these institutions are mostly lacking in Kingdon's as well as Zahariadis' work (with some exceptions, including the structure of policy-communities).

How problematic is this failure to take institutions into account? And can it be rectified? Regarding the first question, the answer depends upon which stage of the policy cycle is to be analysed. For scholars interested only in agenda-setting – as is the case for Kingdon's original contribution – the failure to take institutions into account is not problematic. Baumgartner *et al.* (2009), for example, found that agenda-setting is generally much less shaped by formal institutions than later stages of the policy-cycle. In contrast, if the analysis is to be extended to the decision-making stage of the policy-cycle, it becomes much more problematic to ignore institutions.

There is nothing in the MSF, however, that forecloses the possibility of introducing institutions into the framework. Spohr, for example, in his contribution to this volume (2016, Chapter Fourteen) proposes to combine the MSF with historical institutionalism in order to take institutional effects into account. Herweg, Huß and Zohlnhöfer (2016) argue that institutions define who are the actors who need to accept a proposal and the authors define strategies that policy-entrepreneurs can employ to get the consent of these veto-actors. Other contributions discussing relevant aspects of how to integrate institutions in the MSF include Béland 2005, Ness and Mistretta 2009 and Blankenau 2001.

Moreover, authors like Mucciaroni (1992, 2013) or Bendor *et al.* (2001) question the (relative) independence of the three streams that, according to the model, only flow together during a window of opportunity. Critics argue that problems can become so severe as to lead to changes in the political stream, for example, a change in the national mood or even a change of government. Similarly, public acquiescence as a criterion of survival in the policy stream is obviously related to the political stream. Other examples could be added (see Herweg 2016). Thus, it is hard to deny that streams are not completely independent and proponents of the MSF admit that: 'There are some links between these streams at times other than the open windows and the final couplings' (Kingdon 2003[1984]: 229). Nevertheless, Kingdon, Zahariadis and others argue that the notion of independent streams should be used as a 'conceptual device' (Zahariadis 2014: 42). As each stream, although not entirely independent of the others, operates according to a distinct logic, they should be analysed separately. Moreover, if stream-independence were denied, it would be impossible to make the argument that (at least sometimes) solutions exist before the problem to which they are eventually attached is on the agenda. Thus, Zahariadis (2014: 42) suggests it suffices to assume 'that streams don't have to be independent and only need flow as if they are independent'.

Finally, it is contested if and how the MSF can be applied to other political systems than the presidential one it was developed for; and to other stages of the policy cycle than agenda-setting. As we have seen already, the MSF is actually applied in this way but there is no consensus on how this is to be done.

With regard to other political systems, it was somewhat disputed whether the MSF can be applied to parliamentary systems, which were seen as 'more orderly' (Zahariadis 2003: 1) when compared with the presidential system of the United States. Zahariadis (1995) originally suggested simply replacing the elements of the political stream by party politics, thus omitting the concepts of national mood and interest-group politics. This idea has recently been complemented by a proposal by Herweg, Huß and Zohlnhöfer (2016). These authors also put political parties centre-stage, but in a slightly different way. They argue that parties' policy experts are expected to be members of the policy-communities in the policy stream and to promote viable policy-alternatives in their respective parties, while the party leadership is concerned with adopting policies in the political stream.

The application of the MSF to multi-level systems like the political system of the EU has also been discussed (and tried). With regard to the EU, Zahariadis (2008) has suggested a number of adaptations. Again, it is the concept of the political stream that clearly needs the most modification. In contrast, to the best of our knowledge, we are not aware of any theoretical discussions regarding the applicability of the MSF to federalist countries. Nonetheless, the contributions of Raquel Gallego and co-authors (2016, Chapter Thirteen in this volume) as well as of Iris Reus (2016, Chapter Twelve in this volume) show that such an application is possible.

The extension of the MSF from agenda-setting to decision-making and even sometimes implementation (for example, Exworthy and Powell 2004) is also far from trivial. As is well known from research on the policy-cycle and related studies, different actors become relevant in the various phases of the policy-cycle (Jann and Wegerich 2007). Nonetheless, Zahariadis (1995) suggested understanding agenda-setting and decision-making as belonging to the same process 'by which policy-makers make an authoritative choice from a limited set of previously generated alternatives' (Zahariadis 2003: 10). In essence, this suggestion means to analyse agenda-setting and decision-making together, as both are collapsed into the coupling process. Other authors have suggested more elaborate models. Michael Howlett, Allan McConnell and Anthony Perl, in their contribution to this volume (2016, Chapter Five) argue that after the three streams are coupled they are joined by two other streams (for a more extensive presentation of their model, see Howlett *et al.* 2016). A process stream sets up the procedures for decision-making, such as the timetable for discussions, the institutionally designed steps for procedure, *etcetera*. And the programme stream calibrates the new instruments with the old ones. Herweg *et al.* (2016) instead propose to distinguish between two coupling processes, one for agenda-setting and one for decision-making.

In sum, a number of questions can be asked regarding the MSF: can it be falsified? Are the core concepts clear enough? Does it lack relevant variables? Are the streams independent? Can it be applied in other contexts? Nonetheless, as the above discussion should have proved, not all of these questions must remain unanswered. What is lacking, however, is a lively debate about these questions.

The contributions to this volume

Even though there is remarkable progress in the discussions on the policy-making process in general and the MSF in particular, the editors of this volume wanted to start such a debate about the current state of research in the MSF tradition, the framework's empirical applicability and theoretical refinements, its merits and limitations. Therefore, they organised a workshop on the multiple-streams framework at the ECPR's Joint Session of Workshops in Mainz/Germany in March 2013. This volume contains (sometimes substantially) revised versions of the papers that were presented at that workshop. Different versions of the chapters by Michael Howlett, Allan McConnell and Anthony Perl, by Åsa Knaggård and by Nikolaos Zahariadis were first published in the forum section of the *European Journal of Political Research* 2016 54(3) entitled Theoretically Refining the Multiple Streams Framework.

Most of the chapters suggest that the multiple-streams framework indeed can be a valuable lens through which to analyse policy-making. In principle it can travel to political systems quite different from the US presidential system for which it was originally developed. Moreover, it does seem possible to extend the approach to other stages of the policy-cycle than just agenda-setting. Nonetheless, the chapters also document that the MSF does have some limitations and many papers make an effort to improve it, by clarifying concepts and refining the framework (not least regarding its extension to parliamentary systems or to decision-making). Interestingly, quite a number of papers suggest combining the MSF with other theoretical approaches from policy-analysis (for example, historical institutionalism, partisan theory or punctuated equilibrium theory), but also from social psychology (prospect theory, affect-priming theory).

The individual chapters are grouped into three parts. In Part One, a number of contributions deal with some basic theoretical issues of the MSF. Harald Sætren (Chapter Two) discusses the relationship between the MSF and the garbage-can model of decision-making that Kingdon used as an inspiration for his own model. Sætren argues that a number of important insights of the original garbage-can model were lost in Kingdon's translation – which was associated with a substantial loss of analytical clarity. Sætren points to the streams of participants and choice opportunities that Kingdon uneasily lumped together in the political stream as one example. In this case, Kingdon's translation led to the neglect of institutions in the MSF. On the other hand, Sætren shows that Kingdon should be given credit for introducing a number of important elements to the model, including the role of policy-entrepreneurs.

In the following chapter, Johanna Kuhlmann discusses the micro-foundation of the multiple streams framework (Chapter Three). She refutes Edella Schlager's (2007: 302) claim that the individual in the multiple-streams framework is 'firmly grounded in Simon's boundedly rational individual'. While the two concepts have a family resemblance, bounded rationality cannot be seen as a micro-foundation for the MSF: Kingdon theorises at the macro- rather than the micro-level, as the individual is not the point of departure for the multiple-streams framework. Moreover, the actual basis of the individual's decisions is not discussed at any great length in the MSF. And the connection between the individual and the organisation is different: in the concept of bounded rationality, the organisation compensates individual deficits, while the organisation within the multiple-streams framework increases them.

Friedbert W. Rüb reflects on the notion of time in politics in his contribution (Chapter Four). Time plays a prominent role in the multiple-streams framework and impacts decision-making in two analytically distinct ways. First, treating time as a historical category, the author raises the question of in which time policy-makers are bound to decide and how the structure of political challenges is affected by today's globalising world. Secondly, in the face of 'wicked problems', decision-making is confronted with a dramatic scarcity of time. Decisions are often made on a first-come-first-served basis, challenging the ideal of rational problem-solving. The contribution concludes with a discussion of time paradoxes. Attempts to speed up the process of policy-making in order to keep up with the dynamics of increasingly globalised societies have to preserve the institutionalised time-structures of democratic systems.

Part Two of the book comprises papers that discuss individual elements of the multiple-streams framework. In Chapter Five, Michael Howlett, Allan McConnell and Anthony Perl discuss, among other things, what a stream is and how many streams exist. They argue that Kingdon's model needs to be extended in order to be applicable to different stages of the policy cycle. Thus, they propose their own five-stream model, which they present more extensively in Howlett *et al*. 2016.

Two chapters deal with certain elements of the problem stream. Tom Birkland and Megan Warnement take stock of the literature on focusing events in Chapter Six and present a programme for future research in this field of study that they argue should focus on the policy discourse within policy-domains. The basic idea of Åsa Knaggård's Chapter Seven is that most problems need to be framed in a particular way in order to become politically salient. Thus, she proposes to introduce agency into the problem stream, namely, so-called knowledge-brokers: credible actors with access to decision-makers. In contrast to policy-entrepreneurs, knowledge-brokers do not necessarily pursue a pet project but rather have a problem-definition they want to spread. If successful, knowledge-brokers can, nevertheless, be highly influential; the problem-definition makes some solutions more plausible than others, which may well affect coupling.

In her Chapter Eight, Nicole Herweg discusses the concept of policy-communities in the policy stream. Policy-communities belong to those concepts of the MSF that are not defined particularly precisely in Kingdon's book or the literature based on it. Based on Kingdon's contribution and the literature he worked with, Herweg derives a clear definition of what policy-communities are. Furthermore, she shows that her definition is actually applicable in a case study on the European natural-gas policy-community.

Finally, Nikolaos Zahariadis' Chapter Nine deals with the relationship between political leadership and the national mood. In contrast to some of his earlier work, Zahariadis shows here that the national mood can actually exert a substantial impact on policy under certain conditions. Moreover, he extends the MSF by combining it with affect-priming theory.

Part Three of the book contains a number of case studies applying the multiple-streams framework. These case studies cover very different policy areas (abortion, economic policy, energy policy, non-smoker-protection legislation, internal security and social policy among others), diverse national contexts (Germany, Spain, Sweden, UK) as well as politics in multi-level systems. Thus, questions of the empirical applicability of the core concepts figure prominently in many of these chapters, most explicitly in the one by Zohlnhöfer and Huß (Chapter Ten). These authors find that the MSF travels comparatively well to the veto-ridden corporatist German political system. Nonetheless, they, too, argue that certain adaptations to the framework need to be made in order to apply it to parliamentary systems. Furthermore, they add to the discussion of the problem stream by arguing that a problem is more likely to be addressed by policy-makers when its persistence endangers the governing party's re-election.

Iris Reus' chapter on German non-smoker protection (Chapter Eleven) also confirms the MSF's travelling capacity as she, too, can show that the framework nicely explains why the former 'smoker's paradise' went up in smoke when it did. Moreover, the national mood again turns out to be important, even in the realm of multi-level politics. At the same time, the MSF turns out to be much more apt to explain the agenda-setting processes for which it was conceived originally; in contrast, Reus argues that the framework must be extended by other approaches if it is to explain decision-making.

Dan Hansén's chapter on the policy consequences of the assassination of former Swedish prime-minister Olof Palme (Chapter Twelve) corroborates the claim that the MSF can be applied to a parliamentary system with substantial benefit. From a theoretical point of view, Hansén's chapter is particularly interesting because, on the one hand, he deduces some falsifiable propositions from the MSF and, on the other hand, he complements the MSF with prospect theory.

The chapters by Raquel Gallego, Nicolás Barbieri and Sheila González (Chapter Thirteen) and Florian Spohr (Chapter Fourteen), which empirically analyse labour-market reforms in Sweden and the UK and healthcare reform in Catalonia respectively, come up with similar conclusions. Both suggest combining the original MSF with other approaches in order to extend its analytical leverage. While Gallego and co-authors present their own 'institutional processualism' approach that in some ways builds upon the MSF, Spohr aims at introducing aspects of historical institutionalism into the MSF.

In conclusion, we hope that these papers will spark a debate on the analytical merits and limitations of the multiple-streams framework, and on ways to develop it further and improve its empirical applicability; most authors in this volume seem to believe that the time for a wider application of the framework has finally come.

References

Ackrill, R. and Kay, A. (2011) 'Multiple streams in EU policy-making: the case of the 2005 sugar reform', *Journal of European Public Policy* 18(1): 72–89.

Baumgartner, F. R., Breunig, C., Green-Pedersen, C., Jones, B. D., Mortensen, P. B., Nuytemanns, M. and Walgrave, S. (2009) 'Punctuated equilibrium in comparative perspective', *American Journal of Political Science* 53(3): 603–20.

Baumgartner, F. R., Breunig, C., Jones, B. D., Mortensen, P. B. (2014) 'Punctuated equilibrium theory: explaining stability and change in public policymaking', in Paul A. Sabatier and Christopher M. Weible (eds) *Theories of the Policy Process*, Boulder, CO: Westview Press, pp. 59–103.

Béland, D. (2005) 'Ideas and social policy: an institutionalist perspective', *Social Policy & Administration* 39(1): 1–18.

Bendor, J., Terry M. M. and Shotts, K. W. (2001) 'Recycling the garbage can. An assessment of the research program', *American Political Science Review* 95(1): 169–90.

Birkland, Th. A. (1997) *After Disaster – Agenda setting, public policy and focusing events*, Georgetown, Washington, DC: Georgetown University Press.

— (1998) 'Focusing events, mobilization, and agenda setting', *Journal of Public Policy* 18(1): 53–74.

Blankenau, J. (2001) 'The fate of national health insurance in Canada and the United States. A multiple streams explanation', *Policy Studies Journal* 29(1): 38–55.

Boscarino, J. E. (2009) 'Surfing for problems: advocacy group strategy in U.S. forestry policy', *Policy Studies Journal* 37(3): 415–34.

Boushey, Graeme (2013) 'The punctuated equilibrium theory of agenda setting and policy change', in E. Araral, S. Fritzen and M. Howlett (eds) *Routledge Handbook of Public Policy*, London and New York: Routledge, pp. 138–52.

Bundgaard, U. and Vrangbæk, K. (2007) 'Reform by coincidence? Explaining the policy process of structural reform in Denmark', *Scandinavian Political Studies* 30(4): 491–520.

Cairney, P. and Heikkila, T. (2014) 'A comparison of theories of the policy process', in P. A. Sabatier and C. M. Weible (eds) *Theories of the Policy Process*, Boulder, CO: Westview Press, pp. 363–90.

Cohen, M., March, J. and Olsen, J. (1972) 'A garbage can model of organizational choice', *Administrative Science Quarterly* 17(1): 1–25.

Copeland, P. and James, S. (2014) 'Policy windows, ambiguity and commission entrepreneurship: explaining the relaunch of the European Union's economic reform agenda', *Journal of European Public Policy* 21(1): 1–19.

Exworthy, M. and Powell, M. (2004) 'Big windows and little windows: implementation in the "congested state"', *Public Administration* 82(2): 263–81.

Häusermann, S., Picot, G. and Geering, D. (2013) 'Review article: rethinking party politics and the welfare state – recent advances in the literature', *British Journal of Political Science* 43(1): 221–40.

Herweg, N. (2015) 'Der Multiple Streams Ansatz', in G. Wenzelburger and R. Zohlnhöfer (eds) *Handbuch Policy-Forschung*, Wiesbaden, DE: Springer VS, pp. 325–53.

Herweg, N., Huß, C. and Zohlnhöfer, R. (2015) 'Straightening the three streams: theorizing extensions of the multiple streams framework', *European Journal of Political Research* 54(3): 435–49.

Howlett, M., McConnell, A. and Perl, A. (2015) 'Streams and stages: reconciling Kingdon and policy process theory', *European Journal of Political Research* 54(3): 419–34.

Immergut, E. (1990) 'Institutions, veto points, and policy results: a comparative analysis of health care', *Journal of Public Policy* 10(4): 391–416.

—   (1992) 'The rules of the game: the logic of health policy-making in France, Switzerland, and Sweden', in S. Steinmo, K. A. Thelen and F. Longstreth (eds) *Structuring Politics: Historical institutionalism in comparative analysis*, Cambridge, UK: Cambridge University Press, pp. 57–89.

Jann, W. and Wegrich, K. (2007) 'Theories of the policy cycle', in F. Fischer, G. J. Miller and M. S. Sidney (eds) *Handbook of Public Policy Analysis: Theory, politics and methods*, Boca Raton, FL: CRC Press, pp. 43–62.

Jenkins-Smith, H. C., Nohrstedt, D., Weible, C. M. and Sabatier, P. A. (2014) 'The advocacy coalition framework: foundations, evolution, and ongoing research', in P. A. Sabatier and C. M. Weible (eds) *Theories of the Policy Process*, Boulder, CO: Westview Press, pp. 183–223.

John, P. (2003) 'Is there life after policy streams, advocacy coalitions and punctuations: using evolutionary theory to explain policy change?', *Policy Studies Journal* 31(4): 481–98.

Jones, M. D., Peterson, H. L., Pierce, J. J., Herweg, N., Bernal, A., Lamberta, H. and Zahariadis, N. (2015) 'A river runs through it: a multiple streams framework meta-review', *Policy Studies Journal* online version of record published 17 June: DOI: 10.1111/psj.1211.

Katz, R. S. and Mair, P. (1995) 'Changing models of party organization and party democracy: the emergence of the cartel party', *Party Politics* 1(1): 5–28.

Kingdon, J. W. (2003 [1984]) *Agendas, Alternatives, and Public Policy*, New York: Longman.

Mucciaroni, G. (1992) 'The garbage can model and the study of policy making: a critique', *Polity* 24(3): 459–82.

—   (2013) 'The garbage can model and the study of the policy-making process', in E. Araral, S. Fritzen and M. Howlett (eds) *Routledge Handbook of Public Policy*, London and New York: Routledge, pp. 320–28.

Münter, M. (2005) *Verfassungsreform im Einheitsstaat. Die Politik der Dezentralisierung in Großbritannien*, Wiesbaden, DE: VS Verlag für Sozialwissenschaften.

Ness, E. C. and Mistretta, M. A. (2009) 'Policy adoption in North Carolina and Tennessee: a comparative case study of lottery beneficiaries', *Review of Higher Education* 32(4): 489–514.

Real-Dato, J. (2009) 'Mechanisms of policy change; a proposal for a synthetic explanatory framework', *Journal of Comparative Policy Analysis* 11(1): 117–43.

Sabatier, P. A. (2007a) 'Fostering the development of policy theory', in P. A. Sabatier (ed.), *Theories of the Policy Process*, 2nd edn, Boulder, CO: Westview Press, pp. 321–36.

— (2007b) 'The need for better theories', in P. A. Sabatier (ed.), *Theories of the Policy Process*, 2nd edn, Boulder, CO: Westview Press, pp. 1–17.

Scharpf, F. W. (1997) *Games Real Actors Play. Actor-centered institutionalism in policy research*, Boulder, CO: Westview Press.

Schlager, E. (2007) 'A comparison of frameworks, theories, and models of policy processes', in P. A. Sabatier (ed.) *Theories of the Policy Process*, Boulder, CO: Westview Press, pp. 293–319.

Steinmo, S., Thelen, K. and Longstreth, F. (eds) (1992) *Structuring Politics. Historical institutionalism in comparative analysis*, Cambridge, UK: Cambridge University Press.

Travis, R. and Zahariadis, N. (2002) 'A multiple streams model of U.S. foreign aid policy', *Policy Studies Journal* 30(4): 495–514.

Tsebelis, G. (2002) *Veto Players: How political institutions work*, Princeton, NJ: Princeton University Press.

Weir, M. (1992) *Politics and Jobs: The boundaries of employment policy in the United States*, Princeton, NJ: Princeton University Press.

Zahariadis, N. (1992) 'To sell or not to sell? Telecommunications policy in Britain and France', *Journal of Public Policy* 12(4): 355–76.

— (1995) *Markets, States, and Public Policy. Privatization in Britain and France*. Ann Arbor, MI: University of Michigan Press.

— (1996) 'Selling British Rail. An idea whose time has come?', *Comparative Political Studies* 29(4): 400–22.

— (2003) *Ambiguity & Choice in Public Policy: Political decision making in modern democracies*, Washington, DC: Georgetown University Press.

— (2005) *Essence of Political Manipulation: Emotion, institutions, and Greek foreign policy*, New York: Peter Lang.

— (2007) 'The multiple streams framework. Structure, limitations, prospects', in Paul A. Sabatier (ed.) *Theories of the Policy Process*, Boulder, CO: Westview Press, pp. 65–92.

— (2008) 'Ambiguity and choice in European public policy', *Journal of European Public Policy* 15(4): 514–30.

—— (2014) 'Ambiguity and multiple streams', in P. A. Sabatier and C. M. Weible (eds) *Theories of the Policy Process*, Boulder, CO: Westview Press, pp. 25–58.

Zohlnhöfer, R. and Herweg, N. (2014) 'Paradigmatischer Wandel in der deutschen Arbeitsmarktpolitik: Die Hartz-Gesetze', in Friedbert W. Rüb (ed.) *Rapide Politikwechsel in der Bundesrepublik. Gründe, Akteure, Dynamiken und Probleme*, Baden-Baden: Nomos, pp. 93–125.

PART ONE

THE THEORETICAL ASSUMPTIONS OF THE
MULTIPLE-STREAMS FRAMEWORK

Chapter Two

Lost in Translation: Re-conceptualising the Multiple-Streams Framework Back to its Source of Inspiration

Harald Sætren

Introduction

John Kingdon (1984: 20) makes it perfectly clear that the analytical-theoretical construct he presented in his seminal book was based on a modified and *simplified* version of the equally well known garbage-can (GC) model of organisational decision-making, formulated by Cohen, March and Olsen (1972) a good decade earlier. Kingdon has been richly and rightly praised and awarded for his contribution in demonstrating the relevance of the GC logic at the highest level of decision-making in society – public policy-making – where it is, no doubt, even more appropriate and useful.

Nevertheless, the main argument to be addressed in this paper is that several essential features of the GC model were left out in Kingdon's translation of it to the MS framework, thereby seriously impairing its analytical and theoretical leverage in a broader policy-making context. Lost in this translation were not only some key theoretical concepts but also the intentions of Cohen, March and Olsen in developing their GC model, as well as the assumed relationship between decision streams and how they are connected. Neglecting the organisational-institutional connection to policy streams is by far the most serious omission in this respect. Realising the full potential of the MS framework as a synthesising multi-theoretical policy-making construct requires re-conceptualising it back to the core of its original concepts. This will also greatly facilitate combining and fusing it with some other promising theoretical constructs embedded in the historical institutionalism and policy-design research literature.

A few caveats are in order before we proceed with analysing what got lost (and with what consequences) in the translation from the GC model to the MS framework. First, Kingdon did not name his simplified theoretical construct the 'multiple streams' or 'policy streams' approach or framework. This was done by later policy scholars inspired by his work. Second, Kingdon's ambition was to analyse and theorise about the apparently fluid nature of the agenda-setting stage of the policy process, not the entire policy process from beginning to end. Hence, when we criticise some of the shortcomings of the MS framework, we primarily target those who interpreted and launched Kingdon's simplified version of the GC model under this label as a more comprehensive policy-making theory.

Third, the naming of Kingdon's simplified construct has changed from the *policy streams* approach/framework during the late 1980s and early 1990s (for example, Mumper 1987 and Sabatier 1991) to the *multiple-streams* approach/framework from the mid 1990s; the latter term was coined by one scholar in particular, Nikolaos Zahariadis (1995, 2002). For the sake of simplicity, we use the later nomenclature *multiple-streams* (MS) framework, which seems to have become the more common label.

A nearly universally held misconception must be corrected at the outset. It is the belief that Kingdon was the first to demonstrate the applicability and utility of the logic of the GC model in a public-policy-making context. This is simply not true! One of the GC model co-authors actually published an article in *Scandinavian Political Studies* the same year as the GC model was published (Olsen 1972). Here, the relevance of the logic of the GC model as a more general analytical framework for the policy process was spelled out for the first time, without changing and simplifying the core concepts in the way Kingdon did. Four years later, March and Olsen (1976) followed up by publishing a book containing several case-studies demonstrating empirically the wider applicability of the GC model in a public-policy-making context. There is no reference in Kingdon (1984) to these earlier applications of the multiple-steams framework in a public-policy-making context. This is not mentioned here to detract from the praise Kingdon deserves in promoting the GC model logic so effectively by applying it in his seminal book. Rather, we just want to set the record straight!

On balance Kingdon must also be credited for adding something valuable to the GC model in his translation of it. The most important thing in this respect is probably the more explicit attention to the role of *human agency* – through the *policy-entrepreneur* concept – in the successful coupling of policy streams. Another is the *policy-window* concept which represents more focused attention and elaboration on the *temporal-order* idea so crucial in the *original* GC model by Cohen, March and Olsen. *Policy-design* is another type of highly relevant literature to the MS framework. However, with a few exceptions (for example, Sætren 2009) this link has not been made: though doing so would no doubt enhance the analytical-theoretical leverage of the MS framework even further. Nevertheless, the main purpose of this chapter is not to present and discuss a fully fledged, revised and more comprehensive version of the MS framework, along the lines just suggested above. Rather, our aim is more limited yet of critical importance: pointing out how the *organisational-structural* dimension of the GC model got lost in Kingdon's simplified translation, an omission that, unfortunately, was transmitted in subsequent scholars' interpretation of his work into their own policy streams/multiple-streams frameworks.

A further discussion of the model elements that were lost in Kingdon's translation and which should be retrieved as part of re-conceptualising the revised MS framework requires briefly revisiting the main purpose, features and logic of the GC model and comparing it to Kingdon's modified and simplified version. In this context, we will try to demonstrate how the theoretical leverage of the MS framework will be substantially enhanced just by giving more explicit attention to *organisational* and *institutional* factors as well as by extending its analytical focus to more stages of the policy process, including both policy-authorisation and policy-implementation.

Revisiting the garbage-can model

It is not uncommon to interpret the GC model as one claiming that organisational decision processes are basically *chaotic*, that is, lacking any clear order or structure, thus producing largely unintended and unpredictable decision-outcomes. Cohen, March and Olsen (1972) may have contributed in no small part to this misconception by referring to their object of study in the late 1960s – universities – as *organised anarchies* and by the rather indelicate naming – *garbage can* – of their model. Nevertheless, and perhaps surprisingly, this is clearly not the main message the authors intended to convey.

Their point of departure at that time was an overly rationalistic conception of organisations and related internal decision-processes, stemming from classical economics, that Herbert Simon spent much of his career correcting and modifying. Thus, the ideas of *bounded rationality* and *satisficing* behaviour were launched as more realistic core assumptions than *absolute rationality* and *maximising* behaviour (Simon 1955; March and Simon 1958). In the same vein, the purpose of Cohen, March and Olsen in developing the GC model was not to reject a rational-choice model (based on more or less realistic core assumptions) in favour of a polar-opposite model postulating that organisational choices were predominantly characterised by anarchy and chaos. Rather, they wanted to call attention to the less analytical-rational aspects of decision-making frequently observed by organisational scholars, such as when choices became politicised or appeared to be a result of almost random chance events. Furthermore, and this is the crux of the GC model, the aim was to identify and specify under what conditions the behaviour of organisational decision-makers is likely to appear more, or less, rational.

To make their point, they introduced some very unconventional notions about organisational decision-making, accompanied by a language-style and metaphor-use that many would have found quite provocative:

> … an organization is a collection of choices looking for problems, issues and feelings looking for decision situations in which they can be aired, solutions looking for issues to which they might be the answer and decision makers looking for work.

They went on in the same vein to suggest that:

> … one can view choice opportunity as a garbage can into which various kinds of problems and solutions are dumped by participants as they are generated. The mix of garbage in a single can depends on the mix of cans available, on the labels attached to the alternative cans, on what garbage is currently being

produced, and on the speed with which garbage is collected and removed from the scene (Cohen, March and Olsen 1972: 2).

Nevertheless, forty years later, the same authors caution against the all too common chaos theory interpretation of their GC model, emphasising that these novel ideas were originally presented as '*an aspect* of organizational decision making' and as '*A*...model, not *the* model,' and was 'an attempt to enlarge rather than to replace other interpretations of organizational life' (Cohen, March and Olsen 2012: 22; italics in original).

In their latter work, the authors remind us of the unique context in which their unconventional ideas about organisational decision-making originated. They were based on observations of higher-education institutions during the late 1960s in California, at a time when not only universities but society as a whole seemed to be in state of flux, experiencing fundamental changes in core values as well as in political and social institutions.

Hence, it is now time to spell out in more detail what was lost in Kingdon's translation and the implications of those omissions; and to suggest how this can be rectified.

Lost in translation

The missing policy-stream elements

Cohen, March and Olsen (1972: 3), Olsen (1972) and March and Olsen (1976) identified four decision-stream elements (*see* Table 2.1). Kingdon (1984: 20) reduced these to three, keeping the two first (problems and solutions) but substituting for Cohen, March and Olsen's *participants* and *choice-opportunities* his own choice of concept: *politics*. There are at least two basic problems associated with this. First, participants and choice opportunities do not totally disappear. Instead they are lumped into the hodge-podge concept *politics*, with other potentially important but very different phenomena, like *pressure-group campaigns, public/national mood, election results, partisan or ideological distribution of Congress* and *changes in administration* (Kingdon 1984: 152). Thus, the political-stream concept assumes the function of a very heterogeneous residual category, containing almost anything that does not constitute problems or

Table 2.1: Decision streams as conceptualised by Cohen, March and Olsen (1972) and Kingdon (1984)

Cohen, March and Olsen (1972)	Kingdon (1984)
Problems	Problems
Solutions	Policy-proposals (solutions)
Participants	Politics
Choice-opportunities	

Table 2.2: Core theoretical concepts related to two versions of MS framework

Cohen, March and Olsen (1972)	Kingdon (1984)
Temporal orders	Policy-windows
Organisational structure:	Policy-entrepreneurs
1. Hierarchical	
2. Specialised	
3. Open/unsegmented	

Table 2.3: Implications of decision and access structures following from three ideal-typical organisational structures in GC model

Organisational structure	Decision structure	Access/agenda structure
Hierarchical	Only important/high-ranking organisational members can participate in important choice opportunities/decision arenas.	Important problems/issues have access to many choice opportunities; important choice opportunities/decision arenas are accessible only to important problems/issues.
Specialised	Each organisational member can participate only in one choice opportunity/decision arena.	Each problem/issue has access to only one choice opportunity/ decision arena.
Open/unsegmented	Any organisational member can participate in any choice opportunity/decision arena.	Any problem/issue has access to any choice opportunity/ decision arena.

policy proposals (solutions). Hence, the analytical clarity of the *politics* concept is greatly impaired.

The missing organisational-structure context

The omission of the *choice-opportunities* concept, however, is much more serious: its unfortunate consequence has been to disconnect Kingdon's simplified construct from the *organisational context* so crucial to the GC model. Collective decision-making does not happen in an organisational or institutional vacuum. Thus, the concept of *choice-opportunities* refers to the various formalised and institutionalised settings – decision arenas – in which organisational and political decisions are supposed to be made.

However, even within hierarchical and specialised structures in which decision streams are supposedly more closely connected, there are inevitably certain *ambiguities* and *uncertainties* related to stream elements that might be conducive to lack of process stability and predictability. There are four of these ambiguity-and-uncertainty-creating factors. Two are basic axioms of the GC model. They are: 1) any *decision opportunity* is basically an *ambiguous* stimulus; and, 2) most decision-makers are *part-time participants*. This means that the definition of problems/issues and their solutions is seldom crystal-clear at the outset, implying that there is often some discretionary space for clever and creative interpretation of issues – depending on whoever chooses to exercise her/his privilege to participate. This means that turnover of participants during a decision process could easily result in unstable issue-definition over time. But the opposite could also be the case. That is, the *type of issue* on the decision-agenda and its *content* (proposed solution) could also determine, to a large extent, who chooses to become activate and participate. This suggests that *activation* and *definition* processes respectively may play a dynamic critical role in how decisions are formulated, authorised and implemented.

Table 2.4 suggests how variation in activation and definition processes related to decision-makers may produce results consistent with three different types of decision-making models.

Two other ambiguity-uncertainty factors in the GC model are well known in the organisation-theory literature (Thompson 1967: 134). They relate to whether 1) *goals* and 2) *goals–means* relationships are *clear* or *unclear* or *well understood* or *not*, respectively. Rational decision-making presupposes both clear goals and well understood goal–means relations. Conversely, when goal–means relations, especially, are not well understood, decision-making becomes a risky and unpredictable enterprise, regardless of whether goals are clear or not. It is when all these factors coincide in the ambiguity-and-uncertainty-creating mode in organisational settings that Cohen, March and Olsen use the term *organised anarchies*.

Table 2.4: Patterns of activation and definition processes and how they affect likelihood of three types of organisational decision-models.

	Rational model	**Political model**	**Artifactual/chance model**
Activation process	Low and stable number of participants.	Mobilisation of more and different types of participants.	Changing patterns of participants, especially over longer time periods.
Definition process and solutions	Agreement on definition of decision issues also makes agreement on solutions more likely.	Disagreement on issues along stable cleavages more likely; compromise or forced solutions more likely.	Unstable, changing, unpredictable issue definitions more likely; unexpected, surprising solutions more likely.

Re-conceptualising the MS framework

What we are proposing here is a return to the decision-stream elements in the GC model that can establish the crucial link to organisational context and then extend the MS framework to all observable and relevant policy stages.

As already suggested, this implies that each stage of the policy process, from its beginning to its logical and empirical conclusion, should be analysed in terms of its relevant institutional decision-arenas; what type of actors/participants are included or excluded; and what consequence this has for what problems and solutions are addressed, defined and, eventually, connected or not.

This brings us to the last, but not least important, limitation of Kingdon's version of the MS framework: that he chose to apply it *only* to the *agenda and formulation* stages of the policy process. This was a deliberate choice on his part that we have to respect; though, again, it had the consequence of creating the widespread misconception that the MS framework somehow could *only* be applied fruitfully to these two policy stages. There is, of course, nothing in the MS framework itself that restricts its application to some policy stages at the expense of others. March and Olsen (1976) had already demonstrated this almost four decades ago, by applying the MS framework empirically in this more inclusive manner (see, for instance, Rommetveit 1976). It is only in later years that some scholars seem to have recognised this misconception and extended the MS framework to include later policy stages like authorisation/legitimation and implementation (Zahariadis 2003. This, unfortunately, seems to be a case of policy-scholarship reinventing the proverbial wheel!

Institutions in the MS framework

Elevating the MS framework to the highest societal level of decision-making in the spirit and application of its creators implies linking it to an *institutional* framework. The public-policy-making process epitomises the political system in action. Hence, it follows that the organisational and institutional context of the policy process cannot be ignored in our attempts to understand and explain it. Kingdon does discuss the role of governmental institutions and actors in his book, both in chapter 2 ('Participants inside government') and chapter 7 ('The political stream'). The problem here, however, is that this institutional focus is more *implicit* than explicit, since it is subsumed in a mixture with other, quite different, ideas, under more general broad and heterogeneous concepts such as the political stream. This basic flaw in the MS framework was pointed out in a critique of it more than twenty years ago (Mucciaroni 1992: 465–6). One likely explanation for this is that the case studies reported and analysed by Kingdon (1984), despite his inspiration from the GC model, were nevertheless heavily influenced by the general analytical-theoretical thinking dominating political science in the late 1970s and early 1980s – the so-called *behavioural* approach.

By some ironic twist of events, it so happened that it was March and Olsen who ushered in the *new institutionalism* in political science, through their famous pioneering *APSR* article (March and Olsen 1984), in the very same year Kingdon published his seminal book. As we know, other scholars soon followed suit, bolstering the institutional argument with convincing empirical data. It is no coincidence that the latter contributions originated from comparative politics/public-policy scholarship (for example, Hall 1986; Steinmo *et al.* 1992; Weaver and Rockman 1993), since the impact of institutional factors is much more apparent than real when similar policies are studied across national borders. Since institutional arrangements tend to be more invariant within single countries, unravelling their impact on the policy process would often require a longitudinal methodological approach encompassing several decades – still a relatively rare commodity in policy research. This fact, plus focusing only on the formulation stage of the policy process – which also implies less variation in political institutions involved – could be another explanation for Kingdon's skewed focus on interest-group configurations (such as policy-communities) and a special type of actor (policy-entrepreneurs), at the expense of the wider institutional framework within which they operate.

The institutional argument is more than that institutions are another variable that must be added to the multiplicity of other factors of potential relevance in political science. It goes further, by claiming that institutions play a privileged role by *structuring* the relationship between the many other factors in ways that may crucially affect outcomes of the policy process (Steinmo *et al.* 1992: 3). Other scholars of a more rational persuasion, for example, North (1990) make the same claim by referring to institutions as defining the *rules of the game* in politics.

In cross-national comparative policy studies, the organisation and structure of *constitutions* and higher-tier institutions may play a significant role in explaining marked differences in policy performance across countries on similar policy issues. Scholars like Knill and Lenschow (1998); Lijphardt (1984, 1999); Steinmo *et al.* (1992); Weaver and Rockman (1993); Olsen and Peters (1996); Pollitt and Bouckaert (2011); Sætren (2009); and Treib (2008 have all explored the impact of macro-level institutions on policy processes in cross-national comparative studies. Typically *federal* versus *unitary* or *presidential* versus *parliamentarian* political systems figure prominently as hypothesised important institutional factors. The number of levels from the central to the local level in the political-administrative system as well as the veto-points embedded in institutional arrangements, that is, their types and prevalence, are also potentially important factors at this level of analysis. Nevertheless, often, lower-tier institutional and organisational factors within each of these constitutional systems seem to play a more important role. Thus, the difference between different types of *political regimes* (types of government) within parliamentary systems (single-party majoritarian governments *versus* multi-party coalition and consensus-oriented governments) seem to play a crucial role (see, for example, Lijpart 1984; Pollitt and Bouckaert 2011; Sætren 2009). More informal institutionalised practices, stemming from historically derived *political* and *administrative cultures* and resulting in unique *national policy styles* and *politico-administrative traditions* (Richardson 1982; Freeman 1985; Siedentorpf and Ziller 1988; Knill and Lenschow 1998), have also been suggested and explored as other supplementary and potentially important institutional factors in this respect.

Within the same country, the type of organisation and institution involved in the policy process typically varies from one policy stage (agenda-setting and policy-formulation) to another (policy-legitimisation and -implementation) and this usually implies a changing gallery of actors in the policy process as it progresses from the earlier to the later stages. National policy styles, as suggested above, may play an important role here in regulating the access of various actors and interest groups in some crucial policy stages, like policy-formulation and -implementation.

A common and quite valid criticism of the institutional approach in political science, which applies to many other approaches as well, is that they are better suited to explain policy *continuity* than *change*. This follows from the strong emphasis on the role of *the legacy of the past* and *path-dependency* in historical institutionalism. This critique highlights the important *constraining* function of institutions on political life. What it tends to miss is the other equally important face of institutions: their *enabling* function (Olsen 1992: 257–8; Scharpf 1997: 34). Weaver and Rockman (1993: 447), summing up their impressive cross-national comparative study, confirmed this dual role of institutions: they found that the same institutional arrangements both *facilitate* and *impede* policy-change, depending on policy-context and circumstances. Another frequently cited example that has intrigued many policy scholars in this respect is Sweden in the early decades of the last half of the previous century. Here, an unprecedentedly long-lasting and stable type of government (Social Democrats were in government for more than forty years) developed a policy tradition of initiating and implementing innovative and radical reform programmes (see, for example, Anton 1969; Castles 1976; Richardson 1982).

The congruence between EU directives and the unique national historical-institutional contexts in which they are supposed to be adopted and implemented is one line of research that has tried to investigate this dual role of institutions (Knill and Lenschow 1998; Treib 2008). The assumption here is that the faithful adoption and implementation of EU law is the result of some sort of test of the compatibility of the former relative to political-administrative institutions of the member-states. This again implies that policy-making is a matter of matching policies to institutions and other contextual factors, where policy success supposedly depends on finding a good fit. This matching and compatibility-testing thesis is very similar to the coupling of policy streams so essential in the MS framework, especially if we add the logic of historical-institutionalism and path-dependency to those of serendipity and human agency.

What is the GC model and the MS framework?

The last issue we will discuss, related to both the GC model and the MS framework, is the important question of how they should be understood. There has been considerable confusion surrounding this question from the very beginning. Are they theories, perhaps models or maybe nothing more than ideas and metaphors serving as some kind of analytical framework? The confusion may stem from the fact that Cohen, March and Olsen (1972) presented the GC metaphor both as a new *idea,* that is, an alternative way of thinking about organisations and how they operate, and as a very sophisticated and highly specified organisational *computer-simulation model.* The latter is allegedly one of the most famous computer models in all of social science, according to some of its critics (Bendor *et al.* 2001: 169). Thus, there is no doubt that this computer model represents a highly specified *theory.* However, when Sabatier (1991, 1999) refers to it as a novel and promising *approach* in his discussion of how to improve on policy theory, he seems to interpret it more as a new idea or way of thinking about causation in policy research than as a theory *per se.* In this vein, like some others (for example, Mucciaroni 1992: 482), this author also does not think it is appropriate to refer to the MS framework as a theory. At best it functions as an *analytical framework,* that is, a 'roadmap' that guides investigators in the right direction with respect to what type of explanatory factors to look for and observe. The framework itself, however, does not explain how decision-stream elements interact with each other and with exogenous factors to produce policy results. At least, the version formulated by Kingdon does not. This is where theories about actors, interest-groups, organisational structures and institutions, and their wider context, are needed.

The potential of the MS framework as a multi-theoretical construct

It should be clear by now that the central objective of this paper has been to suggest how the MS framework can be developed into a more comprehensive and integrative policy theory. Before the turn of the century, the conclusion was that no unified theoretical paradigm had emerged so far in the study of public policy (Hill 1997; John 1998). This, of course, reflects the great complexity of the research topic: the multiplicity of institutions and actors at different levels of analysis and the related policy processes, which may take several years from beginning to end. There has, so far, been a, probably necessary, division of labour in theorising about various aspects of this complexity, resulting in different well known theoretical approaches mentioned in many textbooks (Howlett *et al.* 2009; John 1998; Sabatier 1999). These theoretical approaches are not rivals. They complement each other and are all part of an overall explanation. John (1998: 18) puts it this way:

> ... only an integrative framework, one that utilizes important insights from all the approaches, can fully explain the variety and complexity of the practice of policy-making and implementation.

This is the spirit in which this paper has been written. But it is also written in the firm belief that a revised MS framework provides the best platform for a much-needed integrative framework. The strength of a revised MS framework along the lines suggested in this paper is that it could be developed into a genuinely *multi-theoretical* framework that does not privilege one classical theoretical orientation at the expense of others. Thus, it could offer more convincing and realistic causal explanations of many counter-intuitive, paradoxical and surprising policies that are often best understood as resulting from dynamic interaction between factors central in different types of policy approaches/theories and their combination in time and space.

The MS framework is an idea or a solution that has been 'floating' around in the academic literature for a good forty years now. Its potential and promise as a policy theory has been pointed out repeatedly over these years (Bendor *et al.* 2001; Sabatier 1991; Mucciaroni 1992: John 1998; Zahariadis 2003). At the same time, advocates of some of the other leading 'rival' theoretical approaches have suggested the need to bond theirs with those of others (see, for example, Schneider and Ingram 1997: 73–5; Peters *et al.* 2005: 1284–7) to overcome the acknowledged weaknesses of their own favourite approaches. In view of these facts, a *window of opportunity* may have finally opened for work to begin on synthesising the many policy-theoretical approaches within an expanded and integrated MS framework. To stay in the parlance of the MSF, some *entrepreneurship* is probably required to effectuate this long-overdue project.

References

Anton, T. J. (1969) 'Policy-making and political culture in Sweden', *Scandinavian Political Studies Yearbook* 4: 90–102.

Bendor, J., Moe, T. M. and Shotts, K. W. (2001) 'Recycling the garbage can: an assessment of the research program', *American Political Science Review* 95(1): 169–90.

Castles, F. (1976) 'Policy innovation and institutional stability in Sweden', *British Journal of Political Science* 6(2): 203–16.

Cohen, M. D., March, J. G. and Olsen, J. P. (1972) 'A garbage can model of organizational choice', *Administrative Science Quarterly* 17(1): 1–25.

— (2012) '"A garbage can model" at forty: a solution that still attracts problems', in A. Lomi and R. Harrison (eds) *The Garbage Can Model of Organizational Choice: Looking forward at forty*, Research in Sociology of Organizations 36, Bingley, UK: Emerald Group Publishing, pp. 19–30.

Freeman, G. P. (1985) 'National styles and policy sectors. Explaining structured variation', *Journal of Public Policy* 5(4): 467–96.

Hall, P. (1986) *Governing the Economy. The politics of state intervention in Britain and France*, Oxford, UK: Oxford University Press.

Hill, K. Q. (1997) 'In search of policy theory', *Policy Currents* 7(1): 1–9.

Howlett, M., Ramesh, M. and Pearl, A. (2009) *Studying Public Policy. Policy cycles & policy subsystems*, Oxford, UK: Oxford University Press.

John, P. (1998) *Analyzing Public Policy*, London and New York: Pinter.

Kingdon, J. W. (1984) *Agendas, Alternatives, and Public Policies*, Boston, MA and Toronto: Little, Brown & Co.

Knill, C. and Lenschow, A. (1998) 'Coping with Europe. The impact of British and German administrative traditions on the implementation of EU environmental policy', *Journal of European Public Policy* 5(4): 595–614.

Lijphart, A. (1984) *Democracies. Patterns of majoritarian and consensus government in twenty-one countries*, New Haven, CT and London: Yale University Press.

— (1999) *Patterns of Democracy: Government forms and performance in thirty-six countries*, New Haven, CT and London: Yale University Press.

March, J. G. and Olsen, J. P. (1976) *Ambiguity and Choice in Organizations*, Bergen, NO: Universitetsforlaget.

— (1984) 'The new institutionalism: organizational factors in political life', *American Political Science Review* 78(3): 734–49.

March, J. G. and Simon, H. A. (1958) *Organizations* New York: John Wiley.

Mucciaroni, G. (1992) 'The garbage can model and the study of policy making: a critique', *Polity* 24(3): 459–82.

Mumper, M. (1987) 'Review essay: understanding policy agendas', *Social Science Journal* 24(1): 83–6.

North, D. C. (1990) *Institutions, Institutional Change and Economic Performance*, Cambridge, UK: Cambridge University Press.

Olsen, J. P. (1972) 'Public policy-making and theories of organizational choice', *Scandinavian Political Studies Yearbook* 7: 45–62.

— (1992) 'Analyzing institutional dynamics', *Staatswissenschaften und Staatspraxis* 3(2): 247–71.

Olsen, J. P. and Peters, B. G. (1996) *Lessons from Experience. Experiential learning in administrative reforms in eight democracies*, Oslo, Stockholm, Copenhagen, Oxford and Boston, MA: Scandinavian University Press.

Peters, B. G., King, D. S. and King, J. P. (2005) 'The politics of path dependency: political conflict in historical institutionalism', *Journal of Politics* 67(4): 1275–1300.

Pollitt, C. and Bouckaert, G. (2011) *Public Management Reform: A comparative analysis*, Oxford: Oxford University Press.

Richardson, J. (1982) *Policy Styles in Western Europe*, London: George Allen & Unwin.

Rommetveit, K. (1976) 'Decision-making under changing norms', in J. G. March and J. P. Olsen (eds) *Ambiguity and Choice in Organizations*, Bergen: Universitetsforlaget, pp. 140–55.

Sabatier, P. A. (1991) 'Towards better theories of the policy process', *PS: Political Science & Politics* 24(2): 147–56.

— (1999) *Theories of the Policy Process*, Boulder, CO: Westview Press.

Sætren, H. (2009) 'Explaining radical policy change against all odds: the role of leadership, institutions, program design and policy windows', in J. A. Raffel, P. Leisink and A. E. Middlebrooks (eds): *Public Sector Leadership. International challenges and perspectives*, Cheltenham, UK: Edward Elgar Publishing, pp. 53–72.

Scharpf, F. W. (1997) *Games Real Actors Play. Actor centered institutionalism in policy research*, Boulder, CO: Westview Press.

Schneider, A. L. and Ingram, H. (1997) *Policy Design for Democracy*, Lawrence, KY: University Press of Kansas.

Siedentorpf, H. and Ziller, J. (eds) (1988) *Making European Policies Work: The implementation of Community legislation in the member states*, vol. 1, *Comparative Syntheses*, London: Sage Publications.

Simon, H. A. (1955) 'A behavioral model of rational choice', *Quarterly Journal of Economics* 69(1): 99–118.

Steinmo, S., Thelen, K. and Longstreth, F. (1992) *Structuring Politics. Historical institutionalism in comparative analysis*, Cambridge, UK: Cambridge University Press.

Thompson, J. D. (1967) *Organizations In Action*, New York: McGraw-Hill.

Treib, O. (2008) 'Implementing and complying with EU governance outputs', *Living Reviews in European Governance* 3(5): 1–30.

Weaver, R. K. and Rockman, B. A. (1993) *Do Institutions Matter? Government capabilities in the United States and abroad*, Washington, DC: Brookings Institution Press.

Zahariadis, N. (1995) 'Ideas, networks and policy streams: privatization in Britain and Germany', *Review of Policy Research* 14(1–2): 71–98.

Zahariadis, N. (2003) *Ambiguity and Choice in Public Policy*: Georgetown, Washington, DC: Georgetown University Press.

Chapter Three

Clear Enough To Be Proven Wrong? Assessing the Influence of the Concept of Bounded Rationality within the Multiple-Streams Framework

Johanna Kuhlmann

Introduction

The multiple-streams framework (MSF) plays a special role in policy analysis. On the one hand, it is one of the most-cited approaches in policy analysis (Sabatier 2007a: 9); on the other hand, it is also criticised by leading scholars in the field. Sabatier's well-known critique of the approach concentrates especially on three points (Sabatier 2007b: 332). First, the dependent variable is not clearly defined; second, falsification of some important theoretical assumptions is impossible; and, third, causal processes are under-specified, mainly because there is no consistent conception of the individual. So the main assumption of theory construction, '[to] be clear enough to be proven wrong' (Sabatier 2007b: 327), is violated and theoretical progress is complicated.[1]

Nonetheless, the literature disagrees with one point of Sabatier's critique in particular: Many scholars state that the individual in the MSF is boundedly rational and is, therefore, by no means under-specified. When talking about processes underlying the political system, the founder of the multiple-streams approach, John W. Kingdon, points to the limits of rational policy-making by referring to the work of James G. March and Herbert A. Simon (Simon and March 1958). They were the first to analyse organisations by linking them to the concept of bounded rationality (Jones 2003: 396), which was developed by one of the authors, Simon, in 1945. Regarding policy-makers, Kingdon (2003[1984]: 78) claims that the 'ability of human beings to process information is more limited than ... a comprehensive approach would prescribe'. Thus, in a review article comparing different approaches in policy analysis, Edella Schlager (2007: 302) states that the individual in the MSF is 'firmly grounded in Simon's boundedly rational individual'. That is why she characterises the individual as a 'satisficer' (Schlager 2007: 302). So Schlager's conclusion seems to oppose Sabatier's: while the latter denies a consistent model of the individual in the MSF, the former claims the individual in the MSF to be 'firmly' conceptualised in the sense of Simon's concept of bounded rationality.

---

1.   For a critique on Sabatier in this regard, see Herweg 2013.

Against the background of these contradictory assumptions concerning the theoretical premises of the MSF, this article aims to critically analyse the actual influence of the concept of bounded rationality within the multiple-streams approach.[2] This does not imply that it is essential for any approach in policy analysis to have a micro-foundation. However, *if* the multiple-streams approach is considered to have one, this needs to be highlighted; because placing the actors in the MSF within the concept of bounded rationality has implications not only for the micro-theoretical foundation of the approach but for theory construction as a whole: the fundamental relevance of bounded rationality for political science lies in the assumption that human behaviour can be transferred to macro-politics (Jones 2003: 395). Against this background, this chapter will analyse two questions:

1. is the individual in the MSF based on the boundedly rational individual in Simon's sense?; and, based on that,
2. what role does bounded rationality play within the whole MSF?

The chapter, thus, furthers our knowledge of the conception of the individual in the MSF: if bounded rationality is identified as consistently underlying the MSF, Sabatier's critique that the approach lacks logical and causal consistency has to be denied. If, however, the MSF is considered as being inconsistent with bounded rationality, the next question would be: is there another micro-foundation underlying the approach, or does the approach completely lack a micro-foundation? Either way, the chapter aims to contribute to a better understanding of the MSF and – keeping in mind Sabatier's (2007a) call for better theories – also builds a theoretical basis for further development.

The structure of the paper is as follows: the first section gives a short overview of different micro-foundations in important theories of policy analysis. The second section then traces in detail the influence of bounded rationality on the MSF, in order to answer the two research questions. The analysis will be based on five categories: the *theoretical point of departure* briefly identifies whether the concept of bounded rationality and the MSF theorise on the micro- or macro-level. It is self-evident that the *conception of the individual* as well as *handling of rationality* are crucial for understanding the micro-foundation of the two approaches. The *connection between the individual and the organisation* is important because the main notion of the concept of bounded rationality, as already stated, is that the conception of the individual has an effect on the organisation's structures and processes. Thus, to assess the influence of the concept of bounded rationality within the MSF, it is necessary to analyse if there is a similar connection between the individual and the organisation in the MSF. Finally, *decision-making* will be

---

2. By doing this, I will primarily refer to the work of Nikolaos Zahariadis, who has extensively worked with the multiple-streams framework (Zahariadis and Allen 1995; Zahariadis 1998; Zahariadis 2008; Ackrill *et al.* 2013) and elaborated the initial concept as developed by John W. Kingdon. However, it is important to note that Kingdon's and Zahariadis' conceptualisation of the multiple-streams framework differ in some important aspects, for example, regarding certain concepts like the policy-entrepreneur or the politics stream, and also in the scope of the approach.

analysed, because this is where the other principles actually come into operation. The final section summarises the central implications of the analysis and also contains some reflections on the implications of these findings for the MSF.

Discussing the micro-foundation in theories of political science – a short overview of relevant approaches

The most common approach for addressing the question how actors make decisions is still the concept of the 'economic man' (*homo oeconomicus*), which has been developed in the field of economic theory. He possesses preferences concerning possible alternatives, orders these preferences according to their respective benefits, and chooses the option that enables him best to achieve his goals (Dehling and Schubert 2011: 31). Although the concept of economic man is very popular in political science, especially in the field of public choice (Howlett and Ramesh 2003: 22), there are also many approaches that deviate from the notion that individual action is primarily driven by self-interested utility-maximisers – without, however, necessarily completely denying it.

Herbert A. Simon was the first to reject the assumption of comprehensive rationality postulated by the model of economic man; he replaced it by a 'bounded rationality' model. His book *Administrative Behavior: A study of decision-making processes in administrative organizations*, first published in 1945, has become a milestone in a multiplicity of disciplines and was awarded the Nobel Prize in Economics in 1978 (Sherwood 1990: 252). Simon's main assumption – which will be explained in more detail in the next section – is that human rationality is bounded but that these boundaries depend on the individual's administrative environment. Against this background, 'the organization … takes from the individual some of his decisional autonomy, and substitutes for it an organization decision-making process' (Simon 1976: 8). Individual goals, then, become administrative goals, resulting in an outcome that is considered to be more rational. Thus, the concept of bounded rationality does not at all neglect rational action (Rüb 2009: 358) but expounds the problem of achieving it.

Administrative Behavior can be seen as the 'first bold step' (Jones 2003: 396) in the evolution of the concept of bounded rationality. In the meantime, the concept has become both popular and unspecific, where defining central assumptions turns out to be difficult (Campitelli and Gobet 2010). While the influence of the concept of bounded rationality on many disciplines (including, for example, sociology, economics and psychology) is beyond controversy, political science is often said to neglect the concept's assumptions (Bendor 2003; Jones 2003). This is particularly surprising if one considers that the concept, at least implicitly, underlies many established approaches in policy analysis (Schlager 2007; Pump 2011).

Another influential approach that emerged in contrast to the rational model and which sheds light on a specific form of micro-foundation was developed by Charles Lindblom. His article 'The science of muddling through' (Lindblom 1959) provided the basis for the so-called 'incremental model'. Although sharing Simon's opinion on (individual) constraints on comprehensive rationality, Lindblom was sceptical of the likelihood of improving rational decision-making (Parsons 1995: 284). In the incremental model, decision-making is seen as a

> political process characterised by bargaining and compromise among self-interested decision-makers .... In this model, the decisions eventually made represent what is politically feasible rather than desirable, and what is possible rather than 'maximal' (Howlett and Ramesh 2003: 170).

Accordingly, 'The science of muddling through' indicated that decision-making proceeded in rather small steps away from the status quo, due to the high costs of radical change and to bureaucratic hurdles (Howlett and Ramesh 2003: 171). When developing the MSF, Kingdon recognises the importance of the incremental model but claims that it only explains a certain part of the policy process, that is, the development of alternatives (Kingdon 2003[1984]: 83). When it comes to policy-change, however, non-incremental change takes place. That is why the incremental model will not be analysed in the present article.

In recent years, 'prospect theory' has been increasingly used to explain political decision-making (McDermott 2004; Vis 2011). It was initially developed by Kahneman and Tversky (1979) and analyses individual behaviour under risk. In contrast to rational-choice theory, individual action does not depend on final states but on whether individuals are facing gains or losses. Losses are felt more than gains; this means that people are inclined to accept risks when facing losses and to avoid risks when facing gains (Vis 2011). However, as the MSF evolved in a completely different context and does not analyse individual behaviour based on a certain reference point, the influence of prospect theory will not be analysed here.

While these approaches do not completely abandon the notion of rationality, but rather modify it in order to be able to build on more realistic assumptions, the 'garbage-can' model of organisational choice (Cohen, March and Olsen 1972) was the first model that did not place rationality (or partial departures from rationality), but rather ambiguity at the centre of analysis. The model focuses on organisations as 'organized anarchies' (Cohen, March and Olsen 1972: 1). They are characterised by 'problematic preferences', 'unclear technology' and 'fluid participation' (Cohen, March and Olsen 1972: 1), which is the reason why decision-making is no longer considered to be a rational process. Rather, the connection between problem and solution is interrupted so that decisions are made randomly and unpredictably (Rüb 2009: 350).

Although the garbage-can model has been an important and influential innovation in organisation theory (Bendor et al. 2001: 169), it has, among other things, been criticised for its high level of abstraction (Muccarioni 1992: 463) and for being 'cloud-like' (Mucciaroni 1992: 482). Despite the criticism, however, the model has been regarded as an important 'starting point' (Mucciaroni 1992: 482) for further development of agenda-setting approaches. What is more, it is often said that the MSF represents a more elaborate version of the garbage-can model (Bendor et al. 2001: 186). Also, scholars of the MSF stress the central role that the model plays for the approach (Kingdon 2003[1984]: 86; Rüb 2009: 350; Zahariadis 2007: 66). However, as the garbage-can model does not have a micro-foundation at all (Bendor *et al.* 2001: 172), it will also be excluded from the analysis.[3]

The concept of bounded rationality

Theoretical point of departure and conception of the individual

As the concept of bounded rationality theorises at the micro-level, the 'administrative man' is crucial to the whole concept. Starting his explanation, Simon states that 'the social sciences suffer from acute schizophrenia in their treatment of rationality' (Simon 1976: xxvi): while the economists think of the individual as acting perfectly rationally (economic man), social psychology conceives of the individual as being affect-controlled. In contrast, Simon settles his administrative man *between* rational and non-rational behaviour:

> To anyone who has observed administrative organizations or has concerned himself with their theory, it seems obvious enough that human behavior in organizations is, if not wholly rational, at least in good part *intendedly* so (Simon 1976: xxviii) [italicisation in original].

This assumption has two implications (Simon 1976: xxix). First, the administrative man does not seek, as economists state, the best solution for a problem: rather, he looks for solutions that are good enough – in Simon's words: 'satisficing' – because his limited cognitive skills do not allow him to find an optimal solution. So every decision automatically becomes a compromise. Second, the administrative man has a very simplified picture of reality, insofar as he considers most of the factors in the world irrelevant to his personal situation. On the one hand, this enables him to make his decisions faster than the economic man, as he does not have to search for all alternatives and weight them against each other. On the other hand, based on his simplified world view, he can also make his decisions by using 'relatively simple rules of thumb' (Simon 1976: xxx) that do not challenge him intellectually.

Handling of rationality

The conception of the individual is strongly tied to the understanding of rationality. For Simon, the individual is confronted with many complications when he or she tries to act rationally: 'Roughly speaking, rationality is concerned with the selection of preferred behaviour alternatives in terms of some system of values whereby the consequences of behaviour can be evaluated' (Simon 1976: 75).

---

3. Considering that 1) the concept of bounded rationality is claimed to be the micro-foundation on which MSF is built and, 2) the MSF is claimed to be an elaboration of the garbage-can model, which does not have a micro-foundation, the question of the actual influence of the concept of bounded rationality within the MSF gains even more importance.

However, this definition does not make clear what happens with unconscious and unintended processes or with behaviour that is based on erroneous information (Simon 1976: 75). It is also hard to identify measurable benchmarks for rationality. Simon's solution lies in a plural definition of rationality, indicating that a single rationality does not exist but that rationality always depends on the respective frame of reference. To give an example: 'A decision is "organizationally" rational if it is oriented to the organization's goals; it is "personally' rational if it is oriented to the individual's goals' (Simon 1976: 77).

Connection between individual and organisation

What is more, acting fully rationally is, for an individual, at the same time impossible and unnecessary, as people act nearly always within organisations (Simon 1976: ix). These organisations enable individuals to come close to what Simon calls objective rationality, indicating that a decision is 'in fact … the correct behaviour for maximizing given values in a given situation' (Simon 1976: 76). Within this context, for Simon, the term organisation

> refers to the complex pattern of communication and relationships in a group of human beings. This pattern provides to each member of the group much of the information and many of the assumptions, goals, and attitudes that enter into his decisions, and provides him also with a set of stable and comprehensible expectations as to what the other members of the group are doing and how they will react to what he says and does (Simon 1976: xvii).

At the centre of analysis lies the decision-behaviour of an organisational participant. However, he is influenced 'within and by the organization' (Simon 1976: 3). As individual and organisational goals overlap, the individual accepts the influence of the organisation (Simon 1976: 110).

Although the preceding arguments suggest that stability is assured within the organisation by certain routines, 'the organization objective is by no means a static thing' (Simon 1976: 114). Rather, organisational goals have to be permanently adapted. Within this process, the organisation and the organisational participants find themselves in a kind of symbiotic relationship, also called 'the equilibrium of the organization' (Simon 1976: 110).

Even though the organisation controls, to a certain degree, non-rationality, one should not overestimate rationality within the organisation: while choosing alternatives, the organisation is also confronted with boundaries. In addition to that, certain authorities can also refuse to make a decision. In this context, it is also important to specify the role of time (Simon 1976: 67).

Decision-making

The actual decision can be understood as a 'composite decision' (Simon 1976: 221), where the role of a single individual can be neglected as the development of the decision can be traced back to many different members of the organisation (Simon 1976: 221).

In sum, it should have become clear that, on the one hand, the organisation is able to control individual irrationality and to approximate rational decisions; on the other hand, the organisation is far from being a rational entity – which is only natural as it is constituted by boundedly rational individuals.

The influence of the concept of bounded rationality on the MSF

After outlining the concept of bounded rationality as the assumed 'groundwork' of the MSF, the following section will analyse the influence of the concept of bounded rationality within the MSF.

Theoretical point of departure and conception of the individual

Unlike the concept of bounded rationality, the MSF theorises on the macro-level, that is, the (governmental) organisation is considered first. Thus, in this regard, the MSF indeed relies strongly on the garbage-can model. Looking at the micro-level of the MSF as a second step, however, reveals two actors acting in different contexts: the policy-entrepreneur and the policy-maker. Thus, actors do indeed matter in the MSF. Yet – and opposed to the concept of bounded rationality – decisions in the MSF should not be understood as an aggregation of individual efforts (Zahariadis 2007: 66).

Policy-makers are actors who are formally entitled to adopt policies. Policy-entrepreneurs[4] – who are more central in the approach – are 'goal-intending manipulators' (Zahariadis 2007: 70) who can, more precisely, be described as

> advocates who are willing to invest their resources – time, energy, reputation, money – to promote a position in return for anticipated future gain in the form of material, purposive, or solidary benefits (Kingdon 2003[1984]: 179).

So policy-entrepreneurs not only provide particular solutions, they are 'power brokers and manipulators of problematic preferences and unclear technology' (Zahariadis 2007: 74). The MSF does not mention the placement of the entrepreneur; however, as he possesses 'some claim to a hearing' (Kingdon 2003[1984]: 180), he has a certain reputation and is also convincing.

Both kind of actors in the MSF, policy-makers and policy-entrepreneurs, are trying to act rationally in order to achieve their aims (Rüb 2009: 358) but face 'biological and cognitive limitations' (Zahariadis 2007: 68) – a finding that is very much in line with the concept of bounded rationality as described by Simon. Against this background, policy-makers can deal with only a limited number of policy issues (Zahariadis 2007: 68) and are permanently overburdened (Zahariadis 2007: 75) because of the number and the complexity of problems they have to

---

4. For a review of the concept of policy-entrepreneurship, see Mintrom and Norman 2009.

deal with. As they have, in addition to that, unclear preferences (Zahariadis 2007: 70), they can be manipulated by policy-entrepreneurs: relying on their opinion could be, after all, an considerable relief! Policy-entrepreneurs act in a boundedly rational way, insofar as they try to put forward their 'pet projects' (Zahariadis 2007: 68) in different contexts, being unable (due to the biological and cognitive limitations already described) to develop a policy for every special issue and irrespective of whether this 'pet project' is an efficient solution to the problem. Kingdon clearly points out that

> we should not paint these entrepreneurs as superhumanly clever. It could be that they are … [b]ut it could as easily be that they aren't. They push for their proposals all the time; long before a window opens, they try coupling after coupling that fails; and by dumb luck, they happen to come along when a window is open (Kingdon 2003[1984]: 183).

Although it has become clear that policy-makers and policy-entrepreneurs act in a way that is boundedly rational, this does not ensure that the individual within the MSF is deeply rooted within the concept of bounded rationality. This is illustrated by the policy-entrepreneur, who is designed in a fuzzy way (Rüb 2006: 24). Kingdon clearly thinks of the policy-entrepreneur as an individual actor (Kingdon 2003[1984]: 179). Zahariadis, in contrast, states that policy-entrepreneurs can be either individual or corporate (Zahariadis 2007: 74). Here, the concept of bounded rationality and the MSF clearly differ: the central premise of the concept of bounded rationality is that individual and collective rationality are different and that individuals can only act in a rational manner when they find themselves in an organisational environment. However, the MSF does not address the fact that individual and corporate actors may have different resources for achieving their aims.

Handling of rationality

In matters of rationality, important differences can also be stated. Simon focuses on the factor of uncertainty. Although the individual herself is boundedly rational, the organisational environment enables an approximation to so-called objective rationality. In contrast, the MSF does not posit that achieving full rationality is completely impossible; only that it is extremely unlikely (Rüb 2009: 360). Instead of focusing on uncertainty, the approach concentrates on ambiguity, which can be seen as the main ontological premise (Zahariadis 2007: 87). Thus, in this regard, the approach again adopts the garbage-can perspective. Citing Feldman, Zahariadis defines ambiguity as 'a state of having many ways of thinking about the same circumstances or phenomena' (Feldman 1989: 5). Ambiguity is different from uncertainty because the latter can, to a certain degree, be eliminated by more information, for example, with the help of organisations. However, more information does not reduce ambiguity – on the contrary, it even enhances the vagueness because the ambiguity of social phenomena is complexified by more dimensions (Zahariadis 2007: 66).

If ambiguity is central to policy-making, political manipulation is used by actors to control ambiguity (Zahariadis 2007: 69) and, moreover, to change ambiguity into unambiguousness. This is primarily done by the policy-entrepreneur, who can influence the policy-maker's process of choice by specific 'manipulating strategies and skills' (Zahariadis 2007: 77). 'Political manipulation aims primarily to provide meaning, clarification, and identity' (Zahariadis 2007: 69). While political manipulation, from the policy-entrepreneur's point of view, can be regarded as quite egoistic, it does, from a systemic perspective, bring in new ideas (Zahariadis 2007: 69 and 84). An important point here is the so-called 'framing' that gives a dominant interpretation to an ambiguous situation. Here, information plays a crucial role that is, however, never presented in a neutral way (Jones and Baumgartner 2005). Moreover, symbols are important in building support for particular ideas. They particularly address the emotions of those who should be convinced and are also highly responsible for the structuring of attention. 'Salami tactics' refers to the strategic manipulation of time. Finally, 'affect-priming' means the strategic influencing of emotions (Zahariadis 2007: 77-8).

The way the MSF derives ambiguity reveals further differences between the concept of bounded rationality on the one hand and the MSF on the other hand: Simon's understanding of rationality results from the individual's cognitive boundaries. In the MSF, on the contrary, ambiguity is not placed at the micro-, but rather at the macro-level: It is, first of all, social processes that are ambiguous. Here, once again, the different levels of theorising become clear. In general, one can assume that ambiguity, indeed, makes achieving rationality impossible (Zahariadis 2007: 68). It is only *ex post* that the rationality of political processes can be analysed (Rüb 2009: 360).

Focusing on ambiguity leads the researcher to attach special importance to time because political processes and outputs are not determined by rationality but rather by contingency. Against this background, the timing of political processes becomes important at certain moments in time (Zahariadis 2007: 68; Blank *et al.* 2011: 74). In general, focusing on time is the common ground between the MSF and the concept of bounded rationality. It holds true for both approaches that 'the sequence in which solutions are considered strongly affects the decision outcome' (Zahariadis 2007: 68). So, while both emphasise the importance of time in decisions, managing time becomes dominant only in the MSF. That is also why the individual's cognitive boundaries can primarily be considered in the face of time. The first key assumption here is that 'individual attention or processing is serial' (Zahariadis 2007: 68), referring to biological and cognitive limits. The second important assumption highlights that individuals are permanently under time pressure (Zahariadis 2007: 68–9). Both assumptions are compatible with the concept of bounded rationality.

Connection between individual and organisation

The MSF and the concept of bounded rationality both posit that the individual's cognitive boundaries are absorbed by administrative structures: 'Because policy makers at the top are frequently overwhelmed by the number and complexity of problems they encounter, they have designed institutions to ease overload' (Zahariadis 2007: 75). This especially results from the organisation's capacity for 'parallel processing', meaning that an organisation can direct its attention to many problems at the same time. This is enabled through subsystems (Zahariadis 2007: 75). At the same time, the organisation also prioritises problems through temporal sorting. Here, Simon again can be regarded as a pioneer in dealing with parallel processing (True *et al.* 2007: 158); however, this was not yet his main topic in *Administrative Behavior* (Simon 1957; Simon 1983).

By focusing on parallel processing and temporal sorting, the MSF states that managing time can be regarded as the central characteristic of the organisation. This is also reflected in the definition of the organisation as a procedural structure that is in constant flux (Rüb 2009: 350).

In this regard, the concept of bounded rationality on the one hand and the MSF on the other hand indeed differ: first, although it also leaves room for certain dynamics, the organisation in the concept of bounded rationality has a relatively fixed structure that is, for example, supported by routines, hierarchies and so on. In addition to that, the organisation is not at all limited to the management of time but has many more functions in order to control non-rationality. In contrast, the (governmental) organisation in the MSF is a process-oriented structure that is permanently being reconfigured (Rüb 2009: 350). Such an organisation is hardly able to establish routines and so on, or control the process of choice (Zahariadis 2007: 66).

Thus, the connection between the organisation and the individual is different: in the concept of bounded rationality, the individual is, to some extent, integrated in the organisational structure, his autonomy to decide being replaced by the organisation's autonomy in order to make almost rational decisions. As the individual's goals and the goals of the organisation overlap, this does not pose a problem. In the MSF, however, the governmental organisation hardly exerts influence on the individuals, apart from enabling them to manage time more effectively.

To sum up, the preceding explanation calls into question Zahariadis' assumption that the organisation compensates for individual cognitive boundaries: where exactly can this 'compensation' be found? The organisation is, of course, able to carry out parallel processing. However – irrespective of the quality of the outcomes generated by parallel processing – it needs to be highlighted that parallel processing might increase the ambiguity of social processes instead of reducing it.

Decision-making

A final step is to look at the differences in decision-making: while the decision in the concept of bounded rationality results from organisational structures and processes, it remains contingent in the MSF. As the final decision-making is the step in the whole policy-making process in which the analysed principles actually come into operation, the implications of this finding are important for assessing the influence of the concept of bounded rationality within the MSF as such: obviously, the influence of the concept of bounded rationality within the MSF is rather limited.

The next section will summarise the main findings of the analysis in more detail.

Results of analysis

The analysis has revealed that, although the MSF shares some common ground with the concept of bounded rationality, 1) the concept of bounded rationality does not constitute the micro-foundation of the MSF; and, consequently, 2) the influence of the concept of bounded rationality in the MSF as a whole is overall rather limited. This results primarily from the fact that ambiguity is the central ontological premise of the MSF.

The main results of the analysis are summarised in Table 3.1.

While the concept of bounded rationality theorises on the micro-level, the systemic level serves as the initial point in the MSF. At the micro-level the MSF, like the concept of bounded rationality (with the administrative man), characterises the individual (more specifically policy-makers and policy-entrepreneurs) as being boundedly rational. So Schlager's assumption that individuals in the MSF are grounded in Simon's conception of bounded rationality is in one way right. However, if one assumes that the concept of bounded rationality is serving as the micro-foundation of the MSF, Sabatier is also right when he states that the individual in the MSF does not possess a consistent micro-theoretical foundation (Sabatier 2007b: 328). This becomes particularly clear with regard to the policy-entrepreneur, who can be conceived as either individual or corporate, hence ignoring the different logics of action that, at least according to the concept of bounded rationality, underlie the actions of individual and corporate actors. Thus, the MSF 'borrows' from the concept of bounded rationality in a way but it does not, strictly, build on it.

Table 3.1: Results of analysis

	Bounded rationality	**Multiple-streams framework**
Theoretical point of departure	Micro-level	Macro-level
Conception of the individual	Administrative man	Policy-makers and policy-entrepreneurs
Handling of rationality	Uncertainty	Ambiguity
Connection between individual and organisation	Organisation compensates for individual shortcomings	Organisation increases individual shortcomings
Decision-making	Results from organisational structures and processes	Contingent

Based on that, an important difference is the marginal role that rationality plays within the MSF: while the concept of bounded rationality assumes that uncertainty is the dominant principle, which can, however, be compensated by more information, the MSF acts on the assumption that ambiguity can even be reinforced by more information. In addition to that, the MSF emphasises the handling of time, which is, in the concept of bounded rationality, only one aspect among others.

Regarding the connection between the individual and the organisation, the assumptions of the concept of bounded rationality and the MSF also differ. Within the concept of bounded rationality, boundedly rational individuals need organisations in order to control the non-rational. The MSF, however, does not transfer the implications of boundedly rational individuals to the conception of the macro-level: within the governmental organisation, it is not bounded rationality but rather ambiguity that dominates. In addition, the organisation hardly exerts any influence on the individuals. The concept of bounded rationality and the MSF also differ considering the possibilities of the organisation: while the concept of bounded rationality ascribes a role in compensating for the limitations of individual rationality to the organisation, the governmental organisation within the MSF seems to make these limitations worse. This also results from the different understanding of the organisation.

The different understandings of how the actual decision is made are particularly interesting: while it can be regarded as a logical result from the organisational structure and processes in the concept of bounded rationality, it turns out to be contingent in the MSF.

However, it is important to point out that the fundamental difference between the concept of bounded rationality and the MSF is not that bounded rationality is more rational: Indeed, both concepts assign an important role to uncertainty. However, the concept of bounded rationality aims to make this uncertainty, coming from the individual's bounded rationality, explicable at the macro-level and also, finally, something it is possible to overcome by establishing organisational structures and processes. In contrast, the MSF applies a completely different logic by taking the macro-level as a theoretical point of departure. In addition, ambiguity rather than bounded rationality is the dominant principle on the macro-level because the implications that are being drawn from the micro-level are different from those on the macro-level. The connection of boundedly rational individuals on the micro-level, derived from the concept of bounded rationality, and ambiguity on the macro-level, derived primarily from the garbage-can model of choice, poses a theoretical challenge for the micro-foundation of the MSF that has not yet been resolved.

Implications for further research

The analysis has shown that the MSF does not fundamentally rely on Herbert Simon's concept of bounded rationality as a micro-foundation. Rather, it *partially* builds on the concept of bounded rationality and conceptualises two boundedly rational actors, the policy-maker and the policy-entrepreneur, of which the policy-entrepreneur, especially, is a little conceptually fuzzy. The implications of the concept of bounded rationality on the micro-level are, however, not transferred to the macro-level, where a different logic prevails.

What a consistent micro-foundation for the MSF could look like is, of course, far beyond the scope of this article. However, further research could address three possibilities for further theoretical advancement of the MSF.

First, one could give up the idea of a micro-foundation of the MSF (as undertaken in the garbage-can model) as the approach theorises from the macro level. However, this option is extremely unlikely to be helpful as it would mean that policy-entrepreneurs are excluded from the analysis, thereby eliminating one decisive factor for explaining change within the approach.

Second, one could improve the micro-theoretical foundation of the MSF, for example, by comparing it to other perspectives. A comparison could contrast the identified deficits of the micro-foundation of the approach with elements of other approaches, thus creating a basis for a multi-perspective analysis that is currently only loosely applied in policy analysis (Zahariadis 1998; Meijerink 2005; Cairney 2007). Such a perspective could also decrease the very unfortunate tendency of policy analysis scholars to do parallel rather than interacting research (Meier 2009). Moreover, connecting various approaches to a 'synthetic framework' could also compensate for existing insufficiencies (Nowlin 2011). Consequently, for Rüb (2009: 371), the biggest strength of the MSF is that it can be combined with other approaches. For example, Real-Dato (2009) attempted such a synthesis by combining the MSF, the punctuated-equilibrium theory (Baumgartner and Jones 1993; True *et al.* 2007) and the advocacy-coalition framework (Sabatier and Jenkins-Smith 1993; Sabatier and Weible 2007) within the institutional analysis and development framework (Ostrom 2007). Ideally, a synthesis of the MSF with other approaches would provide a more consistent basis for the boundedly rational individual in the MSF. Therefore, the realisation of the concept of bounded rationality within the MSF could at least be achieved indirectly. My presumption is that the punctuated-equilibrium theory would be particularly well suited to such a synthesis, as it is substantially placed within the concept of bounded rationality.

Finally, the third option would simply be to leave the micro-level as it is – but no longer call it bounded rationality.

References

Ackrill, R., Kay, A. and Zahariadis, N. (2013) 'Ambiguity, multiple streams, and EU policy', *Journal of European Public Policy* 20(6): 871–87.

Baumgartner, F. R. and Jones, B. D. (1993) *Agendas and Instability in American Politics*, Chicago: University of Chicago Press.

Bendor, J. (2003) 'Herbert A. Simon: political scientist', *Annual Review of Political Science* 6: 433–71.

Bendor, J., Moe, T. M. and Shotts, K. W. (2001) 'Recycling the garbage can: an assessment of the research program', *American Political Science Review* 95(1): 169–90.

Blank, F., Blum, S. and Dehling, J. (2011) 'Der Faktor "Zeit" und theoretische Ansätze der Policy-Forschung' ['The "time"-factor and theoretical approaches of policy analysis'], in N. C. Bandelow and S. Hegelich (eds) *Pluralismus – Strategien – Entscheidungen. Eine Festschrift für Prof. Dr. Klaus Schubert [Pluralism – Strategies – Decisions. A festschrift for Prof. Dr. Klaus Schubert]*, Wiesbaden: VS Verlag für Sozialwissenschaften, pp. 63–83.

Cairney, P. (2007) 'A "multiple lenses" approach to policy change: the case of tobacco policy in the UK', *British Politics* 2007(2): 45–68.

Campitelli, G. and Gobet, F. (2010) 'Herbert Simon's decision-making approach: investigation of cognitive processes in experts', *Review of General Psychology* 14(4): 354–64.

Cohen, M. D., March, J. G. and Olsen, J. F. (1972) 'A garbage can model of organizational choice', *Administrative Science Quarterly* 17: 1–25.

Dehling, J. and Schubert, K. (2011) *Ökonomische Theorien der Politik. [Economic Theories of Politics]*, Wiesbaden, DE: VS Verlag für Sozialwissenschaften.

Feldman, M. S. (1989) *Order without Design: Information production and policy making*, Stanford, CA: Stanford University Press.

Herweg, N. (2013) 'Der Multiple-Streams-Ansatz Ein Ansatz, dessen Zeit gekommen ist?' ['The multiple-streams-approach – an approach whose time has come?'], *Zeitschrift für Vergleichende Politikwissenschaft* 7: 321–45.

Howlett, M. and Ramesh, M. (2003) *Studying Public Policy, Policy Cycles and Policy Subsystems*, Toronto: Oxford University Press.

Jones, B. D. (2003) 'Bounded rationality and political science: lessons from public administration and public policy', *Journal of Public Administration Research & Theory* 13(4): 395–412.

Jones, B. D. and Baumgartner, F. R. (2005) *The Politics of Attention*, Chicago: University of Chicago Press.

Kahneman, D. and Tversky, A. (1979) 'Prospect theory: an analysis of decision under risk', *Econometrica* 47(2): 263–91.

Kingdon, J. W. (2003[1984]) *Agendas, Alternatives, and Public Policies*, New York: Longman.

Lindblom, C. E. (1959) 'The science of "muddling through"', *Public Administration Review* 19(2): 79–88.

McDermott, R. (2004) 'Prospect theory in political science: gains and losses from the first decade', *Political Psychology* 25(2): 289–312.

Meier, K. J. (2009) 'Policy theory, policy theory everywhere: ravings of a deranged policy scholar', *Policy Studies Journal* 37(1): 5–11.

Meijerink, S. (2005) 'Understanding policy stability and change. The interplay of advocacy coalitions and epistemic communities, windows of opportunity, and Dutch coastal flooding policy 1945–2003', *Journal of European Public Policy* 12(6): 1060–77.

Mintrom, M. and Norman, P. (2009) 'Policy entrepreneurship and policy change', *Policy Studies Journal* 37(4): 649–67.

Mucciaroni, G. (1992) 'The garbage can model and the study of policy making: a critique', *Polity*, 24(3): 459–82.

Nowlin, M.C. (2011) 'Theories of the policy process: state of the research and emerging trends', *Policy Studies Journal* 39(S1): 41–60.

Ostrom, E. (2007) 'Institutional rational choice: an assessment of the institutional analysis and development framework', in P. Sabatier (ed.) *Theories of the Policy Process*, Boulder, CO: Westview Press, pp. 21–64.

Parsons, W. (1995) *Public Policy: An introduction to the theory and practice of policy analysis*, Cheltenham, UK: Edward Elgar Publishing.

Pump, B. (2011) 'Beyond metaphors: new research on agendas in the policy process', *Policy Studies Journal* 39(S1): 1–12.

Real-Dato, J. (2009) 'Mechanisms of policy change: a proposal for a synthetic explanatory framework', *Journal of Comparative Policy Analysis: Research & Practice* 11(1): 117–43.

Rüb, F. W. (2006) 'Die Zeit der Entscheidung. Kontingenz, Ambiguität und die Politisierung der Politik – Ein Versuch' ['The time of decision-making. Contingency, ambiguity and the politicisation of politics – an essay'], *Hamburg Review of Social Sciences* 1(1): 1–34.

— (2009) 'Multiple-Streams-Ansatz: Grundlagen, Probleme und Kritik' ['The multiple streams framework: basic principles, problems and critique'], in K. Schubert and N. C. Bandelow (eds) *Lehrbuch der Politikfeldanalyse 2.0 [Textbook of policy analysis 2.0]*, München, DE: Oldenbourg Verlag, pp. 348–76.

Sabatier, P. A. (2007a) 'The need for better theories', in P. A. Sabatier (ed.) *Theories of the Policy Process*, Boulder, CO: Westview Press pp. 3–17.

— (2007b) 'Fostering the development of policy theory', in P. A. Sabatier (ed.) *Theories of the Policy Process*, Boulder, CO: Westview Press, pp. 321–36.

Sabatier, P. A. and Jenkins-Smith, H. C. (1993) *Policy Change and Learning: An advocacy coalition approach*, Boulder, CO: Westview Press.

Sabatier, P. A. and Weible, C. M. (2007) 'The advocacy coalition framework: innovations and clarifications', in P. A. Sabatier (ed.) *Theories of the Policy Process*, Boulder, CO: Westview Press, pp. 189–220.

Schlager, E. (2007) 'A comparison of frameworks, theories, and models of policy processes', in P. A. Sabatier (ed.) *Theories of the Policy Process*, Boulder, CO: Westview Press, pp. 293–319.

Sherwood, F. P. (1990) 'The half-century's "great books" in public administration', *Public Administration Review* 50 (2): 249–64.

Simon, H. A. (1957) *Models of Man*, New York: John Wiley & Sons.

— (1976) *Administrative Behavior. A study of decision making processes in administrative organization. Third edition with new introduction*, New York: Free Press.

— (1983) *Reason in Human Affairs*, Stanford, CA: Stanford University Press.

Simon, H. A. and March, J. G. (1958) *Organizations*, New York: Wiley.

True, J. L., Jones, B. D. and Baumgartner, F. R. (2007) 'Punctuated equilibrium theory: explaining stability and change in public policymaking', in P. Sabatier (ed.) *Theories of the Policy Process*, Boulder, CO: Westview Press, pp. 155–87.

Vis, B. (2011) 'Prospect theory and political decision making', *Political Studies Review* 9(3): 334–43.

Zahariadis, N. (1998) 'Comparing three lenses of policy choice', *Policy Studies Journal* 26(3): 434–48.

— (2007) 'The multiple streams framework: structure, limitations, prospects', in P. Sabatier (ed.) *Theories of the Policy Process*, Boulder, CO: Westview Press, pp. 65–92.

— (2008) 'Ambiguity and choice in European public policy', *Journal of European Public Policy* 15(4): 514–30.

Zahariadis, N. and Allen, C. S. (1995) 'Ideas, networks and policy streams: privatization in Britain and Germany', *Policy Studies Review* 14(1/2): 71–98.

Chapter Four

Agenda-Setting and Policy-Making in Time: What the Multiple-Streams Approach Can Tell Us – and What It Cannot

Friedbert W. Rüb

Introduction

The multiple-streams framework (MSF) has placed time at the centre of the analysis of policy decisions and has moved away from traditional rationality conceptions of problem-solving. It is also an approach which accepts ambiguity and contingency and integrates them systematically into its concept: the 'window of opportunity' along with the 'political-entrepreneur' are two phenomena that are important. The incidence or appearance of these phenomena depends on contingent conditions, with the approach thus accepting coincidences and unforeseeable occurrences and, therefore, the non-causality of public decision-making within its basic concept.

In my contribution to this volume, I intend to concentrate on time.[1] Although time plays a central role and the management of time dominates the management of tasks and problems in the MSF, time is seldom systematically analysed. I consider the analysis of time to be of central importance in two dimensions: firstly, time is a (contemporary) *historical category*: the MSF should clarify in which historical time agenda-setting and policy-making take place. One must ask: where on the historical time axis are we situated today? Every epoch is anchored in a particular (historical) time, with significant challenges. I will attempt to clarify which time is indicated by the current state of globalisation and which challenges and responses this could entail. Challenges and responses vary according to different historical situations and present different challenges to policy-makers. My first thesis will be that we are faced today with increased complexity, a particularly high degree of contingency and an extraordinary acceleration of social change. This leads to the rise of 'wicked problems' (Rittel and Webber 1973), which cannot be solved in a goal-oriented manner, but which can only be managed in an unending and incremental process.

Secondly, agenda-setting and policy-making are fundamentally shaped by the *temporal rhythms of politics*. The sphere of politics has its own time, which arises due to the institutional, co-ordinative and cognitive requirements of democratic decision-making. Agenda-setting, coupling and decision-making as central activities of the policy-entrepreneur and other political agencies must be

---

1.   I would like to thank Reimut Zohlnhöfer for valuable comments.

translatable into a temporal progression. Policy-making requires time and this political time may not be in harmony with the speed of economic and social changes. Instead, *de-synchronisation* may occur between the time-scale of politics and that of social change, which results in problems becoming even more difficult to solve.

I proceed as follows: first, I will discuss the historical time we are living in, restraining myself from dwelling upon a variety of theories of present age. Instead, I simply use three descriptive terms – complexity, contingency and acceleration – which may capture some of the most important properties of the globalised world. Second, I will attempt to analyse the times of politics through the use of three other terms: momentum, time-span and calendar. Thus, I hope to formulate new concepts of the most important terms and categories of the MSF, thereby making them useful for empirical investigations. Third, I will try to sketch the consequences of policy-making under intense time-pressure. The acceleration of politics leads to a 'motorized legislator' (Schmitt 1950, 2009) and shifts policy-making away from the time-consuming and deliberative parliament to the speedy core executive.

The main argument running through the entire chapter is: in a globalised world, policy-making on the national level is changing from *goal-oriented rationality* to *time–oriented reactivity* (Luhmann 2000: 142). If that holds true, we may have to alter fundamentally the basic premises, analytical tools and theoretical concepts with which policy-analysis has worked hitherto. The MSF started to do just that; but now we have to stand on the shoulders of the fathers of the MSF. And standing there, a dwarf may indeed see further than the giants. Therefore, the main task is to rethink some of the most important building blocks of that approach. To be clear, the chapter deals mainly with theoretical and conceptual challenges that stem from bringing time back into the MSF.

Time as historical time: what the multiple-streams framework can tell us about history and context – and what it cannot

The term 'time' has many dimensions. One of these dimensions is time as historical time, which takes place along a historical time-axis and runs from the past through the present into the future. Every time has its own historical time, since one can position it on the historical time-axis. Many policy theories suffer from the defect that they are de-historicised and made subject to the assumption that all historical situations present the same challenges and thus produce relatively unchanging solutions. A critical theory of the policy process, however, must be in a position to answer a central question: which problems arise in which periods of time? What character do these problems have and are they 'solvable' or not? Can one recognise and understand the often multiple and interconnected causes of problems, or do they remain hidden from us? Can we gain worthwhile access to the complex matrix of causes? In essence, these questions combine into the need for a (critical) diagnosis of the *current* era: in which historical time are we living *today*? Which *effective* problems are we confronted with? And in which *present* national and international contexts are policies decided upon?

I will attempt to provide some clarification of this question. In doing so, I will abstain from 'grand' diagnoses of the current era inspired by social-science theory, such as 'world risk society' (Beck 1999), 'post democracy' (Crouch 2004), 'media society' (Hjarvard 2013), 'multiple modernities' (Eisenstadt 2002) or 'anarchical society' (Bull 2012). Instead, I will attempt to outline some important new elements of the historical situation by using three central terms, namely complexity, contingency and acceleration. These new elements culminate in two phenomena: (a) the impulses for policy-making come mostly from *external* sources and often appear as 'focusing events' (Birkland 1998; Birkland and DeYoung 2013) or as external shocks. They bias attention, they change priorities, they reshuffle power constellations and provoke political parties to reposition in the political spectrum. Politics is compeled to react to those external conditions that set the pace for political action. To the contrary, however, early policy-analysis and democratic theory assumed that policies reflect the normative and programmatic ideas of a government and are decided upon from *within* politics, in order to shape or steer the societal order of a given society into the future.

Today's problems are (b) mostly 'wicked problems' (Rittel and Webber 1973), which cannot be solved, and can only be managed in constantly renewed steps, in an endless process of adaptation and adjustment, of updating and attempting to forget. Rational problem-solving seems all but impossible.

Complexity

The complexity of societies and of social problems is implicitly contained within the MSF. The problem stream is an expression of the functional differentiation of modern societies translated into a temporal process, a flowing stream. The subsystems of modern societies operate each according to its specific code and according to a system-specific logic; this, however, produces challenges for other subsystems, to which they must react. The *internal* logics and subsystem dynamics produce *external* effects that have consequences and side-effects for other subsystems, forcing them to adapt. If the economic process slows down, unemployment grows and the political sector is left with reduced financial means with which to combat the situation then labour market policies become more difficult. If companies rationalise or move their production overseas, problems are created that become relevant in the problem stream. It contains all the potential problems a given society is confronted with and thus its whole complexity. Complexity is a condition of a system, society or a circumstance, which is expressed in three dimensions:

a) In a great *variety* of states in which a (social) system can exist. Variety is a purely numerical or formal criterion and is an indication of the potentially possible states in which an object can subsist. A light bulb displays exactly two states: on and off. A system with five light bulbs can potentially exist in 2^5, that is, thirty-two states, while a system with twenty-five light bulbs has as many as thirty-three million potential states. Every new light bulb doubles the number of states. For social issues, one can thus state the following: the more variables or causes are responsible for a particular state and its alteration, the larger the potential number of possible states and the more complex the issue. Globalisation[2] adds to the possible number of nationally expressed states new states of affairs that are caused by outside variables and which are outside the control of national policy-makers.

b) Complexity is expressed in the *rate of change*. The faster and more often the state of a system, an organisation or a policy-field changes, the greater is its complexity. The temporal dynamics of social and technical change are central here. The faster situations change, the greater the rate of change is; there is no doubt that globalisation accelerates all the important processes in a society, be they social, economic, political or technical.

c) Complexity includes the *unpredictability* of the dynamics of situations. Complex issues always have a multitude of causes and their development is never one-dimensional. Complex systems are kept in motion through internal feedback; they often trigger their own dynamics and are frequently characterised by an erratic rather than a linear dynamic. An object can remain for some time in a stable or minimally altering state until it reaches a 'turning point' (Abbott 1995), when rapid changes take place. Patterns of change conforming to the idea of 'punctuated equilibrium', which Jones and Baumgartner *et al.* were able to identify for the politics of budgeting (Jones and Baumgartner 2005, 2012), are valid, *mutatis mutandis*, for the dynamics of other situations as well.

The factors that I have described here in relatively abstract terms, using system-theory terminology, are dramatised by *globalisation*, which introduces additional *external* factors that alter the states of individual situations, subsystems or an entire society, thus increasing their variety, rate of change and unpredictability. While in relatively closed national states it was the *internal*, and partially controllable, dynamics that altered the state of society, globalisation adds new ones which are systematically inaccessible to national governments and their policy-making initiatives. Furthermore, the dynamics of globalisation take place at an extremely high speed. The high-frequency trade on the international financial markets is only one particular but extreme example. All social issues and circumstances, that is to say, the problems which appear in the problem stream today, are hyper-complex and constantly varying, with constellations changing extremely rapidly. (National) policy-making can now be deemed neither goal-oriented nor rational. It simply starts to respond to the uncontrollable and unforeseeable events with which it is confronted.

---

2. Globalisation, its driving forces, its features and its consequences are contested issues; for critical overviews see Scholte 2005; Rodrik 2012; Baumann 2013; Held and McGrew 2007.

Contingency

Contingency is a consciousness of the fact that everything that exists could also be different; that nothing has a fundamental – that is, indisputable – basis, and that social circumstances are essentially no longer transparent and controllable. Contingency can be substantiated in a constructivist manner. Sociologist Niklas Luhmann pointed out: 'Everything becomes contingent if that *which* is observed is dependent on *who* is observing' (Luhmann 1992: 100 [my translation]). Contingency undermines the durability of the present through the doubt caused by the possibility of difference. And since everything could be different, what currently exists has no fundamental basis and no definitive purpose. While the idea of pluralism assumes that there are a number of different perspectives from which to view an issue, object or occurrence, contingency drives doubt into each and every perspective and makes them all vulnerable to the possibility of being contingent.

Nevertheless, the definition of what is contingent (and what is not) is terminologically ambivalent, historically variable and dependent on certain historical world views and social assumptions (Makropoulos 1997: 14). Every political power constellation and every social order has its own horizon of possibility, which is dependent on the current cognitive, normative and moral capacities of a society.

In the present case, I distinguish between two forms of contingency. *Background* contingency can be traced back to Machiavelli's *Il Principe* (Machiavelli 1990). Here, Machiavelli vividly describes how the new prince is able to achieve and maintain power in a world that is uncontrollable, unrecognisable and ungovernable, and which is laced with coincidences and surprises. *Fortuna* stands for the contingency of the social environment, allowing events to occur haphazardly and without reason that pose challenges to the prince and to which he must respond. Courage and determination are able to curtail the arbitrariness and coincidence of *fortuna* and thus restrain her. But *virtù* is never able to curtail it completely. And while prior to Machiavelli, virtù was always understood as acting morally for the common good, he now dissolves all connections with moral and ethical premises. He reverses the poles of *virtù* in such a way that, for him, any action is possible, from political opportunism to lies and the arbitrary use of violence. And most importantly: *virtù* insists upon quick decisions, for the prince must pre-empt the actions of others if he is to stay in power (or to gain new powers). Today's policy-makers still struggle with *fortuna*, today renamed contingency; skills, professionalism and leadership competence comprise the *virtù* of policy-makers.

Action contingency arises from the interactions of the individuals or groups competing for political power. First, sociologist Talcott Parsons (1951; see also Luhmann 1984; Vanderstraeten 2002) introduced the figure of thought of 'double contingency'. Every social interaction constitutes a situation of double contingency: Ego has to take into account the (unknown) actions of Alter and vice versa. Both know that one could also act differently and that situation brings about structural indeterminacy, which only can be overcome by acting in accordance with some social norms. Norms make the actions of Ego predictable for Alter and Alter's actions for Ego. However, commitment to norms works only if others do the same. If they do not stick to the norms, one is challenged by uncertainty, indeterminacy, and contingency.

The same holds true for action contingency in the realm of politics. It is the result of a certain understanding of politics, which can be traced back to Max Weber and the Finnish political scientist Kari Palonen's interpretation of Weber (Palonen 1998, 2001, 2003). According to Palonen, politics is oriented towards the alteration of the current state of affairs. This, however, does not represent a positive orientation of politics in the sense of goal-oriented changes or improvements to the *status quo*. Instead, it is a negative orientation: an activity that aims to rid itself of the past, initially without adding any further content. According to this view, politics is the pure temporality of action, which aims for change, new chances and new possibilities, but which follows no particular direction or concrete substance. The future is open, as it depends on the actions of others. As Kari Palonen wrote:

> power is a chance-concept. As such, it expresses the contingent character of politics-as-activity, it is 'only' a possibility, an occasion, or an opportunity to do something. It opens a horizon of action, but does not specify how to act within this horizon. In a temporal perspective, chances refer to possibilities that are present and 'real' in the experience of the persons acting politically, while the 'realized reality' is for political agents a contingent result of past political struggles (Palonen 2003: 2).

The 'realised reality' is always a policy which evolves from the contingent situation of the political struggle. It is not predetermined but rather arises in the course of the *interaction of politics* with opposing forces. Since their actions and positions are also contingent, a policy is, in a certain sense, 'born' out of these interactions. Because the result of the struggle for power is not predetermined, the final product is also contingent. A policy is thus created from a combination of many different possibilities: the final version is dependent on a range of contingent factors. The MSF concentrates on two contingent phenomena: the 'window of opportunity' and the 'political-entrepreneur', neither of which is structurally pre-existent; rather, both appear and disappear again in particular historical situations. A policy is only created when they are present, which, in turn, is dependent on the ideational materials flowing in the streams; these are only available in a particular combination in a specific situation in time.

Furthermore, politics as a struggle for chances to participate in political power

> does not indicate a zero-sum-game, but the plurality and mutability of the types of power shares render the struggle an open contest, in which the agents are also obliged to revise their views and redirect their striving for power shares. The struggle against the opposing agents is, in the Weberian view, a 'moving' instance of politics. In particular, he [Weber] writes in 'Politik als Beruf', how in politics the results are in a paradoxical relation to the intentions of any of the participants (Palonen 2003: 3).

The time in which politics-as-activity takes place thus alters not only the motives, intentions and goals of the participating players, but also the relationships and the power distributions between them (Palonen 2006). Taken to the extreme, one could say that every policy is the result of the unintended consequences of intentional actions.

Acceleration

Globalisation is defined by many different characteristics and the social and political sciences have not reached a consensus as to what the central characteristic of globalisation is. One possible way of viewing globalisation, however, is as the *compression of space and time* (Scheuerman 2001: 43–9; Hassan 2009; Rosa and Scheuerman 2009). Acceleration is central here, as it enables the compression of spaces in which everything can move faster and in which distances shrink.

The economy – and in particular the financial sector, which is seen as the most important driving force behind acceleration (Rosa 2005a, 2000b; Hassan 2009) – has its own rhythms of production and consumption and takes place in spaces characterised by the movement of goods and labour. *Technological developments* are occurring across shorter time-spans all the time; the speed of goods-transport and financial services across the globe is constantly increasing; and the computerised high-frequency trade on the international financial markets now occurs at unimaginable speeds governed by mathematical algorithms.

As a result, a *social acceleration* is taking place in which the norms and patterns of action of day-to-day society are changing faster all the time and must adapt to changing technology. Knowledge acquired and collected at one point is no longer sufficient for an entire (working) life but must be repeatedly adapted to the changing parameters of life within a single lifetime. The same is true of *political knowledge*, which is becoming obsolete at an ever increasing pace and may no longer keep up with the unique challenges of the globalised world.

The structure of 'wicked problems'

The important generalisation for my subject matter from the passages above is that which Reinhart Koselleck refers to as a 'contraction of the meaningful present'. This phenomenon is characterised by the fact that in the complex, contingent and accelerated world, the *space of experience* (*Erfahrungsraum*) and the *horizon of expectation* (*Erwartungshorizont*) diverge (Koselleck 2009). That is, the experience, the knowledge, the routines, the practices and the habits of policy-making are no longer sufficient for coping with the events that occur. It is not only a case of too many contingent and unknown events entering the space of experience, be they 'focusing events' or other occurrences of the horizon of expectation. The real problem is that they are appearing more often and with greater speed. This leads to a divergence of the two dimensions, which increases the difficulty of policy-making.

Policy-making is confronted with problems which Rittel and Webber referred to in the 1970s as 'wicked problems', identifying ten defining characteristics (Rittel and Webber 1973; cf. Roberts 2001; Verweij 2011). I will define them slightly differently, reformulating them in a manner appropriate for today's world and reducing the number of characteristics to five:

a) The possible causes of such problems are multidimensional, highly complex, uncertain and interacting; in addition, the causes are contested and there is no consensus on what they are, which are the most relevant and how they interact. Scientific knowledge cannot help to leap over the ditch of uncertainty. Every expert is challenged by a counter-expert.

b) The range of solutions is equally large and uncertain, because the problem is highly ambiguous. Often, solutions are arrived at by accident without any serious relationship to the problem. There are no right and no wrong options; there are only contingent options, a perspective that is shared by the MSF.

c) Wicked problems are often unique and novel and every solution is, therefore, a one-shot operation with serious and often unpredictable and irreversible consequences. Learning is extremely difficult because of the 'structure of ill-unstructured problems' (Simon 1973). The newness and uniqueness of the problems make learning difficult and allow no copying from the experience of the management of other problems.

d) They have no stopping rules and every policy decision leads to new problems. Every option creates new wicked problems and, as a consequence, policy-making always creates new waves of problems, which again await new policies.

e) There is no unified agency; rather, a wide array of actors is involved. During the process of solving wicked problems, new actors become involved and others disappear. Again, this assumption is in line with the MSF. But it has a solution: the contingent occurrence of the political-entrepreneur, who carries out agenda-setting and policy-making.

To summarise: wicked problems call for the *reactive management* of problems and no longer allow for prospective, rational and problem-solving policy-making. Goal-oriented policy-making or the political steering of modern societies seem to be aims that politics is no longer able to achieve. In addition, deliberative policy-making which tries to deal to some degree adequately with 'wicked problems' is extremely time-consuming and no longer in time with the pace of today's problem-production. However, politics allow for processes in which some of the problems are politicised, placed on the political agenda and decided upon.

The time-scales of politics and policy-making

Time plays a significant role in the MSF. In contrast to rationalistic policy-making concepts, it builds upon a different logic based on temporal order. Choice has more to do with the simultaneous evocation of problems and solutions than with any inherent correlation between them. Choice is often made on a first-come, first-served basis. ... because the primary concern of decision makers – whether policymakers, business executives, or top civil servants – is to manage time rather than to manage tasks ... It is reasonable to use a lens that accords significance to time rather than rationality (Zahariadis 2003: 4–5; cf. 1999: 75; 2007: 67–8).

'Managing time' is the key phrase: it is at the centre of the MSF approach and concentrates attention on three particular issues. The first of these is the 'window of opportunity', which opens through external events or political action; only the latter can be viewed as management of time. Nevertheless, once a window of opportunity is opened, regardless of the reasons why, time-management once again begins to play a role, for action must then be taken and the chance must be exploited. The second issue is 'temporal sorting' (Zahariadis 2003: 4) by an entrepreneur or by the political regime, in the course of which they employ their own processes of selection and attention-structuring in order to filter out from the many problems those which should be placed on the political agenda and decided upon. Finally, there is the issue of 'coupling'. Although all three dimensions refer to time, the MSF generally sees them as timeless, in that it does not give any systematic account of how one might conceptualise these activities in terms of time. In the following, I will try to translate them into temporal categories and thus put them in a temporal progression.

The politics of time: dealing with the 'momentum', time-span and calendar

Which terms can we use to renew the concepts of these issues? I distinguish between three temporal levels: the politics of the 'momentum', the politics of the time span and the politics of the calendar (Palonen 2008: 25–32;). All three dimensions are institutional framework conditions for the politics of time and that are strongly underestimated by the MSF. However, they mark the horizon within which opportunities and possibilities for policy-making arise.

The 'momentum'

A *momentum* is defined as a situation in which a chance or possibility arises, which is brought about by institutional factors of the political regime or by external factors. It is similar to a 'window of opportunity', but a 'momentum' is more specific. It is a situation of *discontinuity*, in which the normal flow of time is interrupted by a specific event and in which time is compressed. Often 'focusing events' (cf. Birkland 2007[3]) introduce momentum into the political

---

3. A focusing event is defined as 'as an event that is sudden, relatively rare, can be reasonably defined as harmful or revealing the possibility of potentially greater future harms, inflicts harms or suggest potential harms that are or could be concentrated on a definable geographical area or community of interest, and that is known to policy makers and the public virtually simultaneously' (Birkland 2007: 22).

processes in that they engage the interest of the mass media, the political parties and interest-groups. They trigger social and political actions and intensify political conflicts. They change the dynamics within the three streams: within the policy stream, new ideas may come to the fore, new or recombined options may be developed, and previous policies may be considered as being worth rethinking or being ineffective; within the problem stream, the discussion about the understanding of the focusing problem intensifies; and within the politics stream, we can expect a controversial and often heated debate between governing and opposition parties about the focusing problem and how to react adequately to it.

In such situations, new opportunities arise which are not normally present and contingency is introduced into the situation. The important questions are then whether or not the players involved recognise the situation as a 'turning point'; whether they exploit it to advance their interests; which options are available for politicisation in the policy stream *et cetera*.

In the politics stream, elections are a typical momentum, for they present the chance to overthrow an existing power-constellation and build a new one. The same holds true for a no-confidence motion, a dissolution of parliament and so on. Elections take place in a specific rhythm that is known to all players involved and which interrupts the flow of governing. An election is an interruption of the continuous governing period and marks a new beginning, with a new government and thus new opportunities for policy-making. While the election, as a regularly recurring institution, is nothing more than an interruption to the period of governing, the election *campaign* is a particularly intensive phase, a time-span of politics in which political competition is played out with the highest intensity. During that phase, promised and therefore future policies play a central role in trying to attract segments of the electorate in order to maximise votes.

Time-span

A *time-span*, in contrast to a momentum, marks not the beginning but the end of a period of time. It sets a deadline by which a project, a policy or a programme must be realised. The politics of the time-span must attempt to complete a policy initiative, that is, to have it passed into law, within this time period. The passing of the budget is one example, as is the approaching end of a legislative term. While a momentum opens the horizon for new possibilities, the time-span *closes* it. A policy initiative must be completed by exactly this time, otherwise it must wait once again for a chance, or a momentum.

Calendar

Finally, the *calendar* breaks up a time-span into small and recurring *points in time*. The calendar opens up new possibilities for the management of time and thus also opportunities for policy-making. Examples of this include multiple readings of a law, referral to a select committee following the first reading, set time-periods between subsequent readings and so on. Here, the priority of time over the content of a policy becomes dominant and a political entrepreneur must have control of this calendar. Alongside this institutional-chronological calendar, he or she must keep a parallel calendar in which all time-points are noted that are relevant for 'coupling', such as the point in time for the introduction of a bill, for the reading, for the select committee meetings, for the final vote and so on; only then can a policy be successfully passed into law. One must therefore deal with time reflectively and translate the content of a policy into chronological steps. What occurs here is what Nikolaos Zahariadis referred to as 'management of time', although on the level of the calendar.

Time and the politics of time in the MSF

Before I discuss the various aspects of the politics of time, it is necessary to make a preliminary conceptual remark. Management of time is a process that can be divided into two different activities, namely 'politicisation' and 'politicking' (Palonen 2003, 2008). *Politicisation* makes an object or an issue politically 'playable', either by marking a hitherto non-political issue as political or by reviving an old one. This issue becomes the subject of particular attention. Politicisation then has two main purposes: first, to raise awareness in the course of 'vote-seeking', that is, the mobilisation of potential voter-support (Müller and Strøm 1999); and, second, to change an existing power-constellation in order to improve one's own position. Political players will favour problems or policies that are politically accessible and will orientate themselves according to voter-preferences. Short-term and populist positions will thus always be preferred over long-term and responsible policies. Here, the contingency of all issues and the ambiguity of each individual becomes clear, for politicisation is always a controversial process in which various players with differing interests and norms struggle for dominance. Without politicisation, there can be no agenda-setting and no policy-making. It always precedes these events and its main purpose is to open new possibilities for the future.

Politicking, on the other hand, refers to the game then played with the objects that have been made politically 'playable', that is, those that are already politicised. It is a performance taking place purely in the present, in which the virtuosity of performance – like in early Greek politics – is decisive (Palonen 2003: 5). The most important activities are expressed in different styles of politicking. One may differentiate between cautious and daring styles, between dramatic and realistic, or between symbolic and pragmatic styles (*ibid.*). Politicking has its own time. It is played out in the present only and rests within itself. Politicisation, on the contrary, is future-oriented. By introducing new items to the political agenda, it attempts to change the *status quo* and incubate a new future within the present.

I will now attempt to apply these terms and related activities to the most important dimension of managing time in the MSF.

Temporal sorting

I will begin with the '*temporal sorting*' of the political system. Which issues receive attention and which are placed high on the political agenda 'is a function of opportunity, bias, formal position in an organisation or government, and the number of issues competing for policymakers' attention' (Zahariadis 1999: 76). What could this mean?

First, it is the political players themselves who decide what is to be decided upon. It is a case of internal selection processes and the political players follow their own logics here. One form of logic is the widely known motivation of 'vote-seeking', meaning that those issues are politicised which promise to generate a certain amount of support from voters and which can be expected to produce a reshuffle of a political power-constellation in the course of the political struggle. Whatever fulfils this purpose is the issue that will be politicised. Furthermore, the media and the public sphere play a significant role in temporal sorting, propelling politics forward and exerting pressure to act. The modern mass media are an significantly underestimated agenda-setting force, both in the MSF and in other theories of policy analysis.

How is temporal sorting temporised? The first temporisation is elections and election campaigns. Elections are a momentum, in that the continuous progression of time is interrupted and new opportunities for politicisation and for new power-constellations arise. Elections are of central importance for what is to be placed on the political agenda and for the question of what is to be decided upon. Interestingly, elections and election campaigns are mentioned only indirectly in the MSF. Kingdon describes how in the politics stream, alongside national mood and interest-group pressure, legislative or administrative turnover frequently affects the political agenda in a quite dramatic manner. A sudden influx of new politicians or administrators with new policy ideas may strongly affect the political agenda (Kingdon 1984; Zahariadis 2007: 73). Elections and the time period of the election campaign are not specifically discussed, despite the fact that it is precisely here that temporal sorting plays an important role.

In Kingdon's original approach and in the various subsequent developments of it, elections and election campaigns play virtually no role, although, as institutionalised regularities, they repeatedly throw open the door to temporal sorting. The politics of the time-span also influence the logic of temporal sorting. If a deadline is approaching, political players must politicise and/or place certain issues on the agenda by this date, otherwise the opportunity is wasted. The temporal rhythms of time-spans are of central importance and their effects on temporal sorting have been investigated very little thus far. For what is urgent then comes before any substantial problem and, in very urgent matters, only what can be achieved before the deadline. Other policies are not considered at all. The sorting criterion therefore is which idea is temporally feasible.

Window of opportunity as a process

The metaphor of the window of opportunity is prominent in the MSF. How could it be temporised? It can be subdivided into at least three phases: a) the point in time of opening; b) the chronological structuring of the period of being open; and c) the point in time of closing.

a) The *point of opening* can be divided into coincidences and certain rhythms. The occurrence of coincidences is the very essence of contingency: earthquakes, tsunamis, hurricanes; but social occurrences, such as the appearance and dynamics of financial and/or economic crises, are also typical unforeseeable 'focusing events' (Birkland 2007). However, there are also institutional and regular events, such as elections or the passing of the budget, which are also momentums. Deliberately created windows are possible as well: the dissolution of parliament and the calling of new elections; a vote of no-confidence against the government or a member of the government; or the reconstitution of a second chamber are all good examples of this. Such situations open chronological horizons for new opportunities which can be seized, or indeed not.

b) The period of time for which a window remains open, however, is more difficult to determine. Its rhythm is also structured through institutional frameworks. Here, it is particularly time-span and calendar that play an important role. Since one knows that one must act quickly, the acceleration of processes takes on central importance. Zahariadis mentioned that 'salami tactics' are meant to 'cut the process into distinct stages which are presented sequentially to policy-makers. Doing so promotes agreement in steps.' (Zaharadis 2007: 78). Here, temporisation has the advantage of creating consensus on small issues. However, negotiated agreements take up large amounts of time, which is in short supply. Also, lobbying takes up time and energy (*ibid.*) of both of which only a limited amount is available. However, it seems to me that only the acceleration of these processes can make coupling successful. And that means shifting the policy-making processes from the legislature to the executive. Whereas the legislature slows down the policy-making process by introducing time-consuming deliberative procedures, the executive is able to act more rapidly (I will come back to this topic later).

c) The window can close itself or can be closed from outside. It closes itself when institutional deadlines expire, such as legislature periods or other deadlines, or when media excitement must be calmed down by making a decision. It is closed from outside when political-entrepreneurs can set deadlines themselves, when they predetermine the chronological steps and so forth. In both cases, political agency deals with the politics of the time-span and/or the politics of the calendar. Access to power is an inescapable precondition for these modes of politics.

Coupling as a time structure

The MSF conceptualises coupling as a complicated process of framing, affect-priming, 'salami tactics' and the use of symbols, which definitely holds true. Time is not made an issue of here but coupling always has a temporal structure. If the MSF hopes to analyse the entire process, from agenda-setting through to the passing of a law, the calendar must come into play. The politics of the calendar consist principally of translating the contents of a policy into chronological steps. Here, the neglect of institutional questions becomes particularly clear: decision-making, due to the institutional framework, is a chronologically elongated process. It includes the discussions of the cabinet and the various readings in parliament and the respective committees, as well as the ability to exercise control over the agenda of institutions; voting in a second chamber is also relevant. In this process of coupling, there are several veto-points, which are 'points of strategic uncertainty' (Immergut 1992: 27) and which contain opportunities to block policies or to prevent blocking by others. The management of time plays a particularly important role here.

The acceleration of policy-making or the 'motorisation of the legislator'

As previously mentioned, policy-making is faced with new challenges in a world characterised by complexity, contingency and acceleration. *Time* and *space compression* is the most important factor here and requires a self-acceleration of policy-making. It is not only 'focusing events' with far-reaching consequences that demand very quick reactions; other policy decisions must also be made quickly, if policy-makers indeed wish to keep pace with the high rate of acceleration of today's world. MSF reflects upon this in saying: 'Policy makers operate under significant time constraints' and there is a 'sense of urgency' in the policy-making processes and time constraints 'limit the range and number of alternatives to which attention is given' (Zahariadis 2007: 68–9). But how should or could one deal with the 'sense of urgency'? Which mechanisms provide for the acceleration of the policy-making process?

Focusing events are 'low-probability/high-consequence events' (Birkland 2006) and demand very *rapid adaptations*. One is, nonetheless, confronted with the paradox that because of the far-reaching consequences, the lack of knowledge and the uniqueness of such events, the appropriate solutions must be prepared very carefully. This requires policy-makers to ascertain new information, enlist the help of experts, extensively consult the appropriate institutions and so on. In other words: a deliberative political process must be followed; this, however, is extremely time-consuming. On the other hand, there is an expectation that politics should react quickly, otherwise the conditions may change in such a way that an appropriate reaction is no longer possible. This means that deliberative processes cannot actually be used and that decisions must be made quickly, which involves shifting policy-making to the executive branch of government and a disempowerment of parliament. However, the MSF would assume that some options would be quickly available because the policy stream always contains a surplus of options that policy-makers could have in their political 'hands' to play as 'aces'.

Nevertheless, shortage of time always plays an important role. To provide an example: law-making in the German Bundestag is a time-consuming process and has remained essentially unchanged since World War II. Since 1949, it has taken 225 days, on average, to respond *via* a law to social or political challenges, including all minor and technical changes of laws or governmental orders, and these policies often had only minor consequences. In 2009, during the financial and economic crisis, the speed of law-making was extremely accelerated. The so-called 'Stimulus Package II' (*Konjunkturpaket* II) encompassed a volume of nearly fifty-five billion euros but was decided on within less than forty days in spring 2009. In doing so, the normal procedures of parliament were suspended, with the consent of all political parties, in order to speed up policy-making (Laux 2011: 232).[4] However, some experts and economists claimed that despite that tremendous speed, the legislation – including its implementation through the German federal states – was too slow. Be that as it may, the whole process shifted from parliament to the executive; parliament and political parties abstained from exercising their right of democratic deliberation. During the financial crisis, the same legislative procedures took place as always but at a newly accelerated speed.

Shifting policy-making to the executive has important consequences, especially for problems of time (for the following, see Scheuerman 2004). In liberal-democratic theory, the legislature is future-oriented, whereas the executive is present-oriented. The legislature has the task of deciding in the present on future developments, whether they are anticipated or emerge from present problems. Future-oriented decision-making calls for gathering information, listening to experts, involving various stakeholders, deliberating in parliament, activating the second chamber and so on. In addition, the legislature is expected to take into account future developments and to act pre-emptively.

In contrast to the legislature's slow procedures and orientation to the future, the executive is expected to act in time with the present, and that means to act or react to issues in real time. Shifting legislative competence to the executive comes close to what the German legal theorist and puppet of the Nazi Regime, Carl Schmitt, called the '*motorisierte Gesetzgeber*' or 'motorized legislator' (Schmitt 1950, 2009;[5] *cf.* Scheuerman 2003). The legislator is able to speed up the policy-making process and attempt to overcome the de-synchronisation between the accelerated environment and the institutionalised times of politics.

Given the complex, contingent and accelerated problems of the modern world and the unresolvable character of 'wicked problems', one would expect that law and policy-making would shift increasingly to the executive and would change the system of checks and balances between the three branches of government.

Policy-analysis should pay much more attention to the institutional and procedural changes in policy-making processes. Many theorists focus on the analysis of the 'core executive' (Smith 1999; Burch and Holliday 2004; Rhodes and Dunleavy 1995), which takes over the whole policy-making process. It is a small group of persons, located close to the centre of political power, pulling the strings and deciding, more or less exclusively, on the most important issues.

---

4. The internal rules of procedure for the German Bundestag (§§79 GO BT) do indeed allow for this course of action.

5. A partial translation of Carl Schmitt's text can be found in Rosa and Scheuermann 2009: 65–73.

However, the core executive is like a chameleon; it changes its appearance from policy to policy. But the same holds true for the political-entrepreneur, who also differs from policy to policy. And the core executive may act as the political-entrepreneur in the MSF without displaying its properties.

Conclusion

My contribution on time in the MSF is lopsided and perhaps biased too. However, the main goal was to think more deeply on the issue of time in policy-analysis and to make theoretical concepts more sensitive to aspects of time. The main argument running through the whole paper is that policy-making is changing from goal-oriented rationality to time-oriented reactivity. If that holds true – and I hope to have given some new and convincing arguments – time must capture more of the attention of scholars of theories of the policy process. In addition, we are in need of some new concepts, terms and categories that allow a better theoretical understanding and more sophisticated comparative and empirical research.

Policy-analysis in contemporary modern parliamentary democracies[6] is confronted with a serious paradox: on the one hand, policy-making needs more time because the problems it is confronted with require that a great deal of deliberation and consultation takes place in the process of generating appropriate responses. On the other hand, complexity, contingency and high-speed societies produce a huge variety of problems that compete for attention in the problem stream. To avoid too much de-synchronisation between the time-rhythms of politics and the high speed of social change, politics tries to speed up its decision-making processes. However, the 'motorization of the legislator' shifts policy-making to the core executive and may downgrade the parliament and its deliberative practices. In the end, this comes at a high price: the consequence may be the de-democratisation of modern democracies. Whereas in the early 1960s and 1970s, practically oriented policy-analysis started with the claim to be able to improve the quality of political decision-making and of democracy, in the beginning of the twenty-first century, practically and theoretically oriented policy-analysis may be observing a decline in the quality of democracy. True or false? We only know by investigating more time in theoretical considerations and in empirical research on time.

---

6. I limit myself to parliamentary democracies; similar developments may occur in presidential democracies and are often called 'decreeism' or 'governing by decrees' (see Carey and Shugart 1998; Rudavelige 2006; Healy 2008).

References

Abbott, A. (1997) 'On the concept of turning point', *Comparative Social Research* 16: 85–105.

Bauman, Z. (2013) *Globalization: The human consequences*, Cambridge, UK: Polity Press.

Beck, U. (1999) *World Risk Society*, Cambridge, UK: Polity Press.

Birkland, Th. A. (1997) *After Disaster – Agenda setting, public policy and focusing events*, Washington, DC: Georgetown University Press.

— (1998) 'Focusing events, mobilization, and agenda setting', *Journal of Public Policy* 18(1): 53–74.

— (2006) *Lessons of Disaster: Policy change after catastrophic events*, Washington, DC: Georgetown University Press.

Birkland, T. A. and DeYoung, S. E. (2013) 'Focusing events and policy windows', in E. Araral Jr., S. Fritzen, M. Howlett, M. Ramesh and Xun Wu (eds) *Routledge Handbook of Public Policy*, London and New York: Routledge, pp. 175–88.

Bull, H. (2012) *The Anarchical Society: A study of order in world politics*, 4th edn, New York: Columbia University Press.

Burch, M. and Holliday, I. (2004) 'The Blair government and the core executive', *Government and Opposition* 39(1): 1–21.

Carey, J. M. and Shugart, M. S. (1998) *Executive Decree Authority*, Cambridge, UK: Cambridge University Press.

Crouch, C. (2004) *Post-Democracy*. Cambridge, UK and Malden, MA: Polity Press.

Hassan, R. (2009) *Empires of Speed: Time and the acceleration of politics and society*, Leiden, NL: Brill.

Healy, G. (2008) *The Cult of the Presidency: America's dangerous devotion to executive power*, Washington, DC: Cato Institute.

Held, D. and McGrew, A. (2007) *Globalization Theory: Approaches and controversies*, Cambridge, UK: Polity Press.

Hjarvard, S. (2013) *The Mediatization of Society and Culture*, New York: Routledge.

Immergut, E. M. (1992) *Health Politics: Interests and institutions in Western Europe*, Cambridge, UK: Cambridge University Press.

Jones, B. D. and Baumgartner, F. R. (2005) 'A model of choice for public policy', *Journal of Public Administration Research and Theory* 15(3): 325–51.

— (2012) 'From there to here: punctuated equilibrium to the general punctuation thesis to a theory of government information processing', *Policy Studies Journal* 40(1): 1–19.

Kingdon, J. W. (1984) *Agendas, Alternatives, and Public Policies*, Boston, MA and Toronto: Little, Brown & Co.

Koselleck, R. (2009) 'Is there an acceleration of history?', in H. Rosa and W. Scheuerman (eds) *High-Speed Society. Social acceleration, power, and modernity*, University Park, PA: Pennsylvania State University Press, pp. 113–33.

Laux, H. (2011) 'The time of politics: pathological effects of social differentiation', *Time & Society*, 20(2): 224–40.

Luhmann, N. (1984) *Soziale Systeme. Grundriß einer allgemeinen Theorie*, Frankfurt am Main, DE: Suhrkamp.

— (1992) *Beobachtungen der Moderne*, Opladen, DE: Westdeutscher Verlag.

— (2000) *Die Politik der Gesellschaft*, Frankfurt am Main, DE: Suhrkamp.

Machiavelli, N. (1990) *Der Fürst*, Frankfurt am Main, DE: Insel Verlag.

Makropoulos, M. (1997) *Modernität und Kontingenz*, München, DE: Wilhelm Fink.

Müller, W. C. and Strøm, K. (eds) (1999) *Policy, Office, or Votes? How political parties in Western Europe make hard decisions*, Cambridge, UK: Cambridge University Press.

Palonen, K. (1998) *Das 'Webersche Moment'. Zur Kontingenz des Politischen*, Opladen, DE: Westdeutscher Verlag.

— (2001) 'Politik statt Ordnung. Figuren der Kontingenz bei Max Weber', in H. J. Lietzmann (ed.) *Moderne Politik. Politikverständnisse im 20. Jahrhundert*, Opladen, DE: Leske+Budrich, pp. 9–21.

— (2003) 'Four times of politics: policy, polity, politicking, and politicization', *Alternatives* 28: 1–12.

— (2006) *The Struggle with Time: A conceptual history of 'politics' as activity*, Münster and Hamburg DE and London: LIT.

— (2008) *The Politics of Limited Time. The rhetoric of temporal judgement in parliamentary democracies*, Baden-Baden, DE Nomos.

Parsons, Talcott (1951) *The Social System*, New York: Free Press.

— (1968) 'Social interaction', in D. L. Sills (ed.) *The International Encyclopedia of the Social Sciences*, vol. 7, New York: McGraw-Hill, pp. 429–41.

Rhodes, R. A. W. and Dunleavy, P. (eds) (1995) *Prime Minister, Cabinet, and Core Executive*, London: Macmillan.

Rittel, H. W. J. and Webber, M. M. (1973) 'Dilemmas in a general theory of planning', *Policy Sciences* 4(2): 155–69.

Roberts, N. (2001) 'Wicked problems and network approaches to resolution', *International Public Management Review* 1(1): 1–19.

Rocheford, D. A. and Cobb, R. W. (eds) (1994) *The Politics of Problem Definition*, Lawrence, KA: University Press of Kansas.

Rodrik, D. (2012) *Globalization Paradox: Democracy and the future of the world economy*, New York: Norton & Company.

Rosa, H. (2005a) 'The speed of global flows and the pace of democratic politics', *New Political Science* 27(4): 445–59.

Rosa, H. (2005b) *Beschleunigung. Die Veränderung der Zeitstrukturen in der Moderne*, Frankfurt am Main, DE: Suhrkamp.

Rosa, H. and Scheuerman, W. E. (eds) (2009) *High-Speed Society: Social acceleration, power and modernity*, University Park, Philadelphia, PA: Pennsylvania State University Press.

Rudalevige, A. (2006) *The New Imperial Presidency: Renewing presidential power after Watergate*, Ann Arbor, MI: University of Michigan Press.

Scheuerman, W. E. (2001) 'Liberal democracy and the empire of speed', *Polity* 34: 41–67.

—— (2004) *Liberal Democracy and the Social Acceleration of Time*, Baltimore, MD and London: Johns Hopkins University Press.

—— (2003) 'Emergency powers and the compression of time and space', *Israel Yearbook of Human Rights* 33: 45–62.

Schmitt, C. (1950) *Die Lage der Europäischen Rechtswissenschaft*, Tübingen, DE: Internationaler Universitätsverlag.

—— (2009) 'The motorized legislator', in H. Rosa and W. Scheuerman (eds) *High-Speed Society. Social acceleration, power, and modernity*, University Park, Philadelphia, PA: Pennsylvania State University Press, pp. 65–73.

Scholte, J. A. (2005) *Globalization: A critical introduction*, Basingstoke, UK and New York: Palgrave Macmillan.

Simon, H. A. (1973) 'The structure of ill-structured problems', *Artificial Intelligence* 4: 181–200.

Smith, M. J. (1999) *The Core Executive in Britain*, 2nd edn, Basingstoke, UK and New York: Palgrave Macmillan.

Vanderstraeten, R. (2002) 'Parsons, Luhmann and the theorem of double contingency', *Journal of Classical Sociology* 2(1): 77–92.

Verweij, M. (2011) *Clumsy Solutions for a Wicked World: How to improve global governance*, Basingstoke, UK and New York: Palgrave Macmillan.

Verweij, M. and Thompson, M. (eds) (2006) *Clumsy Solutions for a Complex World: Governance, politics and plural perceptions*, Basingstoke, UK and New York: Palgrave Macmillan.

Zahariadis, N. (1999) 'Ambiguity, time and multiple streams. Theories of the policy process', in P. A. Sabatier (ed.) *Theories of the Policy Process*, Boulder, CO: Westview Press, pp. 73–93.

—— (2003) 'Multiple streams and public policy', in N. Zahariadis (ed.) *Ambiguity and Choice in Public Policy: Political decision making in modern democracies*, Washington, DC: Georgetown University Press, pp. 1–22.

—— (2007) 'The multiple streams framework. Structure, limitations, prospects', in P. A. Sabatier (ed.) *Theories of the Policy Process*, Boulder, CO: Westview Press, pp. 65–92.

PART TWO

THE ELEMENTS OF THE MULTIPLE-STREAMS
FRAMEWORK

Chapter Five

Kingdon à *la Carte*: A New Recipe for Mixing Stages, Cycles, Soups and Streams

Michael Howlett, Allan McConnell and Anthony Perl

Introduction: a mixture of metaphors about the policy process

The academic pursuit of policy analysis often relies on metaphors to simplify complexity and illuminate policy dynamics (Pump 2011; Bardach 2000; Edelman 1988; Stone 1988 and 1989; Schlesinger and Lau 2000; Black 1962). However, these conceptualisations run the risk of confusing a metaphor with a model, which can constrain the development of testable theories and impede theoretical advance (Dowding 1995; Pappi and Henning 1998).

This is true of the multiple-streams model developed by Kingdon (1984) from March and Olson's earlier work on decision-making theory (1979). This conception has been utilised in many studies, both as a metaphor for agenda-setting, as Kingdon originally intended it, and as a larger model for interpreting policy-making as a whole. More recently, McConnell (2010a, 2010b) used a similar approach in his studies of policy success and failure. However the application of Kingdon's framework to wider policy-making dynamics, which extend beyond those found in agenda-setting, poses some questions as to what exactly constitutes a 'stream' and how streams 'flow together' to produce agenda-entrance or subsequent policy outcomes.

This is also true of the classic metaphor about policy-making: the '*stages*' model. This process metaphor originated with the earliest scholarship on public-policy analysis but received varying treatment by different authors. Its attempt to explain policy-making has been criticised for focusing too narrowly on decision-making within government and having little to say about external or environmental influences on government's behaviour, since decision-making is assumed to be limited to a small number of participants working inside government.

This chapter revisits the early literature that used the metaphors of policy streams and policy stages and explores in detail the variables which flow over time and affect instances of policy-making. It suggests that both Kingdon and McConnell's three-stream models offer perspectives that are suited to illuminating the specific aspects of policy-making they examine; but such approaches require augmentation in order to engage the full range of practices that characterise policy-making as a whole. This chapter develops and refines work undertaken by the authors and already published in the *European Journal of Political Research* in a forum section devoted specifically to the multiple-streams framework (Howlett, McConnell and Perl 2016).

The stages model

The conceptual advantages of breaking the policy-making process down into a number of discrete stages for gaining insight into complex public policy-making dynamics were first broached in the early work of Harold Lasswell (1956 and 1971). Lasswell posited that the policy process began with intelligence-gathering, that is, the collection, processing, and dissemination of information needed by those who make policy decisions. It then moved to consider how particular options were assessed by those involved in making the decision. In the third stage, the decision-makers formally ratified a plan of action. In the fourth stage, the approved plan was enacted as a set of sanctions to enforce compliance with the prescribed course of action. The policy was then applied by the bureaucracy and overseen by the courts until it was terminated or cancelled. Finally, the results were appraised and evaluated against the aims of the original policy and the goals of the decision-makers.

One shortcoming of this model was its ordering of stages. The placement of appraisal or evaluation following termination fails to recognise that governments usually evaluate policy *before* winding it down rather than afterwards (Brewer 1974). Nevertheless, with suitable amendment, this model and metaphor influenced a great deal of thinking as the policy sciences developed and Lasswell's formulation served as the basis for numerous similar models put forward in succeeding years (Lyden *et al.* 1968; Simmons *et al.* 1974; Anderson 1975; Jones 1984).

Typical among these was a simplified model created by Gary Brewer (1974). Brewer suggested that the policy process was composed of only five or six stages: 1) invention/initiation; 2) estimation; 3) selection; 4) implementation; 5) evaluation; and 6) termination. According to Brewer, invention or initiation characterised the earliest stage in the sequence, when a problem would first be recognised. In Brewer's model, the initiation stage would be characterised by an unfocused definition of the problem and inchoate solutions. In the second stage, known as estimation, there is a calculation of the risks, costs and benefits associated with each potential solution identified in the earlier stage. Both technical assessment and normative perspectives would guide such estimation. Estimation would facilitate policy development by excluding unfeasible options and thus narrow the range of plausible policy-options to a manageable number whose desirability could be ranked. In the third stage, choices would be made to adopt one, or none, or some combination of solutions that had advanced through the estimation stage. The remaining stages focused on implementing the selected policy option(s), evaluating the results of the subsequent policy and then terminating or modifying the policy, based on findings revealed through policy evaluation (Brewer and deLeon 1983).

Brewer's conceptualisation of the policy process enhanced the insight of Lasswell's pioneering effort. This analytical perspective expanded the search for influences on policy beyond the bounds of government by recognising the dynamic of problem-recognition; and it specified more precise terminology to describe each stage of the process. Moreover, Brewer introduced a second metaphor to assist in thinking through the stages of policy-making: that is, the image of this process as an ongoing 'cycle'. This metaphor recognised that most policies did not go through a linear development from birth to death but, instead, tended to reappear in slightly different manifestations, as one policy succeeded another through incremental modification. Brewer's contribution precipitated several variants of the policy-cycle metaphor that were developed during the 1970s and 1980s. The best known of these were expounded in widely adopted textbooks written by Charles O. Jones (1984) and James Anderson (1975). Both these textbooks varied in their specification of the names, number, and order of stages in the cycle but embraced the same underlying metaphorical construction.

The multiple-streams model

A significant advantage arising from the policy-cycle metaphor is that it offers an analytical approach that facilitates the understanding of policy-making by reducing complex processes into component stages and sub-stages, which can be studied directly or in relationship to any or all subsets of the policy-cycle. This segmentation contributes to theory-building. It enables the evidence from multiple case studies, as comparative examinations of different stages, to be aggregated and the findings from these investigations to be synthesised. The model generated through the use of this metaphor can then be applied to all jurisdictions and places where policy is made, from local boroughs to international political organisations (Fowler and Siegel 2002; Bogason 2000; Billings and Hermann 1998). Furthermore, the cycle model facilitates analysis of the contribution of all actors and institutions to policy development, not just the work of governmental agencies formally accountable for policy.

Despite its aforementioned merits, however, the principal shortcoming of the policy-cycle metaphor is that it also creates the impression that policy-makers pursue solutions to public problems in a straightforward and essentially linear fashion (Jenkins-Smith and Sabatier 1993). Yet we know that in the real world, such a pattern is far from the norm. While the policy-cycle's logic may be elegant in the abstract, in practical applications, stages are often condensed or passed over entirely. Identifying problems, as well as developing and implementing solutions, is often an *ad hoc* and idiosyncratic process, shaped by ideologies, interests and strategies and, at times, beginning with putative solutions (as per 'garbage-can' theory) (March and Olson 1979). The order of operations in practical policy-making may thus bear little resemblance to that specified by the policy-cycle's conceptual logic. For example, the cycle may not run as a single iterative loop but, rather, proceed through a series of smaller loops, in which the results of prior decisions and implementation shape the course of subsequent policy formulation, regardless of the agenda-setting specifics of a particular case.

While the policy-cycle metaphor retains a prominent position among policy researchers, other metaphorical constructions that grapple with this more complex policy-making reality have attracted interest in the effort to overcome these limitations. An elaborate set of policy-making metaphors, for example, can be found in John Kingdon's book, *Agendas, Alternatives, and Public Policy* (1984). Kingdon proposed a means of understanding agenda-setting based upon first-hand and secondary (see, for example, Walker 1977) examinations of agenda processes in the US Congress. His model highlighted the influence of a specific category of policy-actors in subsystems – policy entrepreneurs – who generated policy initiatives both inside and outside of government by taking advantage of agenda-setting opportunities – *policy-windows* – to move items on to government's formal agenda. Kingdon's writing is replete with vivid metaphors, such as 'the *primeval policy soup*' and, most significantly for later work, the images of '*policy streams*' and '*policy-windows*'.[1]

Kingdon's treatise on policy-making dynamics in the US Congress was focused on agenda-setting and formulation but the concepts put forward in his book were soon embraced by others in order to develop explanations of the entire policy process (Zahariadis 1995; Barzelay 2006). Kingdon's model posited that substantive issue characteristics combined with the organisational characteristics of political institutions, and with the development of policy solutions, in a manner which triggered the opening and closing of policy-windows that could enable these issues to enter on to the agenda. Such opportunities could be realised if, and only if, policy-entrepreneurs were able to recognise and act upon them. This 'multiple-streams' model, and its variants, has yielded an ongoing analytical tradition that both describes policy-making and seeks to explain it in terms of the confluence of key factors or variables at particular moments in time.

In Kingdon's particular explanation of how agenda-setting worked in the United States, three categories of independent variables were said to interact. These problem, policy, and political streams were said to have the following characteristics:

- The *problem stream* is filled with perceptions of problems that were seen as 'public' in the sense that government action was needed to resolve them. These problems usually came to the awareness of policy-makers because of dramatic events such as crises or through feedback from existing programmes that gained public attention. People come to view a situation as a 'problem' based upon its variance from their understanding of some desired state of affairs.
- The *policy stream* is filled with the output of experts and analysts who examine problems and propose solutions to them. In this stream, the myriad possibilities for action and inaction are identified, assessed and narrowed down to a subset of ostensibly feasible options.

---

1. Of course, he also uses other less dynamic metaphors, such as 'windows of opportunity' and 'policy-entrepreneurs'.

- Finally, the *political stream* is comprised of factors that influence the body politic, such as swings in national mood, executive or legislative turnover and interest-group advocacy campaigns.

According to Kingdon, these three streams flow along different paths and remain more or less independent of one another until, at a specific point in time, a *policy-window* opens. Only then do their paths cross. As Kingdon viewed agenda-setting: 'The separate streams of problems, policies, and politics come together at certain critical times. Solutions become joined to problems, and both of them are joined to favourable political forces' (Kingdon 1984: 21). Only then does an issue become a recognised problem on the official (or institutional) agenda and the public-policy process begins to address it.

Under certain circumstances, *policy-windows* can be used by particular actors in a policy subsystem in order to advance the engagement of the issues they care about. These policy entrepreneurs play an important role in shaping the course of multiple streams by linking or 'coupling' policy problems and policy solutions together with political opportunities. Kingdon suggested that window openings could sometimes be triggered by apparently unrelated external '*focusing events*', such as crises, or accidents; or the presence or absence of 'policy-entrepreneurs' both within and outside governments. At other times, these windows were opened by institutionalised events such as periodic elections or budget deadlines (Birkland 1997 and 1998). As Kingdon argued:

> windows are opened either by the appearance of compelling problems or by happenings in the political stream. … Policy entrepreneurs, people who are willing to invest their resources in pushing their pet proposals or problems, are responsible not only for prompting important people to pay attention, but also for coupling solutions to problems and for coupling both problems and solutions to politics (p. 21).

This streams metaphor has proven valuable in helping us to explain policy dynamics and envisage the convergence of multiple societal phenomena to precipitate an 'idea whose time has come'. And applying the concept of multiple streams has become common practice in the policy sciences. Among the subjects it has been applied to have been US foreign-policy-making (Woods and Peake 1998); public enterprise privatisation in Britain, France and Germany (Zahariadis 1995; Zahariadis and Allen 1995); US efforts to combat illegal drug use (Sharp 1994); collaborative pollution-control partnerships between business and environmental groups in the US and Europe (Lober 1997); and the wide-ranging dynamics of policy reform and -restructuring in Eastern Europe (Keeler 1993). McConnell (2010a) has applied a similar model in his studies of policy success and failure.

However, the concepts applied in many streams analyses, while appearing similar, have not been identical. For example, the alternative three-stream model developed by McConnell (2010a, 2010b) in his study of policy success and failure uses 'processes, policies and politics' streams (see also Marsh and McConnell 2010; Howlett 2012).

This raises the question of which phenomena should be categorised as 'streams' as well as how these streams flow together and interact to produce policy outcomes. There remains also the question of whether, or how, 'streams' analysis fits in with the earlier understanding of policy-making as a process, which grew out of the policy-cycle or 'stages heuristic' (Jann and Wegrich 2007). These questions have usually been ignored by the multiple-streams literature, which has often viewed itself as antithetical to the stages model. However, as discussed below, this is not the case; and a more subtle interpretation of what a stream is can help reconcile the apparent differences between these two approaches to policy studies.

Kingdon *à la carte*: towards a new recipe connecting cycle and stream models

Some scholars have called for an integration of 'streams' and 'cycle' models, anticipating that incorporating the stream metaphor into policy process models would provide the causal insight necessary to move policy studies beyond competing metaphors and to advance from description to explanation of policy dynamics. Barzelay, for example, proposed in a 2006 symposium that the two approaches simply be synthesised, as is. He argued that Kingdon's work would benefit from a process approach while incorporating elements of a multiple-streams framework would similarly improve policy-cycle models. As he put it:

> Kingdon's book exemplifies the quest for a process understanding of public policymaking (in addition to providing analytic generalizations about statutory change in substantive policy domains within the institutional setup of the U.S. federal government). Kingdon's analytical approach examines the policymaking process systemically, while disaggregating the whole into component processes, drawing on the concept of a policy cycle (Barzelay 2006: 253).

Barzelay advocated a straightforward merger of the cycle model and multiple-streams framework, suggesting that:

> [i]n the overall process, agenda-setting events influence alternative-specification events through two causal channels. First, problem definition trajectories influence the construction and winnowing of alternatives, through the influence of issue framing and the assignment of issues to distinct venues for alternative specification. Second, the prospect of policy change, inferred from an agenda-setting event's past and anticipated trajectory, spurs the efforts of participants in alternative-specification events, whether they are policy entrepreneurs, protectors of the status quo, or just doing their job. The trajectories of decision-making events are, in turn, influenced by agenda-setting and alternative-specification events. This aspect of the overall policymaking

process arises because the rendering of alternatives, in combination with pressures responsible for an elevated issue status, may open the gates to decisional venues and their corresponding decisional agendas (Barzelay 2006: 253–4).

While innovative, such a proposal does not derive directly from the principles found in the multiple-streams framework. Rather, it rests upon an interpretation that abandons some of the presuppositions and postulates from the 'garbage-can' perspective on decision-making (March and Olson 1979; Mucciaroni 1992) which Kingdon incorporated in his work. As such, there remain some lingering problems from this pioneering effort to reconcile the metaphors of stages and streams. Kingdon can be oversold as providing the key for understanding all, or most, policy-making dynamics when, in fact, his analysis was explicitly focused on agenda-setting (Zahariadis 1995; Zahariadis and Allen 1995; Zahariadis 2007). And Kingdon's application of garbage-can metaphors to policy-making becomes murky when it engages the garbage-can model (Mucciaroni 1992). He seems to imply that agenda-setting embraces wider dimensions of policy-making since 'an idea whose time has come' will often be a problem that was dragged out of the garbage can and used to rationalise a solution that was favoured by some subset of policy participants. This linkage between agendas, issues and policy-making doesn't come to grips with the actual dynamics of the processes, in which ideas compete for the attention and engagement of policy-makers (Bache and Reardon 2013).

Given its widespread application, it is surprising that Kingdon's model has received such limited conceptual interrogation. For example, what exactly is a 'policy stream' and what happens to the stream once a problem has made its way on to the formal agenda? Can the stream metaphor continue to explain policy dynamics once problems, politics and policy options move beyond agenda entrance? And if so, what then happens to these 'fluids'? Could certain streams suddenly run dry? Or do they flow differently, with new volumes of policy, problems or politics joining at a particular confluence? Can the waters be transformed through new streams being created?

Notwithstanding these challenges, we believe it is possible to connect these two models and reconcile their insights and assumptions. There is much to gain by seeing how far Kingdon's streams metaphor can be extended to help answer the 'what happens next?' question in policy-process studies, which is so often addressed through application of the stages metaphor in the policy-cycle model. However, this requires re-examining in some detail the adoption and application of the 'soup', 'streams', and 'windows' metaphors that were used by Kingdon.

What is a stream and how does it function?

One of the defining characteristics of a 'stream' in Kingdon's work is its more or less independent trajectory. As a result, events that are initiated by specific actors can occasionally 'intersect' to affect each other and trigger new events;

but without losing their fundamentally autonomous nature. Although some of these questions have been pursued elsewhere (see, for example, Howlett 1998 on types and predictability of policy-windows), a key question embedded within the 'streams metaphor' which is engaged in this chapter, is the primordial search for 'how many' and 'what type' of key factors influence policy processes and how they relate to one another.

Kingdon's focus on the interconnection between a flow of problems, policy and politics to explain policy-making, for example, builds upon Cohen, March and Olson's earlier foundational work on garbage-can decision-making (1972) and has inspired many assessments of policy agenda-setting, as well as more ambitious attempts to illuminate the entire process. A 'stream' in this sense is a collection of variables parameters which develop and change over time. This temporal focus is what differentiates Kingdon's work from many earlier agenda-setting studies (see, for example, Cobb, Ross and Ross 1976; Cobb and Elder 1972) and is what later analysts and students of policy-making found to be intriguing and useful in his work (John 2003).

The garbage-can model and the multiple-streams framework appear to posit different relationships among their streams, however, with Kingdon seeing a more structured interaction than was posited by March and Olson. As John puts it:

> Kingdon uses evolutionary ideas to highlight the dynamic and contingent aspects of his account. It is a useful component of his account of policy change, without being an evolutionary model. There are, however, some useful clues as to how one could emerge. Kingdon argues that possibilities and limits of combinations create unique outcomes because '[e]verything cannot interact with everything else' (John 2003: 488).

In other words, there are certain combinations of ideas and proposals that have the potential to evolve, but not others (2003: 488).

Equally significantly, some streams, for Kingdon, appear to carry more weight than others. In his analysis of agenda-setting, for instance, Kingdon suggested this would occur but never explained exactly why. Thus the opening of a window for agenda-entry was thought by Kingdon to be triggered by one of two flows, in either the 'problem' or 'political' streams rather than in the 'policy' one, although why this would be the case was not examined:

> [b]asically a window opens because of change in the political stream (e.g. a change of administration, a shift in the partisan or ideological distribution of seats ... or a shift in national mood); or it opens because a new problem captures the attention of governmental officials and those close to them (Kingdon 1984: 176).

Although it could also be plausible to suggest that something flowing through the 'policy stream' could open a window for change in the agenda – such as when market mechanisms are proposed to address an existing problem without a change in the problem or the politics surrounding it *per se* (for example de-regulation or privatisation) – this possibility was not considered by Kingdon, despite his well received observation that 'solutions can precede problems'.

Another question that was left hanging in the multiple-streams framework is whether any window is likely to open or close with greater predictability than any other (Howlett 1998). While arguing that random events can be significant, Kingdon stressed that institutionalised windows create more predictable dynamics in the US agenda-setting process than one would expect given a pure garbage-can approach. As he put it 'there remains some degree of unpredictability. Yet it would be a grave mistake to conclude that the processes ... are essentially random. Some degree of pattern is evident.' (Kingdon 1984: 216). This led him to conclude that a majority of policy-windows open on a more or less predictable cycle:

[w]indows sometimes open with great predictability. Regular cycles of various kinds open and close windows on a schedule. That schedule varies in its precision and hence its predictability, but the cyclical nature of many windows is nonetheless evident (Kingdon 1984: 193).

and

[s]ometimes, windows open quite predictably. Legislation comes up for renewal on schedule, for instance, creating opportunities to change, expand or abolish certain programs. At other times, windows open quite unpredictably, as when an airliner crashes or a fluky election produces unexpected turnover in key decision-makers. Predictable or unpredictable, open windows are small and scarce. Opportunities come, but they also pass. Windows do not stay open long. If a chance is missed, another must be awaited (Kingdon 1984: 213).

While such perspectives on the dynamics of policy change may be more or less accurate, depending on the setting they are used to explain, it is not inherent in the idea or metaphor of multiple streams that a particular stream influences the prospects for change in policy-making more than any other, or that any type of window should be inherently more significant or common than any other. Incorporating aspects of policy-cycle models into the streams framework, however, helps to explain why this should be the case. However it also requires, *contra* Barzelay, that some fundamental aspects of the multiple-streams model, such as how many streams there are and how they interact, be modified.

Is 'process' a stream? How many streams are out there?

As Kingdon acknowledged in his 1984 work, the idea of 'policy streams' was inspired by the earlier work of Cohen, March and Olson (1972; see also March and Olson 1979) to explain administrative decision-making processes in complex and fluid organisational environments. But when they created this analytical antecedent to the multiple-streams framework, Cohen, March and Olson posited that there were *four* streams, not the three that Kingdon incorporated into the multiple-streams framework. Cohen, March and Olsen presented policy 'windows' or 'choice opportunities' as another stream which flowed more or less independently of the other three. The original streams were defined by them as:

- *Problems* Problems are the concern of people inside and outside the organisation. They might arise over issues of lifestyle; family; frustrations of work; careers; group relations within the organisation; distribution of status, jobs, and money; ideology; or current crises of mankind as interpreted by the mass media or the next-door neighbour. All of these require attention.

- *Solutions* A solution is somebody's product. A computer is not just a solution to a problem in payroll management, discovered when needed. It is an answer actively looking for a question. The creation of need is not a curiosity of the market in consumer products; it is a general phenomenon of processes of choice. Despite the dictum that you cannot find the answer until you have formulated the question well, you often do not know what the question is in organisational problem-solving until you also understand its answer.

- *Participants* Participants come and go. Since every entrance is an exit somewhere else, the distribution of 'entrances' depends on the attributes of the choice being left as much as it does on the attributes of the new choice. Substantial variation in participation stems from other demands on the participants' time (as much or more than from features of the decision under study).

- *Choice-opportunities* These are occasions when an organisation is expected to produce behaviour that can be called a decision. Opportunities arise regularly and any organisation has ways of declaring an occasion for choice. Contracts must be signed; people hired, promoted, or fired; money spent; and responsibilities allocated (Cohen March and Olson 1972: 2).

Thus Cohen, March and Olson (1972: 3) noted that *all four* sets of dynamic variables were 'relatively independent' that is: 'although not completely independent of each other, each of the streams can be viewed as independent and exogenous to the system'. This differs significantly from treating a policy-window as the exclusive point of intersection among the other three streams, as in Kingdon's framework.

McConnell (2010a, 2010b) also described a policy process in expansive terms, reaching beyond the problem-definition stage of the policy-cycle. A policy process was thus meant to extend beyond the agenda-setting stage to encompass the stages where problems are defined, options examined and decisions taken, implemented and evaluated (Lyden *et al.* 1968). Thus the policy process offers an extension of analytical and political activities on multiple fronts, addressing what Kingdon would characterise as the 'problem' stream but also paying attention to policy solutions and political events that could influence them.

Such variation between Kingdon's original formulation and subsequent applications of the multiple-streams framework reinforces the possibility that utilising only 'three streams' of influence on policy-making dynamics may fail to capture relevant drivers of change, and that more streams – at least four – would better capture key aspects of policy formation, by representing a more complete set of the configurations among variables that could open a window for moving policy on to, or between, the stages of policy deliberation, decision and deployment.

The minimum four would be: *politics*, *problem*, *policy* and *process*. 'Process' in this formulation bears a strong resemblance to Cohen, March and Olson's 'choice opportunity' stream but is centred on the stages of the policy-cycle, with each stage providing a particular intersection point for the other three. This variable flows from the bureaucratic capacities and cultural norms that orient both the state and society in shaping preferences on how to meet the needs of a particular policy context. This choice-opportunity stream thus captures the structural variation that can lead policy subsystems in very different directions when engaging a policy issue as seen through the policy-cycle construct.

This is quite compatible with Kingdon's vision, since he was not driven to engage this fourth 'P': his analysis focused explicitly on understanding only the dynamics of one stage of the policy process: agenda-entrance. Although his book considered plenty of policy formulation efforts, these were addressed by the logic of the garbage-can model (March and Olson 1979), in which the distinction between agenda-setting and formulation effectively disappears. Expanding the three streams to four and looking beyond the agenda-setting stage is logical if we are attempting to apply a multiple-streams logic to the entire range of policy-making activities beyond agenda-entrance.

But adding an additional process stream poses problems for Kingdon's original model, in that the manner in which these four streams interact is not immediately apparent. One way to realign three- and four-stream models is to replace the 'problem' stream with a 'policy' stream after agenda-setting occurs. In this perspective, the 'problem' maintains independent significance during dynamics prior to agenda-entrance, as Kingdon posited, but after the policy process moves on to developing options for dealing with the problem, it drops out and is replaced by the 'process stream', which influences subsequent dynamics as an effort is made to generate a solution to this problem. The temporal shift also carries the streams framework beyond its garbage-can epistemological and ontological foundations, towards a logic that is consistent with conceptual trends in policy studies, which have focused more on the manner whereby institutions affect decision-making and policy development in routine and predictable ways (Araral *et al.* 2012). In this perspective, 'process' takes on a different character from 'politics' or 'problem' or 'policy', since it becomes internal to the policy-making process, rather than an external factor contributing to it.

This conceptualisation may initially appear quite promising as a means of squaring the 3P versus 4P relationship. It offers the advantage of grounding Kingdon's three-stream model in its origins as an agenda-setting analysis, while extending it to cover all the stages of the policy process – without simply ignoring the nuances and differences in the choice-opportunities that exist at each stage (Zahariadis 2007). However, simply turning the 'problem' stream into a 'process' stream after agenda-setting has occurred raises the difficulty that it assumes a problem stream simply stops flowing once agenda-setting has occurred: namely, that the basic problem remains unchanged once policy-making gets underway and discussion focuses on policy (that is, solutions). Although Kingdon successfully avoids this conceptual difficulty by remaining focused on a single stage of the policy cycle, the option of building a problem 'lock-in' into the multiple-streams framework is incompatible with findings from the problem-definition and policy-cycle literature that demonstrate that competing constructs of the problem continue to co-exist through policy-making (Fischer and Forrester 1993; Hajer 2005; Sabatier *et al.* 2007; Howlett 2009).

Other possibilities exist that might be better suited to understanding this complexity, for example, the full confluence of the three streams which converge at the agenda-setting stage of the policy process and from there onwards flow together as a single stream. This confluence yields a fourth policy-making stream, which then flows along through the policy-cycle towards an outcome (Teisman 2000). However this model, too, fails to deal with the alterations of and interactions between policy and problem and politics, which occur as the policy process unfolds.

Adding another 'stream' in addition to the March and Olson four to create a five-stream model is a more promising elaboration that would retain 'process' as an independent stream while separating out a programme stream that focuses explicitly on the instrumentation that is developed to deliver policy outputs. In this model, once Kingdon's three original streams converge and produce actions or inaction to address policy, they would be supplemented by 'process' and 'programme' streams, whose flow is generated from the issue-management and policy output dimensions of policy-making. That is, the choice and application of policy instruments creates its own influences on a policy sub-system as policy implementation influences politics, which would be captured within the programme stream's flow. Thus the flow of the programme stream can include new instruments introduced to deal with a problem (such as public agencies to provide transport security in a number of nations after 11 September 2001) and it can cover refinements of established instruments (such as special inspection of airline passengers' footwear after an attempt to bring down an aircraft using explosive running shoes).

Conclusion

Although the policy-stages idea has a long list of detractors (for example, Sabatier 1991; Colebatch 2006), it retains a predominant place among contemporary policy-science metaphors that influence model-construction and elaboration (deLeon 1999; Burton 2006; Weible *et al.* 2012). As a mode of considering change or stasis in policy development, the cycle employs a metaphor invoking a temporal primacy to matching solutions to problems – breaking an extended and conflictual process into discrete stages and sub-stages whose dynamics can be assessed iteratively, and interconnected – which has been very effective in pursuing policy analyses

(Simmons 1974). Kingdon's work on the multiple-streams idea has also generated a metaphorical construction that has found favour with policy scholars, many of whom object to the linear instrumental rationality of the cycle model. The concept of limited and readily identifiable key variables – the multiple streams affecting policy-making – along with the idea that interactions between these streams create choice-opportunities that affect how policy issues are addressed by governments, has proven alluring to many looking for an alternative to the cycle orthodoxy.

As we have shown, however, Kingdon's notions cannot simply be imported *holus bolus* into stage-models of policy-making without yielding a muddled mixing of metaphors that limits the efficacy of both models. In order to attempt their reconciliation, a way is needed to reconfigure the contingent aspects of the three-streams model that Kingdon developed to make it better fit with the notions about sequential decision-making that the policy-cycle relies upon. Reconciling these two dominant metaphorical constructions requires going back to Kingdon's original treatment of policy-windows or choice-opportunities, which differs from the ideas he borrowed from Cohen, March and Olsen in their foundational work about policy-making as an expression of organised anarchy. Specifically, their idea of at least a fourth 'choice-opportunity' or 'process' stream is a key insight that Kingdon did not elaborate upon in his work, focused as it was on a single 'stage' of the policy process.

This chapter has demonstrated that extending three-stream models into four-stream constructs improves but does not ultimately resolve these challenges; but moving to a five-stream model may have a better potential for the reconciliation of the two approaches, helping to move policy studies forward beyond the present situation of competitive analytical constructs (Cairney 2013). Such a conceptual progression helps extend Kingdon's insights and offers a framework that can help advance future understandings of policy-making and policy dynamics, while also clarifying the existing literature on these subjects.

References

Anderson, J. E. (1975) *Public Policy Making*, New York: Praeger.

Araral, E., *et al.* (eds) (2012) *Routledge Handbook of Public Policy*, New York: Routledge.

Bache, I. and Reardon, L. (2013) 'An idea whose time has come? Explaining the rise of well-being in British politics', *Political Studies* 61(4): 898–914.

Bardach, E. (2000) *A Practical Guide for Policy Analysis: The eightfold path to more effective problem solving*, New York: Chatham House Publishers.

Barzelay, M. (2006) 'Introduction: the process dynamics of public management policymaking', *International Public Management Journal* 6(3): 251–82.

Billings, R. S. and Hermann, C. F. (1998) 'Problem identification in sequential policy decision making: the re-representation of problems', in D. A. Sylvan and J. F. Voss (eds) *Problem Representation in Foreign Policy Decision Making*, Cambridge, UK: Cambridge University Press, pp. 53–79.

Birkland, T. A. (1997) *After Disaster: Agenda setting, public policy and focusing events*, Washington, DC: Georgetown University Press.

— (1998) 'Focusing events, mobilization, and agenda setting', *Journal of Public Policy* 18(1): 53–74.

Black, M. (1962) *Models and Metaphors: Studies in language and philosophy*, Ithaca, NY: Cornell University Press.

Bogason, P. (2000) *Public Policy and Local Governance: Institutions in postmodern society*, Cheltenham, UK: Edward Elgar.

Brewer, G. D. (1974) 'The policy sciences emerge: to nurture and structure a discipline', *Policy Sciences* 5: 239–44.

Brewer, G. and deLeon, P. (1983) *The Foundations of Policy Analysis*, Homewood, IL: Dorsey.

Burton, P. (2006) 'Modernising the policy process: making policy research more significant?', *Policy Studies* 27(3): 172–92.

Cairney, P. (2013) 'Standing on the shoulders of giants: how do we combine the insights of multiple theories in public policy studies?', *Policy Studies Journal* 41(1): 1–21.

Cobb, R. W., and Elder, C. D. (1972) *Participation in American Politics: The dynamics of agenda-building*, Boston, MA: Allyn and Bacon.

Cobb, R., Ross, J. K. and Ross, M. H. (1976) 'Agenda building as a comparative political process', *American Political Science Review* 70(1): 126–38.

Cohen, M., March, J. and Olsen, J. (1972) 'A garbage can model of organizational choice', *Administrative Science Quarterly* 17(1): 1–25.

Colebatch, H. K. (2006) *Beyond the Policy Cycle: The policy process in Australia*, Crows Nest, NSW: Allen and Unwin.

deLeon, P. (1999) 'The stages approach to the policy process: what has it done? Where is it going?', in P. A. Sabatier (ed.) *Theories of the Policy Process*, Boulder, CO: Westview Press, pp. 19–34.

Dowding, K. (1995) 'Model or metaphor? A critical review of the policy network approach', *Political Studies* 43(Supplement 1): 136–58.

Edelman, M. J. (1988) *Constructing the Political Spectacle*, Chicago: University of Chicago Press.

Fischer, F. and Forester, J. (eds) (1993) *The Argumentative Turn in Policy Analysis and Planning*, Durham, NC: Duke University Press.

Fowler, E. P. and Siegel, D. (eds) (2002) *Urban Policy Issues*, Toronto: Oxford University Press.

Hajer, M. A. (2005) 'Setting the stage: a dramaturgy of policy deliberation', *Administration & Society* 36(6): 624–47.

Howlett, M. (1998) 'Predictable and unpredictable policy windows: issue, institutional and exogenous correlates of Canadian federal agenda-setting', *Canadian Journal of Political Science* 31(3): 495–524.

—   (2009) 'Process sequencing policy dynamics: beyond homeostasis and path dependency', *Journal of Public Policy* 29(3): 241–62.

—   (2012) 'The lessons of failure: learning and blame avoidance in public policy-making', *International Political Science Review* 33(5): 539–55.

Howlett, M. McConnell, A. and Perl, A. (2015), 'Streams and stages: reconciling Kingdon and policy process theory', *European Journal of Political Research* 54(3): 419–34.

Jann, W. and Wegrich, K. (2007) 'Theories of the policy cycle', in F. Fischer, G. J. Miller, and M. S. Sidney (eds) *Handbook of Public Policy Analysis: Theory, politics and methods*, Boca Raton, FL: CRC Press, pp. 43–62.

Jenkins-Smith, H. C. and Sabatier, P. A. (1993) 'The study of the public policy processes', in P. A. Sabatier and H. C. Jenkins-Smith (eds) *Policy Change and Learning: An advocacy coalition approach*, Boulder, CO: Westview Press, pp. 1–9.

John, P. (2003) 'Is there life after policy streams, advocacy coalitions and punctuations: using evolutionary theory to explain policy change?', *Policy Studies Journal* 31(4): 481–98.

Jones, C. O. (1984) *An Introduction to the Study of Public Policy*, Monterey, CA: Brooks/Cole Publishing Company.

Keeler, J. T. S. (1993) 'Opening the window for reform: mandates, crises and extraordinary policy-making', *Comparative Political Studies* 25(4): 433–86.

Kingdon, J. W. (1984) *Agendas, Alternatives, and Public Policies*, Boston: Little, Brown & Co.

Lasswell, H. D. (1956) *The Decision Process: Seven categories of functional analysis*, College Park, MD: Bureau of Governmental Research, College of Business and Public Administration, University of Maryland.

—   (1971) *A Pre-View of Policy Sciences*, New York: American Elsevier.

Lober, D. J. (1997) 'Explaining the formation of business-environmentalist collaborations: collaborative windows and the paper task force', *Policy Sciences* 30: 1–24.

Lyden, F. J., Shipman, G. A., Wilkinson, R. W. and Le Breton, P. P. (1968) 'Decision-flow analysis: a methodology for studying the public policy-making process', in Le Breton, P. P. (ed.) *Comparative Administrative Theory*, Seattle, WA: University of Washington Press, pp. 155–68.

March, J. G. and Olsen, J. P. (1979) *Ambiguity and Choice in Organizations*, Bergen, NO: Universitetsforlaget.

Marsh, D. and McConnell, A. (2010) 'Towards a framework for establishing policy success: a reply to Bovens', *Public Administration* 88(2): 586–7.

McConnell, A. (2010a) 'Policy success, policy failure and grey areas in-between', *Journal of Public Policy* 30(3): 345–62.

—   (2010b) *Understanding Policy Success: Rethinking public policy*, Basingstoke, UK: Palgrave Macmillan.

Mucciaroni, G. (1992) 'The garbage can model and the study of policy making: a critique', *Polity* 24(3): 460–82.

Pappi, F. U. and Henning, C. H. C. A (1998) 'Policy networks: more than a metaphor', *Journal of Theoretical Politics* 10(4): 553–75.

Pump, B. (2011) 'Beyond metaphors: new research on agendas in the policy process', *Policy Studies Journal* 39(s1): 1–12.

Sabatier, P. A. (1991) 'Toward better theories of the policy process', *PS: Political Science & Politics* 24(2): 144–56.

Sabatier, P., Hunter, S. and McLaughlin, S. (1987) 'The devil shift: perceptions and misperceptions of opponents', *Western Political Quarterly* 40(3): 449–76.

Schlesinger, M. and Lau, R. R. (2000) 'The meaning and measure of policy metaphors', *American Political Science Review* 94(3): 611–26.

Sharp, E. B. (1994) 'Paradoxes of national anti-drug policymaking', in D. A. Rochefort and R. W. Cobb (eds) *The Politics of Problem Definition: Shaping the policy agenda*, Lawrence, KA: University Press of Kansas, pp. 98–116.

Simmons, R. H. *et al.* (1974) 'Policy flow analysis: a conceptual model for comparative public policy research', *Western Political Quarterly* 27(3): 457–68.

Stone, D. A. (1988) *Policy Paradox and Political Reason*, Glenview, IL: Scott, Foresman.

—   (1989) 'Causal stories and the formation of policy agendas', *Political Science Quarterly* 104(2): 281–300.

Teisman, G. R. (2000) 'Models for research into decision-making processes: on phases, streams and decision-making rounds', *Public Administration* 78(4): 937–56.

Walker, J. L. (1977) 'Setting the agenda in the U.S. Senate: a theory of problem selection', *British Journal of Political Science* 7(4): 423–45.

Weible, C. M. *et al.* (2012) 'Understanding and influencing the policy process', *Policy Sciences* 45(1): 1–21.

Woods, B. D. and Peake, J. S. (1998) 'The dynamics of foreign policy agenda-setting', *American Political Science Review* 92(1): 173–84.

Zahariadis, N. (1995) *Markets, States, and Public Policy: Privatization in Britain and France*, Ann Arbor, MI: University of Michigan Press.

Zahariadis, N. (2007) 'The multiple streams framework: structure, limitations, prospects', in P. Sabatier (ed.) *Theories of the Policy Process*, 2nd edn, Boulder, CO: Westview Press, pp. 65–92.

Zahariadis, N. and Allen, C. S. (1995) 'Ideas, networks, and policy streams: privatization in Britain and Germany', *Policy Studies Review* 14(1/2): 71–98.

Chapter Six

Refining the Idea of Focusing Events in the Multiple-Streams Framework

Thomas A. Birkland and Megan K. Warnement[1]

Introduction

Nearly twenty years ago, Thomas Birkland[2] adapted John Kingdon's notion of focusing events to the study of the agenda-dynamics evident after major accidents and natural disasters (Birkland 1997, 1998, 2006; Kingdon 2003[1984]). Such events have long been postulated as drivers of policy change (Cobb and Elder 1983; Sabatier and Weible 2007; Kingdon 2003), although the policy-process literature is limited in its ability to explain why and under what conditions policy changes after a focusing event. Indeed, the literature on focusing events and their relationships to agenda and policy change remains underdeveloped and several shortcomings have been identified in Kingdon and Birkland's conceptualising of focusing events. If these shortcomings were overcome, our understanding of focusing events in the agenda-setting process would be improved. In this chapter, we re-examine Kingdon's multiple-streams framework (MSF) to better understand how focusing events influence policy-making, while acknowledging that this framework is influenced by, and influences, other theories of agenda-setting. These theories are Paul Sabatier's advocacy-coalition framework (Sabatier and Weible, 2007) and Baumgartner and Jones' (1993) punctuated-equilibrium (PE) approach. We consider the strengths and weaknesses of Kingdon and Birkland's approaches to focusing events and then turn to a discussion of how it will be difficult to show, in a systematic way, that focusing events are crucial to policy change. We conclude with comments on methodological considerations for future research that would show the circumstances under which event-motivated agenda-change might yield actual policy change.

Kingdon's streams metaphor

Kingdon's streams metaphor is most often invoked in studies of agenda-setting, which is interesting for political scientists because 'the definition of the alternatives

---

1. This first draft of this paper was originally presented at the ECPR forty-first Joint Sessions of Workshops, workshop on Decision-Making under Ambiguity and Time Constraints: Assessing the Multiple Streams Framework, at the Johannes Gutenberg Universität, Mainz, Germany, 11–16 March 2013. This is a substantially revised version of that paper.

2. Because this chapter is co-written, we have decided, despite the slight awkwardness, to refer to Birkland in the third person.

is the supreme instrument of power' (Schattschneider 1975: 66): alternatives can mean issues, events, problems and solutions. Groups, or agglomerations of such groups, called *advocacy coalitions* (Sabatier and Weible 2007) engage in rhetorical debates, in different venues, to elevate these issues on to the agenda, while attempting to deny agenda-access to other actors (Cobb and Ross 1997). Group competition is fierce because agenda-space is limited by individual and organisational constraints on information-processing, so that no system can accommodate all issues and ideas (Walker 1977; Baumgartner and Jones 1993; Cobb and Elder 1983).

The competition in agenda-setting is both about getting an issue on to the agenda *and* about propagating the preferred story about how a bad condition came to be and how the problem might be prevented or mitigated in the future (Stone 2002). This story-telling is important because stories of problem-definition compete with other problem-definitions and strongly signal pre-existing preferences for particular policies (Hilgartner and Bosk 1988; Birkland and Lawrence 2009). The agenda-setting process is, therefore, a system of shifting issues, problems and ideas and for implicitly assigning priorities to these issues. Kingdon argues that agenda-setting is driven by three broad phenomena: *changes in indicators* of underlying problems, which lead to debates over whether and to what extent a problem exists and is worthy of action; *focusing events*, sudden shocks to policy systems that lead to attention, agenda-change and potential policy change; and *feedback* within and across policy domains, which can also yield greater attention to problems and their potential solutions.

Thus, Kingdon agrees with Cobb and Elder (1983) that an event itself is not enough to bring an issue to the public's attention. He states that only rarely does this occur and only with extremely prominent events. More often, focusing events need to be accompanied by something else, such as the alignment of the political stream, the policy stream and promotion by policy-entrepreneurs. Focusing events then serve as a way to highlight existing problems, reinforce pre-existing perceptions of a problem, serve as an early warning and also affect problem-definition (Kingdon 2003[1984]: 98–9).

John Kingdon used the term 'focusing event' within a general discussion entitled 'Focusing events, crises, and symbols' (Kingdon 2003[1984]: 94–100). Kingdon calls focusing events a 'little push', 'like a crisis or disaster that comes along to call attention to the problem, a powerful symbol that catches on, or the personal experience of a policy maker'. One such type of event will 'simply bowl over everything standing in the way of prominence on the agenda' (Kingdon 2003[1984]: 96). Birkland's work on focusing events is based on this 'bowling over' effect and he assumes that the event so dominates the agenda that talk of policy change – that is, learning the 'lessons' of the recent event – is the normatively desirable result because the event itself often reveals policy failures from which we normatively expect to learn (Birkland 2006).

Birkland refined Kingdon's definition of a focusing event, defining a *potential focusing event* as an event that is sudden, relatively rare, can be reasonably defined as harmful or revealing the possibility of potentially greater future harms, inflicts harms or suggests potential harms that are or could be concentrated on a definable geographical area or community of interest, and that is known to policy-makers and the public virtually simultaneously (Birkland 1997: 22).

The term *potential* sharpens our definition of *focusing event*. We begin with the term 'event', which is defined by the Merriam-Webster online dictionary as 'something (especially something important or notable) that happens'. But it is difficult to know in advance how 'important' an event will be. Will the event remain an aspect of policy debate for some time? Will the event continue to have a discernible influence on the agenda when other events and issues overtake the more recent event? Will that event have any discernible influence on policy changes? Will it have a greater influence on the agenda, and on policy, than did similar events in the past? The basic idea is that the event is *likely* to elevate attention to a problem among elites and mass publics, which, in turn, leads to pressure for policy change. But it is not a certainty that any one particular event will gain a great deal of attention. We can usually only understand the effects of an event retrospectively. But we can isolate and monitor *potential* events as they happen to see if they develop into important milestones in agenda-setting and policy change.

The traditional assumptions about focusing events hold that a focusing event opens these windows because events provide an urgent, symbol-rich example of claimed policy failure (May 1992; Birkland 2006). Of course, other interests may argue that an event is atypical, that existing systems can and will bring the acute problems under control and that therefore sweeping change is not necessary. Regardless of the ultimate outcome, pressure for policy change increases in most focusing events and debate over ideas increases, both among policy-makers and in the attentive public, to the extent that an attentive public exists. Focusing events may cause greater attention to be paid to problems and solutions because they increase the likelihood that more organised interests, including some that are influential and powerful, could advocate policy change (Schattschneider 1975; Baumgartner and Jones 1993).

Baumgartner and Jones note that increased attention to a policy problem is usually *negative* attention, which often motivates further political debate, moving issues closer to the decision-agenda in which change is more likely. However, political elites do not always resist change. Focusing events, particularly in policy domains characterised as 'policies without publics', (May 1990) yield 'internal mobilization' efforts to promote the change that policy elites or experts prefer (Cobb and Elder 1983). Indeed, Best (2010) cites Molotch and Lester's (1975) claim that 'actor-promoted events' (APEs, in her term) are more likely to generate attention when the actors are elites with which news media already have regular contact, and whose actions are considered important by virtue of the actors' positions in society. This is consistent with Grossman's (2014) claim that policy-making is much more often driven by established political actors than by public mobilisation, a point that we return to below.

The messages these actors seek to convey are generally pro-*status quo*, or at least pro-elite, to the extent that elites sometimes desire policy change. This is not to say that such elite-driven mobilisation and change is unimportant. Many policy-domains prone to sudden events like natural disasters, are domains that deal with technical matters invoking science and engineering; these are fields of expertise with which the public and most elected officials are unfamiliar. The professions, whose people work both in and out of government, may mobilise both because of their desire to participate in policy-making as policy-entrepreneurs and because they believe their ideas are technically, professionally and ethically correct.

Assessing focusing-event theory

Kingdon's work provides a rich font of ideas from which we can draw to understand focusing events. However, Kingdon's definition of focusing events is imprecise and difficult to operationalise in a way that allows for systematic study of the phenomenon. Birkland attempts to define the concept and operationalise the definition by relating event 'impact' attributes – scope and scale, mostly – to agenda-change. But in doing so he washes out much of the richness of the history of policy change, even in those policy-domains subject to attention-grabbing events, because modelling relationships along the lines Birkland proposes fails to explain the *reasons* why some events didn't gain attention or yield policy change, even though the features of the event would have predicted a much greater effect.

More fundamentally than what Birkland offers, we must consider that, when studying focusing events, we need to ask, 'What kind of events gain more attention than other kinds of events?' even in the same problem domain. Birkland did so in his comparison of the agenda-setting dynamics of hurricanes and earthquakes (1998) but, again, in a more strictly quantitative and structured way. But why do some earthquakes gain more attention than others? Why do we pay more attention to the technical attributes of earthquakes compared with hurricanes? Why do crises nearer to home gain more attention than even larger crises in foreign countries? What attributes of an event make it more or less focal? We can measure how sudden an event is; we can measure its rarity; and we can measure its associated damage to life and property. But we can only model correlates of agenda-attention.

By doing so, we cannot really predict policy change. Consider school-violence incidents in the United States, which attract considerable attention and generate calls for change. Most prominent among these events recently was the murder of 20 students and six teachers at Sandy Hook Elementary School in Connecticut in 2012. As Grossman notes, this event gained a great deal of attention, but 'bans on "assault" weapons and high-capacity magazines made little progress in Congress. Even a bipartisan bill to expand background checks to gun purchases on the Internet and at gun shows failed to clear the Senate' (Grossman 2014: 85). Similar dynamics have been seen in earlier school-shooting cases; Lawrence and Birkland (2004) found that the 'gun problem' frame in school-violence cases is common in news coverage and in the general pronouncements of elected officials. However, as the problem moves 'up' the agenda to the point of policy decisions, more contentious policy ideas, such as gun-control, are de-emphasised in favour of familiar and routine styles of policy that serve multiple goals. In this case, Congress favoured spending more money on school-violence 'programmes,' both because such programmes were uncontroversial and because they fulfilled Congress's strong imperative to distribute funds to local governments.

Birkland's approach to the study of focusing events in this chapter has some significant advantages. The theory is limited to policy domains that are 'prone to focusing events' so that we can select a class of events and use historic and longitudinal data over several decades to understand their agenda-setting influence in a particular policy domain. This theory is designed to be able to compare the relative influence of focal attributes across an entire class of physical event-types, such as natural disasters, or of a particular kind of accident, such as oil spills or aircraft crashes. This avoids anecdotal descriptions of 'critical events' which are often identified after the fact, rather than being rigorously analysed as part of an entire class of events. And the determinants of agenda-change are systematically and empirically analysed, using readily available data about the event and the area in which the event took place.

Challenges to Birkland's approach

Birkland's approach – and research that adopts his claims uncritically – has some significant disadvantages, however. Like most theories of the policy process, Birkland's theory of focusing events is not a predictive theory; it is largely retrospective, because it relies upon the collection of a great deal of data after an event to assess whether or not the event had an influence on agenda-setting. If it did, Birkland assumes that it *may* therefore have had an effect on policy change, although the policy literature is clear that agenda-setting and even alternative-selection do not yield immediate change, particularly when the interests that constitute a 'policy monopoly', in Baumgartner and Jones's term, actively seek to prevent change. Kingdon's framework does not explain the connection between focusing events, agenda-setting, and policy change. Indeed, the literature that cites Birkland reduces his argument to 'big events get lots of attention'. This does not really go very far beyond Birkland's own findings.

Similar to most of the agenda-setting literature, Birkland's work does not link well *empirically* to policy change. He attempts to bridge the two questions using the 'policy-learning' framework but has yet to assess this process beyond case studies (2006). These cases are not as well developed as his original theory, because one could argue that he selects on the dependent variable, picking instances where learning actually did happen. Birkland's book and subsequent work have attempted to fill in the gaps in the relatively simple statistical modelling with narrative stories about how, for example, the earthquake and hurricane policy-domains – both of which are part of broader 'natural hazard' or 'public safety' or even 'homeland security' domains – are so different in terms of the nature of the ideas discussed in these domains and the availability of policy-entrepreneurs to argue for change. But Birkland focuses on event-attributes without accounting for the politics in which the event is embedded. His dependent variable is a measure of agenda-change in the news media and in Congress. But it doesn't measure the effect of other attention-grabbing features of the event among the general public in such a way that we can understand whether or not Congress and the public seized upon the issues simultaneously; whether the public pressured Congress to act; or whether Congress, in an effort of 'internal mobilisation', led the public to believe the problem needed immediate attention.

In reviewing both Kingdon's and Birkland's approach to focusing-event theory, it is clear that Birkland's logic focuses on the attributes of the event itself and seeks to understand its effect on the agenda by analysing aspects like the size and scale of the event. Kingdon, on the other hand, is more concerned with the *symbolic meaning* of the event as an avenue for policy-entrepreneurs to engage in advocacy and promote greater attention and, ultimately, policy change. In both ways of looking at focusing events, we see that the fact of an event itself is not as important as the political environment in which the event occurs and the ways in which policy-actors in that environment use the event to promote different interpretations of the event, which, in turn, will shape the development of arguments about the event.

Why does this matter? As a matter of democratic theory, citizens and scholars often believe that politics should be a problem-solving endeavour that identifies problems and engages in an active search for solutions. In this normative sense, governments and officials 'should' find the 'real problems' that can be addressed through well understood interventions. This, however, is not how the MSF views politics, nor is it, in reality, the way most modern theories of the policy process regard politics. Policy changes proposed after major events may simply reanimate old debates about pre-existing solutions applied to new problems. Or they may raise policy ideas that, from a technocratic perspective, would be very effective, but that would be unworkable in a democracy that values other things more, like liberty or equity. And, of course, many 'solutions,' like the 'problems' themselves, are often defined and circumscribed by the preferences of members of interest-groups, who will advocate a preferred framing of the problem and solution to achieve their policy goals. Any theory of event politics, therefore, must account for the tension between technocratic, democratic and group-driven definitions of problems and solutions.

An additional shortcoming of Birkland's approach is that his model greatly narrows the scope of the very idea of focusing events as proposed by Kingdon. In *After Disaster*, Birkland concentrates on focusing events that 'bowl everything over' (Birkland 1997). But Kingdon notes that a focusing event can be not just 'a crisis or disaster that comes along to call attention to the problem' but can also be 'a powerful symbol that catches on, or the personal experience of a policymaker' (Kingdon 2003[1984]: 95). Kingdon's definition of a focusing event is obviously very broad, including personal events and the sudden and rapid propagation of powerful symbols. Birkland models the 'bowling over' style of focusing events – and this use of the term 'focusing event' has become a term of art, often divorced from its theoretical origins – to describe this very sort of event. Birkland and others adopt this definition because it is simpler to conceptualise and model, while the other types of focusing events are really features of the story of how issues gain attention and can yield policy change.

In Birkland's original study, he argued that future research on focusing events should look at other types of events beyond those he studied. Figure 6.1 depicts a 'taxonomy' of drivers of agenda-change, in terms both of Birkland's definition and of Kingdon's conceptualisation of the streams metaphor. The first category of events are 'normal' focusing events – the kind that bowl things over. We don't mean that events are themselves 'acceptable' or 'typical'. Rather, we use the term 'normal' in the sense used by Charles Perrow (1999), who argues that, in complex systems, unanticipated problems will eventually occur. By this definition, earthquakes, hurricanes, oil spills and nuclear plant accidents – as well as wars, economic crises and environmental disasters of other kinds – can be expected to happen eventually, even if they cannot be predicted.

Figure 6.1: Conceptual map of focusing-event theory

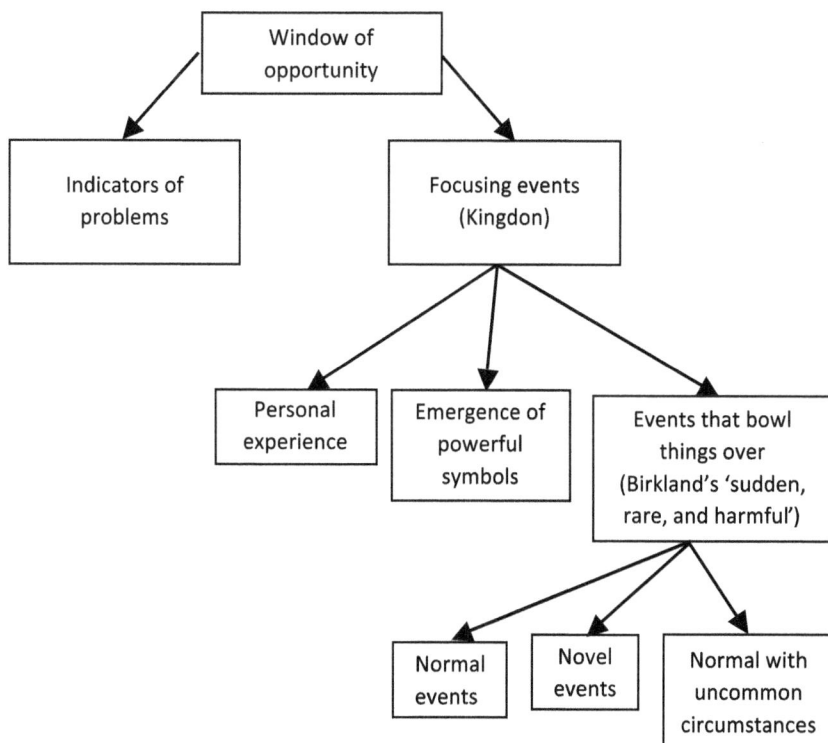

The second type is 'new' focusing events. Fishman (1999) makes a similar distinction between Type One (common) and Type Two (novel) focusing events. This distinction is crucial in how an event will have varying contextual factors that will influence possible policy solutions, as well as on framing and symbol-propagation. A new focusing event will seem utterly novel to all participants in policy discussion. For example, the Tylenol product-tampering cases of the early 1980s were 'new' because, while minor examples of product-tampering had occurred before the Tylenol case, there had been no nationwide scare over the safety of such a ubiquitous consumer product. Indeed, engineer Henry Petroski notes that 'it was a time when consumers were unsuspecting of such unconscionable behavior, and the poisonings shocked the world' (Petroski 2005: 117). The problem gained widespread attention and actual policy change, such as a mandate for new packaging practices, was the result.

The Oklahoma City bombing was novel because, while there had been terrorist incidents on United States soil before this bombing – most notably, the bombing of the World Trade Center in New York City in 1993 – no such terrorist attack had, in living memory, killed so many people or done so much property damage in one place in the United States.[3] The bombing was focal on several levels: it increased the attention given to the issue of terrorism in the United States and it increased, if for a short time, media and government scrutiny of the anti-government 'militias' that had become more active in the early 1990s. *Prima facie* evidence of the focal importance of this event was the introduction of anti-terrorism legislation after the bombing and the imposition of greater security measures at government office buildings nationwide. And the event changed the way the news media covered terrorism, thereby elevating the issue on the national agenda, whereupon the 'terrorism' issue became, at this time of writing, a near-permanent feature of early twenty-first century American politics.

The third type of event is a 'common event[s] under uncommon circumstances'. Such events are generally not-unusual ones, such as accidents, that gain greater-than-normal attention due to some unique and unusual feature that makes them newsworthy and, not coincidentally, worthy of greater government attention and potential policy change. One such event cited by Birkland is that of the death of Jessica Dubroff, a seven-year-old 'pilot' who sought, in 1996, to set a record for youngest pilot to fly across the United States in a small plane. Her death in a crash – attributed to very poor decision-making on the part of her flight instructor, who decided to take off in a thunderstorm – attracted great attention to the race, at that time, among young trainee pilots to set the 'youngest pilot' 'record', even though such records were accepted by no aviation-sanctioning body nor by the Guinness Book of Records and the attempt to set it may well have violated US national aviation regulations. Because of

---

3. Indeed, this event is called 'unprecedented' by the Oklahoma City National Memorial and Museum and the museum quotes a journalist as saying: 'There was no way to grasp the scale of it because we hadn't seen anything like it before.' See: http://newsok.com/article/3836988 (accessed 28 September 2016).

the youth of this pilot and the tragic circumstances of her death, Congress enacted the Child Pilot Safety Act, which, as the FAA administrator put it, was intended to prevent children not from being in cockpits but from being part of 'media-driven publicity stunts', in which young people would be, even briefly, manipulating the controls of an aircraft.[4] This was, from the private-pilots-lobby's perspective, a victory, since the first proposal would have prevented *anyone* under sixteen from manipulating the controls at all, which would have restricted the ability of pilots and their groups from introducing aviation to children. But this case shows how an event, accompanied by a very powerful symbol, can yield ideas for policy change that would not have arisen had the event been a more routine one, such as the typical small-aircraft accident.

Broader applications of the focusing-event idea

Since Birkland's attempts to refine Kingdon's (2003[1984]) definition of focusing events, other scholars have applied or mentioned focusing-event theory as an important aspect of the policy process, in three ways: research that cites Kingdon or Birkland uncritically, accepting the definitions without any critical analysis, often simply to acknowledge that events matter; work that cites Kingdon or Birkland and use the focusing-event theory to build, reinforce, or expand the definitions of focusing events and their causal mechanisms; and work that seems to us to misapply the focusing event concept to other phenomena that better explain the processes being described.

A great deal of work relies on Kingdon's or Birkland's discussion of focusing events by simply acknowledging the importance of focusing events, without careful dissection of agenda-setting theory. Works that cite Kingdon alone are works that contain overviews of major agenda-setting theory, with a focus on the streams model, but that fall short of carefully differentiating focusing events from other drivers of agenda-change. Similarly, works that cite Birkland but not Kingdon (for example, Ackleson 2005; Chenoweth and Clarke 2010; Davis 2006; Einsiedel 2000; Melis and Pulwarty 2001; Verhulst and Walgrave 2009) often simply recapitulate Birkland's definition of a focusing event without testing the definition or challenging or improving on the underlying theory.

The second body of literature expands on theory by applying a case and then building an argument for whether the case or event can be considered as a focusing event, usually by using quantitative and qualitative data to reinforce or analyse how the case adheres to the focusing event concept. These studies may also reconsider the definition of focusing events in light of the new data and interpretation. For example, Busenberg (2001) makes an interesting case for the

---

4.   The transcript of the congressional hearing on this matter is available at: http://commdocs.house. gov/committees/Trans/hpw104-58.000/hpw104-58_0.HTM (accessed 18 September 2016). A pilots' group noted that the event and subsequent legislation 'redefined general aviation'; see: http://www.aopa.org/News-and-Video/All-News/2006/November/4/An-accident-that-redefined-GA (accessed 9 October 2014).

second-order effects of policy changes that can be engendered by focusing events. He showed how the enactment of the Oil Pollution Act (OPA) of 1990, soon after the Exxon Valdez oil spill, created an atmosphere in which coalitions and oil companies were more willing to collaborate to prevent and mitigate future spills, and that the OPA induced companies to be more open to innovative strategies than they had been before the spill and the OPA.

A particularly promising study is Best's (2010) analysis of how local newspapers in Denver treated news events related to homelessness. Best coded story-frames to consider, among other things, whether stories were episodic or thematic and whether the events being covered were 'actor-promoted events'(APEs) or 'non-actor-promoted events' (NAPEs). Best found that NAPEs were highly likely to trigger thematic stories about the problem of homelessness, which appears to support the idea, implicit in Birkland's work and explicit in work by Lawrence (2000) and Molotch and Lester (1975), that NAPEs will trigger greater thematic coverage. Contrary to her expectations, APEs were found to be more likely to challenge the *status quo*, which Best claims is contrary to Molotch and Lester's theory that APEs promote the *status quo*. But focusing-event theory and agenda-setting theory could explain the pro-change orientation of elites as a form of internal mobilisation among a set of the elite who perceive homelessness to be a problem deserving of attention and policy change. Best also notes that the articles that contained content that promoted change and homelessness-amelioration were most often written or promoted by organisations that were dedicated to social change (2010: 87).

The third category of literature is characterised by a form of over-reaching, in which other phenomena are characterised as focusing events. For example, Collins and Kapuçu (2008) discuss the importance of warning systems for tornadoes, using 'tornadoes as focusing event'. But their use of the term to mean a class of phenomena is synonymous with a presumably attention-grabbing event (the tornado itself). Indeed, many uses of the term do not delve beyond this meaning.

Another common use of the concept comes when the surprising result of an election is cited as a focusing event, as when Béland (2005) and Blankenau (2001) suggest that the 1991 election of Harris Wofford to the US Senate was a focusing event that propelled health-care reform on to the agenda. In Kingdon's streams metaphor, these surprising results might be understood as a change in the political stream that could be harnessed by reformers to attempt to drive forward policy change. After all, these reformers could sense that the political atmosphere had opened a window of opportunity for change. An election is not a focusing event because it is expected, planned and part of normal governmental routine. But the *rationale* for Wofford's election was indeed a focusing event in the sense of Kingdon's definition: a symbol that gains attention. Wofford's election symbolised the power of health-care reform as an issue, with profound effects on the conduct and outcome of the 1992 presidential and congressional elections.

Among the works we reviewed for this paper, there seems to be a sense – not explicitly stated, however – that Birkland's definition of *focusing event* may be so restrictive that there would be few events to study, thereby defining too-small a set of phenomena as focusing events. The variability of the implicit or explicit definitions of the term focusing event suggests that it may be useful to attempt to create some categories or typologies of events, much as Birkland (1997, chapter 6) did. Neither Birkland nor other scholars have followed up on these tentative categories with more careful research but Fishman's (1999) ideas of Type One and Type Two events are promising. To the extent that future research is undertaken on focusing events, our goal should be to improve the explanatory and predictive power of any theory of these events. Such a theory should lend itself to replication and testing across multiple policy-domains over many years. A good foundation has been laid in the social sciences and, with continued sudden, dramatic and unsettling events gaining attention, there is no paucity of cases or of policy-domains subject to these events, all of which provide fruitful material for research.

Refining our understanding of focusing events and agenda-change

Kingdon's notion of focusing events is, despite some of the challenges it poses for empirical analysis, a remarkably rich body of ideas that should drive a programme of research, employing many methods, to help us better understand the policy process. As we noted earlier, Birkland's idea of focusing events tends to consider the characteristics of the events themselves and pay little attention to change in the political and social environment. Any model of event-driven agenda-setting should take into account three aspects of policy-making. First is the relatively stable parameters of a policy domain. Second, any model should take into account external or system events, in Sabatier and Wimble's terms. These events include changes revealed by indicators, but also by sudden events.

The third dimension is the features of the event itself. Birkland's earlier work largely measured these features in terms of the dollar value of damage done by the event; the number of people killed; the number of people in the affected area; and the increase in media attention to the event. Birkland found that, even with these estimators of the magnitude of agenda-change, there were significant differences between policy-domains, even within a similar policy-regime (earthquakes and hurricanes in the natural-hazards policy-regime, for example). Birkland explained why these differences exist but did not undertake a careful analysis, based on textual-analysis tools, of the discourse that surrounds focusing-event politics.

We can also, through qualitative analysis, examine various documents in order to understand whether and to what extent the event caught elites and the public by surprise. Some events may be a shock to the public because they had not been aware of any prior debate over the underlying problem, the likelihood of its occurrence and the precursors of the event. In any case, such events are often followed by 'after action' or 'lessons learned' reports that may reveal learning from experience or that may represent 'superstitious learning' in the form of 'fantasy documents' that reflect the most fervent hopes of their authors but which may bear little relation to reality (Birkland 2006; Clarke 1999). Such efforts may also reveal to the public that the problem was well known to policy-makers but that their efforts to prevent the event were inadequate. Such inadequacy may be an act of commission – an affirmative choice that the likelihood of a bad event was *believed* to be small, only later to be proven wrong – or an act of omission, such as inattention to the problem at all, due to the usual shortage of available attention in any decision-making or agenda-setting opportunity.

These ideas suggest that, when one is studying focusing events, there are actually two levels of analysis we must consider: the nature of discourse in the policy-domain itself and the attributes of individual events. Much of the research cited here has been quite adept at understanding the latter, the attributes of events. But the research has yet to take a careful look at the former: what do people *say* about events, where do they say it and to what political and policy effect? How do people and the groups they represent strategically use information made available by the event – or made more *salient* by the event – to shape the decision-agenda such that their desired outcomes are achieved? This analysis of discourse is vital to understanding the motivations of policy-actors; a promising way to study these interactions is through the 'narrative policy analysis' framework, or NPF (McBeth, Jones and Shanahan 2014). Such an approach lends itself well to understanding the dynamics of focusing events in the multiple-streams framework; story-telling is a way to *frame* debate, and the information central to that debate, so as to achieve policy goals. As Zahariadis (2007) notes, policy debates are not generally characterised by a need for more information; rather, they are characterised by the exploitation of the ambiguity of a particular phenomenon by policy-actors, who amass information and rhetoric in such a way as to promote some policy options and constrain others. And, as Birkland's work has consistently noted, a major part of the politics of focusing events is the story-telling surrounding how the event yielded evidence of policy failure, following Stone's (1989) ideas of 'causal stories'.

The NPF systemises our study of policy narratives by considering four elements of any narrative: setting, characters, plot and moral. With this in mind, we propose that policy scholars interested in better understanding the dynamics of focusing events undertake the analysis of documentary evidence of policy-discourse in policy-domains prone to focusing events. This textual analysis would derive from a database of a wide range of documents. Arraying these documents along a continuum from 'popular' to 'technical' documents, we should come to understand news coverage of a policy-domain over several decades. News coverage could be divided into the popular and elite press, although the line between the two is not clear. In the United States, there are also sound datasets of television news clips, such as at Vanderbilt University, that would be useful for illuminating popular understandings of events as depicted in TV news. The elite press would involve professional and technical journals in fields such as engineering or emergency management, in the natural-hazards case.

Figure 6.2 depicts the sources of documentary evidence that would be most useful in studies of focusing events informed by the NPF. In the United States,

Figure 6.2: Documentary sources for narrative policy analysis: key sources and subjects of policy-discourse in domains prone to focusing events

Sources of discourse:

- *News media*:
  - Popular press
  - Elite press
  - Technical press
  - Social media
- *Legislative branch*:
  - Bills introduced and enacted
  - Congressional testimony
  - Congressional Record
- *Executive branch*:
  - Presidential documents
  - Executive orders
  - Notices of proposed rules
  - Adoption of final rules
- *Judicial branch*:
  - Court decisions about policies

Subjects of discourse:

- Extent to which events are mentioned, the main topic, or ignored
- Claims as to causes of the problems revealed by the event
- Claims as to the solutions to the problems revealed by the event
- Claims as to the motivations of other actors in the policy domain

a bridge between popular and elite discourse might be found in statements in the *Congressional Record*, the daily, albeit somewhat artificial, record of Congress's debates. The testimony of witnesses before Congress is a particularly important body of discourse to track. As the agenda narrows to the decision-agenda, we find manifestations of the results of this discourse in introduced and enacted legislation and proposed and adopted regulations. Also in the executive branch, documents like the Weekly Compilation of Presidential Documents[5] offer insights on the key issues of the day.

Any document should be coded with information about who is talking (both personally and in their institutional role); the subject of their remarks; and whether and to what extent the speaker is discussing a particular event, a class of events, or no event at all. Such an analysis should carefully consider how the speakers or writers frame the causes and consequences of events. Content-analysis would

---

5.   Available at: http://www.gpo.gov/fdsys/browse/collection.action?collectionCode=CPD.

be the preferred approach to this analysis, although the primary challenge is in finding full-text, machine-readable text of these documents, particularly for older documents that were not 'born digital' and that have yet to be converted to a machine-readable format.

Bits and pieces of this approach have been undertaken (Lawrence and Birkland 2004; Birkland and Lawrence 2009; Bennett and Lawrence 1995; Birkland 1998; Best 2010). But none of these methods has been systematically applied, to our knowledge, to a body of discourse in a policy-domain. Such an undertaking would certainly be challenging but one model of a similar event that might be examined is the Policy Agendas Project, originated by Frank Baumgartner and Bryan Jones and now hosted at the University of Texas.[6] This project is a compendium of data about congressional hearings, bills introduced, news-media coverage and presidential documents, on every policy matter in the United States since 1947. It is a remarkable asset; and similar projects have been undertaken in Europe.[7] These datasets are not sufficiently detailed for our research programme but they would provide an excellent starting point for finding the data we need. Data collected to study focusing-event politics should be coded in such a way as to cross-reference new data with these existing datasets, thereby improving data-sharing and continual testing of hypotheses and conclusions.

---

6. Available at: http://www.policyagendas.org (accessed 9 October 2014).

7. Available at: http://www.comparativeagendas.org (accessed 9 October 2014).

References

Ackleson, J. (2005) 'Border security technologies: local and regional implications', *Review of Policy Research* 22(2): 137–55.

Baumgartner, F. R. and Jones, B. D. (1993) *Agendas and Instability in American Politics*, Chicago: University of Chicago Press.

Béland, D. (2005) 'Ideas and social policy: an institutionalist perspective', *Social Policy & Administration*, 39(1): 1–18.

Bennett, W. L. and Lawrence, R. G. (1995) 'News icons and the mainstreaming of social change', *Journal of Communication* 45(3): 20–39.

Best, R. (2010) 'Situation or social problem: the influence of events on media coverage of homelessness', *Social Problems* 57(1): 74–91.

Birkland, T. A. (1997) *After Disaster: Agenda-setting, public policy and focusing events*, Washington, DC: Georgetown University Press.

—   (1998) 'Focusing events, mobilization, and agenda-setting', *Journal of Public Policy* 18(1): 53–74.

—   (2006) *Lessons of Disaster*, Washington, DC: Georgetown University Press.

Birkland, T. A. and Lawrence, R. G. (2009) 'Media framing and policy change after Columbine', *American Behavioral Scientist* 52(10): 1405–25.

Blankenau, J. (2001) 'The fate of National Health Insurance in Canada and the United States: a multiple streams explanation', *Policy Studies Journal* 29(1): 38–55.

Busenberg, G. J. (2001) 'Learning in organizations and public policy', *Journal of Public Policy* 21(2): 173–89.

Chenoweth, E. and Clarke, S. E. (2010) 'All terrorism is local: resources, nested institutions, and governance for urban homeland security in the American federal system', *Political Research Quarterly* 63(3): 495–507.

Clarke, L. (1999) *Mission Improbable: Using fantasy documents to tame disaster*, Chicago: University of Chicago Press.

Cobb, R. W. and Elder, C. D. (1983) *Participation in American Politics: The dynamics of agenda-building*, Baltimore, MD: Johns Hopkins University Press.

Cobb, R. W. and Ross, M. H. (1997) *Cultural Strategies of Agenda Denial: Avoidance, attack, and redefinition*, Lawrence, KA: University Press of Kansas.

Collins, M. M. and Kapuçu, N. (2008) 'Early warning systems and disaster preparedness and response in local government', *Disaster Prevention & Management* 17(5): 587–600.

Davis, C. (2006) 'Western wildfires: a policy-change perspective', *Review of Policy Research* 23(1): 115–27.

Einsiedel, E. F. (2000) 'Cloning and its discontents – a Canadian perspective', *Nature Biotechnology* 18(9): 943–4.

Fishman, D. A. (1999) 'ValuJet Flight 592: crisis communication theory blended and extended', *Communication Quarterly* 47(4): 345–75.

Grossmann, M. (2014) *Artists of the Possible: Governing networks and American policy change since 1945*, Oxford, UK and New York: Oxford University Press.

Hilgartner, J. and Bosk, C. (1988) 'The rise and fall of social problems: a public arenas model', *American Journal of Sociology* 94(1): 53–78.

Kingdon, J. W. (2003[1984]) *Agendas, Alternatives, and Public Policies*, 2nd edn, Longman Classics in Political Science, New York: Longman.

Lawrence, R. G. (2000) *The Politics of Force: Media and the construction of police brutality*, Berkeley, CA: University of California Press.

Lawrence, R. G. and Birkland, T. A. (2004) 'Guns, Hollywood, and school safety: defining the school-shooting problem across public arenas', *Social Science Quarterly* 85(5): 1193–1207.

May, P. J. (1990) 'Reconsidering policy design: policies and publics', *Journal of Public Policy* 11(2): 187–206.

— (1992) 'Policy learning and failure', *Journal of Public Policy* 12(4): 331–54.

McBeth, M. K., Jones, M. D. and Shanahan, E. A. (2014) 'The narrative policy framework', in P. A. Sabatier and C. M. Weible (eds) *Theories of the Policy Process*, 3rd edn, Boulder, CO: Westview Press.

Melis, T. S. and Pulwarty, R. S. (2001) 'Climate extremes and adaptive management on the Colorado River: lessons from the 1997–1998 ENSO event', *Journal of Environmental Management* 63(3): 307–24.

Molotch, H. and Lester, M. (1975) 'Accidental news: the great oil spill as local occurrence and national event', *American Journal of Sociology* 81(2): 235–60.

Perrow, C. (1999) *Normal Accidents: Living with high-risk technologies, with a new afterword and a postscript on the Y2K problem*, Princeton, NJ: Princeton University Press.

Petroski, H. (2005) 'Engineering painful design', *American Scientist* 93(2): 113–17.

Sabatier, P. A. and Weible, C. M. (2007) 'The Advocacy Coalition Framework: innovations and clarifications', in Sabatier, P. A. (ed.) *Theories of the Policy Process*, 2nd edn, Boulder, CO: Westview Press, pp. 183–223.

Schattschneider, E. E. (1975) *The Semisovereign People*, Hinsdale, IL: Dryden Press.

Stone, D. A. (1989) 'Causal stories and the formation of policy agendas', *Political Science Quarterly* 104(2): 281–300.

— (2002) *Policy Paradox: The art of political decision making*, New York: Norton.

Verhulst, J. and Walgrave, S. (2009) 'The first time is the hardest? A cross-national and cross-issue comparison of first-time protest participants', *Political Behavior* 31(3): 455–84.

Walker, J. L. (1977) 'Setting the agenda in the U.S. Senate: a theory of problem selection', *British Journal of Political Science* 7(4): 423–45.

Zahariadias, N. (2007) 'The multiple streams framework: structure, limitations, prospects', in Sabatier, P. A. (ed.) *Theories of the Policy Process*, 2nd edn, Boulder, CO: Westview Press, pp. 65–91.

Chapter Seven

Framing the Problem: Knowledge-Brokers in the Multiple-Streams Framework

Åsa Knaggård

Introduction

In the multiple-streams framework (MSF), as outlined by John Kingdon (2003[1984]), the policy-entrepreneur is the actor who makes things happen. By suggesting alternative policies and connecting them to problems at certain points in time, policy-entrepreneurs have a major role in determining what issues end up on the political agenda. In coupling problem and policy-alternative, policy-entrepreneurs place problems in categories that will fit their 'pet proposals' (Kingdon 2003[1984]: 115, 204). In this sense, policy-alternatives come first and policy-entrepreneurs search for problems that, in the right category, can make their proposal seem reasonable. Indeed, Kingdon (2003[1984]: 93) states that '[d]emonstrating that there is indeed a problem to which one's solution can be attached is a very real preoccupation of participants in the policy process'. What this account lacks is an understanding of how policy-entrepreneurs come upon these problems. As Kingdon (2003[1984]: 109) states, problems come into being when we believe that something needs to be done about a condition. This belief can be triggered by an apparent difference between the values one holds and a certain state of affairs, or be raised by comparisons of similar situations (Kingdon 2003[1984]: 110–11). How a condition is categorised also affects the kind of problem that is created (*ibid.* 111–13). Thus, policy-entrepreneurs categorise conditions as specific problems to fit their pet proposals.

What I find problematic in this account is that it narrows the process of defining problems to something that is done foremost to enable coupling of policy-alternatives and problems. Focus is thereby placed on the policy stream of the MSF. I argue that if we look deeper into the problem stream we will find a lot of action that does not fit what policy-entrepreneurs do but very much affects their possibilities of coupling streams. There are actors that categorise, or frame as I prefer to call it, conditions as political problems without the intention of coupling them to specific policy-alternatives. I will refer to these actors as knowledge-brokers. Framing problems is thus not only done to increase the likelihood of successful coupling but also to define problems. This does not mean that solutions are always developed in response to problems. Rather, it means that problems and policy-alternatives are developed partly independently of one another and that the coupling that policy-entrepreneurs do in important ways is structured by the availability of problem-frames. This implies that what is happening in the problem stream ought to be as important for our understanding of which issues receive political priority as what goes on in the policy stream.

If we want to clearly separate the problem and policy streams analytically, we have to develop a more elaborate account of what is happening in the problem stream. To assign agency to policy-entrepreneurs in both the problem and policy streams risks blurring the lines between streams and what goes on within them. In this chapter, I expand on Kingdon's account of the problem stream and try to separate it more clearly from the policy stream. I do this by using insights and concepts from agenda-setting and IR theory. I will use the concepts of framing and knowledge-broker to develop a more elaborate account of agency in the problem stream.

The concepts of framing and knowledge-broker will be elaborated below. Further, it will be argued that access to policy-makers, persistence and credibility are important determinants for successful framing. Finally, I will also argue that the reason why actors tend not to move between streams is due to institutional constraints. Depending on the problem studied and what actors are active, the degree of institutional constraint will vary. The argument is based on a case study of the Swedish and international climate change policy process from 1975 to 2007 (Knaggård 2009, 2014).[1] Examples from the case study, including both the Swedish and international contexts, will be used to illustrate my argument.

The process of problem-framing

One problem with Kingdon's account of the problem stream is the relative lack of agency. In some sense, problems seem to just appear out of indicators, focusing events and feedback from already enacted policies. According to Kingdon (2003[1984]: 90), indicators are numbers that are routinely measured and can signal that something needs to be done. Focusing events can be accidents or a crisis of some sort that illustrates the problem (2003[1984]: 94–5). Finally, feedback is assessments of adopted policies and running programmes (2003[1984]: 100). I argue that indicators, focusing events and feedback can be used to frame a condition as a problem but cannot induce action on their own. This is where framing can be useful in the MSF. It establishes a link between the belief that something is wrong and needs to be managed politically and the tools for measuring the problem. The concept of framing fits well with Kingdon's discussion about categorisation and has also already been applied in connection to the MSF by Zahariadis (2003).

By framing a condition as a problem, certain aspects of it are highlighted and others are toned down. The concept of framing thereby points out that there are

---

1. The study is based on a wealth of material. It includes interviews with a broad range of politicians, political appointees, civil servants and scientists; a broad range of official political documents, like committee work, government propositions, parliamentary debates and decisions; newspaper material (mostly debate articles); and reports from a broader scientific community addressed at policy-makers. The study has been presented in more depth in Swedish (Knaggård 2009).

several ways in which a condition can be understood. According to Schön and Rein (1994: 30)

> [t]here is no way of perceiving and making sense of social reality except through a frame, for the very task of making sense of complex, information-rich situations requires an operation of selectivity and organization, which is what 'framing' means.

Which problem-frame will catch on determines how the issue will be perceived, what actors will be attracted to it and what solutions will seem relevant. This is because frames are based on 'specific models of agency, causality, and responsibility' (Jasanoff and Wynne 1998: 5). Frames tell us what the problem is about, why it occurred, who is to blame and what can be done about it (for a more elaborate discussion on problem-framing see Knaggård (2016)).

Indicators, focusing events and feedback reveal conditions that, without framing, are meaningless. They can, however, all be used in framing a condition as a political problem. In the climate case, important indicators are, for example, the increase in carbon dioxide emissions and changes in the global temperature. Focusing events are storms and floods. Feedback can consist of decreasing emissions from transport and the heating of houses. However, these do not mean anything without a frame that can tell us what the problem is about. For example, climate change is framed as caused by human emissions of greenhouse gases and as a threat to societies. This frame draws on a number of different indicators as well as symbols, like the hurricane Katrina that hit the US in 2005. Climate change can be managed politically according to this frame. The possible political response is to decrease the human emissions that create the problem.

Framing is a highly political activity as it affects how issues are perceived. In Kingdon's words (2003[1984]: 110): '[t]here are great political stakes in problem definition'. It can be strategically used to gain support for an issue or for a solution (see Stone 1989: 133; Schattschneider 1960). As a frame not only entails an understanding of the problem but also, implicitly, a possible course of action, the difference between framing in the problem and policy streams is not self-evident. This is reinforced by the fact that Kingdon as well as other scholars have seen policy-entrepreneurs as the ones defining problems. For example, Zahariadis (2007: 70) argues that '[p]olicy makers and entrepreneurs use labels and symbols that have specific cognitive referents and emotional impact ... Employing these elements strategically alters the dynamics of choice by highlighting one dimension of the problem over others.' I argue that we have to make a more clear-cut distinction between the two streams. Seeing policy-entrepreneurs and policy-makers as the main problem-framers blurs the analytical distinction between streams and thereby undervalues what is going on in the problem stream. Framing in the problem stream is about portraying a condition as a political problem. This entails there being an idea about some sort of action to counter the problem, but without suggestions of actual alternatives. In the climate case, the problem-frame included the idea that emissions should be decreased but nothing more specific on how it should be done. The difference between the problem and policy streams, therefore, is that, in the latter, policy-entrepreneurs develop specific policy-alternatives and couple these to certain problem-frames; in the former, however, problem-frames only include a general understanding that something needs to be done. The analytically important distinction between knowledge-broker and policy-entrepreneur makes it possible to further develop the problem stream theoretically.

Confusing actors and roles

My argument for including the role of knowledge-broker in the problem stream is based not only on the need to separate the streams analytically but also on the unfortunate confusion between actors and roles that we can find both in Kingdon and in work that criticises him.

In his book, Kingdon explores, as I would see it, two different and not entirely consistent ways of studying the policy process. In the first part of his work, he focuses on actors and what role they play in agenda-setting. For example, he makes statements about what actors are important in the different streams of his American cases (2003[1984]: 68f). Actors in the policy stream are often not so visible, for example, career bureaucrats and academics. More visible actors, like the president, parts of Congress and the media, are more active in the problem stream. This part of the book is used to explore the dynamics involved, which are then theorised in the second part of the book. Here, Kingdon shifts focus from actors to process, with the separation of the problem, policy and political streams. He also introduces the role of the policy-entrepreneur, who plays a crucial part in placing issues on the political agenda. I argue that the preoccupation with actors in the first part of his work unnecessarily narrows the applicability of the framework. As the actor configuration will vary over different types of political systems, the focus on actors makes the framework difficult to apply to other systems without adjustment. It might also run into problems explaining the developments in certain policy areas. Robinson and Eller (2010) have shown that in local school policy-making in the US, the actors in the problem and policy streams were the same and, further, not the ones anticipated by Kingdon. On these grounds, they criticise the MSF for assuming the independence of streams.

I find this critique misguided as Kingdon never claimed that the streams were absolutely independent of each other. Rather, the separation of streams should be seen as analytical. However, Kingdon's focus on actors does invite critique of this kind. The unfortunate aspect of it is that there is no need for the preoccupation with actors, as there exists the alternative of roles in the framework. I would argue that the strength of the MSF is exactly the rather limited importance of what actors are, in terms of the position they hold and the significance of what they do. With this approach, we can go beyond simply looking at which actors are active and instead study what role they play in agenda-setting. The policy-entrepreneur is crucial in this respect. Differences in how problems are understood and positioned on the agenda in different countries can be studied as a matter of framing rather than as foremost a question of timing by policy-entrepreneurs. The problem, as I have already presented, is that a lot of work on the MSF, including Kingdon's, conflates what the policy-entrepreneur does in the policy stream with what is going on in the problem stream. The person acting as policy-entrepreneur can, of course, be active in both streams; but what he or she does in the two streams has to be analytically separated. Therefore, I introduce the role of the knowledge-broker.

Which actors will play the role of knowledge-broker and policy-entrepreneur will, of course, vary between policy areas and countries. In school politics, teachers and parents will play both roles, as Robinson and Eller have shown (2010). In climate politics, scientists are crucial in their role as knowledge-brokers (Knaggård 2009, 2014), contrary to Kingdon's argument that scientists will be important foremost in the policy stream. It is important to separate what actors in these two roles do as this enables us to make a clear analytical distinction between streams. By focusing on roles, the MSF is strengthened as a framework that can travel over policy areas and countries.

The role of knowledge-broker

The concept of knowledge-broker was presented by Karin Litfin (1994, 1995), in a study of international ozone politics. She sees knowledge-brokers as 'intermediaries between the original researchers, or the producers of knowledge, and the policy-makers who consume that knowledge' (1994: 4). What knowledge-brokers do is to frame some sort of knowledge, be it research or indicators, to make it understandable in the political world. According to Litfin (1995: 253, footnote 14) 'what is fundamentally important is not their identities, but rather their ability to translate and interpret knowledge in accordance with new or pre-existing sets of linguistic practices which entail specific constructions of the world'. They interpret knowledge and frame it to be understandable in a political context. This does not mean that these actors do not hold beliefs about the right political course of action or that their frames do not include value judgments – they do. However, for different reasons they refrain from stating these outright. Here lies the difference between knowledge-broker and policy-entrepreneur. In the case study of climate change politics, it was quite obvious that some actors tried to frame climate change as a political problem and called for action; but deliberately refrained from coupling the problem to policy-alternatives. This will, of course, be more pronounced in some policy areas.

In Litfin's account of knowledge-brokers, the knowledge that actors use to frame problems is scientific in character. However, this does not necessarily have to be the case. In order to frame conditions as problems, some form of knowledge about them needs to be present. It could be scientific knowledge, as is often the case in environmental issues. It could be bureaucratic knowledge about indicators or feedback from enacted policies. It can also be what is often called local knowledge (for example, Jasanoff and Martello 2004), which is based on personal experience. Even if scientific or expert knowledge is often regarded as more important for policy-making, visible, for example, in the call for evidence-based decision-making, research has shown that local knowledge can be just as important for understanding problems (for example, Wynne 1992). Knowledge, perceived broadly, opens up the role of the knowledge-broker to a whole range of actors. Which actors are successful as knowledge-brokers is open to empirical examination. Crucial for the perspective taken here is that the quality of knowledge is not the only, or even the most important, determinant of the successful framing of problems. I have elsewhere suggested the concept 'problem-broker' to capture a broader span of problem-framing, in which knowledge, of any kind, is not necessarily the most important part of the frame (Knaggård 2016). Here, focus will be on the concept 'knowledge-broker', with its focus on the role of knowledge in problem-framing.

What determines successful problem-framing?

The argument in this section is based on results from the case study on the Swedish and the international climate change policy process (Knaggård 2009, 2014). As climate change politics is highly dependent on scientific knowledge, scientists came forth as important knowledge-brokers and, in some cases, as policy-entrepreneurs. What the study shows is that access to policy-makers and persistence are crucial for successful problem-framing. These two qualities are comparable with the ones that determine success for policy-entrepreneurs –access and time. A third factor that can be added is the credibility of knowledge-brokers. Finally, the characteristics of the problem-frame and how it is connected to the national mood will also be discussed.

Successful problem-framing cannot be equated with placing a problem on the agenda. Rather, when people in the political system come to accept a certain frame as given, problem-framing is successful. This, of course, becomes obvious once the problem is placed on the agenda. However, a knowledge-broker does not need to sell a problem-frame at high political levels; he or she can just as well present a problem-frame to lower civil servants. They, in turn, can act as knowledge-brokers and pass the frame on and so it can take root in an organisation. Kingdon (2003[1984]: 32) discusses this as 'elevating a problem'. Problem-framing is an on-going process of framing and reframing, in which competing frames offer different understandings of the world. Policy-entrepreneurs and policy-makers can choose the one among these frames that best fits their purposes. However, as already argued, existing problem-frames not only offer opportunities to policy-entrepreneurs and policy-makers but restrict them in important ways.

Access to the political system

The case under consideration shows clearly the importance of the connection of the knowledge-broker to the political system for successful problem-framing. Throughout the studied period, 1975–2007, knowledge-brokers with access to the political system managed to popularise their problem-frames. A few policy-makers acted as knowledge-brokers, with major impact. The Swedish professor of meteorology, Bert Bolin, with strong connections to the Social-Democratic government, was also highly influential. Finally, the Intergovernmental Panel on Climate Change (IPCC), consisting of scientists but with institutionalised communication with national governments, had an enormous impact on how climate change was perceived as a political problem.

That access to policy-makers is crucial should be expected. Kingdon (2003[1984]: 56) sees this as a critical aspect for the success of policy-entrepreneurs as well as for scientists. He argues that scientists who pursue an 'inner–outer career' – a career both in academia and in the political system – will have the advantage of connections in both worlds. This is also a strong argument in Peter Haas' (1989: 388–9) work on epistemic communities, which are international groups of experts that share both scientific and political opinions. The success of epistemic communities in spreading knowledge and framing conditions as political problems, he argues, depends on their contacts with national governments. Several of the scientists that he studied later became civil servants in different countries and thus could advocate their problem-frame from within.

Arenas in which knowledge-brokers and policy-makers can meet seem crucial. In the Swedish context, a number of committees, of which some were expert-based and others parliamentary, functioned as institutionalised arenas for this exchange. The committee work evidently spread knowledge of the issue and established a certain problem-frame in wider circles. At an early stage, it was only scientists who acted as knowledge-brokers, foremost Bert Bolin. The committees came to function as a place where these scientists could communicate with other experts, civil servants and even politicians. The dialogue between knowledge-brokers and policy-makers seems to have been crucial for the spread of a certain problem-frame and for the increasing importance of climate change as a political problem.

The IPCC also functions as such an arena. The major work of the IPCC is scientific – a number of scientists, divided into several working groups, assess current scientific knowledge on climate change. However, for all the major IPCC reports so-called *Summaries for Policymakers* are created. These are negotiated between the scientists involved in the IPCC work and national political representatives. These national representatives in many instances are civil servants, as is the case with Sweden; in some cases, though, they are diplomats involved in negotiating the UN climate regime. In this way, the construction of the IPCC has established an arena for communication between the IPCC as knowledge-broker and policy-makers around the world. This can explain the massive penetration of the problem-frame advocated by the IPCC. If we want to understand the difference in impact that the IPCC has had in different countries, one important aspect to look at is how the connections between knowledge-brokers and policy-makers are institutionalised in specific countries.

Persistence and willingness to act

A second aspect that is important for successful problem-framing is that actors actually choose to act as knowledge-brokers. It takes a lot of time to establish one's problem-frame among policy-makers. As a knowledge-broker, you have to maintain a contact network and, just as policy-entrepreneurs, be persistent in presenting your frame. Some actors, like lobbyists and interest organisations, are devoted foremost to this task. For other actors, like scientists, advocating a problem-frame is not a primary task. In the international as well as Swedish context, many scientists were unwilling to act as knowledge-brokers. They were anxious that involvement in what they perceived as political issues would have a negative impact on their scientific credibility. When scientists act as knowledge-brokers it is very common for them to be criticised by their peers for making claims that go beyond what science can prove. This is visible also in the later climate debate and criticism of the IPCC.

In the Swedish context, Bert Bolin chose actively to act as knowledge-broker. That he was first in doing so gave him a first-mover advantage. When other knowledge-brokers presented alternative frames, he had already secured the ear of important policy-makers and his problem-frame had been established as the way to understand the issue.

Credibility of knowledge-brokers

A third aspect of successful problem-framing is the credibility of the knowledge-broker. The credibility of knowledge-brokers determines to a large degree what power they hold. To be seen as a credible actor in a policy area gives that actor a legitimate voice. Credibility can be based on knowledge but also on other resources, like normative appeal.

The IPCC problem-frame was criticised after its first report in 1990. Alternative framings were advocated and took hold in some countries. In the US, the debate around different framings came earlier and has been more acrimonious than in many other countries (Grundmann 2008). Also, in Europe, there are clear differences in how much attention the alternative frames attracted. In Germany, the Netherlands and Belgium they received some attention, whereas in France and Great Britain they had no impact at all (Skolnikoff 1997: 4f.). In Sweden, knowledge-brokers came forth with alternative frames in the beginning of the 1990s. They tried to frame climate change as something natural on which human influence was minor. According to Swedish politicians and civil servants involved in climate politics at the time, these alternative frames had no impact whatsoever on the understanding of climate change as a political problem.

The influence of the knowledge-brokers with alternative frames was thus rather limited in most countries. This can, of course, be explained by a lack of access to policy-makers – many knowledge-brokers simply did not have someone to speak to. However, their credibility as knowledge-brokers is also important. Whereas Bert Bolin was an active researcher in meteorology, which was seen as the most important discipline for understanding climate change, many of the other knowledge-brokers were scientists from other disciplines, which were seen as more peripheral. Further, Bolin also had a high scientific reputation. To accept the problem-frame presented by a knowledge-broker with a high reputation – if scientist, interest-group, or policy-maker – can lend legitimacy to political decisions (see Boswell 2009). Therefore, to whom they should listen is a strategic decision for policy-makers.

Knowledge-brokers on the inside of the political system can also have different levels of credibility. Some of the civil servants working in national agencies had higher credibility as they came from academia. When climate change was first framed as a political issue, the civil servants with an inner–outer career, as described above, could more easily perceive climate change as a political problem and, of course, had more credibility in disseminating that problem-frame than their colleagues with no such double career. How commonly civil servants go back and forth between academia and the political system could influence both the impact of problem-frames and the credibility of civil servants as knowledge-brokers. This is likely to be particularly pronounced in scientifically grounded issues. This line of thinking can be translated to fit other groups acting as knowledge-brokers, although the base of credibility might differ.

Credibility could also be connected to what Robert Dahl (1991: 40) calls rational persuasion – to convince someone of the correctness of one's view with rational arguments. Also Litfin (1995: 254) argues that the influence of knowledge-brokers is partly determined by the 'plausibility of their interpretation'. This implies that policy-makers might accept a certain problem-frame for other than strategic reasons. If a policy-maker becomes convinced of the rightness of a certain problem-frame, it will be more persistent and difficult to challenge. There is evidence that this was the case in Sweden. At the time when the alternative framings were made, Swedish policy-makers were unwilling to take action on climate change. In the international context, as well as in other countries, these problem-frames were used to legitimise the *status quo*. In Sweden, though, the alternative frames were never alluded to, even if they could have been used to avoid action. This indicates that Bert Bolin, among other knowledge-brokers, had been able to convince Swedish policy-makers, irrespective of their political opinion, that climate change was caused by humans and serious enough to warrant political attention.

The problem-frame

So far I have discussed the knowledge-broker as such; I will now turn to the problem-frame and what characteristics can explain successful problem-framing. I will use Rochefort and Cobb's (1994) account of the aspects of a problem-definition that generate political attention. They list causality; severity; incidence; novelty; proximity; and crisis.

Causality is about who to blame. Here we find a connection to framing as the allocation of responsibility, as discussed above. If the problem is caused by humans, it is more likely that it will be seen as a political problem than if it has natural causes. This was visible in the struggle between knowledge-brokers supporting the IPCC frame and those opposing it. Many of those opposing it framed climate change as, foremost, a natural process on which humans had very little impact, whereas the IPCC framed climate change as, to a large extent, caused by humans. The effort to reframe the issue therefore aimed for a de-politicisation of the problem.

The more *severe* a problem is perceived to be, the more likely it will get attention. In the 1970s and early 1980s, climate scientists focused only on the effects of carbon dioxide on climate change. In 1985, the scientific debate expanded to include other gases as well, collectively called greenhouse gases (Agrawala 1999: 160; Hecht and Tierpak 1995: 380). This implied a change in the framing of the problem as well. The new frame emphasised human impact on climate change and described the impact as larger than previously thought. It also meant that climate change could not be seen as solely an energy and transport problem that had been partly addressed in the wake of the energy crisis in the 1970s. Bert Bolin (1994a: 26) later wrote in an article that '[s]uddenly, the climate change issue became much more urgent'.

Incidence is about the frequency and prevalence of the problem. If it is a common problem it will get more attention. For a long time, this was an issue for knowledge-brokers trying to frame climate change as a political problem. Climate change was understood as something that would hit people in the South foremost, and in the future. This made it less interesting for policy-makers in the North. This has changed in the last ten years with, for example, the perception that flooding is increasing in central Europe.

Rochefort and Cobb (1994) argue that the *novelty* of an issue can work to attract political attention. They also argue that the novelty might be problematic, in the sense that there are no prior examples that policy-makers could draw on. This could make it harder to couple problems and policies initially and thereby to place a problem on the political agenda. Climate change was a truly novel issue when it was placed on the political agenda in 1988. Nothing in the studied case indicates that this was an advantage in terms of agenda-setting. Rather, there were problems in framing the issue in a way that policy-makers would understand. An additional problem was that knowledge of climate change was purely theoretical at that point and scientists highlighted the possibility of surprises – effects that they simply did not know about or could not predict with any reliability. This made it hard to determine the severity of the problem. With older issues this is less of a problem, as there will be statistics to support problem-framing. In the climate case, knowledge accrued since 1995 is also based on actual observations (IPCC 1995).

This change in framing from future to current problem did not just mean a change in how novel the issue was but also in its *proximity*. One of the major difficulties for knowledge-brokers in the 1970s and 1980s was that climate change was seen as a problem for the future, connected also to how incidence was understood. Although knowledge-brokers framed the issue as requiring immediate political action, Swedish policy-makers in the 1970s reframed the problem as a problem for the future. When the IPCC reported actual climate changes, it became impossible to reframe the issue as something distant.

Finally, to frame a problem in terms of *crisis* means to increase the perceived severity and proximity of the problem. Climate change has, by some, been framed as the crisis of our age. However, this has been rejected by most knowledge-brokers as counter-productive. Despite the fact that not a single natural accident can be connected to climate change, the belief that the incidence and severity of, for example, floods and storms have increased has, at times, generated heightened public and political attention. Focusing events, as Kingdon would call them, like the hurricane Katrina that hit New Orleans in 2005 or the storm Gudrun that hit Sweden the same year, have definitely given framings of climate change a sense of crisis and, through that, of severity and proximity.

It is not clear from Rochefort and Cobb's argument which factors are more crucial and under what circumstances they will be important. One way of understanding the different factors is that, together, they build a frame. The frame needs both an idea of the problem – as captured in numbers or indicators about severity and incidence as well as in an understanding of causality – and an idea of what to do about it, including symbols of proximity, crisis and who is to blame. However, what is missing in Rochefort and Cobb's account is an appreciation of how problem-framing relates to the political context in which it is made. One could argue that the listed factors will always be important for getting political attention for a problem. However, the MSF highlights that there is more to problem-framing than this – policy-entrepreneurs need to be in the right place at the right time. Also, knowledge-brokers need to know something about what is going on in the political stream. This includes the national mood, which partly determines what issues can be considered and how, as well as possible policy-windows. In the Swedish case, this became obvious in the 1980s. In 1980, Sweden held a referendum on nuclear power and decided to phase out nuclear energy. This reduced the political interest in framings of climate change as an urgent political issue, as coal, oil and gas were seen as the natural alternatives to nuclear energy. Therefore, it became non-strategic for policy-entrepreneurs to use climate change as the problem to which they would couple their pet proposals. This situation endured until the publication of the Brundtland report in 1987[2]. In these years, it was virtually impossible to get policy-makers to consider climate change seriously. This means that successful problem-framing cannot be seen as separated from the political context; but when a problem-frame resounds with the national mood, the frame is likely to take hold.[3]

The conclusion about successful problem-framing is that we need to study both the knowledge-broker who tries to introduce a certain problem-frame to policy-makers and whether the frame is accepted by policy-makers. Based on the case study, knowledge-brokers' access to policy-makers is crucial as well as their persistence and willingness to act. Fundamental also is their credibility as knowledge-brokers. To understand successful problem-framing, we also have to

---

2.   The so called Brundtland report (WCED 1987) was the result of the work of a UN commission, the World Commission on Environment and Development, tasked with finding a possible route for the world towards sustainable development.

3.   It should be emphasised that this is not the only way to understand what 'successful' means. If a knowledge-broker aims to change the perception of a problem radically, it might be more effective to challenge the national mood than to frame the problem in congruence with it (see Ferree 2003). This strategy would, of course, be more time-consuming if it were to be successful.

study the problem-frame as such and how it is connected to the general political debate and national mood.

Moving between streams

In the MSF there is no theoretical assumption that actors act only in one stream. However, Kingdon (2003[1984]: 18–19) argues that even though it is possible for actors to move between streams, many becomes specialised in one. Nevertheless, some criticism of the MSF focuses on the movement of actors between streams and uses this to argue that the independence of streams is falsified (for example, Robinson and Eller 2010). There will surely be differences between policy-areas and types of actors: some types will be more prone to move between streams than others. This is an empirical question to a large extent. It is the non-movement between streams that needs to be explained, rather than the movement. One way of understanding why actors choose to stay in one stream is that movement can be limited by institutional constraints. Different types of actors will be subject to a varying degree of institutional constraint. The less constraint there is, the higher the likelihood actors will move between streams. This is the case with parents in Robinson and Eller's (2010) study of school politics. In climate change politics, it was obvious that some actors were bound by institutional constraints. This was especially the case for scientists. The long-standing tradition of science as a neutral actor, based on the Mertonian ideals of universalism, communism,[4] disinterestedness, and organised scepticism (Merton 1973), constitutes a strong norm for scientists in academia. In this view, the role of science in society is based on its separateness from the political system. Even if this understanding of science is incorrect, it is still normatively powerful for scientists. This implies that many scientists are unwilling to move into the policy stream, which is seen to be about values rather than facts. Bert Bolin, for example, strongly believed that scientists could act as knowledge-brokers but should avoid the role of policy-entrepreneur (see Bolin 1994b, 2007: 48–9.). In the Swedish case, some scientists were criticised for taking a stance even just in the role of knowledge-brokers. The critics argued that the scientific uncertainty about climate change was too large for safely drawing the conclusion that climate change should be framed as a political issue (see also Colglazier 1991).

There will most likely be a large difference between scientists in 'pure science' and in applied science. In the latter, focus is moved from problems to the solutions and their applications, often in close collaboration with industry and bureaucracy. Scientists working within applied science cannot restrict themselves to acting as knowledge-brokers but must advocate a particular solution. Therefore, their institutional framework pushes them into the role of policy-entrepreneur. This coincides with Kingdon's (2003[1984]: 55) finding that scientists will be more influential in the policy stream.

---

4. By communism, Merton meant that scientific results should be seen as a common property within the scientific community.

For different types of actors, apart from scientists, these institutional constraints will be felt to different degrees. Some categories of actors will probably be only slightly influenced by these constraints, whereas others will be steered by them to a significant degree. Moving between streams therefore depends on the institutional context for a certain type of actor; it will also differ between countries. This is a question for further study.

Conclusion

My argument in this chapter is that by introducing the role of knowledge-broker into the MSF, a clear analytical separation between the problem and policy streams can be established, which enables a closer study of the problem stream. Moreover, it shifts focus from Kingdon's preoccupation with types of actors to what these actors actually do. This makes the question of who does what into an empirical issue rather than a theoretical one. The focus on knowledge-brokers and the way they frame conditions as political problems builds on the MSF and makes it easier to apply in different contexts. This inclusion also enables us to study who gets to talk and who is listened to – in other words, what makes problem-framing successful. Based on a case study of climate change politics (Knaggård 2009, 2014), I argue that access to policy-makers and time to advocate a certain frame are crucial, just as it is for the success of policy-entrepreneurs. The credibility of knowledge-brokers was also important in the studied case. In agenda-setting theory, the focus has been on the characteristics of the problem-frame. This also had significance in the Swedish case but I argue that it has to be seen in context. This means analysing how the problem-frame corresponds to the national mood and how that mood determines what issues can attract attention at a particular point in time. Knowledge of this has to be possessed by knowledge-brokers. The final argument of the paper is that there is a need to focus on institutions and how they constrain actors from moving between streams. The main contribution of the inclusion of knowledge-brokers and framing in the MSF is that it emphasises agency in the problem stream.

The theoretical development of the MSF suggested here makes the framework even more complex. The benefits of the development will be most visible in studies where actors chose to stay in the problem stream. Their impact on agenda-setting is difficult to capture with Kingdon's version of the MSF, even if the essence of framing conditions as political problems is there. However, the benefits go beyond such studies. The largest benefit of strengthening the focus on roles in the MSF is that many issues that today are discussed as theoretical can be seen as empirical and therefore possible to study in different contexts. We can then study what roles different actors play in different countries and problem areas. Depending on how the communication between knowledge-brokers and policy-makers is institutionalised, we will see different results in terms of both types of actors and the success of problem-framing. This could be just as important for understanding agenda-setting as the work of policy-entrepreneurs. More studies of differences between countries and problem areas pertaining to problem-framing and its effects are needed.

References

Agrawala, S. (1999) 'Early science–policy interactions in climate change: lessons from the Advisory Group on Greenhouse Gases', *Global Environmental Change* 9(2): 157–69.

Bolin, B. (1994a) 'Science and policy making', *Ambio* 23(1): 25–9.

— (1994b) 'Next step for climate change analysis', *Nature* 368(6467): 94.

— (2007) *A History of the Science and Politics of Climate Change: The role of the Intergovernmental Panel on Climate Change*, Cambridge, UK: Cambridge University Press.

Boswell, C. (2009) *The Political Uses of Expert Knowledge: Immigration policy and social research*, Cambridge, UK: Cambridge University Press.

Colglazier, B. W. (1991) 'Scientific uncertainties, public policy, and global warming: how sure is sure enough?', *Policy Studies Journal* 19(2): 61–72.

Dahl, R. A. (1991) *Modern Political Analysis*, 5th edn, Englewood Cliffs, NJ: Prentice Hall.

Ferree, M. M. (2003) 'Resonance and radicalism: feminist framing in the abortion debates of the United States and Germany', *American Journal of Sociology* 109(2): 304–44.

Grundmann, R. (2007) 'Climate change and knowledge politics', *Environmental Politics* 16(3): 414–32.

Haas, P. M. (1989) 'Do regimes matter? Epistemic communities and Mediterranean pollution control', *International Organization* 43(3): 377–403.

Hecht, A. D. and Tierpak, D. (1995) 'Framework agreement on climate change: a scientific and policy history', *Climatic Change* 29(4): 371–402.

IPCC (1995) *IPCC Second Assessment: Climate Change 1995. A report of the Intergovernmental Panel on Climate Change*.

Jasanoff, S. and Wynne, B. (1998) 'Science and decisionmaking', in S. Rayner and E. L. Malone (eds) *Human Choice and Climate Change*, vol. 1, *The societal framework*, Columbus, OH: Battelle Press, pp. 1–87.

Jasanoff, S. and Martello, M. L. (2004) 'Conclusion. Knowledge and governance', in S. Jasanoff and M. L. Martello (eds) *Earthly Politics: Local and global in environmental governance*, Cambridge, MA: MIT Press, pp. 335–50.

Kingdon, J. W. (2003[1984]) *Agendas, Alternatives, and Public Policies*, 2nd edn, New York: Longman.

Knaggård, Å. (2009) *Vetenskaplig osäkerhet i policyprocessen. En studie av svensk klimatpolitik. [Scientific uncertainty in the policy process. A study of Swedish climate policy]*, unpublished thesis, Lund, Sweden: Lund University.

— (2014) 'What do policy-makers do with scientific uncertainty? The incremental character of Swedish climate change policy making', *Policy Studies* 35(1): 22–39.

— (2015). 'The Multiple Streams Framework and the problem broker', *European Journal of Political Research* DOI: 10.1111/1475–6765.12097.

Litfin, K. T. (1994) *Ozone Discourses: Science and politics in global environmental cooperation*, New York: Columbia University Press.

— (1995) 'Framing science: precautionary discourse and the ozone treaties', *Millennium* 24(2): 251–77.

Merton, R. K. (1973) *The Sociology of Science: Theoretical and empirical investigations*, Chicago: University of Chicago Press.

Robinson, S. E. and Eller, W. S. (2010) 'Participation in policy streams: testing the separation of problems and solutions in subnational policy systems', *Policy Studies Journal* 38(2): 199–215.

Rochefort, D. A. and Cobb, R. W. (1994) 'Problem definition: an emerging perspective', in Rochefort, D. A. and Cobb, R.W. (eds) *The Politics of Problem Definition: Shaping the policy agenda*, Lawrence, KA: University Press of Kansas, pp. 1–31.

Schattschneider, E. E. (1960) *The Semisovereign People: A realist's view of democracy in America*, New York: Holt, Rinehart and Winston.

Schön, D. A. and Rein, M. (1994) *Frame Reflection: Toward the resolution of intractable policy controversies*, New York: BasicBooks.

Skolnikoff, E. B. (1997) 'Same science, differing policies; the saga of global climate change', Joint Program Report Series, MIT Joint Program on the Science and Policy of Global Change, available at: http://mit.edu/globalchange/www/MITJPSPGC_Rpt22.pdf (accessed 2 March 2009).

Stone, D. A. (1989) 'Causal stories and the formation of policy agendas', *Political Science Quarterly* 104(2): 281–300.

WCED (World Commission on Environment and Development) (1987) *Our Common Future*, Oxford, UK: Oxford University Press.

Wynne, B. (1992) 'Uncertainty and environmental learning. Reconceiving science and policy in the preventive paradigm', *Global Environmental Change* 2(2): 111–27.

Zahariadis, N. (2003) *Ambiguity and Choice in Public Policy: Political decision making in modern democracies*, Washington, DC: Georgetown University Press.

— (2007) 'The multiple streams framework: structure, limitations, prospects', in Sabatier, P. A. (ed.) *Theories of the Policy Process*, 2nd edn, Boulder, CO: Westview Press, pp. 65–92.

Chapter Eight

Clarifying the Concept of Policy-Communities in the Multiple-Streams Framework

Nicole Herweg

Introduction

John W. Kingdon's *Agendas, Alternatives, and Public Policies* (1984) is a curiosity in itself: on the one hand, it is considered one of the most important public-policy-related books (Shoup 2001: 14), a claim which is mirrored in an outstanding citation frequency (King 1994). On the other hand, it is seen as one of the 'least elaborated or systematically applied' contemporary policy theories (McLendon and Cohen-Vogel 2008: 31). Although contributions markedly less well elaborated than Kingdon's multiple-streams framework (MSF) surely exist, it is true that not all its concepts are well defined. The concept of policy-communities is a case in point. Most likely resulting from Kingdon's focus on other aspects, his explanatory notes regarding policy-communities are derived from case studies; they are descriptive and not sufficient to produce a workable definition. Furthermore, Kingdon's reference to policy-communities and issue-networks when discussing the participants involved in the process of agenda-setting and specification of alternatives leads to further confusion, as these concepts are commonly seen as opposites.

These theoretical difficulties hamper the operationalisation of the concept of policy-communities. As a consequence, it becomes difficult to deduce falsifiable hypotheses regarding the characteristics of policy-communities and their influence on generating alternatives. This difficulty might, at least partly, explain the gap between the number of citations and the number of systematic applications of the framework. As the development of alternatives falls in the realm of policy-communities, and their availability is a necessary condition for agenda-change, clarifying the definition of policy-communities would contribute directly to answering Kingdon's main question: why do ideas arise when they do? (Kingdon 1984: vii). A clearly outlined definition of policy-communities as applied in the MSF might facilitate the systematic application of the framework to case studies; this chapter aims at contributing in this regard. In order to meet this goal, it focuses on the definition of policy-communities and deliberately refrains from testing hypotheses about the state of a policy-community and its influence on policy-dynamics. Instead, it discusses the difficulties arising from concept-application within the MSF, as well as ways to deal with those difficulties, in depth. In order to demonstrate that the revised definition of policy-communities allows for an empirical determination of who the members of a policy-community are, and whether or not the policy-community changes (prerequisites for hypotheses-deduction regarding policy-dynamics), a case study of the European natural gas policy-community was conducted.

Clarifying the policy-community concept is a challenging task, as it is not only vaguely formulated in the MSF but also the subject of controversy in the policy-network literature. In fact, a consensus regarding the definition of this concept has not yet emerged. This concept was first introduced by Jack L. Walker in the United States, in 1974 (Jordan and Maloney 1997: 558). Since then, a '"Babylonian" variety of different understandings and applications of the policy network concept' (Börzel 1997: 1) evolved in the study of policy-making. Unfortunately, this 'Babylonian variety' makes sound scientific debate very difficult because 'contributors offer their arguments in a private code that cannot be refuted' (Jordan 1990: 319).

In order to achieve a clear analysis, this chapter elaborates on Kingdon's understanding of policy-communities, based on a summary of his explanatory notes on them. This is supplemented by a discussion of how Kingdon mingles policy-communities with issue-networks when referring to the participants involved in agenda-setting and specification of alternatives.[1] Since the publication of Kingdon's monograph in 1984, the ascription of certain attributes to different network concepts has gained importance in the theoretical development of the policy-network literature. In order to avoid conflating the meaning of the terms policy-communities and issue-networks in today's academic parlance with the meaning they had when Kingdon wrote his monograph, the contributions he refers to are summarised and their inter-relatedness discussed.[2] These contributions are the works of Hugh Heclo (1978) on issue-networks and of Jack L. Walker (1981) on policy-communities. On this basis, the present chapter suggests a definition of policy-communities for the MSF. Going beyond Kingdon's remarks concerning policy-communities, it also develops an answer to the question of how policy-communities evolved in the first place. The European natural gas policy-community was chosen as an example for testing the utility of the derived definition.[3] This policy-community emerged in the late 1990s, which corresponded to the passing

---

1. In fact, the latter concept is seen to be highly influential for Kingdon's line of reasoning (Berry *et al.* 2004: 542). This does not come as a surprise: fluidity is one of the main characteristics not only of issue-networks but also of the idea of 'organized anarchies' (Cohen, March and Olsen 1972), on which the MSF draws heavily.

2. Resulting from the paper's focus on the state of research in the mid 1980s, the time of publication of Kingdon's (1984) monograph, the huge amount of research done since then is not considered. This applies particularly to the literature on policy-networks, network-governance and governance-networks (for overviews, see Blanco *et al.* 2011; Rhodes 2007; Torfing 2005).

3. Kingdon (1984) derived the MSF from observations of agenda changes at the federal level of the United States. However, several researchers have already indicated that the MSF is applicable to the European level (Richardson 2001: 23; Zahariadis 2008), or have even applied it to EU policy-making (Ackrill and Kay 2011). Therefore, this case study's set-up is suitable to elaborate the framework's policy-community concept.

of three European gas directives dealing with the introduction of common rules for the natural gas market, and has shown an enormous dynamism since. As the policy-community's core, the European Gas Regulatory Forum was set up so issues relating to the creation of an internal natural gas market could be discussed. Strikingly, the policy process for the second and third directives was significantly shorter than the first one, although they were of a greater political complexity.[4] Thus, this example suitably proves the influence of a policy-community's state on the availability of alternatives as well as the usefulness of the introduced theoretical refinements.

Empirically, the analysis is based on primary sources: in particular, legislative documents and any available documentation originating from the European Gas Regulatory Forum. These are complemented with secondary sources, such as media reports and information gathered from the European Public Affairs Directory. Due to data limitations, the time-span considered ranges only from 1993 until 2009.

The notion of policy-communities in the multiple-streams framework

This section begins by summarising Kingdon's explanatory notes on policy-communities and discusses the difficulties that arise from conflating policy-communities with issue-networks. Subsequently, the contributions of Walker and Heclo are summarised, since Kingdon refers to them explicitly.[5] On this basis, Kingdon's understanding of policy-communities is unveiled and, where necessary, made concrete.

Network concepts in the multiple-streams framework

In line with the usual practice in early policy-community literature (Thatcher 1998: 391), Kingdon's explanatory notes regarding policy-communities are closer to a description than to a definition. The most accurate definition Kingdon introduces is that, '[p]olicy communities are composed of specialists in a given policy area … scattered both through and outside of government' (Kingdon 1984: 123). These specialists share a concern with policy problems occurring in a given policy area. Furthermore, they interact with each other, which results in the development of policy alternatives. Activities that Kingdon counts as examples of engagement in working out policy alternatives range from 'going to lunch, circulating papers, publishing articles, holding hearings, [and] presenting

---

4. Following Kaeding 2006 and Steunenberg and Rhinard 2010, the number of recitals in a directive is a good proxy for estimating the degree of political complexity. Generally speaking, recitals explain a directive's purpose and provide factual information. In addition, member states, the European Parliament, and the Commission use them in order to express reservations or to clarify issues. While the first gas directive contains thirty-two recitals, there are already thirty-four recitals in the second one, which becomes sixty-six in the third gas directive.

5. For introductory readings to the network literature see, for instance, Jordan 1990; Jordan and Schubert 1992; van Waarden 1992; Marsh 1998a; Thatcher 1998; Berry *et al.* 2004. An overview of future research needs is provided in Marsh 1998b and Lewis 2011.

testimony' to 'drafting and pushing legislative proposals' (Kingdon 1984: 122). Before this chapter addresses the question of who these specialists are, I elucidate in which context Kingdon applies the concept of issue-networks.

Kingdon refers to issue-networks in order to describe exchanges among policy specialists. According to him, '[t]he communication channels between those inside and those outside of government are extraordinarily open, and ideas and information float about through these channels in the whole *issue-network of involved people*, somewhat independent of their formal positions' (Kingdon 1984: 48, my emphasis). Although policy-communities also consist of participants within and outside government, we cannot conclude that Kingdon uses the terms policy-communities and issue-networks synonymously. The reason is that Kingdon distinguishes between the specification of alternatives and agenda-setting.

According to Kingdon, two clusters of participants are involved in these two activities (*see* Table 8.1): a visible cluster affecting agenda-setting and a hidden cluster affecting the specification of alternatives. How do these clusters relate to each other?

Table 8.1: Clusters of participants involved in specification of alternatives and agenda-setting

Participants	Involvement in specification of alternatives and/ or agenda-setting	Visibility of participants
Inside government		
Administration	Agenda-setting	Visible
Civil servants	Specification of alternatives	Hidden
Capitol Hill	Specification of alternatives and agenda-setting	Visible
Outside government		
Interest groups	Specification of alternatives	Hidden and visible (depending on their activities)
Academics, researchers, consultants	Specification of alternatives	Hidden
Mass media	Agenda-setting (indirect involvement *via* impact on public opinion)	Visible
Specialised media	Agenda-setting (*via* its function as a policy-community's communication channel)	Visible
Election-related participants	Agenda-setting	Visible
Public opinion	Agenda-setting	Visible

Source: Author's own compilation, based on Kingdon (1984).

The governmental agenda is set by visible participants who exploit changes in the problem and/or politics stream (Kingdon 1984: 208). A change in one of these two streams coincides with the opening of a policy-window and the opportunity to change the decision agenda.[6] At this point, visible participants 'turn to specialists in *the less visible policy-community* ... for the alternatives from which an authoritative choice can be made' (Kingdon 1984: 74, my emphasis). Thus, the policy-community is composed of a smaller fraction of the issue-network.

This conclusion conflicts with the established understanding that issue-networks and policy-communities represent two opposing concepts in the network literature, with the latter being characterised by closed, restricted and stable relationships and the former by open, unrestricted and unstable relationships (Marsh 1998a: 16; Thatcher 1998: 391). However, this seeming contradiction can be resolved when we take into account that the practice of ascribing certain attributes to different network concepts was in its infancy in the 1980s. Instead of drawing on today's academic understanding of these concepts, Walker's (1981) writings on policy-communities[7] and Heclo's (1978) work on issue-networks are addressed and related to each other in the next section, since Kingdon refers to them explicitly.

Back to the roots: Heclo's issue-networks and Walker's policy-communities

Heclo's issue-networks

Heclo's issue-networks are a reaction to the sub-government literature, which refers to 'clusters of individuals that effectively make most of the routine decisions in a given substantive area of policy' (Ripley and Franklin 1984, quoted in Jordan and Schubert 1992: 20). The most prominent concept of this literature is the 'iron triangle', which describes a closed and stable relationship between at least one interest-group, a central government agency and a congressional committee (Marsh 1998a: 4–5).

Contrary to the idea that access to policy-making is restricted in the United States, Heclo sees a 'large number of participants with quite variable degrees of mutual commitment or of dependence on others in their environment' (Heclo 1978: 102) aiming at influencing policy formation. In Heclo's view, networks consist of 'powerful interest groups', 'individuals in or out of government who have a reputation for being knowledgeable' and 'issue-skilled [individuals] ... regardless of formal professional training' (Heclo 1978: 102–3). These so-called *issue-networks* vary in their composition as '[p]articipants move in and out of the

---

6. Peters makes the criticism that the MSF does not specify how the emergence of policy-windows is related to the nature of networks (Peters 1998: 26). This criticism overlooks that networks (or policy-communities in Kingdon's usage) can determine only whether a coupling process is successful, as this requires the availability of a worked-out proposal, but not whether policy-windows emerge as they are opened by changes in the problem or politics stream.

7. Although Kingdon also refers to Walker's writings from the years 1969, 1974 and 1977, the focus is on Walker 1981, as this contribution deals explicitly with policy-communities.

networks constantly', which makes it 'almost impossible to say where a network leaves off and its environment begins' (Heclo 1978: 102).

Jack L. Walker's policy-communities

Based on case studies dealing (among other things) with agenda-setting in the United States, Walker refers to 'policy-communities' (Walker 1974: 113) in order to 'describe a network of policy professionals who shape policy agendas through professional consensus' (Jordan and Maloney 1997: 558). To refer to the same phenomenon, he uses several labels, such as 'specialized communication networks' (Walker 1969: 894), 'communities of policy professionals' (Walker 1981: 79), 'professional forums' (Walker 1981: 79), or 'para-bureaucratic communities of policy specialists' (Walker 1989: 2).[8] According to Walker, policy-communities consist of people who are concerned with a specific set of policy problems. They comprise

> those primarily engaged in studying the policies and procedures being employed in an area, as well as administrators of the major agencies with operating programs. The communities involve bureau chiefs and officials in operating agencies, academics and consultants employed by research-and-development firms, publishers or editors of professional journals and magazines, representatives from business firms that are major suppliers of goods and services employed in the area, members of legislative staffs and legislators themselves who specialize in the subject, and other elected officials and lobbyists with interest in the policies (Walker 1981: 79).

How John W. Kingdon combines these contributions

In what sense does Kingdon apply the terms issue-networks and policy-communities? Regarding the latter, Kingdon seems to have been greatly inspired by Walker's writings. That there had been an academic exchange between them is not surprising, as they were colleagues at the University of Michigan. This exchange is best documented in their acknowledgments (Kingdon 1984: vii, Walker 1977: 423), in which they mention each other.[9] In fact, Kingdon adopted several of Walker's ideas, which can be deduced from references to them in two-thirds of his chapters.[10]

---

8. For reasons of clarity, the term 'policy-community' is used exclusively in the following.

9. This personal acquaintance is also reflected in the obituary Kingdon wrote for Walker after his unexpected death (Kingdon 1990).

10. Furthermore, some elements of Kingdon's MSF had already been addressed in Walker's writings. For instance, Walker hinted at, first, the similarities between the process-dynamics described by the garbage-can model of organisational choice and public policy-making (Cohen, Marsh and Olsen 1972) and, second, the importance of policy-entrepreneurs for the matching of problems and solutions (Walker 1981: 89–91).

Kingdon applies the concept of issue-networks in two ways: first, as a means of referring to the different participants involved in agenda-setting and the specification of alternatives; and, second, to highlight the fact that communication channels between them are open. Apart from these references to issue-networks, he focuses on policy-communities.

Heclo's and Walker's contributions share more commonalities regarding the actors considered than today's received wisdom would suggest. There is a great overlap between Heclo's enumeration of participants involved in issue-networks and Walker's list of people forming a policy-community. In comparison to Heclo, Walker devotes more attention to the roles of researchers and expert knowledge. According to him, the supply of new ideas is generated by the research sector of a policy-community (Walker 1981: 86), and one prerequisite for policy change is that these researchers are able to provide 'clear justification for the use of a given solution' (Walker 1981: 91). Hence, not all participants of the policy-community are of equal importance. Kingdon adopts this idea when differentiating participants involved in policy-making according to their engagement in agenda-setting and the specification of alternatives. He departs from Walker's understanding insofar as he considers not only a policy-community's research sector (academics, researchers and consultants) to be important for the specification of alternatives but also civil servants and interest-groups.

Apart from listing the different participants in policy-communities, Walker devotes attention to the structure of the network. According to him (1981: 86), there is a link between the organisation of a policy-community's research sector and the supply of new ideas: '[T]he more autonomy, interchange, and competition among researchers in a policy field, the more likely they will have the initiative in defining the area's goals, problems, and objectives'. Put differently, because researchers put their own agendas first, their research is not guided by the needs and interests of administrators and political leaders. As a consequence, they produce a limited amount of new ideas suitable for addressing the problems with which administrators and political leaders are confronted. Although Walker (1981: 80) stresses that the policy-community is held together 'by a set of agreed doctrines or theories', the underlying consensus is comparatively weak (Walker 1981: 83). Consequently, opportunities to redirect the attention of the research sector arise if its members are divided and at odds with each other (Walker 1981: 80). From this passage, we can infer that Walker does not assume policy-communities to be stable. Additionally, he considers anonymous refereeing processes a valid means of choosing articles for publication in specialised media (Walker 1981: 86), which also indicates that policy-communities can be characterised by open access and an enlarged group of participants.

Kingdon adopts the idea of differently structured policy-communities when taking into account the relationship between their fragmentation and agenda-stability. According to him, the level of policy-community integration has an effect on which ideas remain as a result of the softening-up process.[11] The more

---

11. The term 'softening-up' refers to the process of getting policy communities and larger publics used to new ideas and building acceptance for proposals (Kingdon 1984).

integrated a policy-community is, the more easily a common language, outlook, orientation and way of thinking evolves among its members (Kingdon 1984: 126). Less integrated policy-communities, on the other hand, lack internal co-ordination. Consequently, it is easier to float new ideas in the latter, a process which leads to higher agenda-instability and disjointed policies. As in more integrated policy-communities, new ideas must match the policy specialists' commonly shared values in order to be considered, thus tending to result in higher agenda-stability (Kingdon 1984: 124–8). Unfortunately, Kingdon does not specify the conditions that must be met in order to deem a policy-community as more or less integrated. Referring to his case study of the transport community, he describes it as fragmented in several respects, for instance, because of its division into different modes (Kingdon 1984: 125). In sum, neither Walker nor Kingdon assume policy-communities to be necessarily closed, restricted and stable; both allow varying manifestations among them.

Policy-communities in the MSF revisited

In order to deduce falsifiable hypotheses regarding the characteristics of policy-communities and their influence on the generation of alternatives, Kingdon's understanding of policy-communities must be clarified. After taking into account the preceding sections, the following definition results:

> A policy-community is mainly a loose connection of civil servants, interest-groups, academics, researchers and consultants (the so-called hidden participants), who engage in working out alternatives to the policy problems of a specific policy field.

For the sake of clarification, the constraining 'mainly', as well as what is meant by 'a loose connection', must be explained. Regarding the participants in the policy-community, Kingdon states that it is possible, in principle, that both groups of participants, the hidden and the visible ones, are involved in the specification of alternatives *and* agenda-setting. Nonetheless, he regards it as more probable that they restrict themselves, due to a tendency to specialise in one specific activity (Kingdon 1984: 20). Put differently, it is possible that other actors than the hidden ones are part of the policy-community but the hidden ones are present in any case. With respect to applying the MSF, the boundary of a policy-community has to be drawn empirically for each case study, with an actor's engagement in working out policy alternatives serving as a distinction-criterion for that actor's being considered a member of a policy-community. Further research is required to determine the impact that differences in the composition of policy-communities have on agenda-setting.

What does a loose connection between the participants of the policy-community look like? According to Kingdon, members of a policy-community interact with each other. He exemplifies these interactions with the description that they 'know each other's ideas, proposals, and research, and often know each other very well personally' (Kingdon 1984: 123). Hence, a researcher whose ideas are published and considered by other members of the policy-community belongs to the community. From this description, it follows that the only prerequisite to become a part of the policy-community is to contribute policy solutions for a specific policy field in a way that enables the policy-community's participants to notice them. In this sense, the connection between the participants is loose and network access is open.

Kingdon remains silent, however, about how policy-communities evolve in the first place, and why they change. Campbell *et al.* (1989: 89)[12] deal with this issue and differentiate between two stimuli for changes in network structures: one coming from the demand side and the other from the supply side. Demand-side stimulus comes from policy-makers who are dealing with new problems and therefore ask for policy experts' input. Supply-side stimulus, on the other hand, is given if a solution is transferred from one policy-sector to another, a phenomenon Kingdon refers to as 'spillovers' (Kingdon 1984: 200).

A study of the European natural gas policy-community

This section analyses the European natural gas policy-community. It aims at demonstrating how the concept of policy-communities can be applied in a case study in a way which allows us to test whether changes in the structure of the policy-community have had an impact on policy dynamics.

Before delving into the case study, the policy-community's participants must be adjusted to the European level, as the MSF was originally derived to explain agenda-setting at the federal level of the United States. Whereas the terms 'academics', 'researchers' and 'consultants' can be transferred without adjustments 'European civil servant' needs a definition and 'interest-groups' a word of explanation.

Regarding the former, civil servants are officials who have 'been appointed … to an established post on the staff of the institutions of the Union' (Regulation No 31 (EEC), 11 (EAEC), Art. 1a) and are predominantly located within the European Commission (hereinafter referred to as the Commission). 'Interest groups' needs further explanation because Kingdon (1984: 50) not only considers 'business and industry, professional, labor, public interest groups' but also 'governmental officials as lobbyists' to fall within this category. In the European context, the latter refers to member states' governmental officials.

Additionally, European functional equivalents of the visible participants that Kingdon mentions, who can potentially take part in the policy-community, are the European Parliament, the Council and the Commission, with the Council being

---

12. In this contribution, Campbell *et al.* apply an understanding of policy-communities different from Kingdon's. But as they explicitly refer to Kingdon when introducing the idea of supply-side stimulus (Campbell *et al.* 1989: 89), it seems appropriate to combine their ideas with the MSF.

constituted of the member states' governmental officials.[13] Thus, two actors in particular have an outstanding position because they belong to both the visible and the hidden group of participants, which means that they engage in both agenda-setting *and* the specification of alternatives: member states' governmental officials and the Commission. Of these two actors, the Commission is the more important, because it enjoys a monopoly on formal agenda-setting (Pollack 1997: 122).

The inception of the policy-community

Since the 1950s, the Commission (or its equivalent) had repeatedly been trying to develop a common energy policy but had not succeeded (McGowan 1989: 548; Hancher 1990: 221). One reason for its failure can be seen in the absence of a European natural gas policy-community (Matlary 1997: 102), which coincided with a lack of worked-out proposals. This failure primarily resulted from given market-structures and the fact that energy matters remained within the member states' domestic jurisdiction. The latter were characterised by predominantly state-owned, monopolistic energy sectors, consisting of vertically integrated companies that were bound in long-term and (partly) anti-competitive contracts. The states granted those companies exclusive rights in exchange for the fulfilment of certain public-service obligations. Hence the actors simply had no incentive to initiate or participate in a policy-community that would engage in working out proposals with a European dimension.

Although there was no natural gas policy-community at the European level, there was an exchange of views on the international level. For instance, the International Gas Union, founded in 1931, organised the World Gas Conference every three years. Furthermore, moves from liberalisation pioneers like the USA, Canada and the United Kingdom were observed carefully, both by the vast majority of (member) states with less liberalisation impetus as well as by the few (member) states that supported liberalisation. However, the liberalisation pioneers' experiences did not act as a catalyst for spreading the liberalisation gospel but served, instead, as a point of reference for liberalisation's opponents (Stern 1992: 47).

Hence, what initiated the development of a European policy-community in the natural gas sector? As the Commission had been a pivotal actor in the liberalisation of network industries (see Schmidt 1998), it seems plausible to expect that it also took advantage of the key roles arising from its dual membership in the clusters of visible, as well as hidden, participants to put its pet solutions on the agenda.

Indeed, in the shadow of the Single European Act, the Commission explicitly demanded policy-expert input regarding the question of how a liberalised European natural gas market could be achieved. As a first step, it contracted the

---

13. The European Council can be added to the list of visible participants since the Treaty of Lisbon, which states that the Council 'shall provide the Union with the necessary impetus for its development and shall define the general political directions and priorities thereof' (Art. 15(1), Treaty on European Union).

Brussels-based policy think-tank C&L Belmont, in association with Prognos AG, to conduct research on the pros and cons of the introduction of a common carrier system as one way of introducing competition.[14] The resulting reports were completed in the first half of 1989 and circulated throughout the industry, although they have never been officially accessible to the public (Stern 1992: 56).

The Commission's Communication accompanying the proposal for a transit directive for natural gas seized the suggestion listed in the above-mentioned reports to set up two Consultative Committees in order to discuss third-party access in depth (COM (89) 334 final: 3, 14).[15] These Committees were established in mid 1990 and chaired by the Commission. One committee was composed of member states' representatives and the other consisted of gas-industry representatives and consumer representatives (International Gas Report 13 June 1991, COM (91) 548 final: 6). Thereby, the Commission had addressed the relevant participants in a policy-community: interest-groups (among which, according to Kingdon (1984: 50), governmental officials also count as lobbyists); the research sector (although limited to just one consultancy); and itself, in its function as a civil servant.

Instead of creating a climate of co-operation, however, both committees failed to hold constructive talks as they – including, in part, the Commission – 'came to the discussions with their negotiating positions mapped out, lacking a willingness to compromise and engage in new thinking' (Stern 1992: 74). Although these Committees did not result in a policy-community, however, they set the creation of such a community in motion. The affected industries' growing interest in a European policy-community counts as a first step. This interest shows their turn to the European level, which led to increasing numbers of representative offices of the natural gas and electricity sectors, as documented in the Landmarks Publications (1992, 1994, 1996, 1998, 2000, 2002, 2004, 2006, 2008) (see Figure 8.1). Unfortunately, this directory does not exist for the 1980s. The categories listed stem from the European Public Affairs Directory.

However, from a mere turn to the European level it does not follow that the actors exchanged their views or indeed spoke with one voice, as evidenced by the example of Eurogas, the association representing the European gas wholesale, retail and distribution sectors, founded in 1990. Although Eurogas claimed to speak for the natural gas industry as a whole, its members pursued different, conflicting interests, due to differences in size (smaller distributors were opposed to monopoly suppliers), for instance, or to differences in the regulatory environment they faced (such as British Gas, operating in a liberalised country, as opposed to companies enjoying protection from competition) (*EC Energy Monthly*, 1 July 1991). According to Kingdon, this lack of cohesion hampers an interest-group's ability to

---

14. A common carrier system obliges pipeline companies to carry as much gas as its capacity allows for third parties. If the demand is higher than the capacity of the pipeline, capacity *pro rata* has to be offered to all parties (Stern 1992: 23).

15. Third-party access means that pipeline companies either agree, or are obliged, to carry as much gas as their capacities allow against the payment of a charge for the services of which the third party has made use (Stern 1992: 21).

Figure 8.1: Number of representative offices of natural gas and electricity sector at European level

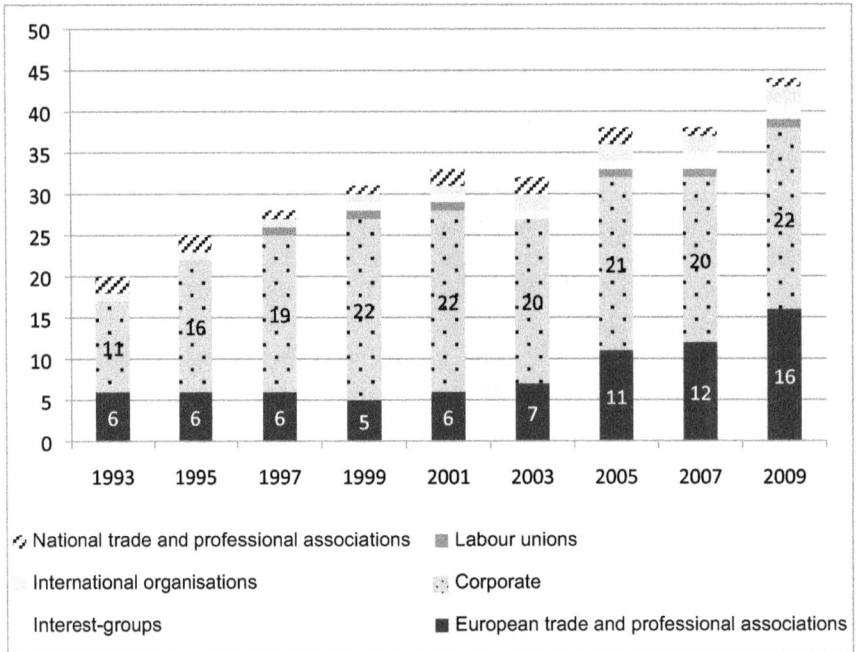

Source: Author's own compilation, based on Landmarks Publications 1992, 1994, 1996, 1998, 2000, 2002, 2004, 2006, 2008.

affect the governmental agenda (Kingdon 1984: 55). Furthermore, in order for an alternative to be considered seriously, its compatibility with the policy specialists' values must be considered (Kingdon 1984: 140). If agreement on proposals and, consequently, on values is lacking even within an interest-group, it is unlikely that a consensus will be reached in the relevant policy-community. Regarding the liberalisation of the natural gas sector, the affected actors failed to speak with one voice and, consequently, to come up with and agree upon at least one proposal. The fact that a directive was passed in 1998 against their will (Stern 1998: 91) illustrates the poor success record of the opponents of the directive. Given their low level of cohesion, the interest-groups' lack of influence is in line with Kingdon's reasoning.

What remains to be elucidated is how the Commission succeeded in drafting a directive in the absence of a vibrant policy-community. The Commission took the chance and simply chose ideas as it suited. In this context, there emerged a win–win situation between the Commission and the United Kingdom (UK). The Commission had always been receptive to lessons drawn from the UK liberalisation experience. The UK, on the other hand, was keen on minimising possible costs resulting from regulatory adjustments and on eliminating economic disadvantages. The latter desire arose from the possible penetration of UK's domestic, liberalised natural gas market by European companies that could draw on their (national) monopoly (*Europe Energy*, 14 June 1991; cf. Héritier, Knill and Mingers 1996: 331). Hence, the UK provided the Commission with worked-out alternatives derived from their domestic regulations and, indeed, the Commission's draft directive mirrored many of them (Multinational Service 08-09/1991). As a result, the liberalisation of the natural gas market rose up the decision-agenda, even though the policy-community concerned was in a nascent state.

It took another six and a half years for the directive to be finally passed. This delay can be related to the fact that the (visible) actors could not agree on solutions, even to a point where they decided not to return to the gas directive until an agreement on the less controversial electricity directive could be reached (*European Report*, 26 November 1994; *Financial Times*, 25 May 1995). During the negotiation process, the involved actors started accepting the idea that the European Union had emerged as a new venue for regulating the natural gas market. As a consequence, they became more interested in developing European solutions for this policy sector. The Commission took advantage of this changed attitude and initiated the European Gas Regulatory Forum, commonly referred to as the Madrid Forum, in 1999.

This shift and the above-mentioned formation of the two Consultative Committees are examples of demand-side stimuli that set the formation of a European natural gas policy-community in motion. The Madrid Forum (MF) developed as the policy-community's cornerstone. Its objective was 'to provide an informal EU level framework for the discussion of issues and the exchange of experience concerning the establishment of a competitive internal market for natural gas' (Conclusion of the Madrid Forum, 30 September–1 October 1999: 1).[16] Thereby, the exchange of views was institutionalised immediately after the passing of the first gas directive. Since then, the MF has met once or twice a year and has kept the discussion and development of viable solutions ongoing. Therefore, the present chapter concentrates on its activities in the subsequent section.

The core of the European natural gas policy-community: the Madrid Forum

The MF was closely modelled on the Electricity Regulatory Forum, which was institutionalised in 1998. Following Eberlein (2005), these forums have four tasks:

   i. The gathering, generation, and assessment of relevant information or data relating to regulatory issues in liberalized ... markets. ...
   ii. The elaboration of regulatory proposals and solutions from the variety of technically feasible solutions. ...

---

16. The documents released by the Madrid Forum between September 2005 and May 2009 and referred to in this chapter are available at: https://ec.europa.eu/energy/en/madrid-forum-previous-meetings (accessed 28 September 2016). The documents released between September 1999 and December 2004 can be obtained by contacting the author.

    iii. The building of institutions that, in turn, help to structure the dialogue between regulators and market players and to drive forward the process of change. …

    iv. To build voluntary consensus and to deliver agreements (Eberlein 2005: 69–75).

The first two tasks clearly correspond to the actors' engagement in working out alternatives to policy problems in a specific field. In fact, since the third meeting of the MF, the exchange of experiences regarding existing legal provisions, as well as the discussion of legislative proposals concerning directives, guidelines for good practice (which are included in the annexes of the directives) and regulations are explicitly mentioned as agenda-items for the third to sixteenth MFs.

A policy-alternative's survival in the policy 'primeval soup' depends on its being accepted within the policy-community and by elected decision-makers (Kingdon 1984: 138). Therefore, the third task in the list above, building voluntary consensus and delivering agreement, is in line with Kingdon's conception of the activities that take place within a policy-community. Hence, the only task that goes beyond the reach of policy-communities and their activities, according to the MSF, is the building of institutions. An example of such an institution arising from the MF is the creation of Gas Transmission Europe (GTE). This body was established by the European gas industry, following an invitation from the Commission, the member states and the Council of European Energy Regulators, to create 'as quickly as possible, a new body or grouping that brings together representatives of all those responsible for the operation of the transmission network for gas in Europe'. Its task is to provide 'technical data regarding the transmission systems within Europe' (Conclusions of the Madrid Forum, 11–12 May 2000), which is required in order to work out policy solutions. Thus the policy-community's engagement in institution-building resulted from the absence of a European transmission network addressing natural gas issues. In order to develop workable policy solutions, input from such a network is indispensable. Hence the policy-makers' appeal to bring GTE into being is a further example of a demand-side stimulus for change in the policy-community.

The lists of participants in the MFs could be analysed in order to determine how closely the composition of the MF matches that of the actors Kingdon describes. Unfortunately, such lists are only available for five meetings (the tenth, twelfth, thirteenth, fifteenth, and sixteenth MFs). Information about participants in the remaining meetings can be deduced from the available documentation, most importantly, the agendas and conclusions, as well as from presentations given by participants, which were later made available to the public.[17]

Table 8.2 summarises the participants' affiliations according to the lists of participants. As some participants held various roles in the forum's meetings, multiple affiliations are possible. These data show that the research sector is of only minor importance. This finding is less surprising if the highly technical nature

---

17. The only exception is the second MF, for which only a summarised conclusion is available.

Table 8.2: Participants' affiliation

Participants' affiliation*	
(according to all available documents)	
Interest group	101
National regulatory authority	90
National ministry/ representative	56
Company	44
European Commission	26
Council of European Energy Regulators	16
European Regulators' Group for Electricity and Gas	12
Consultancy	7
Organisation**	6
European Presidency	1

* Multiple selection possible
** Representatives from European Free Trade Association and Energy Community Secretariat
Source: Author's own compilation, based on available lists of participants (for meetings of tenth, twelfth, thirteenth, fifteen and sixteenth Madrid Forums).

of the natural gas market is taken into consideration, which requires that the actors involved in this market have a profound knowledge of the sector. The remaining participants correspond with the introduced list of European policy-communities' participants.

The openness of the forum can be assessed by looking at the number of meetings the participants attended. The picture here is clear: the vast majority of actors attended only a single meeting and only a few actors attended more than three (*see* Figures 8.2 and 8.3). From this finding, it follows that meeting-participation was fluid and, hence, that there was open access to meetings.

A look at the contributors reveals the particular importance of specific actors (*see* Table 8.3). As might be expected, the Commission contributed most to the discussions at the meetings of the MF and, hence, influenced the direction of the discussions. As the Commission had been the policy-entrepreneur in times of open agenda-windows, its large share of speaking time becomes even more important, because this provided the Commission with the opportunity to push forward the search for policy alternatives most suited to the proper operating of an internal market in natural gas.

The European regulators (ERGEG, CEER) and the association of gas transmission companies (GTE, GTE+) had the next biggest share of speaking time to the Commission. ERGEG (for which the Agency for the Cooperation of Energy Regulators has since been substituted) and CEER mainly consisted of the same actors. They differed in so far as ERGEG was formally set up by the Commission (2003/796/EC), while CEER has been a voluntary co-operation of

Figure 8.2: Number of meetings of Madrid Forum attended by participants I

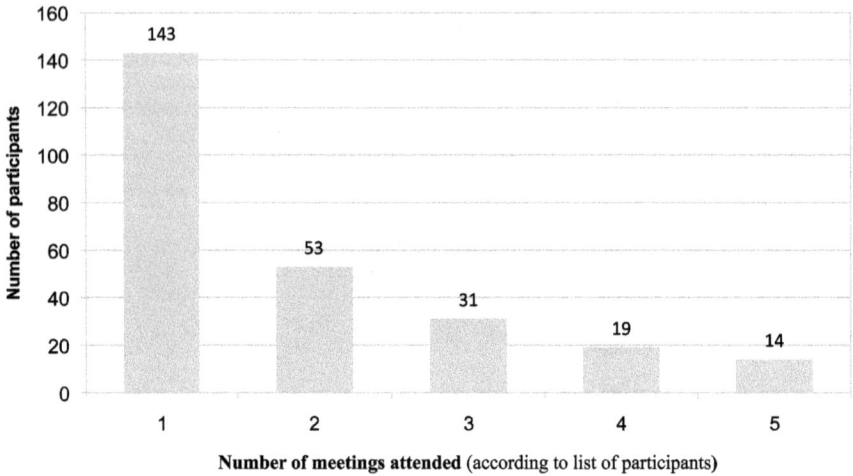

Source: Author's own compilation, based on list of participants for meetings of tenth, twelfth, thirteenth, fifteen and sixteenth MFs.

Figure 8.3: Number of meetings of Madrid Forum attended by participants II

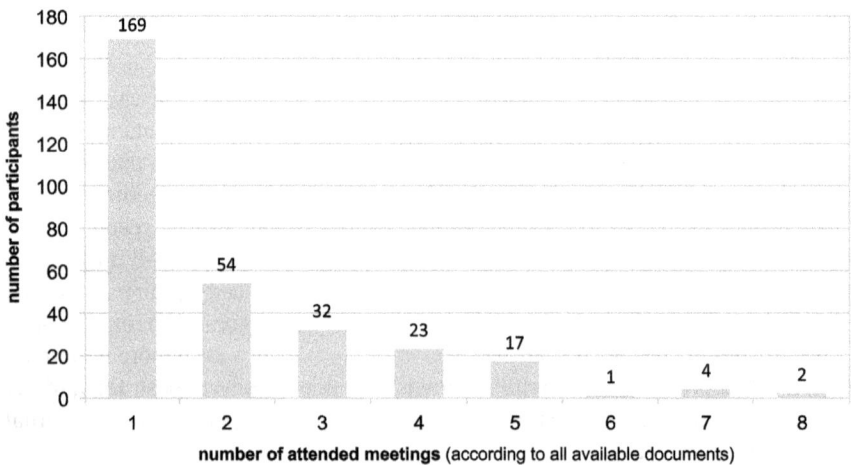

Source: Author's own compilation, based on all available documents for the first to sixteenth meetings of Madrid Forum (except second MF, for which available documents do not mention participants by name).

Table 8.3: Weighted importance of participants in Madrid Forum in terms of possible contribution due to time of incorporation, September 1999 to May 2009

Listed contributor	%
European Commission	22.5
European Regulators' Group for Electricity and Gas (ERGEG)	19.4
Council of European Energy Regulators (CEER)	13.1
Gas Infrastructure Europe (GIE)*	2.7
Gas Transmission Europe (GTE)	9.5
Gas Transmission Europe (GTE+) [precursor of ENTSOG]	7.6
Gas Storage Europe (GSE)	0.9
Gas LNG Europe (GLE)	0.3
European Council Presidency*	7.0
European Federation of Energy Traders (EFET)	4.2
EASEE-Gas	4.2
Comisión Nacional de la Energía (CNE)**	4.2
International Federation of Industrial Energy Consumers (IFIEC)	2.6
Eurogas	2.4
Fundación de Estudios de Regulación	1.7
Eurelectric	1.3
Representative of the United Kingdom	1.0
BG Storage	0.8
Edison Gas	0.8
Gas Natural	0.8
Gasunie	0.8
Ofgem	0.8
OXERA	0.8
Representative of Germany	0.8
Marcogaz	0.7
Brattle Group	0.6
GEODE	0.6
International Association of Oil & Gas Producers (OGP)	0.5
European Chemical Industry Council (CEFIC)	0.4
BP Gas & Power Europe	0.3
Centrica Energy Management Group	0.3
Gas Industry Standards Board (GISB)	0.3
German gas industry association	0.3
Gazprom	0.2

* GIE emerged in 2005 as the umbrella organisation for GTE, GSE, and GLE.
** Opening addresses only
Source: Author's own compilation.
Note: Information is extracted from minutes of first and agendas of third to sixteenth Madrid Forums. The second MF is not included as its documentation consists only of a summarised conclusion.

European national energy regulators. As the establishment of GTE resulted from the forum process, almost 40 per cent of the contributions were influenced by the Commission, in the sense that the Commission (solely or together with further actors) initiated the establishment of the participants.

Conclusion

In attempting to clarify the concept of policy-communities in the multiple-streams framework, this chapter refines Kingdon's definition and suggests viewing policy-communities as loose connections consisting mostly of civil servants, interest-groups, academics, researchers and consultants, who engage in working out alternatives to policy problems within a specific policy field. This chapter advocates an empirical assessment of whether a policy-community consists solely of its hidden participants or if these participants are joined by visible ones, too. Furthermore, it stresses that the connections between participants are not necessarily stable and that changes in the structure of a policy-community caused by either demand-side or supply-side stimuli are possible.

The analysis of the European natural gas policy-community shows that this community's structure changed tremendously during the period under investigation. The policy-community emerged in the 1990s, resulting from a demand-side stimulus as the Commission kept on calling for policy-experts' input. Since then, the policy-community has become very active, which is best reflected in the activities of the Madrid Forum, the policy-community's cornerstone.

The analysis of this policy-community's composition reveals a characteristic all European policy-communities share: the dual membership of the Commission and of the member states' governmental actors of both the cluster of visible and the cluster of hidden participants. In this regard, the Commission's dual membership is particularly important because of its formal agenda-setting competence. In fact, the analysis of contributors at the meetings of the MF documents the Commission's importance, as it contributed more than 20 per cent of the speaking time at these occasions and influenced almost 40 per cent of the other contributions.

Regarding the directives passed so far, the second and third gas directives were of a greater political complexity and had stronger conflict-generating potential than the first one. Nonetheless their negotiation periods were considerably reduced compared to the first directive: The second gas directive (2003/55/EC) was passed in only two and a quarter years and the third gas directive (2009/73/EC) took less than two years.

These findings open a new research agenda dealing with the relation between a policy-community's composition and its influence on policy-dynamics. The case study suggests that changes in the state of the policy-community and the Commission's position explain a good deal of the reduced negotiation period. This refined definition of policy-communities allows us to focus on this relation as it takes into account a policy-community's composition. However, further research guided by the multiple-streams perspective is needed in order to prove whether and possibly how a policy-community's composition influences policy dynamics.

References

Ackrill, R. and Kay, A. (2011) 'Multiple streams in EU policy-making: the case of the 2005 sugar reform', *Journal of European Public Policy* 18(1): 72–89.

Berry, F. S., Brower, R. S., Choi, S. O., Goa, W. X., Jang, H., Kwon, M. and Word, J. (2004) 'Three traditions of network research: what the public management research agenda can learn from other research communities', *Public Administration Review* 64(5): 539–52.

Blanco, I., Lowndes, V. and Pratchett, L. (2011) 'Policy networks and governance networks: towards greater conceptual clarity', *Political Studies Review* 9(3): 297–308.

Börzel, T. A. (1997) 'What's so special about policy networks? An exploration of the concept and its usefulness in studying European governance', *European Integration Online Papers* 1(16): 1–28.

Campbell, J. C., Baskin, M. A., Baumgartner, F. R. and Halpern, N. P. (1989) 'Afterword on policy-communities: a framework for comparative research', *Governance: An International Journal of Policy & Administration* 2(1): 86–94.

Cohen, M., March, J. and Olsen, J. (1972) 'A garbage can model of organizational choice', *Administrative Science Quarterly* 17(1): 1–25.

Eberlein, B. (2005) 'Regulation by cooperation: the "third way" in making rules for the internal energy market', in P. Cameron (ed.) *Legal Aspects of EU Energy Regulation: Implementing the new directives on electricity and gas across Europe*, Oxford, UK: Oxford University Press, pp. 59–88.

Hancher, L. (1990) 'A single European energy market. Rhetoric or reality?', *Energy Law Journal* 11(2): 217–42.

Heclo, H. (1978) 'Issue-networks and the executive establishment', in A. King (ed.) *The New American Political System*, Washington, DC: American Enterprise Institute for Public Policy Research, pp. 87–124.

Héritier, A., Knill, C. and Mingers, S. (1996) *Ringing the Changes in Europe: Regulatory competition and the transformation of the state: Britain, France, Germany*, Berlin: Walter de Gruyter.

Jordan, G. (1990) 'Sub-governments, policy-communities and networks. Refilling the old bottles?', *Journal of Theoretical Politics* 2(3): 319–38.

Jordan, G. and Maloney, W. A. (1997) 'Accounting for sub governments: explaining the persistence of policy communities', *Administration & Society*, 29(5): 557–83.

Jordan, G. and Schubert, K. (1992) 'A preliminary ordering of policy network labels', *European Journal of Political Research* 21(1–2): 7–27.

Kaeding, M. (2006) 'Determinants of transposition delay in the European Union', *Journal of Public Policy* 26(3): 229–53.

King, D. C. (1994) 'John Kingdon as an agenda item', *Policy Currents* 4(3): 17–20.

Kingdon, J. W. (1984) *Agendas, Alternatives, and Public Policies*, Boston, MA: Little, Brown & Co.

Kingdon, J. W. (1990) 'Jack L. Walker, Jr', *PS: Political Science & Politics* 23(2): 214–15.

Landmarks Publications (1992) *The European Public Affairs Directory 3 (1993). The comprehensive guide to opinion-formers in the capital of Europe*, Brussels: Landmarks Publications.

— (1994) *The European Public Affairs Directory 5 (1995). The comprehensive guide to opinion-formers in the capital of Europe*, Brussels: Landmarks Publications.

— (1996) *The European Public Affairs Directory 7 (1997). The comprehensive guide to opinion-formers in the capital of Europe*, Brussels: Landmarks Publications.

— (1998) *The European Public Affairs Directory 9 (1999). The comprehensive guide to opinion-formers in the capital of Europe*, Brussels: Landmarks Publications.

— (2000) *The European Public Affairs Directory 11 (2001). The comprehensive guide to opinion-formers in the capital of Europe*, Brussels: Landmarks Publications.

— (2002) *The European Public Affairs Directory 13 (2003). The comprehensive guide to opinion-formers in the capital of Europe*, Brussels: Landmarks Publications.

— (2004) *The European Public Affairs Directory 15 (2005). The comprehensive guide to opinion-formers in the capital of Europe*, Brussels: Landmarks Publications.

— (2006) *The European Public Affairs Directory 17 (2007). The comprehensive guide to opinion-formers in the capital of Europe*, Brussels: Landmarks Publications.

— (2008) *The European Public Affairs Directory 19 (2009). The comprehensive guide to opinion-formers in the capital of Europe*, Brussels: Landmarks Publications.

Lewis, J. M. (2011) 'The future of network governance research: strength in diversity and synthesis', *Public Administration* 89(4): 1221–34.

Marsh, D. (1998a) 'The development of the policy network approach', in D. Marsh (ed.) *Comparing Policy Networks*, Buckingham, UK and Philadelphia, PA: Open University Press, pp. 3–17.

Marsh, D. (1998b) 'The utility and future of policy network analysis', in D. Marsh (ed.) *Comparing Policy Networks*, Buckingham, UK and Philadelphia, PA: Open University Press, pp. 185–97.

Matlary, J. H. (1997) *Energy Policy in the European Union*, London: Macmillan.

McGowan, F. (1989) 'The single energy market and energy policy. Conflicting agendas?', *Energy Policy* 17(6): 547–53.

McLendon, M. K. and Cohen-Vogel, L. (2008) 'Understanding education policy change in the American states. Lessons from political science', in B. S. Cooper, J. G. Cibulka and L. D. Fusarelli (eds) *Handbook of Education Politics and Policy*, New York: Routledge, pp. 35–50.

Peters, G. (1998) 'Policy networks: myth, metaphor and reality', in D. Marsh (ed.) *Comparing Policy Networks*, Buckingham, UK and Philadelphia, PA: Open University Press, pp. 21–32.

Pollack, M. A. (1997) 'Delegation, agency, and agenda setting in the European Community', *International Organization* 51(1): 99–134.

Rhodes, R. A. W. (2007) 'Understanding governance: ten years on', *Organization Studies* 28(8): 1243–64.

Richardson, J. (2001) 'Policy-making in the EU. Interests, ideas and garbage cans of primeval soup', in J. Richardson (ed.) *European Union: Power and policy-making*, London: Routledge, pp. 3–26.

Schmidt, S. K. (1998) *Liberalisierung in Europa. Die Rolle der Europäischen Kommission*, Frankfurt, DE and New York: Campus.

Shoup, B. (2001) 'Policy section members vote for the most important works in public policy', *Policy Currents* 11(2): 14–15.

Stern, J. P. (1992) *Third Party Access in European Gas Industries: Regulation-driven or market-led?*, London: Royal Institute of International Affairs.

—   (1998) *Competition and Liberalization in European Gas Markets: A diversity of models*. London and Washington, DC: Royal Institute of International Affairs, distributed worldwide by Brookings Institution.

Steunenberg, B. and Rhinard, M. (2010) 'The transposition of European law in EU member states: between process and politics', *European Political Science Review* 2(3): 495–520.

Thatcher, M. (1998) 'The development of policy network analyses. From modest origins to overarching frameworks', *Journal of Theoretical Politics* 10(4): 389–416.

Torfing, J. (2005) 'Governance network theory: towards a second generation', *European Political Science* 4(3): 305–15.

Waarden, F. van (1992) 'Dimensions and types of policy networks', *European Journal of Political Research* 21(1–2): 29–52.

Walker, J. L. (1969) 'The diffusion of innovations among the American states', *American Political Science Review* 63(3): 880–99.

—   (1974) 'Performance gaps, policy research, and political entrepreneurs: toward a theory of agenda setting', *Policy Studies Journal* 3(1): 112–16.

—   (1977) 'Setting the agenda in the U.S. Senate: a theory of problem selection', *British Journal of Political Science* 7(4): 423–45.

—   (1981) 'The diffusion of knowledge, policy communities and agenda setting: the relationship of knowledge and power', in J. E. Tropman, M. J. Dluhy and R. M. Lind (eds) *New Strategic Perspectives on Social Policy*, New York: Pergamon Press, pp. 75–96.

—   (1989) 'Introduction: policy communities as a global phenomena[sic]', *Governance: An International Journal of Policy and Administration* 2(1): 1–4.

Zahariadis, N. (2008) 'Ambiguity and choice in European public policy', *Journal of European Public Policy* 15(4): 514–30.

Chapter Nine

Political Leadership, Multiple Streams and the Emotional Endowment Effect: A Comparison of American and Greek Foreign Policies

Nikolaos Zahariadis

Why do leaders continue to pursue policies even in light of mounting losses? In this chapter, the multiple-streams framework (MSF) and insights from affect-priming theory are used to explore the persistence of emotion, a phenomenon termed the 'emotional endowment effect'. Emotion (affect or mood – I use the terms interchangeably)[1] is defined here as a temporary state of feeling. Two MSF elements are stressed, leaving the others constant: national leaders (a sub-set of a broader group the MSF calls policy-entrepreneurs) and affective processing strategies of coupling. Successful political leaders use stories, images and other symbols to rouse passion, capturing public attention, building support and, at the same time, undermining opposition to their preferred policy (Neuman *et al.* 2007). When they and the public find themselves emotionally vested in a particular policy, change is highly unlikely. Emotion contains 'weight', which acts as inertia. A rational response would point to the desirability of policy-change in light of significant negative consequences but emotional endowment predicts continuity of policy. When novel focusing events open a policy-window pointing to an urgent problem, they tend to stir fear based on perceived threats. I hypothesise that the more intense the fear and the longer it persists under high salience, task unfamiliarity and complexity, and inconsistent preferences, the less likely it is that policy will change.

Using a most-different-systems design and a replicating logic (Yin 2014), I examine the impact of emotional endowment in two cases: the Greek attempt to block international recognition of the Former Yugoslav Republic of Macedonia (FYROM) in 1990–3 and, from the US, the Bush administration's policy in Iraq from 2001–4. Emotion is placed within the MSF for two reasons. First, the MSF is the only policy-framework that pays explicit attention to emotion *via* the concept of the national mood. Second, and despite its wide application, the MSF

---

1. Psychologists concede it is very difficult to differentiate conceptually and empirically between emotion and mood. Some argue moods are typically diffuse and last longer but Beedie, Terry, and Lane (2005) contend that subjective context matters when empirically differentiating between the two. Affective components may be found in either emotion or mood. Although I use theory related to mood, I conflate the two because mood in my case has specific causes and consequences (items normally associated with emotion).

has not been fully applied to issues of foreign policy, leaving considerable room for clarification and amendment. I analyse foreign policy because it is an area in which the role of emotion remains under-researched (Sasley 2010). To make the dependent variable comparable across cases, I restrict foreign policy to a series of choices and actions that are collectively characterised as confrontational, such as verbal aggression, embargoes or open warfare. Stimuli in theoretically different cases give rise to a similar emotion (fear) which, in turn, leads to similarly confrontational foreign policies that endure over time, despite significant losses.

The empirical cases were chosen for two theoretical and one methodological reason. First, they are very important to the respective countries' political life. Iraq was the defining moment of US President G. W. Bush's period in power, perhaps on par with the events of 9/11. The same holds for Greek Prime Minister Constantine Mitsotakis. His inability to deal effectively with the FYROM issue ended his government (it was toppled because of it) and his political career. In the US case, leaders manipulate; in the Greek case, leaders are manipulated. Second, there is sufficient contrast between the two cases to maximise the range of applicable scope conditions: the presence of ample ambiguity which encourages (re)framing; high salience, which rouses widespread emotion; and the time-frame of a single administration/government, which discounts for policy-changes due to changes in personnel. More substantive contrast in the empirical cases enhances the weight of scope conditions and lends more credibility to the findings.

Methodologically, the cases aid the construction of a most-different-systems design. There are significant differences in personality, institutional structure and issue characteristics; yet both leaders are subject to the same emotional endowment effect. First, the two leaders differ in terms of personality, a concept often thought to affect a leader's performance (for example, George and George 1998). Though both leaders are politically polarising figures, Prime Minister Mitsotakis is viewed as a non-charismatic, calculating and moderate politician. In contrast, President Bush is viewed as an impulsive partisan populist; once committed to a policy he would not tolerate doubt (Langston 2007). Second, governmental structure in each country differs dramatically, as does the process of making foreign policy. While institutional considerations affect politicians' responsiveness to public opinion and, consequently, shape policy-outputs (Chan and Safran 2006), endowment effects cut across presidential and parliamentary systems. Finally, issue characteristics differ significantly. The decision to go to war in Iraq was part of the broader 'war on terror' in the US, making it a security-oriented issue. The Greek case differs in that there is no open conflict, while the issue has a peculiar blend of security and cultural-identity aspects. Nevertheless, carefully manipulated fear in both cases gave rise to endowment effects. Discussion focuses on a single negative emotion, fear, because it is important and widely used in political discourse (Gardner 2009).

I highlight the ability of leaders within the MSF to rouse and manipulate public passions in pursuit of policy objectives. To be clear, I don't examine the national mood *per se* or the emotional state of leaders; rather I look at how, once roused, the mood affects policy change. In the empirical sections, I analyse the Greek case, drawing chiefly from material published elsewhere (Zahariadis 2016).

The findings are then used as a benchmark to be replicated in the US case. The additional richness of detail strengthens (or amends) the conclusions drawn in the original (Zahariadis 2016) study. I conclude with implications for the MSF and for theories of policy-change. The more leaders seek to foster a political climate of emotive appeal, the more successful they become in getting their way but the more constrained they subsequently are when they attempt to change course. Short-term expediency often circumscribes long-term success.

Leadership and emotion in public policy

Assuming conditions of ambiguity (and, more specifically, problematic preferences among policy-makers), the MSF describes the policy-making process as the skilful joining together of problems, solutions and politics by policy-entrepreneurs during open policy-windows (Kingdon 1995; Zahariadis 2003). Policy-windows provide the context within which policy-making takes place. Windows are changes in the problem or politics streams that catalyse the appearance of a limited number of issues on the agenda. For example, the events of 9/11 opened a policy-window in the problem stream that directed attention to a number of issues and provided the context for profound changes in foreign policy (Birkland 2004; Mazarr 2007).

In light of problematic preferences, the key actors who couple the three streams together and help shape policy are policy-entrepreneurs. They are skilled corporate actors or individuals who are willing to invest time, energy, and resources to couple the streams by attractively packaging their pet solution to the problem of the day and 'selling' the package to policy-makers (Kingdon 1995). I concentrate on a specific subset of policy-entrepreneurs, national leaders. Leaders are more ambitious and more capable of steering policy during open policy-windows (Wallis and Dollery 1997). Their institutional 'bully pulpit' gives them access beyond what ordinary entrepreneurs can muster. Position allows them to signal commitment to change (Mintrom and Norman 2009: 653–4), while reputation also adds a sense of legitimacy and consequentialism that go beyond ordinary policy-entrepreneurs. Finally, national leaders have unique resources at their disposal that can be used to gain credibility and, under certain conditions, alter the calculations of risk-averse legislators. How and under what conditions do leaders rouse and prolong public passions?

Emotion and attention

Issues contain empirical information and emotive appeals. As Fischer (2009: chapter 10) informs us, policy-deliberation is an emotionally-laden activity that interacts with cognition in complex ways. Both components may be manipulated to get attention (Zahariadis 2005) but I focus here on how emotion colours information, activates relevance and biases attention (Pfister and Böhm 2008). Although emotion is generally theorised at the individual level, I examine its impact at the collective level. Despite some differences between individual and collective decision-making, a meta-analytical study by Kühberger (1998) shows a high degree of similarity of effects between studies where the individual or the group is the unit of analysis, suggesting affect-congruence is applicable at the collective level. Information is transmitted through affect-congruent processing, which refers to the idea that people tend to selectively attend to information that agrees with their emotional state. Unhappy people are more attentive to stimuli that feature unhappy aspects – such as death or war.

Attention may be cognitively aroused by events but it is biased by emotion (Simon 1983: 29–30). What we perceive has as much to do with what has stimulated our attention as it does with our current state of being. Negative moods created by certain situations make greater demands for attention than positive ones (Fiedler 1990). Threats or novel situations activate our surveillance system and demand greater cognitive efforts and attention to survey the degree of environmental safety (Marcus, Neuman and MacKuen 2000: 55–6).

The MSF conceptualises the existence of a national mood in the political stream. It refers to the idea that many individuals in a country tend to think along similar lines (Kingdon 1995). Affect resides in national mood. Leaders are attuned to this mood, which swings from time to time, and seek to capitalise on it by adopting policies that coincide with it. Hence, skilled policy-entrepreneurs seek to influence a policy decision not only by taking advantage of the current national mood but also by framing it in politically expedient ways (for example, Slothuus 2008).

Public opinion has a big role to play in shaping the national mood but it does not determine it. As Kingdon (1995: 148) argues, although the concept is hard to pin down, it refers to the prevailing climate of opinion, that is, how opinion-leaders, activist-groups, the media and the public think about an issue. Policy-makers rely on numerous sources of information to perceive trends and swings in the mood. For example, nationalisation of the health-care industry during the first Clinton Presidency was doomed partly because the national mood was against the idea of a national health-plan. Not only were the public and interest-groups not animated by the prospect of a national plan, they were actively against it, preferring less radical and less expensive ways of containing health-care costs. Similarly, the national mood swung significantly in support of sacrificing some civil liberties in the interest of national security after the events of 11 September 2001. Motivated by fear, many Americans seem to agree with, or at least acquiesce to, the idea that the government should have significantly more power to invade privacy, and to a far greater extent than it did before, and in ways that would have been virtually impossible prior to 2001 (Huddy *et al.* 2005).

I propose to look for evidence of a national mood in public opinion polls as well as in writings and interviews by politicians and other important opinion-leaders. A negative mood is defined as one dominated by the perception of threat. The concept of threats refers to the perceived inadequacy of resources to deal with the demands of the situation (Blascovich and Mendes 2000: 60). Greater resource inadequacies lead to greater perceived threats. When governments are perceived as unable to meet situational demands, fear is likely to set in.

Leaders and the national mood

Political leaders sense the mood created by a novel event, such as the events of 9/11, and assume leadership in nurturing and perpetuating it, depending on the default option. If, for example, current policy favours leaders' preferences, raising affective intensity erects roadblocks for changing the policy. Successful leaders build networks and coalitions, which they activate in support of their preferences (Mintrom 2000, chapter 5; Kotter 1999 chapter 7). There exist many ways to build coalitions – such as resource-exchange or rhetoric (Wenzelburger 2011) – but a good way that has not been adequately explored is through affect-congruence. Preferences are shaped around manipulable emotions such as fear, which can then be articulated and crystallised into specific policies. Because emotion-laden individuals selectively attend to information that encodes that emotion (Peters 2006), it follows that collective agreement can be built around the same emotional response to an issue. For example, abortion is an issue that routinely glues together otherwise disparate activists from libertarians to some feminists, and from Catholics to evangelicals and Muslims (Munson 2009).

Political leaders rouse the national mood to build political coalitions, set the agenda, undermine the opposition and couple the streams. Once they do, however, they become highly constrained by the same emotions they evoked because emotion carries across tasks (Lerner, Small and Loewenstein 2004) and over time. In the next section, I argue that this happens when leaders stress the novelty of the situation and nurture and sustain a negative national mood.

The emotional endowment effect

What factors explain the persistence of emotion? Two conditions are proposed: novelty of events and affect-congruence strategies. Novel events open policy-windows that may evoke negative emotions. The latter are expected to linger for a longer period of time than positive emotions. Although not every novel situation will evoke negative emotions, general apprehension is likely because of the uncertainty of novelty. The underlying principle is that emotion is used as a source of information (Schwarz 2001). Affect provides contextual cues as to the type of situation people face. Stimuli contain information not only about perceptual features, for example, shapes or colours, but also the emotional responses associated with these perceptions. For example, representations of fireworks, kittens and rats include the degree of happiness or enjoyment involved with these concepts. Focusing on the emotional state of happiness (and ignoring others aspects) leads perceivers to view kittens and fireworks, which are emotionally equivalent, as more similar than kittens and rats. In this way, emotion pulls together specific informational dimensions of stimuli within a particular context while ignoring others.

H1: Novel events that evoke negative emotions (fear) have greater inertia than those evoking positive emotions.

Manipulating emotions helps ration attention and orders priorities (Sasley 2010). Not only do individuals selectively orient their attention to emotion-associated information; they also use this information more, and non-emotion-associated information less, than emotion-neutral people (Niedenthal and Halberstadt 2000). Novel events that evoke negative affect require greater attention because they interrupt ongoing behaviour to assess potentially threatening stimuli (Marcus, Neuman and MacKuen 2000). Doing so implies that policy-makers and the public will fixate on them longer than would otherwise be the case. Such novelty requires explanation and debate in the face of ambiguity and uncertainty. Precisely because of the novelty of the situation, people are more susceptible not only to wildly different interpretations but also to longer debates. Affect is likely to linger.

Once a policy-window opens, individuals have the opportunity to (re)frame problems and solutions in political expedient ways. This is because information and the relevant emotions are appraised within particular contexts (Martin 2000). Threats imply the possibility of losses. Negative information fed back from threats generates negative emotions. The greater the distance between demands and resources, that is, the greater the threat, the higher the potential losses are perceived to be and, hence, the more intense are fear and insecurity. Negative affect tends to elicit more confrontational responses than positive affect because information is retrieved and used to elicit behaviour that matches fear and insecurity. Of course, threat-appraisal need not necessarily generate confrontational behaviour to allay fear; the conundrum of 'fight or flight' is well known (Brader *et al.* 2011). When demand-appraisal of threats far exceeds resources, or when flight is viewed as acceptable, non-confrontational action is likely. When none of these conditions are met, which is the case in most instances involving threats between governments, confrontational action is the probable outcome.

The more afflicted by emotion people are, the more likely they are to look for and process information that is congruent with that emotion (Keltner and Lerner 2010). Fear and consequent insecurity act as filters of reality, leading people to look for more evidence of threats, which leads to more insecurity. Expressed in MSF terms, the national mood shapes and constrains policy by affecting receptivity for a proposed solution in the political stream and by helping to define the problem during coupling. Fear begets information-search that conforms to fear, perpetuating a cycle of confrontational action.

H2: More intense and longer-lasting fear, under high salience, task unfamiliarity and complexity, and inconsistent preferences, makes policy less likely to change.

Under certain conditions, affect-congruence strategies overshadow cognitive thinking processes. To understand the rationale behind this coupling strategy, we need to identify the conditions under which one is likely to witness either emotional or cognitive effects. Noted neurologist Donald B. Calne (1999: xi) writes in no uncertain terms that 'we are motivated by instinctive urges and emotions linked to cultural forces – reason is their servant and not their master.' But it is more likely that humans process information differently depending on the conditions (Schwarz 2001).

Forgas (2001) specifies the affect-infusion model to predict the conditions under which affect may exert influence on judgmental processes. It postulates four processing strategies used by people to solve a social cognitive task. *Direct access* refers to evaluations or appraisals based on strong retrieval cues, such as opinion on abortion or political-party affiliation. Many people have a crystallised opinion that does not need much processing. *Motivational* and *substantive* strategies assume strong objectives guiding the process. Negotiation to achieve a specific and clear objective is an example. These mechanisms or processing strategies lead to low affect-infusion, which basically means that emotion will have a weak influence on behaviour.

In contrast, *heuristic* strategies suggest affect should have a strong impact on behaviour. Heuristic strategies involve short-cuts and open-ended searching for information. For example, parents feeding a child for the first time need to employ memory short-cuts and other devices to be able to perform the task because it is so novel. Another would be attributing blame in conflict situations. Because an open-ended search for information that is not immediately accessible is involved, affect is more likely to have an impact.

When are heuristic strategies activated? Forgas (2001) lists a host of factors, three of which are important and relevant to my study: salience; inconsistent beliefs; and task unfamiliarity and complexity. First, highly salient issues are more likely to result in heuristic processing. People want to take their time in learning and evaluating information about issues they care about. Second, inconsistency of beliefs suggests that people don't have any specific motives or direction about what it is they are seeking. If they don't know exactly what they want, they are more likely to take time and engage in creative or substantive thinking. Third, tasks that are unfamiliar and complex involve heuristic thinking. For example, when individuals are asked to evaluate little-known products they are more likely to take their time. Complex tasks make similar demands on processing strategies. The MSF makes many of the same assumptions, placing it in a unique position to probe the applicability of the argument.

Under high salience, belief inconsistency, task unfamiliarity and complexity and threat conditions, the MSF expects coupling to be biased against policy-change. Losses in the form of money spent, lives lost or diplomatic capital wasted are likely to be viewed as evidence for continuing with rather than changing policy. Losses normally constitute negative feedback that prompts search for corrective action in the form of policy-reversal or -change (Pierson 2004). In the presence of strong affect-infusion, however, the process of looking for information that validates the current national mood overshadows the process of calculating costs or benefits. In political terms, the argument implies that those who share the intensity of the national mood will view losses not as a stimulus for corrective action but as validation of their emotional state. Higher losses increase the gap between current resources and situational demands, amplifying the threat and perpetuating affect-infusion. Intense fear promotes selective attention to information that validates fear. Negative affect created by a threat is more likely to elicit confrontation to eliminate the threat. When foreign policy is confrontational and under conditions of ambiguity and affect-infusion, losses operate as signals that validate more rather than less confrontation, that is, continuity rather than change. The process counter-intuitively resembles positive feedback, in that the effects are amplified rather than reduced (Pierson 2004). Solutions are matched with problems in emotionally appropriate ways, resembling what March and Olsen (2008) term the 'logic appropriateness'. Policies under certain conditions are not the outputs of a cost/benefit calculus designed to solve a problem but the coupling outcome of solutions framed to fit to problems: solutions which validate the emotional state of actors in the political stream. Politicians manipulate emotions in the short-term in support of major policy initiatives. However, the same ingredient of short-term success constrains the range of long-term options, leading policy-makers down a path they may not have intended to take.

In sum, the emotional endowment effect helps explain why leaders continue to pursue policies even in the face of mounting losses. The dependent variable is confrontational foreign policy. The independent variable is the national mood and its effects on sustaining confrontational policy. When novel focusing events open a policy-window and point to an urgent problem, they simultaneously tend to create a negative national mood, such as one created by fear. Political leaders seek to carefully nurture and perpetuate affect when it suits their interests. The more intense the negative mood and the longer it persists under high salience, task unfamiliarity and complexity, and inconsistent preferences, the more likely policy-entrepreneurs are to use affect-congruence strategies and the less likely it is for policy to change. In the next two sections, I probe the empirical validity of the argument. I examine the Greek case first to establish a benchmark and then replicate the findings in the US case.

Greece's policy toward FYROM, 1990–3

Why did the Greek government of Prime Minister Constantine Mitsotakis continue to pursue a confrontational policy *vis-à-vis* international recognition of FYROM's statehood even after mounting losses, admitting more or less that it was a lost cause? It is argued the fearful national mood was deliberately stoked, making the Prime Minister a prisoner of a policy he was unhappy with and reluctant to follow. Using data from Zahariadis 2016, I first explain why fear set in and then explore how it affected policy-change.

On 25 January 1991, the Assembly of the Socialist Republic of Macedonia declared independence from the Yugoslav federation. Closely mirroring events in the northern Yugoslav republics of Croatia and Slovenia, the Assembly expressed the nationalist fervour that brought to power the nationalist party VMRO and a new president. Greece has since pursued a confrontational policy designed to deny recognition of this state under the name Macedonia and its derivatives because it claims the name implies territorial demands against Greece. The independence declaration called, among other things, for measures to promote and safeguard 'the situation and rights of parts of the Macedonian people living as national minorities in neighbouring countries' (Valinakis and Dalis 1994: 37). Coupled with the old Yugoslav view of seeing parts of neighbouring territories as 'unredeemed lands', many in Greece viewed the declaration and the use of the name Macedonia, which is also the name of a region of Greece, as provocative and a security threat (Lygeros 2008: 81–4, Zahariadis 2005: 82–9).

This focusing event predictably opened a policy-window. Confirming our expectation, novelty and high salience resulted in apprehension and fear. The last time Greece had dealt with the issue was during its traumatic civil war (1946–9), when some Slav-speaking Greeks sided with the communists against the nationalist Greek government. Up to 1990, Greece continued the same policy it had followed since 1950, the essence of which may be summarised as follows: 'Greece does not harbor territorial or minority challenges in the Macedonian lands of Yugoslavia and Bulgaria, but neither does it accept the existence of a "Macedonian" minority in its territory' (Skylakakis 1995: 25).

Policy-makers claimed the new republic, whose existence Greece continues to support but not under the name Macedonia, represented a threat. Recognition under the name Macedonia was viewed as a triple threat: a cultural threat, because it negated part of Greek national identity by appropriating the name Macedonia (Kofos 2001); a low-intensity security threat, by raising mostly unsubstantiated minority issues (Zahariadis 1994); and a potential geopolitical threat in conjunction with other regional powers (Kamm 1994; Lygeros 2008). As a result, Greek attitudes hardened and policy became confrontational (Zahariadis 2005). But preventing other governments from recognising FYROM proved to be an extremely complex and unfamiliar task, to use Forgas's (2001) terms.

In the presence of ambiguity, the MSF expects the national mood to help steer policy and prolong affect-infusion. Preferences were very inconsistent and volatile, in that few actually knew what they wanted; most could only agree on what they didn't want. Fear fixed attention on the issue but the ambiguity of preferences allowed skilled manipulators to focus on aspects that pushed policy to extremes. Consistent with MSF thinking, the mood in the politics stream helped bound the limits of the possible but it did not, by itself, determine the outcome. There still needed to be coupling of the three streams. But ambiguity provided ample ground for politically contested frames. In his foreword to Skylakakis's book, Prime Minister Mitsotakis clearly states: 'what bothered me from the start was not the name of this state ... The issue was not to have a second minority problem in Western Macedonia.' (1995: 4). However, his foreign minister and the majority of Greeks focused on the name. Mass mobilisation and a colossal demonstration in February 1992 played a catalytic role in pushing Greek policy to extremes. More than a million Greeks, according to some estimates, descended upon the Macedonian capital in Greece to express their support for the 'Greekness' of Macedonia. No politician can ignore the voice of so many voters gathered in a single place and determined to make themselves heard. The demonstration electrified public opinion and confirmed the argument made by Greek politicians at the time to their counterparts in Europe that Macedonia was a major issue for the Greek people (Tziampiris 2000).

Consistent with the MSF's expectations, emotion reverberating across policy publics helped to keep the issue high on the agenda. Whereas foreign policy was not on the minds of the public in November 1991 – it was ninth in terms of importance – it shot up to second by June 1992. Public opinion polls in June 1992 revealed that 60.2 per cent of Greeks considered the Macedonian issue to be the most important foreign-policy issue. In a different poll two years later, although 88.5 per cent were in favour of a dialogue with FYROM, 60 per cent did not support compromise over the name (Loulis 1995: 123–4, 130). The Greek foreign minister at the time, Antonis Samaras, made it clear: 'there are strong emotions in northern Greece, in Greek Macedonia' (Tziampiris 2000: appendix I). This argument was used by the reluctant Prime Minister to justify rejecting any compromise that included recognition of the new state under the name Macedonia or its derivatives. Any other option was viewed as a national loss and a public humiliation.

The emotional-endowment effect expects persistence of fear and inconsistent preferences to make policy less likely to change, despite acknowledged failure. This was indeed the case. Within the politics stream, many members of the prime minister's own party and policy-makers across the political spectrum in Greece and abroad openly considered Greek policy to be a failure. Samaras dates 'defeat' to have begun in March 1992, when the Greek government openly began talking about a compromise over the name. Michalis Papakonstantinou (1994: 65), foreign minister from August 1992 to October 1993, became highly discouraged by the 'hyperbole', as he calls it – the emotional attachment to a particular dimension of the issue that made Greece see threats and enemies everywhere. 'We appeared unreasonable,' he told me in an interview (August 1995), 'while [FYROM's] Gligorov comes across as the moderate even though he, too, refuses to compromise'. Outside Greece, commentators and diplomats thought Greeks were simply paranoid; they argued instead for a 'rational' compromise (for example, Rizopoulos 1993). Indeed, it was the high level of emotion that made Greeks unable or unwilling to accept the EC's compromise offer in April 1992. According to a well informed academic, that was the best deal the Greeks could have achieved: 'The game was lost after that' (interview with the author, November 1994).

As the logic of appropriateness suggests, whereas rational leaders view loss-accumulation as negative feedback prompting corrective action, the presence of an emotionally charged national mood leads to policy continuity, further amplifying losses (defined as loss of domestic political and external diplomatic support for current policy). Not believing in a policy they were publicly advocating, Mitsotakis and Papakonstantinou privately tried to compromise over the name. But a fearful public and an emotionally charged section of the policy-making elite successfully averted what Lygeros (2008: 158) calls 'nationally detrimental solutions'. Although the emotional outburst can be traced back to the Greek sense of cultural heritage, some politicians and journalists also carefully cultivated fear and insecurity. Andreas Papandreou and Antonis Samaras were the biggest culprits. Papandreou, the opposition leader, used deliberately inflammatory language to attack the 'government of Athens' for following 'a treasonous, appeasing policy that sells out a little part of our country every day' (Skylakakis 1995: 172). Walden (1994: 76–7) explains the national hysteria as the result of the nationalist lobby that cuts across parties and of Papandreou's tactic of extremism. 'With much surprise we discover enemies everywhere: everyone is against us.' An analysis of local media reports leads Roudometof (1996: 260) to conclude the same thing. Intellectuals, journalists, and politicians contributed to this campaign of creating extremism and fear (Kyrkos 1994), a Greek 'crusade' as Loulis (1995: 127) called it. While all analysts saw Greek policy at the time as too costly to be sustainable, any change of course was also viewed domestically as defeat.

Confirming the MSF's expectations, high salience and inconsistent preferences magnified the effects of fear, which prevented any policy change. The more the Greek government tried to reach some form of compromise, the more vocal the opposition became against a compromise. Prime Minister Mitsotakis (in Skylakakis 1995: 4) puts it best. While explaining why he was tied to an unsustainably costly policy with which he did not agree, he says: 'an uncontrollable dynamic developed ... A tidal wave just swept us under.' When FYROM was accepted as a member of the UN under a provisional name, politicians saw it as capitulation. The foreign minister at the time defended the action as a triumph in light of a nearly hostile environment in the Security Council, especially among its non-aligned members (Papakonstantinou 1994: 277). But Stelios Papathemelis (n.d.: 21–2), a prominent member of the opposition Socialists, saw it as one more loss in the government's 'sell-out' policy: 'How is it possible for the government to "triumph" and for the country to lose? ... Hellenism stands before national humiliation.' Samaras (1994: 82) was even more critical of his former boss: 'In the negotiations at the UN, we will only give in, only Gligorov will win, we will encounter only insults and humiliations ...' Any dialogue and the consequent give-and-take would be regarded as a loss. Even members of the governing party summarily rejected the proposed compromise offered by UN mediators, Cyrus Vance and Lord Owen, in 1993 (Papakonstantinou 1994: 408). The government's decision to resume the dialogue through direct negotiations in New York ultimately led to defections, which caused the dissolution of parliament. General elections were called in October 1993. The winning Socialists withdrew from the negotiations at the UN, altering the dynamics of Greek foreign policy.

In sum, a novel focusing event drew attention to the problem of recognising FYROM as an independent state. The task was very complex, making it extremely difficult for the Greek government to accomplish its objective. While the prime minister favoured one option, a fearful national mood deliberately stoked and manipulated by his foreign minister and several of his colleagues and opposition policy-makers forced him to choose otherwise. The policy of no compromise proved very costly but the more he tried to implement it, the less he accomplished and the costlier the policy became. In line with the emotional-endowment effect, accumulating losses were viewed as capitulation to outside pressure, which strengthened the resolve for more continuity than change. The power unleashed by stirring up fear shaped preferences in ways that elevated the political cost of subsequent change, effectively rendering the prime minister powerless.

US policy in Iraq, 2001–4

The events of 11 September 2001 opened a policy-window. The consequent emotions of fear and insecurity were carefully nurtured and targeted for political gain. Looking at the first Bush administration, I probe US policy and the war in Iraq. It is reminiscent of strategies crafted by some Greek politicians to manipulate a negative national mood in pursuit of policy continuity despite heavy losses. In the US case, however, leaders were manipulators rather than manipulated. They cultivated fear to rationalise policy and used it as an argument to stifle opposition, despite increasingly heavy losses. While I don't argue that US politics mirrors Greek politics, I do claim the emotional-endowment effect is applicable in many settings. The policy that led to war in Iraq had all the elements of heuristic thinking. It involved a highly complex, unfamiliar task and a salient issue that dominated the headlines for many years, triggered by a novel event that resulted in fear. Consistent with the MSF's expectations, the mood biased coupling toward some solutions and away from others.

The terrorist attacks of 11 September 2001 on the World Trade Center and the Pentagon were major and novel events that are said to have changed everything (Birkland 2004). Although the attacks were not similar in intensity or material consequences for the US as FYROM's declaration of independence was for Greece, they damaged the national psyche. Being novel events, the attacks captured attention and instilled fear, anger, and insecurity in the national mood and the policy-making elites (Bennett 2002). As the *Economist* put it succinctly in an editorial:

> an increasing number of people say they think the future for their children got worse after September 11th … Americans … felt secure … They no longer do … The peace ended that day. As a result, personal insecurity was added to the mix [of less prosperity and no peace] (editorial reprinted in Cigler 2002: 6).

Beliefs were problematic because no one knew what to do. How does one fight a war on terror? There was no blueprint from the nation's past, although entrepreneurial leaders such as President Bush, Vice President Dick Cheney, Secretary of Defense Donald Rumsfeld, and Deputy Secretary of Defense Paul Wolfowitz had very concrete ideas about what to do: in addition to all else, topple Saddam (Woodward 2004; Daalder and Lindsay 2005).

Consistent with expectations, in the presence of ambiguity, terrorism became a symbol whose affective elements could easily travel to other issues and be attached to Iraq, however tangential the cognitive association may have been. President Bush and Secretary Rumsfeld deny ever postulating a direct link between the masterminds of the attacks on 9/11 and Iraq, even though most Americans – according to a poll by the *Washington Post* – and former Vice President Cheney believed in mid 2003 that Saddam Hussein was personally involved in the 9/11 attacks (*USA Today* 2003). As the MSF predicts, all three policy-entrepreneurs in addition to Wolfowitz carefully framed the problem by cultivating the idea of the terrorist threat posed by Saddam and the need to eliminate him. They knew how to 'sell' the war to a fearful public by claiming an imminent threat and by marginalising presidential advisers who disagreed (Bye 2004; Packer 2005). For example, in his 2002 State of the Union address, President Bush famously posited the existence of an 'axis of evil' and the urgency of war. 'I will not stand by as peril draws closer and closer.' And he continued: 'we cannot wait for the final proof' (Daalder and Lindsay 2005: 147).

With the mounting cost of maintaining a presence in Iraq, why did America continue its policy in Iraq throughout the first Bush administration, despite increasingly heavy casualties in both material and human terms? Foreign policy is likely to change, as prospect theorists inform us (Welch 2005), when leaders expect the *status quo* to produce even more painful losses. Vis (2009) further argues that a failing political position will trigger policy reversal. And yet policy in this case remained the same. The reason is that Americans were emotionally vested in the policy. The MSF predicts no change because changing policy would not only imply the admission of error in judgment on the part of the administration but also a change in affective response. A reversal of policy would be an affront to all the lives lost in the war (Ginsberg and Davies 2007: 94). Candidate John McCain made it even more explicit during his 2008 presidential campaign:

> It would be an unconscionable act of betrayal, a stain on our character as a great nation, if we were to walk away from the Iraqi people and consign them to the horrendous violence, ethnic cleansing and possibly genocide that would follow a reckless, irresponsible and premature withdrawal (Kornblut and Shear 2008).

To take the counter-factual, if current policy was crafted partly as a result of the fear and insecurity brought about by an act of terrorism, a dramatic change in policy would imply a causal shift in emotion to happiness or at least relaxation. If fear leads to confrontation, a shift to co-operation would logically imply that it is in response to a more positive emotion. By the end of 2004, there was no indication that Americans were appreciably less worried about terrorism or less fearful and insecure about the potentially catastrophic consequences of terrorism. For example, according to Gallup/CNN/*USA Today* polls, 51 per cent of Americans were worried or somewhat worried that they might fall victims to terrorist attacks in 14–15 September 2001. By 14–16 October 2004 the number had dropped by only 4 per cent. Did the war in Iraq make Americans feel more or less safe? According to polls by the same companies, on 10 April 2003, 51 per cent of Americans felt safer. The emotional endowment effect in the MSF predicts continuation of confrontational policy as the result of a fearful mood. By 21–4 June 2004, the number of Americans who felt safer dropped to 37 per cent (AEI 2009: 63). The fearful national mood prevented other solutions from being coupled in Iraq.

The task of fighting the war and subsequently occupying Iraq proved to be a very complex, unfamiliar and loss-making proposition in lives, material, and diplomatic goodwill, fostering affect-infusion. The administration was caught completely unprepared and unwilling to rebuild Iraq, at least initially, because the task proved to be too complex and the expertise too scarce (Packer 2005). In terms of human losses, the situation got grimmer by the day. US confirmed military casualties quickly mounted from sixty-five in March 2003 to 1,126 on the eve of the presidential election in early November 2004. The number of American wounded climbed from 208 to 8,446 during the same period (Icasualties.org). Estimating the overall cost of Operation Iraqi Freedom is tricky because the administration was not forthcoming with numbers, for obvious reasons. The more reliable figures came from the Congressional Budget Office. It estimated that up to March 2004, the US cost for routine military operations alone, not including reconstruction, amounted to $71.3 billion (CBO 2004).

Diplomatic losses began to mount but, consistent with the MSF's expectations, policy remained the same. Public opinion in most developed countries did not support military action in Iraq (Chan and Safran 2006). The more militarily assertive US policy became, the more strained relations became between the US and many of its allies, as their governments struggled to balance support for US policy in the face of public opposition. Spain is a good example. As the number of wavering allies grew, fear and insecurity in the US intensified. As the argument predicts, more losses fuelled more fear, which strengthened American resolve to continue the policy.

Even if it could have been shown that the country might gain from adopting a more co-operative posture, the confrontational nature of US policy would not have changed. Emotional inertia negates any immediate re-framing effects. Just as the negative image that many Iraqis and Arabs throughout the Middle East have of the US will be long-lasting and hard to change because of the emotional trauma caused by the Iraq invasion (Turner 2004), America's ability to change policy was constrained by the public fear generated by the trauma of 9/11 and subsequent events. Although beliefs can be altered in light of new evidence, emotions are not as easily susceptible. The negative emotion that nurtures and reinforces confrontation is locked in closed-loop iteration. The power to dominate through affect-arousal biased coupling in ways that supported an unchanged policy, even when mounting losses and increasing opposition strongly pushed for change.

If the argument holds, how can the eventual withdrawal from Iraq be explained? Wouldn't the national mood have kept President Barack Obama from pulling out US forces as well? The answer is no, for two reasons. First, as the scope conditions in the beginning of this chapter make clear, a change in government opens a policy-window that favours new solutions and problem-frames. The new leadership is no longer attached to the national mood in the same way the old one was, because it did not cultivate any emotional links to the particular solution coupled to the mood. Indeed, President Obama was able to argue convincingly for a withdrawal by stressing the cost and toning down the benefits of the policy. During his campaign in 2008, he makes it clear:

> I opposed the war in Iraq before it began, and would end it as president. I believed it was a grave mistake to allow ourselves to be distracted from the fight against Al Qaeda and the Taliban by invading a country that posed no imminent threat and had nothing to do with the 9/11 attacks (Obama 2008).

Second, the passions raised in 2003 in support of invading Iraq had subsided by 2008. For example, a Gallup poll in October 2004 showed 44 per cent of the Americans asked considered the war in Iraq was a mistake. By October 2008 that figure rose to 58 per cent (Gallup 2014). Once fear subsided, the mood swung against staying in Iraq, making it possible for then-candidate Obama to overcome emotion as an obstacle to policy-change.

Conclusion

Why do leaders continue to pursue policies in light of heavy losses? Consistent with the MSF's expectations, the Greek and US cases empirically support the claim that affect has a strong impact for a longer period of time when governments face novel events that evoke negative emotions and when they are engaged in heuristic processes. The MSF proves useful not only in explaining domestic policy-agendas, which it was originally developed to do, but also foreign-policy decisions. The propositions enrich the MSF and amend arguments about policy-change and political leadership.

The role of the national mood has been downplayed in some applications of the MSF (for example, Zahariadis 2003). The argument here amends this conceptualisation by strengthening the mood's impact in the political stream, linking it to political leadership and coupling in two different national settings. As the national mood becomes more intense, policies accompanying the mood become inextricably tied to it. The Greek case suggests (Zahariadis 2016) and the US case validates: the higher the intensity of emotion, the higher the political cost will be of changing the policies used to arouse it. The more leaders seek to foster a political climate of emotive appeal, the more successful their coupling strategy becomes; but the more constrained they subsequently are when they attempt to change course. Moreover, sustaining coalitions under certain conditions is more effective through cultivating a negative mood. Enriching the MSF, the study finds the mood is a blunt but effective instrument of opposition. Raising fear can effectively block policy-change.

March and Olsen (2008: 690) describe policy-making as often driven by matching appropriate rules or expectations to specific types of situations, using cognitive criteria of similarity and congruence. My argument enriches the MSF's coupling strategies by adding the impact of emotion. Political leaders, especially in foreign policy, often act as policy-entrepreneurs. But they can do one more thing that entrepreneurs do not. While entrepreneurs pursue numerous strategies to define problems and build teams (Mintrom 2000; Mintrom and Norman 2009), leaders may also pursue affective-congruence strategies by coupling the political and problem streams because they have a 'bully pulpit'. They not only take advantage of the national mood, they also nurture and steer it toward defining problems in a specific and public way. In other words, they build political coalitions around similar values or objectives *and* around similar emotions, especially through cultivating negative emotions. As emotions grow more intense, policies accompanying those emotions become inextricably tied to them.

The MSF logic adopted here amends theories of policy-change and the role of losses as corrective mechanisms. Losses are traditionally viewed as negative feedback but high sunk costs may lead rational policy-makers to hang on to a costly policy. For example, Thaler's endowment effect under prospect theory (1980) shows that people overvalue their possessions, altering the standard cost/benefit ratios. As losses accumulate, pressures for corrective action continue to build. The issue is recognising the point at which losses outweigh gains. The problem with this way of thinking is that it assumes there is a critical threshold. Determining a threshold level in public policy is extremely difficult because that is never specified beforehand, even if such a level exists. In the absence of prior specification, it becomes subject to reinterpretation and *post-hoc* rationalisation.

Consider the case of the Iraq war. The argument that policy had to stay the same despite heavy losses because of high sunk costs is intuitively appealing but fundamentally flawed. It assumes benefits are clearly defined and losses are viewed as a stimulus for corrective action (beyond a certain level). There is no evidence to indicate there was ever a tipping point or a calculus signifying the point at which losses might outweigh benefits. The definition of benefits shifted from eliminating weapons of mass destruction to liberating the Iraqi people to establishing democracy in the Middle East. When there is a constant redefinition of benefits and no exit strategy (the tipping point), the concept of losses as sunk costs is irrelevant. The latter makes sense only when costs are valued in comparison to consistently measured benefits.

Under conditions of ambiguity, the emotional-endowment effect implies that losses constitute positive feedback with no tipping point. Consistent with the MSF's logic of appropriateness, losses amplify the emotive appeal of an issue. In contrast to rational choice and prospect theories, the concept of loss in the MSF is perceptually twisted by affect. Losses fuel fear, which strengthens the resolve for continuity rather than change. Whereas rational leaders consider loss-accumulation as reason for corrective action, the emotional-endowment effect views it as validation for staying the course. Confrontation is 'sticky' when governments are faced with emotionally charged publics. Not only will they pursue more confrontational policies to avoid losing more, but their public is also likely to stifle the opposition and stick with this option, making it very difficult to change course. Under certain conditions, emotional inertia negates any immediate (re)framing effects, fuelling path-dependence.

Success also contains the seed of its demise. As political leaders succeed in changing the world, they also undermine the political coalition that keeps them in power. The paradox is that the same emotion that leaders use to couple the problem, policy and political streams by steering support and undermining opposition to their pet policies also constrains their freedom to act later. The MSF highlights the point that emotion is both an asset and a liability in public policy.

References

American Enterprise Institute (AEI) (2009) *Public Opinion on the War with Iraq*, available at: https://www.aei.org/wp-content/uploads/2012/01/-aeipublic opinioniraq2009_133351682593.pdf (accessed 28 September 2015).

Bennett, W. J. (2002) *Why We Fight: Moral clarity and the war on terrorism*, New York: Doubleday.

Birkland, T. A. (2004) 'The world changed today: agenda-setting and policy change in the wake of the September 11 terrorist attacks', *Review of Policy Research* 21(2): 179–200.

Blascovich, J. and Mendes, W. (2000) 'Challenge and threat appraisals: the role of affective cues', in, J. P. Forgas (ed.) *Feeling and Thinking: The role of affect in social cognition*, Cambridge, UK: Cambridge University Press, pp. 59–82.

Calne, D. B. (1999) *Within Reason*, New York: Pantheon Books.

Chan, S. and Safran, W. (2006) 'Public opinion as a constraint against war: democracies' responses to operation Iraqi Freedom', *Foreign Policy Analysis* 2(2): 137–56.

Cigler, A. J. (ed.) (2002) *Perspectives on Terrorism: How 9/11 changed US politics*, Boston, MA and New York: Houghton Mifflin.

CBO (Congressional Budget Office) (2004) Letter to the Honorable Kent Conrad, 25 June, available at: http://www.cbo.gov/doc.cfm?index=5587&type=0 (accessed 18 September 2014).

Daalder, I. H. and Lindsay, J. M. (2005) *America Unbound: The Bush revolution in foreign policy*, rev. edn, Washington, DC: Brookings Institution Press.

Fiedler, K. (1990) 'Mood dependent selectivity in social cognition', in W. Stroebe and M. Hewstone (eds) *Special Issue: European Review of Social Psychology* 1(1): New York: Wiley, pp. 1–32.

Fischer, F. (2009) *Democracy and Expertise: Reorienting policy inquiry*, Oxford, UK: Oxford University Press.

Forgas, J. P. (2001) 'The affect infusion model (AIM): an integrative theory of mood effects on cognition and judgments', in L. L Martin and G. L Clore (eds) *Theories of Mood and Cognition: A user's handbook*, Mahwah, NJ: Lawrence Erlbaum, pp. 99–134.

Gallup (2014) *Iraq*, available at: http://www.gallup.com/poll/1633/iraq.aspx (accessed 18 September 2014).

Gardner, D. (2009) *The Science of Fear*, New York: Plume.

George, A. L. and George, J. L. (1998) *Presidential Personality and Performance*, Boulder, CO: Westview Press.

Ginsberg, R. and Davies, T. G. (2007) *The Human side of Leadership*, Westport, CT: Praeger.

Huddy, L., Feldman, S., Taber, C. and Lahav, G. (2005) 'Threat, anxiety, and support of antiterrorism policies', *American Journal of Political Science* 49(3): 593–608.

Icasualties.org (2009) 'Iraq coalition casualty count', available at: http://icasualties. org/Iraq/index.aspx (accessed 15 August 2009).

Kamm, H. (1994) 'Greek prime minister insists Macedonia endangers his country', *New York Times*, April 7, available at: http://www.nytimes. com/1994/04/07/world/greek-prime-minister-insists-macedonia- endangers-his-country.html] (accessed 10 September 2014).

Keltner, D. and Lerner, J. S. (2010) 'Emotion', in D. T. Gilbert, S. T. Fiske and G. Lindzey (eds) *The Handbook of Social Psychology*, New York: Wiley, pp. 317–52.

Kingdon, J. W. (1995) *Agendas, Alternatives, and Public Policies*, 2nd edn, New York: HarperCollins.

Kofos, E. (2001) 'Greek policy considerations over FYROM independence and recognition', in J. Pettifer (ed.) *The New Macedonian Question*, New York: Palgrave, pp. 226–62.

Kornblut, A. E. and Shear, M. D. (2008) 'Candidates refine their stances on a changing Iraq', *Washington Post*, July 9, suburban edn, available at: http://www.washingtonpost.com/wp-dyn/content/article/2008/07/08/ AR2008070803127.html] (accessed 15 September 2014).

Kotter, J. P. (1999) *On What Leaders Really Do*, Cambridge, MA: Harvard Business Review Press.

Kühberger, A. (1998) 'The influence of framing on risky decisions: a meta- analysis', *Organizational Behavior & Human Decision Processes* 75(1): 23–55.

Kyrkos, L. (1994) *The Dead-End Path of Nationalism* [in Greek], Athens: Themelio.

Langston, T. S. (2007) 'The "decider's" path to war in Iraq and the importance of personality', in G. C. Edwards III and D. King (eds) *The Polarized Presidency of George W. Bush*, Oxford, UK: Oxford University Press, pp. 145–72.

Lerner, J. S., Small, D. A. and Loewenstein, G. (2004) 'Heart strings and purse strings: carryover effects of emotions on economic decisions', *Psychological Science* 15(5): 337–41.

Loulis, G. (1995) 'Public opinion and foreign policy: 1994 as a turning point', in Hellenic Foundation for European and Foreign Policy (ELIAMEP) *Yearbook of Defense and Foreign Policy '95* [in Greek], Athens: ELIAMEP, pp. 121–35.

Lygeros, S. (2008) *In the Name of Macedonia* [in Greek], Athens: Livanis.

Neuman, W. R., Marcus, G. E. and Mackuen, M. (eds) (2007) *The Affect Effect*, Chicago: University of Chicago Press.

March, J. G. and Olsen J. P. (2008) 'The logic of appropriateness', in R. E. Goodin, M. Moran and M. Rein (eds) *The Oxford Handbook of Public Policy*, Oxford: Oxford University Press, pp. 689–708.

Marcus, G. E., Neuman, W. R. and MacKuen, M. (2000) *Affective Intelligence and Political Judgment*, Chicago: University of Chicago Press.

Martin, L. L. (2000) 'Moods do not convey information: moods in context do', in J. P. Forgas (ed.) *Feeling and Thinking: The role of affect in social cognition*, Cambridge, UK: Cambridge University Press, pp. 153–77.

Mazzar, M. J. (2007) 'The Iraq war and agenda setting', *Foreign Policy Analysis* 3(1): 1–24.

Mintrom, M. (2000) *Policy Entrepreneurs and School Choice*, Washington, DC: Georgetown University Press.

Mintrom, M. and Norman, P. (2009) 'Policy entrepreneurship and policy change', *Policy Studies Journal* 37(4): 649–67.

Munson, Z. W. (2009) *The Making of Pro-life Activists*, Chicago: University of Chicago Press.

Neuman, W. R., Marcus, G. E., Crigler, A. N. and Mackuen, M. (eds) (2007) *The Affect Effect*, Chicago: University of Chicago Press.

Niedenthal, P. M. and Halberstadt, J. B. (2000) 'Emotional response and conceptual coherence', in E. Eich *et al.* (eds) *Cognition and Emotion*, Oxford, UK: Oxford University Press, pp. 169–203.

Obama, B. (2008) 'My plan for Iraq', *New York Times*, 14 July, available at: http://www.nytimes.com/2008/07/14/opinion/14obama.html?_r=0 (accessed 15 September 2014).

Packer, G. (2005) *The Assassin's Gate: America in Iraq*, New York: Farrar, Straus & Giroux.

Papakonstantinou, M. (1994) *The Diary of a Politician*, [in Greek] Athens: Estia.

Papathemelis, S. (n.d.) *National Awakening*, [in Greek] Thessaloniki: Barbounakis.

Peters, E. (2006) 'The functions of affect in the construction of preferences', in S. Lichtenstein and P. Slovic (eds) *The Construction of Preference*, New York: Cambridge University Press, pp. 454–63.

Pfister, H-R. and Böhm, G. (2008) 'The multiplicity of emotions: a framework of emotional functions in decision making', *Judgment & Decision Making* 3(1): 5–17.

Pierson, P. (2004) *Politics in Time*, Princeton, NJ: Princeton University Press.

Rizopoulos, N. X. (1993) 'A third Balkan war?', *World Policy Journal* 10(2): 1–5.

Roudometof, V. (1996) 'Nationalism and identity politics in the Balkans: Greece and the Macedonian question', *Journal of Modern Greek Studies* 14(2): 253–301.

Samaras, A. (1994) 'The Skopjean issue', in Hellenic Foundation for European and Foreign Policy (ELIAMEP) *Yearbook of Defense and Foreign Policy '94* [in Greek], Athens: ELIAMEP, pp. 75–83.

Sasley, B. E. (2010) 'Affective attachments and foreign policy: Israel and the 1993 Oslo Accords', *European Journal of International Relations* 16(4): 687–709.

Schwarz, N. (2001) 'Feelings as information: implications for affective influences on information processing', in L. L. Martin and G. L. Clore (eds) *Theories Of Mood and Cognition: A user's handbook*, Mahwah, NJ: Lawrence Erlbaum, pp. 159–76.

Simon, H. A. (1983) *Reason in Human Affairs*, Stanford, CA: Stanford University Press.

Skylakakis, T. (1995) *In the Name of Macedonia* [in Greek], Athens: Elliniki Euroekdotiki.

Slothuus, R. (2008) 'More than weighting cognitive importance: a dual-process model of issue framing effects', *Political Psychology* 29(1): 1–28.

Thaler, R. (1980) 'Toward a positive theory of consumer choice', *Journal of Economic Behavior & Organization* 1(1): 39–60.

Turner, M. (2004) 'Dashed hopes leave scars on Iraqi hearts and minds', *Financial Times*, 23 July, p. 14.

Tziampiris, A. (2000) *Greece, European Political Cooperation and the Macedonian Question*, Burlington, VT: Ashgate.

USA Today (2003) 'Rumsfeld sees no link between Saddam Hussein, 9/11', 16 September, available at: www.usatoday.com/news/world/iraq/2003–09–16-rumsfeld-iraq-911_x.htm (accessed 15 September 2014).

Valinakis, G. and Dalis, S. (eds) (1994) *The Skopjean Issue* [in Greek], Athens: Sideris.

Vis, B. (2009) 'Governments and unpopular social policy reform: biting the bullet or steering clear?', *European Journal of Political Research* 48(1): 31–57.

Wallis, J. and Dollery B. (1997) 'Autonomous policy leadership: steering a policy process in the direction of a policy quest', *Governance* 10(1): 1–22.

Welch, D. A. (2005) *Painful Choices: A theory of foreign policy change*, Princeton, NJ: Princeton University Press.

Wenzelburger, G. (2011) 'Political strategies and fiscal retrenchment: evidence from four countries', *West European Politics* 34(6): 1151–84.

Woodward, B. (2004) *Plan of Attack*, New York: Simon & Schuster.

Yin, R. K. (2014) *Case Study Research: Design and methods*, 5th edn, Thousand Oaks, CA: Sage.

Zahariadis, N. (1994) 'Is the Former Yugoslav Republic of Macedonia a security threat to Greece?', *Mediterranean Quarterly* 5(1): 84–105.

— (2003) *Ambiguity and Choice in Public Policy*, Washington, DC: Georgetown University Press.

— (2005) *Essence of Political Manipulation: Emotion, institutions, and Greek foreign policy*, New York: Peter Lang.

— (2015) 'The Shield of Herakles: multiple streams and the emotional endowment effect', *European Journal of Political Research* 54(3): 466–81.

PART THREE

THE APPLICABILITY OF THE MULTIPLE-STREAMS FRAMEWORK IN PARLIAMENTARY AND MULTI-LEVEL SYSTEMS

Chapter Ten

How Well Does the Multiple-Streams Framework Travel? Evidence from German Case Studies

Reimut Zohlnhöfer and Christian Huß

Introduction

The multiple-streams framework (MSF) was developed by John Kingdon (2003[1984]) with the presidential system of the United States in mind (Herweg 2013). Despite the substantial differences between presidential and parliamentary systems regarding key aspects of the MSF, a number of scholars, most notably Zahariadis (1995, 2003), have shown that the framework can also be applied to the more 'orderly parliamentary systems' (Zahariadis 2003: 1), with only a few modifications. Zahariadis (1995: 34), for example, suggested collapsing 'the three dimensions in the political stream labeled national mood, interest groups, and turnover into one conceptual variable: the ideology and strategy of governing parties'. He showed that, with this adaptation, the MSF was fit to be applied to parliamentary systems, too.

Nonetheless, the approach has mostly been applied to parliamentary systems with a low level of institutional pluralism and pluralist interest-group systems, like France, the UK and Greece (Zahariadis 1995, 2003; Münter 2005). These might be easy cases for an application of the framework, however, because the existence of single-party governments reduces the number of relevant actors substantially. In contrast, Germany – still a black spot for the MSF (Rüb 2009: 349) – is a polity characterised by its many veto-points, which allow many actors to have a say in policy-making. In this respect, Germany resembles the US political system, for the analysis of which the MSF was first devised. In contrast to the United States, however, Germany is a 'party state', that is to say, political parties play a central role in policy-making. Moreover, Germany is often classified as rather corporatist (see, for example, Siaroff 1999), which means that interest-groups, particularly trade unions and business associations, are integrated in economic and social policy-making more often than not. As reasonable policy-theories need to be applicable in a wide variety of different constitutional settings and policy-fields (see, for example, Sabatier 2007: 8), Germany should thus be a critical case for testing the MSF's empirical applicability.

In this chapter, we report how the MSF fared when applied to the veto-ridden German political system. The chapter is based on the analysis of several key decisions in the Federal Republic of Germany. In order to control for the effects of different government constellations and different policy-fields, these key decisions are taken from various time-periods and policy-fields. In detail, we follow the most important reforms in social policy, labour-market policy, tax policy and economic policy between the early 1980s and 2013. These reforms cover the most salient cleavage in German politics, namely, the socio-economic cleavage. As an example of 'morality politics', we looked at the abortion reforms in the 1970s and 1990s. In addition, we analysed policies regarding nuclear energy as the most salient issue of the post-materialist cleavage in Germany. Moreover, foreign policy is represented by the reform of policy towards the Eastern Bloc, including the GDR, of the Social-Democratic–Liberal coalition in the 1970s ('*Neue Ostpolitik*') as well as by the political processes that led to German unification (1989–90). Thus, our analysis covers policy processes from all coalition governments in power in Germany since 1969. Moreover, while some of these reforms were results of unforeseen problems that forced the responsible governments to act quite fast (particularly, unification and the reaction to the recent financial crisis), others were adopted in the face of much less pressing problems and thus reflected other factors, most notably, government ideology – or, put in MSF terminology: while in some instances policy-windows opened in the problem stream ('problem-windows' in Kingdon's terminology) allowing for consequential coupling (Zahariadis 2003: 72), other policy-windows opened in the politics stream ('political windows'), thus making doctrinal coupling (Zahariadis 2003: 72) possible. Therefore, the cases analysed here offer a lot of variation across different dimensions, which allows a thorough test of the MSF's applicability. The paper will not present the detailed case studies but will rather discuss how well the MSF was able to explain these different reforms and where it has to be amended to fit the veto-ridden, corporatist parliamentary system of Germany.

Our paper adds to various aspects of the literature. First, MSF is applied to a veto-ridden and somewhat corporatist parliamentary system while the overwhelming majority of previous contributions has been concerned either with presidential or with majoritarian parliamentary systems.[1] Second, the framework is systematically tested over very different political constellations, time-periods and policy-fields – to our knowledge, it is the first attempt at such an encompassing application of the framework. Finally, while our analysis generally proves the framework's travelling capacity, we suggest a number of adaptations which might make the MSF even better-apt to be applied empirically. This is true, in particular, regarding the policy and the political streams. With regard to the policy stream, we argue that parties play an important role in the generation and, above all, 'softening-up'[2] of ideas, at least in parliamentary systems like the German one. Thus, they have to be taken into account. As parties also play

---

1. Zahariadis and Allen (1995) are a partial exception as they, too, look at the German case. Zohlnhöfer and Herweg (2014) present a case study of a German labour-market reform.

2. The term 'softening-up' refers to the process of getting policy communities and larger publics used to new ideas and building acceptance for proposals (Kingdon 2003[1984]).

a role in the political stream, this might further qualify the independence of the streams, which was conceptualised as relative rather than absolute from the outset in the multiple-streams framework. Furthermore, further criteria of survival in the policy primeval soup can be added as policies also seem to stand less chance of surviving if their constitutionality is in doubt, if they do not conform to EU legislation and if they contradict previous regulations in areas in which path-dependence is relevant. Regarding the political stream, it turns out that it does not suffice to concentrate on parties, as suggested by Zahariadis (1995), because interest-groups and even the national mood can play important roles. Thus, in this respect, we suggest returning to Kingdon's original conception. Finally, regarding the problem stream, we show that policy-makers in a party-driven parliamentary system are more likely to perceive a condition as a problem when the condition might put the government's re-election at risk.

The chapter is organised as follows. We will discuss the five main elements of the multiple-streams framework, that is, the three streams, the policy-window and policy-entrepreneurs, separately and discuss whether and to what extent these concepts could be applied to our cases and where modifications seemed necessary or helpful. The final section concludes.

The streams

In this section, we discuss in which ways (if in any) the three streams of the multiple-streams approach need to be adapted to fit policy-making in the veto-ridden corporatist German polity.

Policy stream

The policy stream turns out to be the stream that most needs to be amended. Given the dominance of political parties in parliamentary democracies in general and in Germany in particular, it is not surprising that parties do play a more important role in the policy stream than theorised by Kingdon and Zahariadis. Moreover, as Germany also counts as corporatist, we also need to take a look at the role interest-groups play in the policy stream. Moreover, the case studies conducted for this chapter show that more criteria for the survival of policy-proposals in the policy primeval soup can be distinguished.

The role of parties in the policy primeval soup

The adaptation of the concept of the policy-stream to German policy-making (and probably more generally to policy-making in parliamentary democracies) is not trivial. One major reason for this difficulty is the much more important role of political parties in parliamentary democracies (see Herweg, Huß and Zohlnhöfer 2015). German parties, just like parties in most other West European polities, are not only concerned about fighting election campaigns; they also work out policy proposals. It is certainly true that a number of policies put forward by parties are based on ideas from outside experts, bureaucrats, interest-groups or individual ministers. Nonetheless, in many fields, parties work out proposals themselves in specialised groups of MPs and/or party-activists. The revision of foreign and inner-German policy priorities after 1969, which led to the negotiation of treaties with most East European countries, including the GDR, is a case in point. These policy-options were worked out inside the two parties that would eventually form the government after 1969. The Social-Democratic party position was very much influenced by Willy Brandt, who became Chancellor in 1969. Brandt's position evolved over the 1950s and 1960s and reflected input from a number of people (Schmidt 2003: 533, 542, 549–51) but none of these people (among them American diplomat George Kennan and British philosopher Bertrand Russell) were themselves members of the (German) policy-community. The foreign-policy position of the Liberal party was also mainly influenced by contributions of party members and MPs like Wolfgang Schollwer, Hans Wolfgang Rubin and Hans Dieter Jaene (for details, see Baring 1982: 211–29). What is more, much of the softening-up of proposals did not occur in a policy community of experts that engage in arguing about which is the most convincing proposal. Rather, the process of softening-up often took place in the parties themselves (see Schmidt 2003: 546–7 for the SPD and Baring 1982: 218–20 for the FDP) and later in the coalition government.

One might, of course, argue that foreign policy is not representative of other policy-fields; but examples in which parties played a central role in the softening-up process also abound in domestic policy. Take the economic policy of the government of Christian-Democrats and Liberals in the 1980s as an example (for the following, see Zohlnhöfer 2001: 48–50). Two politicians from the Christian-Democrats' business wing, Ernst Albrecht and Haimo George, acted as policy-entrepreneurs and started circulating policy papers that proposed far-reaching reforms to the tax system, the labour market and the welfare state. Although the ideas themselves were well known from supply-side economic thinking, these policy-entrepreneurs were the ones who introduced them into the debate of their party. The policy papers, in turn, sparked a debate inside the party about the best way to deal with the economic problems and found their way (although in a much-diluted form) into an official party document and later into some relevant bills. Interestingly, the softening-up in this case was very much confined to the party itself, too, while the coalition partner discussed similar proposals independently – and with different outcomes, which, in turn, necessitated a second step, of bargaining over government policy.

Moreover, in some cases, policy-proposals are indeed worked out in policy-communities not directly linked to party-politics. The reform of German abortion legislation in the 1970s is a case in point. In 1970, a group of liberal law professors produced a concept for a reform of criminal law in general and of abortion regulation in particular that served more or less as a blueprint for the reform (Gante 1991: 121). Nonetheless, parties played an enormously important role here, too, as the dominant figures of the group of law professors were, at the same time, leading politicians of the Liberal Party (FDP).[3] Similarly, in many other fields parties took up ideas from outside experts but adapted them or merged them with other proposals.

In sum, it can be concluded that parties are an integral part of the policy stream in Germany. In quite a number of instances they have worked out proposals themselves. But even when the original ideas came from bureaucrats or outside experts, a substantial part of the softening-up takes place inside political parties, which regularly adapt proposals to their programmatic stance before they adopt them. Given the important role of parties in the policy stream and their equally important role in the political stream, this finding, however, could put the (even relative) independence of the streams in question. Nonetheless, in our interpretation this is not a serious problem for the MSF as long as the two streams operate in different ways – and the case studies generally point to the fact that this is indeed the case.

Do interest-groups matter in the policy stream?

Given that Germany usually scores reasonably high on corporatism rankings (see Siaroff 1999), one might wonder whether this integration of interest-groups in economic and social policy-making also results in a significant role for interest-groups in the policy-community. In contrast to some other Western European countries, notably the Scandinavian countries, Austria and the Netherlands, German corporatism is not particularly strong at the macro (national) level, however. The few attempts that were made to introduce macro-level consultation and co-operation failed (see, for example, Streeck 2003). Thus, macro-level corporatism would not need to be included in the policy stream.

Nonetheless, at least in some cases, it turns out that representatives of interest-groups were indeed extremely influential in the policy stream. One example is Walter Riester, a secretary of the metal-workers' union and later Minister of Social Affairs, who had advocated the introduction of a further private (or, initially, occupational) pillar of the pension system (for the details, see Trampusch 2006: 67–70). On the one hand, this case is very important: it is rather difficult to imagine how the 2001 pension reform could have been adopted without Riester's proposals. On the other hand, large parts of the trade-union movement were opposed to the plan and it is thus difficult to argue that the trade unions were relevant themselves. It was rather Riester himself and – again – partisan actors who were active in the softening-up of the initial proposal.

---

3.   Werner Maihofer was a member of the party's executive committee (*Präsidium*), chairman of the FDP's programme commission and, later, Minister of Interior; Jürgen Baumann was deputy head of the party's working-group (*Bundesfachausschuss*) on justice and home affairs and later Minister of Justice in the *Land* government of Berlin; Ulrich Klug was also a member of the party's working-group on justice and home affairs and later served as state secretary in the Ministry of Justice in North Rhine-Westphalia and as Minister of Justice in the *Land* government of Hamburg (Gindulis 2003: 98; with authors' own additions).

A more compelling case of interest-groups being active in the policy stream is the so-called 'scrapping bonus', which was introduced in reaction to the financial crisis in 2009 in order to prevent the collapse of the market for automobiles. According to this provision, which was in force for less than a year, buyers of a new car got €2,500 if they scrapped their current automobile – provided it was at least nine years old. This provision can be traced back directly to an initiative from the German Association of the Automotive Industry (VDA).

In sum, interest-groups do, at times, play a role in the policy stream but, overall, that role is limited – which is quite surprising, given that Germany is often classified as a corporatist system in the literature. Quite certainly, much more research is needed in this regard but, for now, it seems reasonable not to overstate the importance of interest-groups when it comes to working out proposals for new policies (rather than in organising campaigns against certain reforms, which we will discuss later).

Further criteria for survival?

As a result of our case studies, more criteria for the survival of proposals in the policy primeval soup can be added to Kingdon's list. One highly relevant criterion in the German case is the constitutionality of a bill. Klaus von Beyme (1997: 304) found that 40 per cent of German key decisions were actually brought before the Federal Constitutional Court. The proportion of bills for which questions of constitutionality are critically discussed in the agenda-setting stage is even larger. For example, Zohlnhöfer (2001: 38), in his study on economic policy-making in the 1980s and 1990s, argues that questions of constitutionality were relevant for almost all the bills he analysed; and, for some of them, committees even held hearings specifically on matters of constitutionality. A case in point is tax policy. According to Ganghof (2006), arguments on constitutionality were one of the main reasons why it took two decades to lower German business-tax rates to levels that were internationally competitive. The reason was, essentially, that constitutional lawyers argued that a cut in the corporate-tax rate had to be accompanied by a more or less similarly large cut to the top income-tax rate, to satisfy the constitutional rule of equal treatment. This meant that governments had to choose between keeping business-tax rates at levels much higher than elsewhere in the OECD (with the likely consequence of investment going elsewhere) or accepting substantial revenue losses, most of which benefitted wealthy individuals (a policy option that was rather unpopular among the voters). Therefore, proposals that aimed at limiting tax cuts to companies without reducing the tax burden for high-income individuals did not stand a chance in the policy stream as soon as doubts about their constitutionality became serious. Other examples for the relevance of constitutionality in the policy stream include foreign policy, where a formal recognition of the GDR was seen as unconstitutional (for example, Wolfrum 2005: 374) or the attempts to reform abortion law, which were very much influenced by the fact that the Federal Constitutional Court had declared a policy as unconstitutional in 1975 that allowed the termination of a pregnancy without further reasons during the first three months of the pregnancy (Gindulis 2003: 111).

The menu of policy-options is further restricted in member-states of the European Union by the fact that new policies have to conform to European law. Economic policy certainly is the most important example in this respect. Many proposals that aimed at restricting market forces (particularly in the public utilities) had a difficult time surviving in the policy stream as they were in conflict with the internal-market programme. For example, the coalition of Social-Democrats and Greens would have liked to restrict competition in the postal market in 2001 but was not able to do so, at least in some market segments, because of EU regulations (Zohlnhöfer and Herweg 2010: 270). Thus, for EU member-states, conformity to EU regulations is an important criterion for survival in the policy stream, too.

What is more, in many policy areas the EU not only restricts the menu of policy-choices but also itself feeds policy-options into the policy stream. The liberalisation of many sectors was advocated by the EU Commission and, in most cases, it was able to get these proposals adopted, although member-states were initially quite reluctant at times (see Scharpf 1999). Once the EU has decided, the policy-options available to actors in member-states are dramatically narrowed, to those few that are compatible with the EU regulation – even in cases in which liberalisation was initially not a relevant proposal in the domestic policy-community. What is more, even in policy areas for which the EU does not have the competence to issue hard law but in which it aims at influencing member-states' policies by soft law, these proposals can have a (limited) effect on the policy primeval soup, as Zohlnhöfer and Ostheim have demonstrated for some German labour-market programmes (Zohlnhöfer and Ostheim 2005).

Moreover, the selection criteria also implicitly incorporate path-dependent developments. Although pension reform was on German governments' agenda almost constantly from the mid 1980s, proposals suggesting a radical departure from the country's pay-as-you-go-system have never been considered seriously. The reason is the well known path-dependent development of these pensions systems. Thus, a departure from the pay-as-you-go-system would mean that one generation would have to double-pay – for existing pensioners as well as for themselves. Obviously, this option is seen as unfeasible by policy-makers, due to the unsolvable financial question, and thus relevant proposals did not survive in the policy primeval soup.

One could certainly subsume this criterion under 'value acceptability' or anticipated 'public acquiescence', which has the advantage of not adding more variables to the framework. Nonetheless, given that the MSF is criticised for not being able to consider path-dependent developments (Rüb 2009: 368), it is important to stress that the framework is indeed able to integrate path-dependence.

The problem stream

The problem stream posed the fewest problems when the MSF was applied to German policy-making. In all cases, relevant problems could be identified and it could be shown that actors perceived certain conditions as problems. Interestingly, some conditions were around for quite a long time until they were defined as problems that needed to be addressed by key policy-making actors; others needed only months or even weeks to be taken very seriously. Examples of the latter kind of problem include the fall of the Berlin Wall, which opened the way for German unification, and the financial crisis of 2008 and the recession that followed it. Conditions that took longer to be defined as problems include demographic ageing and, to some extent, unemployment. It should not take scholars of agenda-setting processes by surprise that it took a while for demographic ageing to be perceived as a problem by policy-makers as it is the prime example of a 'big, slow-moving process' (Pierson 2003) that does not produce swift changes in indicators or generate focusing events.

More interestingly maybe, we argue that unemployment also took some time to be taken seriously, at least in some periods. This might sound surprising as unemployment was rising more or less continuously between the early 1970s and the mid 2000s and had been an important issue for voters most of the time since the 1970s. Nonetheless, governments of differing partisan complexion have not regarded unemployment as a serious problem for substantial periods of time. The reason for this lack of attention was that although unemployment was high, it was not rising and it thus did not endanger the government's re-election. Only when unemployment threatened to cross – or actually crossed – certain symbolic thresholds, did governments start to perceive joblessness as a problem they had to deal with. One example is the Christian-Democrat–Liberal coalition that was confronted with a rise in unemployment to more than 4 million in January 1996, the highest number of unemployed in the Federal Republic's history at the time. The government reacted by adopting structural reforms of all major social-security programmes and labour-market policy and by proposing a massive tax reform (Zohlnhöfer 2001).

Similarly, the government of Social-Democrats and Greens that succeeded the Christian-Democrat–Liberal coalition also dealt with unemployment only when the issue put its re-election in question. Again, this fact is difficult to reconcile with functionalist thinking, as unemployment was very high when the coalition came to power in 1998. What is more, it was also one of the most important issues in the 1998 election campaign. In that election, the Social-Democratic candidate for Chancellor, Gerhard Schröder, promised to reduce the number of unemployed to 3.5 million by the next election, to be held in 2002. In the first years of the coalition of Social-Democrats and Greens, the unemployment figures indeed moved in the direction the government had hoped for (although the government could not claim much credit for this development as it did not adopt relevant reforms in the area of labour-market policy). In October 2000, unemployment was even down to slightly over 3.6 million, close to the level of 3.5 million envisaged for 2002. Therefore, the government could hope to reach its target by 2002 and unemployment was thus not seen as a problem that the government needed to tackle. When the economy slowed down and unemployment started to rise again in 2001, however, it became highly unlikely that unemployment would fall to 3.5 million by 2002 (Hassel and Schiller 2010: 17), which meant that the Chancellor would not be able to keep his election promise concerning the number of unemployed. Therefore, the number of unemployed clearly operated as a problem indicator then: not only did the development of the number of unemployed clearly deviate from what the government wished (indicating that there actually was a problem) but, at the same time, this problem was highly relevant for decision-makers as it concerned one of their central election pledges. Thus, only the fact that the development of the labour market endangered the government's re-election transformed the condition of high unemployment into a problem the government felt it had to deal with.

The problem of unemployment also opened a sudden and unexpected problem-window at the beginning of 2005, when the number of unemployed crossed the symbolic threshold of five million people for the first time in post-war history. Given this state of affairs, doing nothing was not an option for the government, particularly as elections in the largest German state were looming that were important for the Federal government because the results of state elections indirectly affect the composition of the second chamber. So, again, a condition which put the governing parties' re-election at risk led these parties to perceive the condition as a problem. Nonetheless, as a labour-market reform just had been passed – in effect, the rise in unemployment was essentially a 'statistical artefact' (Zohlnhöfer and Egle 2007: 18; our translation) of this reform, as the far-reaching labour-market reforms adopted in the previous years changed the way unemployment was calculated to the effect that more people were counted as unemployed from January 2005 onwards – it was possible for a policy-entrepreneur to attach a corporate-tax reform to the problem of unemployment (see Zohlnhöfer 2009: 385).

In sum, our case studies suggest that a condition is more likely to be perceived as a problem when policy-makers believe that the condition in question may put their re-election at risk (for an elaboration of this argument, see Herweg, Huß and Zohlnhöfer 2016).

The political stream

Zahariadis (1995: 35) suggested that the variables of the political stream should be collapsed into the single category of party politics when parliamentary systems are analysed. According to our case studies, this is not convincing, however. Therefore, we concentrate on the two other elements (apart from government and parties) of the political stream in Kingdon's (2003[1984]) work, namely the national mood and interest-groups, and discuss whether they can contribute to an explanation of policy-making in Germany.

The national mood

Kingdon (2003[1984]: 146) defines the national mood as 'the notion that a rather large number of people out in the country are thinking along certain common lines'. As Kingdon points out that the national mood cannot be read off opinion polls, Zahariadis (1995: 35) argues that it is close-to-impossible to pin it down empirically – which is why he suggests dropping the concept. Convincing as this argument is, there are numerous cases in which something like a national mood indeed did play a role. The most obvious instance among our case studies was German unification. A number of observers not at all attached to the MSF have emphasised the importance of what was perceived as public opinion for the politics of German unification (for example, Lehmbruch 1990: 463; Busch 1991: 197–9). More importantly, even the actors involved said that they perceived something like a national mood. For example, Chancellor Helmut Kohl (1996: 135) repeatedly argued that one could 'feel' that Germany was approaching unification after the fall of the Berlin Wall. Similarly, Wolfgang Schäuble, another politician involved in the relevant policy processes, explained that 'no-one could have afforded it politically to openly oppose the completion of German unity' (1991: 110; our translation). Indeed, it is hard to deny that when the Berlin Wall came down in 1989 and unification increasingly became a real option, actors on all sides of the political spectrum perceived that voters were expecting politicians to aim at unification.

Thus, the government could suspend all standard policy-making routines (including the central bank's legal right to be consulted prior to important decisions regarding exchange rate and monetary policy) when it offered monetary union to the GDR. Similarly, the Social -Democrats, who were in opposition but controlled the second chamber of parliament and thus possessed veto-power, were unable to substantially influence policy because they believed that any action that might be seen as slowing down or impeding the process of unification was unfeasible, given the national mood.

One might argue that unification is a special case but there are other cases, too, in which something like a national mood is part of an explanation of policy-making processes. This is true for the attempt to ban smoking in restaurants (Reus 2010) but also for abortion legislation. One study argued that public opinion ('*das öffentliche Meinungsklima*') had an important impact on the way abortion was discussed in the 1970s (Gindulis 2003: 101). Only after the subject was discussed on the front pages of newspapers did parties take up the issue (Gante 1991: 144). Similarly, a number of historians argue that the '*Neue Ostpolitik*' of the coalition of Social-Democrats and Liberals after 1969 was helped by something akin to a 'national mood'. Wolfrum, for example, explicitly argues that 'the change in the policy towards East Germany was facilitated by a change in public opinion' (2005: 362; our translation) and Baring (1982: 202) makes it clear that the later Social-Democratic Chancellor Brandt seems to have been already certain in 1963 that it would be impossible for future governments not to talk to the Soviets.

The decision of the coalition of Christian-Democrats and Liberals to shut down all nuclear power plants in 2011 (see Huß 2014) is another example for the relevance of the national mood. The same coalition had extended the lifespan of nuclear power-plants only a few months previously but performed a spectacular U-turn after the nuclear disaster in Fukushima (Japan). Although Germany was not directly affected by it, the accident had a tremendous effect on the national mood in Germany. When the government decided on the extension of the lifespan of nuclear power-plants in autumn 2010, a slight majority of the voters was against this policy but the supporters of the governing parties were in favour (for the following data, see Zohlnhöfer and Engler 2014); moreover, the salience of this issue was limited: only between 3 and 6 per cent of respondents rated environmental and energy policy as one of the most important problems at the time. After the nuclear disaster in Fukushima, however, nuclear energy came to be perceived as one of the most pressing problems and the number of people who demanded a rapid exit from nuclear energy sky-rocketed: according to a poll in April 2011, 55 per cent of respondents were in favour of a nuclear energy phase-out as quickly as possible and another 34 per cent preferred a phase-out within the next ten years, while less than 10 per cent still thought the run-time extension of nuclear power-plants the government had adopted a few months previously was a good idea. To make things worse for the government, important state-level elections were to be held only weeks after the Fukushima disaster and the Greens enjoyed increasing popularity. Therefore, the government's decision to abandon nuclear energy shortly after the nuclear accident in Japan was, to a large extent, triggered by the development of the national mood. Thus, we find remarkable evidence for Kingdon's (2003[1984]: 164) notion that a combination of the national mood and approaching elections can 'create extremely powerful impacts on policy agendas'.[4]

In sum, we can conclude that it may well be possible to find indications of what policy-makers may have thought the national mood was like at certain points in time. At times, policy-makers themselves may indicate that they felt public opinion or the national mood was on their side in their memoirs; likewise, observers of policy processes may provide relevant clues. More importantly, probably, the national mood (or rather the perception of the national mood by policy-makers) may indeed help explain the development of particular policy processes, as can be seen from German unification, the reform of abortion regulation and the decision to phase out nuclear energy.

Interest-groups

Interest-groups also seem to be relevant to agenda-setting. Policy-making regarding abortion in the 1970s is a case in point. Alice Schwarzer, the figurehead of the 1970s women's movement, organised a media campaign in 1971 in which 374 women publicly admitted to having had an abortion (Gante 1991: 123–9; Gindulis 2003: 100–1). This campaign had an immense impact on public opinion and is described in the literature as the turning point in the abortion debate. While no party had been interested in a reform of abortion legislation in any substantial way prior to 1971, the campaign generated a momentum that the government (which

---

4.   Admittedly, Kingdon (2003) makes it very clear that the national mood cannot be read off opinion polls; but it seems difficult to argue that the government's U-turn was not induced by the huge swing in public opinion that survey data depict.

saw itself as reformist and progressive) could no longer resist (for the details, see Gante 1991). At the same time, the churches were highly important in this policy process as they were the main opponents of a more permissive regulation of abortion and organised demonstrations and the like in order to influence policy (Gindulis 2003: 102).

But interest-groups do not only play a role in issues concerning morality. To the contrary, trade unions and business associations tried to influence almost all bills in economic, fiscal and social policy. In some instances, these interest-groups were indeed able to shape certain aspects of reforms. Health-policy provides numerous, sometimes rather spectacular examples. The pharmaceutical industry, for example, was able to prevent a policy in which a list was drawn up of all pharmaceuticals for which the health funds would cover the costs (the so-called 'positive list') – meaning that drugs not on the list would not be paid for by health insurance. The industry's opposition was quite successful: at one point, a State Secretary from the Ministry of Health gave the chief executive of the industry's lobby group a very special birthday present: a shredded version of the positive list (Hartmann 2003: 268)!

As might be expected, trade unions fiercely opposed all attempts to cut benefits under social-security programmes or liberalise the labour market – more or less regardless of which government tried to adopt these measures. They, too, were successful at times. For example, the government of Social-Democrats and Greens revoked many reforms of its predecessor that the trade unions had fiercely opposed (see, for example, Streeck 2003). What is more, the same government granted the trade unions a number of concessions in the 2001 pension reform (Merkel 2003: 177). In other cases, unions were less successful in blocking disliked reforms once they were on the agenda. Nonetheless, there is ample evidence that governments have tended to avoid such policies for as long as possible, in order to prevent a conflict with the unions (see Zohlnhöfer 2001; Merkel 2003).

Nuclear energy is an interesting case, too. On the one hand, anti-nuclear social movements demanding a rapid phase-out of nuclear energy were very strong in Germany from the 1970s (see Roose 2010; Rucht 2007). These groups made it very difficult for any government to pursue a pro-nuclear energy policy. Thus, not least due to their public campaigns, no government seriously considered building new nuclear power-plants from the end of the 1980s on. Anti-nuclear groups were not strong enough, however, to push through the rapid shut-down of nuclear power plants and the Christian-Democrat–Liberal government even dared to extend the run-time of nuclear power-plants somewhat in 2009/10 – despite the fierce opposition of these groups, which were able to mobilise thousands of voters against nuclear energy. The energy industry, on the other hand, was quite successful in preventing governments from rapid withdrawal from nuclear energy, by threatening legal action. This balance of power circumscribed the room for manoeuvre in nuclear-energy policy for any government – neither an extension nor a rapid abandonment of nuclear energy were feasible. The balance was tipped towards an exit from nuclear energy after the nuclear disaster in Japan, however. At that point, the governing parties' electoral motivations became dominant and overrode the energy industry's resistance. This strongly corroborates Kingdon's (2003[1984]: 164) claim that a combination of the national mood and elections produces strong impacts on policy agendas, 'impacts capable of overwhelming the balance of organised forces'.

Therefore, according to the cases under study here, interest-groups play much the same role in policy-making in Germany as they do in the case of the USA for which the MSF was originally devised. They can be quite influential at times; and not only by pushing for particular regulations: rather, German policy-makers, just like their counterparts in the US, have calculated the political costs of a confrontation with important interest-groups and have, at times, decided that it was not worthwhile to invest resources in a project that was likely to provoke fierce opposition from strong and well organised forces. In sum, our study suggests that Kingdon's (2003[1984]) original conception of the political stream is applicable – and indeed, analytically valuable – in parliamentary systems as well as presidential ones: in addition to political parties, the national mood and organised interests were relevant players in at least some of the cases investigated here.

Policy-windows

The concept of policy-windows works quite nicely for essentially all cases under investigation in this chapter. Problem-windows opened when the Berlin Wall came down, which allowed Chancellor Helmut Kohl to put German unification on the agenda. Similarly, the financial crisis and the recession that followed it opened a policy-window. In the face of a systemic banking crisis and the deepest recession in post-war history, not doing anything was obviously not an option (see Zohlnhöfer 2011). As the government did not really have any idea how to react to this double crisis, policy-entrepreneurs had excellent opportunities to push through their pet solutions, as can be seen in the case of the scrapping bonus (*see* above). Similarly, when more than four million people were registered as unemployed for the first time in post-war history in January 1996, that was an important indicator that had changed dramatically and had passed a symbolic threshold, opening a problem-window. The business wing of the coalition government of Christian-Democrats and Liberals in turn used this problem-window to get a number of liberal labour-market and welfare reforms adopted that the government had shied away from when economic performance was better.

As can be expected in a parliamentary system that is dominated by political parties, political windows open up in the politics stream quite frequently and are often related to changes of governments. Thus, the new policy towards Eastern Europe was put in place right after the new government of Social-Democrats and Liberals had come to power in 1969. Many economic and social policy-reforms that were introduced after changes of governments are also cases in point. For example, the newly formed government of Christian-Democrats and Liberals introduced a number of expenditure cuts and revenue increases shortly after it came to power in 1982 and also started to liberalise the labour market somewhat (Zohlnhöfer 2001). Similarly, when a new government of Social-Democrats and

Greens came to power in 1998, it did not take them long to revoke some reforms of its predecessor government; to introduce what was called an ecological tax reform; to stipulate the phasing-out of nuclear energy; and to reform citizenship law (for details, see Egle *et al.* 2003).

What is more, politics-windows sometimes opened as a result of changes in the national mood. The case of the exit from nuclear energy in 2011 discussed above is a case in point. Similarly, the case of the liberalisation of abortion in the 1970s can be used as an example. This case even suggests that policy-windows can be opened by policy-entrepreneurs, as it was Alice Schwarzer's media campaign that opened a political window. Similarly, it seems that Chancellor Gerhard Schröder opened a problem-window in early 2002 (see Zohlnhöfer and Herweg 2014). As pointed out above, unemployment was not decreasing as hoped and seriously put the government's re-election in question. Thus, it was imperative for the government to win back the initiative in labour-market policy. And, indeed, Schröder was able to open a problem-window: in response to a scandal regarding wrong placement statistics from the Federal Labour Office that became known in February 2002 (Kemmerling and Bruttel 2006: 91; Hassel and Schiller 2010: 20), he appointed an expert commission that reported back shortly before the election and presented ambitious reform proposals to improve the overall employment situation in Germany. This problem-window was not an obvious one, however, as the problem of wrong placement statistics would not have necessitated a substantial reform of labour-market policy in itself.

In sum, we may conclude that the idea of policy-windows travels very well across policy-domains. In most cases, it is not very difficult to identify policy-windows; at the same time, it is clear they exert much leverage, as it is difficult to understand the timing of reforms without reference to policy-windows. We can only explain why the Schröder government put labour-market reforms on the agenda in the last few months of its first term or why the government of Social-Democrats and Liberals got involved with a reform of abortion legislation in 1971 – even though neither party had shown any interest in those issues before – by reference to policy-windows.

Policy-entrepreneurs

In contrast to policy-windows, the concept of policy-entrepreneurs is not always easily applicable to the cases analysed here. Certainly, there are a number of instances in which it is possible to identify policy-entrepreneurs. For example, it is highly unlikely that a smoking ban in public buildings, on public transport and in restaurants would have come on the agenda in the mid-2000s without Lothar Binding, a backbencher from the governing Social-Democrats (Reus 2010: 15). Similarly, when the recession after the 2008 financial crisis opened a policy-window for new expenditure programmes, Matthias Wissmann, the chairman of the German Association of Automotive Industry (VDA), was quick to suggest the scrapping bonus (*see* above). Both of these policy-entrepreneurs were quite successful, which is completely in line with the MSF's expectations; both had not only a pet solution but also access to policy-makers: Binding as an MP for a governing party; Wissmann as a former MP and Federal Minister of Transport for another governing party.

The reform of business taxation in 2005 provides a nice example of collective entrepreneurship (for collective entrepreneurship, see Roberts and King 1991). The coupling process was initiated by Jürgen Thuman, at the time leader of the German Business Association, who met the Minister of Economic Affairs, Wolfgang Clement, and then opposition leader, Angela Merkel, in a TV talk-show in February 2005, when he convinced them that a business-tax reform could be a way to fight unemployment (which had just reached record-breaking levels). Afterwards, Clement and Merkel themselves called for a business-tax reform and acted as policy-entrepreneurs, while Thuman tried to convince Chancellor Schröder and Thuman's staff worked out a bill in collaboration with the Ministry of Economic Affairs.

Other cases are less clear, however. Take the reform of abortion-regulation in the early 1970s as an example. Clearly, Alice Schwarzer, a leading figure of the feminist movement, pushed for the liberalisation of abortion and initiated a public campaign that was supposed to mobilise the public. But she equally clearly did not have access to policy-makers and did not figure prominently during the rest of the policy-making process. What is more, she did not even work out a proposal that satisfied the criteria for survival.[5] In a way, she only opened a policy-window for somebody else's pet solution, namely the pet solution of the majority of liberal criminal-law professors!

If we want to go beyond agenda-setting and turn to policy-making, quite frequently more than one policy-entrepreneur can be found. The far-reaching labour-market reforms of the early 2000s are a case in point (see Zohlnhöfer and Herweg 2014). While the ideas of activating labour-market policies were around for quite some time and had been advocated by a great number of people in the policy community, this was not enough to put these proposals on the agenda, let alone to get them into the statute books, given the resistance of parts of the governing Social-Democratic party and its close allies, the trade unions, with their strong links to the Ministry of Labour. Rather, Chancellor Gerhard Schröder, not a labour-market expert at all himself, gave the policy-experts the opportunity to put their proposals on the agenda by appointing an expert commission, in which the proponents of activating reforms were easily in a majority position while the Ministry of Labour and the trade unions were hardly represented at all. What is more, Schröder even saw the bills through the legislative process together with his new Minister of Labour, overcoming substantial resistance from the trade unions and his own party in the process. In this case, Schröder certainly must be seen as

---

5. Schwarzer advocated the abolition of the relevant paragraph in the criminal code, a proposal that did not satisfy the criterion of value-acceptability. Moreover, to advocates of a permissive reform it was clear that the abolition of that paragraph would not have a chance in parliament, i.e. they anticipated future constraints and dropped this proposal.

a policy-entrepreneur, although the reforms were equally certainly not among his long-pursued pet policies.

This observation points to a more general pattern. Given the tremendous importance of political parties in parliamentary systems, outside experts only rarely act as policy-entrepreneurs throughout the whole policy process. Rather, once their ideas are taken up by a party, the responsible minister or spokesperson of the party or even, as we have just shown, the head of the executive, becomes policy-entrepreneur and looks for policy-windows to get the proposals on the agenda.

Conclusion

In this paper we have applied the multiple-streams framework to German policy-making processes in different policy-fields at very different points in time. We were able to corroborate earlier research in showing that the framework is indeed able to travel to different political systems: in this case, to a party-dominated, somewhat corporatist parliamentary system. At the same time, we suggest a few amendments that may help to apply the MSF more successfully to parliamentary systems.[6] Regarding the policy stream, we argue that the prominent role of political parties in working out policy-proposals must be recognised – parties are not only relevant in the political stream but also need to be accounted for in the policy stream. What is more, it can be helpful to specify the criteria for survival in the policy stream a little more. We suggest that in addition to the criteria Kingdon (2003[1984]) mentions, a proposal stands a better chance of surviving in the policy primeval soup if its constitutionality is not in question; if it conforms to EU regulations; and if it fits with extant policies in the field.

The other two streams need to be modified much less in our opinion. Regarding the political stream, we propose considering all three factors Kingdon (2003[1984]) puts forward, rather than concentrating only on the ideology and strategy of governing parties, as Zahariadis (1995) suggests. What is more, we show that conditions are more likely to be perceived as problems by key policy-makers when a problem endangers the policy-makers' re-election.

The concept of policy-windows again travels nicely and we were able to show that it may be possible for policy-entrepreneurs to open policy-windows deliberately. Further research is needed, however, to specify conditions under which this is actually possible. Finally, the concept of policy-entrepreneurs is somewhat more difficult to apply to parliamentary systems because it seems that, in a large majority of cases, a representative of a political party becomes a policy-entrepreneur at one point.

Nonetheless, in sum, the MSF has turned out to be a very helpful framework for analysing policy-making in a political setting for which it was not devised. In

---

6. Some of these suggestions have recently been elaborated on theoretically and introduced more systematically into the MSF in a joint paper with Nicole Herweg (Herweg, Huß and Zohlnhöfer 2015).

particular, the MSF proves to be particularly suitable for the analysis of 'unlikely' reforms, that is, for reforms we would not expect on the basis of traditional theoretical approaches. Examples include the liberal labour-market reforms under a Social-Democratic government and the phasing-out of nuclear energy under a Christian-Democrat–Liberal coalition. As these 'unlikely' reforms are growing more frequent, because many parliamentary systems are becoming less 'orderly' due to growing problem-pressures, more volatile voters and an increasingly fragmented party landscape, the MSF might become even more relevant for the analysis of these political systems in the future.

References

Baring, A. (1982) *Machtwechsel. Die Ära Brandt-Scheel*, Stuttgart, DE: DVA.

Beyme, K. von (1997) *Der Gesetzgeber. Der Bundestag als Entscheidungszentrum*, Opladen, DE: Westdeutscher Verlag.

Busch, A. (1991) 'Die deutsch-deutsche Währungsunion: Politisches Votum trotz ökonomischer Bedenken', in U. Liebert and W. Merkel (eds) *Die Politik zur deutschen Einheit. Probleme – Strategien – Kontroversen*, Opladen, DE: Leske+Budrich, pp. 185–207.

Egle, C., Ostheim, T. and Zohlnhöfer, R. (eds.) (2003) *Das rot-grüne Projekt. Eine Bilanz der Regierung Schröder 1998–2002*, Wiesbaden DE Westdeutscher Verlag.

Ganghof, S. (2006) *The Politics of Income Taxation: A comparative analysis*, Colchester, UK: ECPR Press.

Gante, M. (1991) *§218 in der Diskussion. Meinungs- und Willensbildung, 1945–1976*, Düsseldorf: Droste.

Gindulis, E. (2003) *Der Konflikt um die Abtreibung. Die Bestimmungsfaktoren der Gesetzgebung zum Schwangerschaftsabbruch im OECD-Ländervergleich*, Wiesbaden, DE: Westdeutscher Verlag.

Hartmann, A. (2003) 'Patientennah, leistungsstark, finanzbewusst? Die Gesundheitspolitik der rot-grünen Bundesregierung', in C. Egle, T. Ostheim and R. Zohlnhöfer (eds) *Das rot-grüne Projekt. Eine Bilanz der Regierung Schröder 1998–2002*, Wiesbaden, DE: Westdeutscher Verlag, pp. 259–81.

Hassel, A. and Schiller, C. (2010) *Der Fall Hartz IV. Wie es zur Agenda 2010 kam und wie es weitergeht*, Frankfurt and New York: Campus.

Herweg, N. (2013) 'Der Multiple-Streams Ansatz – ein Ansatz dessen Zeit gekommen ist?', *Zeitschrift für Vergleichende Politikwissenschaft*, 7(4): 312–45.

Herweg, N., Huß, C. and Zohlnhöfer, R. (2015) 'Straightening the three streams: theorizing extensions of the multiple streams framework', *European Journal of Political Research* 54(3): 435–49.

Huß, C. (2014) 'Energy transition by conviction or by surprise? Environmental policy from 2009 to 2013', *German Politics* 23(4): 430–45.

Kemmerling, A. and Bruttel, O. (2006) 'New politics in German labour market policy? The implications of the recent Hartz reforms for the German welfare state', *West European Politics* 29(1): 90–112.

Kingdon, J. W. (2003[1984]): *Agendas, Alternatives, and Public Policies*, Boston, MA: Little, Brown & Co.

Kohl, H. (1996) *Ich wollte Deutschlands Einheit*, Berlin: Propyläen.

Lehmbruch, G. (1990) 'Die improvisierte Vereinigung: Die Dritte deutsche Republik', *Leviathan* 18(4): 462–86.

Merkel, W. (2003) 'Institutionen und Reformpolitik: Drei Fallstudien zur Vetospieler-Theorie', in C. Egle, T. Ostheim and R. Zohlnhöfer (eds) *Das rot-grüne Projekt. Eine Bilanz der Regierung Schröder 1998–2002*, Wiesbaden, DE: Westdeutscher Verlag, pp. 163–90.

Münter, M. (2005) *Verfassungsreform im Einheitsstaat: Die Politik der Dezentralisierung in Großbritannien*, Wiesbaden, DE: VS Verlag für Sozialwissenschaften.

Pierson, P. (2003) '"Big, slow-moving, and ... invisible": macrosocial processes in the study of comparative politics', in J. Mahoney and D. Rueschemeyer (eds) *Comparative Historical Analysis in the Social Sciences*, Cambridge, UK: Cambridge University Press, pp. 177–207.

Reus, I. (2010) *Die Nichtraucherschutzgesetzgebung in den deutschen Bundesländern nach der Föderalismusreform*, unpublished diploma thesis, University of Bamberg, DE.

Roose, J. (2010) 'Der endlose Streit um die Atomenergie. Konfliktsoziologische Untersuchung', in P. H. Feindt and T. Saretzki (eds) *Umwelt und Technikkonflikte*, Wiesbaden, DE: Verlag für Sozialwissenschaften, pp. 79–103.

Rucht, D. (2007) 'Umweltproteste in der Bundesrepublik Deutschland: eine vergleichende Perspektive', in K. Jacob, F. Biermann, P.-O. Busch and P. H. Feindt (eds) 'Politik und Umwelt', *Politische Vierteljahresschrift* 7(39): 518–39.

Rüb, F. (2009) 'Multiple-Streams-Ansatz: Grundlagen, Probleme und Kritik', in K. Schubert and N. C. Bandelow (eds) *Lehrbuch der Politikfeldanalyse 2.0*, München, DE: Oldenbourg, pp. 353–80.

Sabatier, P. A. (2007) 'The need for better theories', in P. A. Sabatier (ed.) *Theories of the Policy Process*, 2nd edn, Boulder, CO: Westview Press, pp. 3–17.

Schäuble, W. (1991) *Der Vertrag. Wie ich über die deutsche Einheit verhandelte*, Stuttgart, DE: Deutsche Verlags-Anstalt.

Scharpf, F. W. (1999) *Regieren in Europa. Effektiv und demokratisch?*, Frankfurt, DE and New York: Campus.

Schmidt, W. (2003) 'Die Wurzeln der Entspannung. Der konzeptionelle Ursprung der Ost- und Deutschlandpolitik Willy Brandts in den fünfziger Jahren', *Vierteljahreshefte für Zeitgeschichte* 51(4): 521–63.

Siaroff, A. (1999) 'Corporatism in 24 industrial democracies: meaning and measurement', *European Journal of Political Research* 36(2): 175–205.

Streeck, W. (2003) *No Longer the Century of Corporatism. Das Ende des "Bündnisses für Arbeit"*, Cologne: Max-Planck-Institute for the Study of Societies, working paper 03/4 available at: http://www.mpifg.de/pu/workpap/wp03-4/wp03-4.html (accessed 20 October 2015).

Trampusch, C. (2006) 'Sequenzorientierte Policy-Analyse. Warum die Rentenreform von Walter Riester nicht an Reformblockaden scheiterte', *Berliner Journal für Soziologie* 16(1): 55–76.

Wolfrum, E. (2005) *Die Bundesrepublik Deutschland, 1949–1990*, Gebhardt Handbuch der deutschen Geschichte, vol. 23, Stuttgart, DE: Klett-Cotta.

Zahariadis, N. (1995) *Markets, States, and Public Policy. Privatization in Britain and France*, Ann Arbor, MI: University of Michigan Press.

Zahariadis, N. (2003) *Ambiguity and Choice in Public Policy: Political decision making in modern democracies*, Washington, DC: Georgetown University Press.

Zahariadis, N. and Allen, C. (1995) 'Ideas, networks, and policy streams: privatization in Britain and Germany', *Review of Policy Research* 14(1–2): 71–98.

Zohlnhöfer, R. (2001) *Die Wirtschaftspolitik der Ära Kohl. Eine Analyse der Schlüssel entscheidungen in den Politikfeldern Finanzen, Arbeit und Entstaatlichung, 1982–1998*, Opladen, DE: Leske+Budrich.

—— (2009) *Globalisierung der Wirtschaft und finanzpolitische Anpassungsreaktionen in Westeuropa*, Baden-Baden, DE: Nomos.

—— (2011) 'Between a rock and a hard place: the German response to the economic crisis', *German Politics* 20(2): 227–42.

Zohlnhöfer, R. and Egle, C. (2007) 'Der Episode zweiter Teil – ein Überblick über die 15. Legislaturperiode', in C. Egle and R. Zohlnhöfer (eds) *Ende des rot-grünen Projektes. Eine Bilanz der Regierung Schröder 2002–2005*, Wiesbaden, DE: VS, pp. 11–25.

Zohlnhöfer, R. and Engler, F. (2014) 'Courting the voters? Policy implications of party competition for the reform output of the second Merkel government', *German Politics* 23(4): 284–303.

Zohlnhöfer, R. and Herweg, N. (2010) 'Das Verhältnis von Markt und Staat unter der Großen Koalition: Entstaatlichung in der Ruhe und Verstaatlichung während des Sturms?', in C. Egle and R. Zohlnhöfer (eds) *Die zweite Große Koalition. Eine Bilanz der Regierung Merkel, 2005–2009*, Wiesbaden, DE: VS, pp. 252–76.

Zohlnhöfer, R. and Herweg, N. (2014) 'Paradigmatischer Wandel in der deutschen Arbeitsmarktpolitik: Die Hartz-Gesetze', in F.W. Rüb (ed.) *Rapide Politikwechsel in der Bundesrepublik. Theoretischer Rahmen und empirische Befunde*, Baden-Baden, DE: Nomos, pp. 93–125.

Zohlnhöfer, R. and Ostheim, T. (2005) 'Paving the way for employment? The impact of the Luxembourg Process on German labour market policies', *Journal of European Integration* 27(2): 147–67.

Chapter Eleven

The Expulsion of the Smokers from Paradise: A Multiple-Streams Analysis of German Non-Smoker-Protection Legislation

Iris Reus

Introduction

Smoking has always been a controversial issue and, for reasons ranging from fire-prevention to religious motives, smoking has been restricted and sometimes even banned. As smoking's health impacts became more and more well known from the middle of the twentieth century, many states tried to reduce tobacco-consumption by political means, such as bans on advertising, increases in tobacco taxes and information campaigns. All these activities initially concentrated on the health of smokers but, in the 1970s, a further problematic aspect emerged: so-called passive smoking, that is, inhalation of noxious smoke by non-smokers. Accordingly, the issue of smoking bans concerns every citizen, no matter of what age or part of society, because everybody is either a smoker or a non-smoker. Moreover, as personal needs and everyday habits of life are affected, the debate is often very emotional. While smokers argue for their right of individual freedom of choice, non-smokers counter with their right of physical inviolability.

Until 2007, by international comparison, Germany was often called a 'smoker's paradise' due to the low level of restriction that smokers faced. An evaluation of European countries by two experts for tobacco-control policy (Joossens and Raw 2007: 8–9) ranked Germany twenty-seventh out of thirty in terms of the severity of its controls on smoking. In fact, Germany had slipped down the scale even since 2005 (when it was ranked twenty-second), because several other European countries had engaged in tobacco-control activities in the meantime. By contrast, for more than three decades, all attempts to establish restrictive laws in Germany had failed; nor did European discussion about smoking bans lead to legislative activity at first. This all changed significantly and rapidly starting in 2006, leading important weekly news magazine *Die ZEIT* to ask 'Why now?' and 'What has happened in the "smoker's paradise"?' [own translation] (*Die ZEIT* 1 March 2007). These questions guide the following analysis, which takes the multiple-streams framework as a basis because, as I will show, other theories are not able to explain this policy-change sufficiently.

German non-smoker-protection legislation

Smoking bans can potentially affect all kinds of public buildings and areas: state agencies; public transport and stations; cultural buildings like schools and theatres; and catering establishments. Due to division of legislative competence in Germany's federal system, responsibility for different areas was divided between the federal government and the individual state governments. The catering industry, on which my analysis concentrates, comprises all forms of enclosed areas in which food and/or drink is served and consumed, such as restaurants, pubs, bars and discos. Catering was by far the most controversial area for a smoking ban and responsibility for it was located at the federal level when the political discussion started in June 2006. Simultaneously, discussions started within the states, which were responsible for legislation concerning public as well as cultural buildings. However, in September 2006, the Federalism Reform became effective, one of the most important-ever German constitutional reforms, which aimed at disentangling the interdependent German decision-making system and assigning policy areas either to federal or to state level exclusively. Due to the reallocation of legislative competences, in the middle of the political process, the responsibility for the catering industry was transferred to states.

Kingdon's original version of the multiple-streams framework focuses on agenda-setting: it does not explain 'how issues are authoritatively decided by ... decision-makers, but rather how they became issues in the first place' (Kingdon 1984: 2). However, as do most recent studies, my analysis includes the whole legislative process, from agenda-setting to decision-making. According to Zahariadis (1992: 359), the application of the multiple-streams framework is just as relevant in both these situations because 'the operating structure of the three streams – policies, problems, and politics – is the same'. For reasons of analytical clarity, Herweg (2013: 335) has suggested two coupling processes with regard to agenda-setting and decision-making and therefore distinguishes between the agenda-window (which equates to the policy-window in Kingdon's terminology) and the decision-window. In the present case, the Federalism Reform caused a separation of the phases in two respects. First, it represented a break in the temporal development between agenda-setting and decision-making. Second, in contrast to normal legislative processes taking place in the same political arena, the reform shifted the process from the federal to the state level. The opening of the agenda-window and the first coupling process took place at the federal level and put the issue on the agenda. But the decision-making process failed due to the Federalism Reform, which transferred the responsibility for the catering industry to the states. But because a worked-out proposal that could be the starting point for state-level legislation already existed, the policy stream opened the decision-window and the legislative process continued in the states. The second coupling process then took place at the state level and resulted in a general smoking ban by law in all sixteen states, yet with differences in detail. Still later, a decision of the Federal Constitutional Court opened a second decision-window and almost all states had to revise their laws.

Following the political developments, my analysis is divided into three sections: the federal legislation; the states' original legislation; and the amendment of the states' legislation. Each section starts with a short introduction, providing some general information about the political development; in the second part of the section this development is examined in detail, using the multiple-streams framework.

The federal legislation

The public debate on non-smoker-protection in Germany started in 2004, when Ireland and Norway (followed by Italy and Sweden in 2005) enacted relatively strict smoking bans concerning public buildings and the catering industry. These laws attracted much attention in Germany and were accompanied by extensive news coverage. Nevertheless, no discussion about legislative activities started; the general view in the media was that smoking bans were unthinkable in the German context. Accordingly, rather than adopting legislation, the federal government started bargaining with the Federal Hotel and Restaurant Association (DEHOGA) about a voluntary self-commitment. In March 2005, they agreed that 90 per cent of restaurants (bars and discos were not included) with more than 75 square meters or forty seats should offer half of their seats to non-smokers by 2008 (*Spiegel Online*, 2 March 2005). As the agreement did not demand any physical separation of the non-smoking section, it offered a very low level of protection because smoke can easily get from smokers to non-smokers sitting in the same room. In December 2005 the German Cancer Research Centre published the study 'Passive smoking – an underestimated health risk', concluding that every year, 3,300 people in Germany died as a consequence of passive smoking (German Cancer Research Centre 2005). The study made huge waves but, again, no discussion about legislative activities followed.

In June 2006, Lothar Binding, a member of the Bundestag (federal parliament), made public his plans concerning a legal initiative for a smoking ban covering all areas of public life (*Frankfurter Allgemeine Zeitung*, 12 June 2006). Given the rapidly rising positive feedback from the public, political support also rose within a short time, although top-ranking politicians from both governing parties still hesitated. Yet, in the face of continuing pressure, the governing Grand Coalition of Christian-Democrats (CDU/CSU) and Social-Democrats (SPD) installed a working group to talk about legislative measures. The final compromise contained a general smoking ban in restaurants (no matter their size) and discos, with the exception of separate rooms for smokers (*Die Welt*, 27 September 2006). Bars would be excluded from the smoking ban, which meant that the level of protection was lower than in Binding's original proposal. Only a few days later, however, constitutional problems arose because, meanwhile, the reform of federalism had transferred legislative competence for the catering industry to the states, for which reason the project was cancelled (*n-tv*, 7 December 2006).

The problem stream at the federal level

That there are health risks connected with tobacco-use is not a new finding, but there were no meaningful scientific studies available with regard to passive smoking in Germany. The study published by the German Cancer Research Centre offered concrete data describing the German situation for the first time. According to the study, tobacco smoke is the most important and most dangerous indoor contaminant, causing several serious diseases. In contrast to other contaminants, tobacco smoke is harmful even in low concentrations, with almost no difference between smoking and passive smoking and currently no technical equipment protecting safely against tobacco smoke. The study concluded that, every year, 3,300 people in Germany died as a consequence of passive smoking. Hence, the report demanded the adoption of a general smoking ban.

The publication of the study achieved a huge response in the media and focused public attention on the problem. Every newspaper ran the headline 'Passive smoking *kills* 3,300 Germans every year', which became a catchphrase. According to Kingdon (2003[1984]: 95), 'an issue becomes a burning issue when it reaches crisis proportions'. In this case, for the first time, people got to know the problem in terms of numbers. Health aspects had always been central in the discussion about smoking but the study and the concrete numbers concerning the situation in Germany made people aware of the seriousness of the problem. Thus, the health-frame became the dominant frame while others, like smokers' and the restaurant-owners' rights, were considered less important. The pressure for political action was strengthened by the media, which strongly emphasised German backwardness in comparison with the political development in many other European countries.

The policy stream at the federal level

The German Cancer Research Centre offered a detailed legislative proposal (which later became the basis for Binding's initiative) but, even without that proposal, the policy-options to be considered were already known from the laws other European countries had passed. The basic choice was between a general smoking ban by law and a voluntary ban by each catering establishment. Furthermore, a potential law could cover the whole catering industry or be limited to certain branches, like restaurants, bars or discos; grant or refuse exceptions for special forms of catering, like folk festivals; and set particular requirements concerning the number and configuration of the rooms for non-smokers.

A look at Kingdon's (2003[1984]: 131–9) survival criteria for proposals shows no serious obstacles: budget constraints were not important because the implementation of smoking bans would hardly generate costs for the state. The technical feasibility was also not problematic because prohibiting smoking inside a room needs no special technical installations. Value-acceptability within the policy-community was a given; smoking bans were considered to be the only appropriate solution to the problem of passive smoking. Regarding the public's acquiescence, the pioneer experiences of other European countries justified the assumption that smoking bans could be implemented with few problems and overall positive feedback from the public. Therefore, receptivity to the idea among elected decision-makers increased within a short time.

The politics stream at the federal level

According to Kingdon, the politics stream consists mainly of three elements: political parties, interest-groups and the national mood. Political parties have a central position within the political process. In the conceptualisation of the multiple-streams framework their aims and positions are often not clear at the beginning but formed during the process (Rüb 2009: 359). This ambiguity in preferences is essential for the policy-entrepreneurs because it creates room for strategic manipulation. With regard to non-smoker-protection legislation, that is exactly what we find. Only the two opposition parties communicated clear positions: the Greens (Bündnis 90/Die Grünen) expressed support for a smoking ban in restaurants while the Liberals (FDP) vehemently protested. The governing Grand Coalition, was split, however: in his own party, the SPD, Binding gained more and more supporters, though there were still opponents. The majority of actors in the SPD's coalition partner, CDU/CSU, were against a general smoking ban in the catering industry, however. Top-ranking politicians, in particular from both governing parties, hesitated to begin concrete action at first. Owing to public pressure, the situation changed increasingly in favour of the ban's proponents.

Regarding interest-groups, there was a huge imbalance between those in favour and those against a smoking ban. Although several organisations promoted the protection of non-smokers – such as Pro-Smoke-Free, Non-Smokers' Initiative Germany and various agencies and associations for health education, addiction, cancer and other diseases – their potential for successful lobbying was marginal. Among the opponents of a smoking ban, the Hotel and Restaurant Association (DEHOGA) is important because more than one million employees work in the business, generating average sales of more than €50 billion in recent years. The catering industry claimed that a smoking ban would keep customers away, which would cause a big drop in sales and thus lead to the loss of jobs. Although they did not dominate the headlines, these claims were frequently mentioned in the media. The most important actor was the tobacco industry, represented by the Association of the Tobacco Industry (VdC). The tobacco industry also feared a massive drop in sales, because restaurants and bars were popular places for smoking. The strength of the tobacco industry's argument was primarily related not to jobs but to the revenue raised by the tobacco tax, which has a volume of about €13 billion per annum. Plenty of studies have examined the influence of the tobacco lobby and its remarkable access to relevant authorities, agencies and politicians (Grüning, Strück and Gilmore 2008; Cooper and Kurzer 2003). Detailed insights were gained during US lawsuits, which forced several transnational tobacco companies to make public millions of internal documents (Bornhäuser et al. 2006). According to these documents, by the 1980s, (unpublished) surveys had already shown that the public was becoming more and more aware of the problem of passive smoking;

the tobacco lobby reacted with a broad counter-strategy. New scientific findings were systematically inhibited by casting doubts on the reputation of the scientists behind them and by financing research fitting with the tobacco industry's aims, in combination with massive public-relations efforts. In 1996, for example, a group of members of the Bundestag started an initiative for a smoking ban that failed owing to the activity of the tobacco lobby. The head of the initiative commented: 'We had plenty of supporters, but then the pressure of the lobbyists became too extreme' [own translation] (*Der Spiegel*, 26 June 2006). Again in 2006, the tobacco lobby tried to influence the legislation and actually managed to bring a proposal for a very limited smoking ban into the working group of the Grand Coalition (*Neue Westfälische*, 12 October 2006).

The national mood is, according to Kingdon (2003: 147), defined as 'a rather large number of people out in the country ... thinking along certain common lines'; a change in the national mood has an important impact because that 'creates the "fertile ground"'. Kingdon (2003: 148) himself admitted that it is 'a rather vague presence that people in and around government sense, something that is palpable to them but hardly concrete'. Zahariadis (1995: 34–5) therefore questioned how such a 'nebulous definition' could be operationalised and stated that the term is 'far too imprecise to be empirically useful by itself'. Yet Kingdon (2003[1984]: 149) offered some indications regarding the way politicians sense the national mood: information received from interest-group leaders; newspaper editorials; people's reactions at public events; correspondence with voters and so forth. Thus, the national mood can be seen as a puzzle; by combining these 'pieces', it is possible to detect the whole picture.

With regard to non-smoker-protection, first of all, it is important that the image of smoking has become more and more negative over the last decades. Until the 1980s, smoking was often seen as a symbol of freedom, coolness and attractiveness; today, smoking is rather associated with addiction and toxins. The change was embedded in a general development towards a healthier lifestyle. In the 1980s, fitness and wellness became social trends, accompanied by a higher awareness of ecologically produced food, which all stands in contrast to toxic cigarettes. Market-demand for offers for non-smokers increased; for instance, providing non-smoking rooms in hotels became standard. Overall, the *de facto* situation in 2006 (the start of the legislation process) differed from the *de jure* situation: numerous state agencies, public transport and particularly schools, as well as private businesses, had individually implemented smoking bans. Moreover, without further laws being passed, the legal situation had been changed, step by step, by court decisions. The number of lawsuits increased and, as Rahmede (1983: 125) recognised, a clear tendency from the 1970s on to grant protection to non-smokers based on a new, broader interpretation of the constitutional right of physical inviolability. This represents a change in society as a whole that took place not only in Germany but all over Europe. Although Kingdon cautioned against equating the national mood with the results of opinion polls, the continuous change in national mood is also reflected in opinion polls during the previous two decades. In 1989, for instance, 49 per cent of the

German population favoured smoking bans in public buildings and only a small minority, 10 per cent, in restaurants (Bornhäuser *et al*. 2006: 76). But in 2006 (Eurobarometer Spezial 239, 2006: 27), 77 per cent were 'completely in favour' or 'rather in favour' of smoking bans in restaurants. After Binding's initiative the data was spread by the media, so the majority became aware of its own position and felt strengthened. When the public later learned that the working group of the Grand Coalition had discussed a proposal of the tobacco lobby, it was so outraged that both the CDU/CSU and SPD instantly distanced themselves from the tobacco lobby and publicly accused the other coalition partner of being responsible (*Neue Westfälische*, 12 October 2006). The broad and exceedingly positive public feedback to Binding's initiative illustrates the profound change that had taken place during the previous decades. The decision-makers also clearly perceived the change in national mood and the strong dynamic that had emerged. Only a few weeks after Binding's initiative, Chancellor Merkel signalled her support and stated that the time was ripe for action: large parts of society demanded better protection for non-smokers (*Berliner Morgenpost*, 20 June 2006). One newspaper even commented some days later: 'Meanwhile almost nobody in Berlin dares to take a position openly against general smoking bans' [own translation] (*Der Spiegel*, 29 June 2006). Leading politicians continued to avoid concrete statements and the area of the catering industry remained highly controversial. Yet the need for better protection of non-smokers in general was beyond all question.

Policy-entrepreneur, policy window and coupling at the federal level

Policy-entrepreneurs, according to Kingdon (2003[1984]: 179), are 'advocates who are willing to invest their resources – time, energy, reputation, money – to promote a position'. Their success depends on three characteristics: the person should have some ability to get a hearing and political connections, as well as persistence (Kingdon 2003[1984]: 180–1). Moreover, a policy-entrepreneur has to have the ability to influence the perception of issues, for example, by framing (giving ambiguous issues a dominant interpretation) or by affect-priming (strategic manipulation of emotions concerning an issue) (Zahariadis 2003: 14–16). During the so-called 'softening-up'[1] stage (Kingdon 2003[1984]: 127–131), policy-entrepreneurs try to achieve acceptance and support for their pet proposals. Later, when a policy-window opens, the entrepreneur has to couple the three streams.

Regarding non-smoker-protection legislation, two important actors can be identified. The first is Martina Pötschke-Langer, head of the Department for the Prevention of Cancer within the German Cancer Research Centre, the institution that published the ground-breaking study in December 2005. She acted like a policy-entrepreneur in her massive public-relations efforts, such as interviews, lectures about the issue and the spread of informative material (*Frankfurter Allgemeine Zeitung*, 23 February 2007). Framing the problem of passive smoking in the way

---

1. The term 'softening-up' refers to the process of getting policy communities and larger publics used to new ideas and building acceptance for proposals (Kingdon 1984).

described, she brought 'meaning, clarification, and identity' (Zahariadis 2007: 69) to the public. By focusing attention on the high number of potential victims of passive smoking, she stoked public fears and therefore led public emotion in her favoured direction. However, Pötschke-Langer was not a policy-entrepreneur as defined by Kingdon because she lacked access to politics. When Lothar Binding visited the German Cancer Research Centre, Pötschke-Langer was successful in winning him over to her project; but this happened partly by accident, during a general media event (Binding 2008: 18).

In the following period, Binding became the decisive policy-entrepreneur: a newspaper even called him the 'father of the non-smokers' protection law' [own translation] (*Die Welt*, 10 June 2008). He was a budget expert and not a health expert and, furthermore, a back-bencher and not a top-ranking politician; nevertheless, as a member of the federal parliament, he had access to decision-makers. Binding adopted Pötschke-Langer's argumentation and strategy and invested lots of time and energy, as well as his reputation, in persuading his colleagues and the public. Because, at the beginning, almost nobody believed he could be successful, the project carried a high risk of attracting ridicule (*taz*, 6 March 2008). A key to its success was the use of 'salami tactics' (Zahariadis 2007: 78; Rüb 2009: 362), that is, the strategic handling of time and a skilful alternation between argumentation and threat. By his initiative, which achieved almost 150 supporters in Parliament within a few weeks, Binding put pressure on leading politicians. As they hesitated to take action, he threatened them with an official ballot in Parliament. When the government offered to install a working group, he put his initiative on ice, became a member of the working group and went down the bargaining route.

An open window, according to Kingdon (2003[1984]: 165), 'is an opportunity for advocates of proposals to push their pet solutions' and an indispensable condition for successful coupling. Kingdon emphasised that windows normally stay open only briefly. In this case, a window was opened in the problem stream, particularly by the publication of the study by the German Cancer Research Centre. Yet the opening of the window had no effect at first, as no policy-entrepreneur appeared to take advantage of the public reaction to the study.

When Binding started fighting for a smoking ban, more than six months later, public attention had already drifted away from the study. However, relating the initiative to the study produced the same reaction from the public as six months before, when the study was first published, and therefore Binding reopened the previous window. Thus, I agree with Zohlnhöfer and Huß (2016: Chapter Ten of this volume), who assumes that 'policy windows can be opened by policy entrepreneurs'.

Binding presented the general smoking ban as a solution to what the public perceived as the problem of passive smoking following the Cancer Research Centre study and thus he engaged in 'consequential coupling' (Zahariadis 2003: 72). Given the lobby power of the tobacco industry, nobody expected success but Binding was successful in coupling the problem stream and the policy stream with the strong national mood from the politics stream so that the issue reached the decision-agenda, which includes, according to Kingdon (1984: 4), those subjects 'that are up for an active decision'. The decision failed, however, as constitutional problems arose because meanwhile, owing to the reform of federalism, the legislative competence for the catering industry had been taken away from the federal level (*Badische Zeitung*, 5 December 2006). Yet several newspapers, as well as Binding and his supporters, supposed that the government had, in fact, surrendered to pressure from the tobacco lobby (*n-tv*, 8 December 2006) as some experts also claimed that the federal government still had legislative competence in this area (see Siekmann 2006; Stern and Geerlings 2008). Irrespective of the actual reason, because the process was not completely interrupted but only relocated, the opportunity for a legislative decision still existed.

The states' legislation

Between January and March 2007, the states showed typical behaviour within German unitary federalism[2] by trying to harmonise their policies (cf. Reus 2014: 165). The efforts resulted in an agreement between all sixteen states about a smoking ban affecting state agencies and public transport as well as cultural buildings like schools and theatres. The agreement also contained an official general smoking ban for the entire catering industry, which was more restrictive than the previous federal compromise (which had excluded bars and discos). This success was emphatically emphasised to the public. Yet, as demanded by several states (which were, indeed, not named in the protocol), a deviation clause allowed the exclusion of certain forms of restaurants from the smoking ban.

The policy stream and the decision-window at the state level

When legislative competence for the catering industry was transferred to the German states, there was already a worked-out proposal, which was the starting point for the states' policy-making. According to Zohlnhöfer and Herweg (2012: 5), 'the decision window is opened by the policy stream because once an issue is set on the decision agenda, it will be dealt with irrespective of the pressure to address a particular problem'. At this stage, 'the main emphasis ... is on the politics stream' (Zohlnhöfer and Herweg 2012: 11). As the actors involved were now different from those at the federal level, it is evident that the political situation in each individual state was of central importance for the policy-decision (*see* below). The issue was a fixture on the decision-agenda of all sixteen states but, because the deviation clause had created a potential loophole, depending on

---

2. While many federal states are shaped by the principle of reflecting and encouraging diversity, it is often argued that the Federal Republic of Germany has a unitary political culture. Surveys regularly confirm the lack of citizen support for divergent individual *Land* policy; a clear majority prefers solidarity to federal competition. To some extent this aim is given by the Basic Law, namely, the 'welfare state postulate', which commits all state levels to the aim of ensuring equal living conditions across the territory. The consequence is that Germany is organised like a federal state but, nevertheless, there is often policy uniformity across the states similar to that in centralised states.

the current political situation in the different states, further options beside the federal compromise and the states' agreement were also discussed, both more and less restrictive ones.

The problem stream at the state level

This stream remained the same as at the federal level: the health-frame was dominant and rival frames were marginalised. In all sixteen states, the problem-definition established by the study of the German Cancer Research Centre determined the limits of the political discussion. Argumentation concentrated on whether restaurants and bars should be treated as public or private rooms, the latter presumably not being subject to state regulation. However, almost no politician cast doubt on the existence and importance of the problem of passive smoking in general.

The politics stream at the state level

As mentioned above, the politics stream was essential for the final policy-decision. The chances for restrictive non-smoker-protection laws differed greatly, according to the political situation in the sixteen states. Basically, the issue developed in the same way in political parties at the state level as at the federal level. At the beginning of the process, the parties' aims and positions were often not clear; they were formed *during* the process. Every state party of the Greens was in favour of as restrictive a smoking ban as possible, the definition of which varied between the states. The Liberals (FDP) in almost all states argued against a general smoking ban. Christian-Democrats (CDU) and Social-Democrats (SPD), as well as the Left Party, were split. After some time, the SPD state parties became more or less unanimously in favour of a general smoking ban, while the CDU parties remained split in some states. This led to sometimes acrimonious struggles between the coalition partners within CDU–SPD and CDU–FDP state governments.

The situation with regard to interest-groups was also similar to that at the federal level – marginal lobbying-potential in favour of and much higher lobbying-potential against a smoking ban – but with one significant difference: since the Association of the Tobacco Industry was organised at the federal level, exerting its influence was more difficult in the face of sixteen state counterparts instead of a single federal one.

The national mood was still strongly in favour of better protection for non-smokers and became even more so over time. The media reported increasingly positive feedback from the public and so supported the changing dynamic. Most politicians clearly perceived this and pointed out explicitly the wide consensus among the public. Health Senator Lompscher (Berlin), for instance, saw a 'broad majority in society' (*Berliner Morgenpost*, 16 January 2007) in favour of a smoking ban in Germany; and Health Minister Dreyer (Rhineland-Palatine) recognised 'a clear societal paradigm shift' (Landtag Rhineland-Palatine Printed Matter 15/23: 1322). Within a short time, even initial opponents of a smoking ban were overwhelmed by the development of public opinion: in November 2006, the Hessian CDU politician Alfons Gerling was still arguing for voluntary solutions and characterised the draft law of the opposition (at the state level) SPD as 'typical social-democratic over-regulation' (*Frankfurter Rundschau*, 22 November 2006) but, some months later, his own party passed a relatively restrictive law and Gerling emphatically emphasised the support of 'the predominant majority of citizens' for a smoking ban by law (Landtag Hesse Printed Matter 16/141: 9945).

Policy-entrepreneurs and coupling at the state level

According to Zohlnhöfer and Herweg (2012: 5) 'the second coupling process focuses on policy formulation and captures the political struggle about the concrete design of the proposal'. The result of the legislation process was, in all sixteen states, a general smoking ban by law. Compared to the legal situation previous to 2007 (no restrictions by law), a paradigm shift that turned Germany from the 'paradise of smokers' to the 'paradise of non-smokers' took place. Nevertheless, there were substantial differences between the laws in the different states. Table 11.1 shows the overall level of protection of the sixteen laws – the lower the score, the more restrictive the law (for index-construction, *see* Appendix).

Table 11.1: Strictness of non-smokers-protection in German states and partisan composition of government

State	Score	Government
North Rhine-Westphalia	10	CDU /FDP
Saarland	8	CDU
Hamburg	8	CDU
Schleswig-Holstein	7	CDU/SPD
Hesse	6	CDU
Rhineland-Palatinate	6	SPD
Saxony-Anhalt	6	CDU/SPD
Thuringia	6	CDU
Bremen	6	SPD/Greens
Mecklenburg-West Pomerania	5	SPD/CDU
Lower Saxony	5	CDU/FDP
Saxony	4	CDU/SPD
Baden-Württemberg	4	CDU/FDP
Berlin	4	SPD/Left
Brandenburg	3	SPD/CDU
Bavaria	2	CSU

Source: author's compilation; www.bundeswahlleiter.de (results of elections)

The role of policy-entrepreneur was often taken over by the responsible minister within the state after the transfer of legislative competence. Equating success with the enactment of a comparatively restrictive law, four case groups can be distinguished:

1. Minister takes over role of policy-entrepreneur → success
2. Minister takes over role of policy-entrepreneur → failure
3. Nobody takes over role of policy-entrepreneur → success
4. Nobody takes over role of policy-entrepreneur → failure

The majority of the cases have to be put in case group 1. For example, the health minister of Brandenburg, Dagmar Ziegler (SPD), had been an advocate of more protection for non-smokers for quite some time and thus, in 2004, started the political campaign Smoke-Free Brandenburg. After the states received the legislative competence, she signalled her willingness to fight for a restrictive general smoking ban and she presented a draft bill only a few days later. When several members of the Cabinet (both SPD and CDU) argued vehemently against her plans, Minister Ziegler started one-on-one talks with her colleagues in order to convince them (*Schweriner Volkszeitung*, 13 July 2007). Finally, she succeeded, and the government passed her bill without a dissenting vote, resulting in one of the strictest laws of all the German states.

In Nordrhein-Westfalen and Saarland, on the other hand, nobody promoted a restrictive smoking ban (case group 4) and, as we would expect from a multiple-streams perspective, the result was a relatively lenient law. In North Rhine-Westphalia, for instance, instead of fighting for the protection of non-smokers like most of his counter-parts, Health Minister Laumann (CDU) examined ways to exempt certain forms of catering establishments from the smoking ban. The CDU parliamentary group was internally split and Prime Minister Rüttgers (CDU) and the FDP rejected a smoking ban by law. In response to an expert hearing and the development of public opinion, the CDU parliamentary group adopted a confrontational attitude towards Rüttgers and Laumann and demanded a general smoking ban; but the law passed was comparatively lenient.

Case group 2 contains those states in which a minister took over the role of the policy-entrepreneur but failed. A closer look at the legislation processes shows that these ministers failed owing to resistance from a coalition partner. In other words, the politics stream was only partly ripe; not all parties involved in government favoured restrictive regulations. In Schleswig-Holstein, for instance, Social Minister Gitta Trauernicht (SPD) fought for a restrictive smoking ban but leading politicians of the coalition partner CDU were against her plans. After a serious conflict lasting several months, the CDU was able to modify the bill to make it more flexible, which meant more exceptions; a representative of the SPD commented that his party had been in favour of a more restrictive law but could not stand up to their coalition-partner the CDU (Landtag Schleswig-Holstein Printed Matter 16/72: 5200). Coalition-partners play an important role as veto-players because their agreement is necessary for a change in the *status quo*. If a proposed policy is not compatible with their position, resistance will arise that usually cannot be bypassed, even by the most skilled policy-entrepreneur. Table 11.1 shows that SPD-led governments always enforced laws with a comparatively high degree of restrictiveness; the laws never received scores higher than 6 (with 10 being the most lenient law). In contrast, the CDU and FDP state parties did not act according to a consistent pattern. Thus, the largest range of positions could be found within the CDU.

Case group 3, in which nobody takes over the role of the policy-entrepreneur leading to success, is a serious problem for the multiple-streams framework because the policy-entrepreneur has a central position in coupling the three streams while a window is open. Put differently, if there is no policy-entrepreneur, we would expect no policy change to occur. Münter (2005: 251–5) assumed that the five elements of the multiple-streams framework – problem stream, policy stream, politics stream, policy-window and policy-entrepreneur – do not all have the same potential for obstruction. If the three streams flow in a positive way and a window opens, he asserted, overcoming the lack of a policy-entrepreneur is not problematic because other actors will take over that role. However, we find states without any entrepreneur during the whole process that still passed relatively restrictive laws. As the policy-entrepreneur is essential from the multiple-streams perspective, these cases without the engagement of such an actor show that the approach can be invalidated.

The positive dynamic among the public was so immense that all state governments – even those not originally in favour of a smoking ban by law – feared disadvantages in terms of election losses by not satisfying public demand. In Rhineland-Palatinate, for instance, nobody specifically engaged with this issue but, nevertheless, the law passed is ranked in the middle (6 points) in terms of restrictiveness. Health Minister Malu Dreyer (SPD) expressed her and her party's preference for voluntary solutions and referred to great achievements in schools and state agencies in recent years. Yet owing to the clear trend towards better protection for non-smokers, the government would introduce a draft law (Landtag Rhineland-Palatinate Printed Matter 15/23: 1322). In Lower Saxony, Prime Minister Christian Wulff (CDU), in complete agreement with the coalition partner FDP, initially proposed a labelling duty without substantial restrictions for the catering industry. Confronted with massive public protest – 900 comments in his website visitor's log within two days as well as extremely critical news coverage (*taz*, 3 April 2007) – Wulff performed a complete U-turn. The government proclaimed that 'obviously the people had other preferences' (*Frankfurter Rundschau*, 5 April 2007 [author's own translation]) and, shortly afterwards, one of the most restrictive laws of any state was passed.

The amendment of the state laws

Shortly after the first state anti-smoking laws took effect, catering establishments from different states filed lawsuits against them. Most states had enacted a general smoking ban with the exception of establishments with separate rooms for smokers. Single-room establishments now claimed they had been disadvantaged because they were not able to create a separate room for smoking guests. The Federal Constitutional Court (30 July 2008: 1 BvR 3262/07, 1 BvR 402/08, 1 BvR 906/08, available at: http://www.bverfg.de/e/rs20080730_1bvr326207.html) upheld the claims of these establishments and declared that state laws must include an additional exception for small, single-room bars that offered only drinks and gave no access to minors, because otherwise their existence would be threatened.

The policy stream and the decision-window

This judgment of the Federal Constitutional Court opened a second decision-window. The window made possible several options: if a state intended to make sure that every restaurant and bar offered places for non-smokers, it had to implement an absolute smoking ban without any exemption to fulfil the constitutional requirements. A general smoking ban had to include the exemption for single-room bars, which means that certain bars would not offer places for non-smokers. Of course, abolition of the smoking ban was also possible, as well as further exemptions.

The problem stream

While the problem was clearly framed in just one way at the beginning, now a rival frame emerged. Restaurant-owners claimed that the smoking bans had led to fewer customers and, as a result, to lower sales and, possibly, to job-losses. The media reported these claims extensively and with a strong tone of sympathy for the situation of the restaurant owners (for example, *Thüringer Allgemeine*, 7 June 2008). The health risks of passive smoking sometimes seemed to be forgotten and, instead, commentary on empty restaurants and bars dominated the news coverage. This development shows, in accordance with Kingdon (2003[1984]: 100–3) and Zahariadis (2007: 72), that feedback, particularly from the public, can have a problem-producing function.

The politics stream

Particularly those parties that had initially opposed a general smoking ban for the catering industry – the FDP and, to some extent, the CDU – again became rigorous opponents of it. Moreover, in the face of the economic risk, numerous politicians from all parties began to question the relevance of the problem of passive smoking and openly considered excluding the whole catering industry from the general smoking ban.

The interest-groups fighting against restrictive smoking bans gained influence again. The Hotel and Restaurants Association was especially successful in getting its demands into the media.

With regard to the national mood, the role of the media itself should be highlighted. The media are not only a vehicle for transmitting the national mood of the public but also set trends and thus, to some extent, manipulate the national mood (Rüb 2009: 368). Based on the positive public feedback during the first legislation period and the experiences of other European countries, a relatively unproblematic implementation of the smoking bans had been expected. However, discussion went on after the laws came into effect. Smokers as well as restaurant-owners started initiatives, held demonstrations and tried to bypass the new laws. Beside the new economic frame of the problem, the media published negative feedback from the public and therefore created an impression of a changed national mood. Accordingly, Mario Czaja (CDU) justified the softening of the current Berlin law by referring to 'lots of people in Berlin being noticeably annoyed with the smoking ban in their favourite pubs' (Abgeordnetenhaus Berlin Printed Matter 16/27: 2485). In North Rhine-Westphalia, Health Minister Laumann (CDU) stated that a broad majority supported the protection of non-smokers by law but preferred 'a law with a sense of proportion' (Landtag North Rhine-Westphalia Printed Matter 14/120: 13934), which likewise refers to a less restrictive law. Indeed, surveys (*Rhein-Zeitung*, 30 May 2008) depicted a persistent and large majority in favour of general smoking bans, including for the catering industry, with only a few exemptions. Furthermore, all popular petitions trying to abolish the laws in the states failed. By contrast, in Bavaria the popular petition for an absolute smoking ban without any exception was successful. My analysis thus confirms Kingdon's assumption that the *perception* of the national mood is decisive: 'Researchers on public opinion will long debate the validity of these perceptions, but for our purposes the critical fact is that important people held them strongly' (Kingdon 2003: 147). If decision-makers believe that there is a national mood widening or limiting the possible range of their policy options, these perceptions will guide their behaviour whether they are accurate or not.

Policy-entrepreneurs and coupling

After the Constitutional Court's decision, almost all states except Bavaria were forced to amend their laws and to consider giving the exemption to small, single-room bars (for the individual outcomes, *see* Table 11.2). Overall, there was ambiguity due to the perception of an unexpected change in the public mood. During the original legislative process, politicians had perceived strong public support for restrictive policies but, during the amendment legislation, no such clear trends could be identified. Hence, to be on the safe side, many state governments stayed close to the proposal of the Federal Constitutional Court.

In some cases the differences between the laws can be explained by the actions of a policy-entrepreneur. During the original legislation processes, there was only one policy-entrepreneur per state (or no policy-entrepreneurs at all) fighting for an improvement in protection for non-smokers. During the amendment processes, competing policy-entrepreneurs appeared, who tried to take advantage of the window the Federal Constitutional Court had opened, that is, to push through more exemptions than the court had decreed. These competing policy-entrepreneurs were normally ministers, especially the ministers for economic affairs. Some of them succeeded in coupling the streams while the second decision-window was open and realised significant exceptions. Others failed, sometimes owing to resolutely opposed health ministers.

But the result of legislation can be better explained by the partisan composition of the state governments. Successful entrepreneurs always acted with the support of their parties and mostly also with the support of their coalition partners. The table shows that, with the exception of the CDU–Greens coalition in Hamburg, CDU-led governments, in particular with the FDP as coalition partner, passed less restrictive laws. By contrast, SPD-led governments, except in the outlier Rhineland-Palatinate, passed more restrictive laws. Later, based on changes of government, further amendments were made. Both North Rhine-Westphalia (after the SPD had entered the government) and Saarland (after the Greens had entered the government) tightened their laws and passed absolute smoking bans without any exemptions. Accordingly, after the CSU lost its majority in Parliament in Bavaria in 2008, the FDP required a less restrictive law as a condition for forming a coalition.

Table 11.2: Strictness of original/amended state laws and partisan composition of government

State	Original score	Amended Score
North Rhine-Westphalia	10 (CDU/ FDP)	11 (CDU/FDP)
Rhineland-Palatinate	6 (SPD)	9 (SPD)
Saarland	8 (CDU)	8 (CDU)
Saxony	4 (CDU/FDP)	8 (CDU/FDP)
Baden-Württemberg	4 (CDU/FDP)	7 (CDU/FDP)
Hesse	6 (CDU)	7 (CDU/FDP)
Saxony-Anhalt	6 (CDU/SPD)	7 (CDU/SPD)
Bavaria	2 (CSU)	6 (CSU/FDP)
Lower Saxony	5 (CDU/FDP)	6 (CSU/FDP)
Schleswig-Holstein	7 (CDU/SPD)	6 (CDU/SPD)
Thuringia	6 (CDU)	6 (CDU/SPD)
Berlin	4 (SPD/The Left)	5 (SPD/The Left)
Bremen	6 (SPD)	5 (SPD/Greens)
Mecklenburg-West Pomerania	5 (SPD/CDU)	4 (SPD/CDU)
Brandenburg	3 (SPD/CDU)	4 (SPD/CDU)
Hamburg	8 (CDU)	3 (CDU/Greens)

Source: author's compilation.
Note: partisan composition of government during relevant legislative period in parentheses.

Conclusion

It turns out that the multiple-streams framework is suitable for explaining the German non-smoker-protection legislation – but only in combination with other theories of policy-analysis. Regarding the agenda-setting process, the approach works nearly perfectly; no other theoretical approach is able to explain why the issue reached the decision-agenda in 2006. The legislation process would hardly have started at all without Lothar Binding's engagement as a policy-entrepreneur coupling the three streams, particularly with respect to the national mood. Therefore, I follow Zohlnhöfer and Herweg (2012: 14) in concluding that 'the MSF proves to be particularly suitable for the analysis of "unlikely" reforms, i.e. [reforms] we would not expect on the basis of traditional theoretical approaches'.

However, other theories outperform the multiple-streams framework when it comes to explaining the outcome of the legislation process, that is, decision-making. Once the unlikely reform was under way, the process followed likely patterns. In these phases, partisan ideology, party-competition and veto-player theory sufficiently explain the development: seeing overwhelming public support emerging, all sixteen state governments passed a general smoking ban by law and included the whole catering industry. The differences between the laws largely depend on partisan preferences, with coalition partners as veto-players preventing extreme solutions in either direction. As mentioned above, the influence of partisan preferences became even more obvious with regard to the amendment of the laws after the decision of the Federal Constitutional Court. Although Herweg (2013: 337–42) has demonstrated that these theoretical approaches can be integrated with the multiple-streams framework, the additional explanatory factors do not offer additional value here. In some cases these elements, notably, the policy-entrepreneur, may even have been absent from the coupling process. Thus, the multiple-streams framework is a fruitful addition to other theories but does not make them dispensable.

References *(newspaper and online news articles listed separately, below)*

Binding, L. (2008) *Kalter Rauch. Der Anfang vom Ende der Kippenrepublik,* Freiburg, DE: Orange Press.

Bornhäuser, A., McCarthy, J. and Glantz, S. A. (2006) 'German tobacco industry's successful efforts to maintain scientific and political respectability to prevent regulation of secondhand smoke', University of San Francisco: Center for Tobacco Control Research and Education, available at: http:// escholarship.org/uc/item/5ds4w4f5 (accessed 13 September 2014).

Cooper, A. H. and Kurzer, P. (2003) 'Rauch ohne Feuer. Why Germany lags in tobacco control', *German Politics & Society* 21(3): 24–47.

Eurobarometer Spezial 239 (2006) 'Einstellungen der Europäer zu Tabak, durchgeführt von TNS Opinion & Social im Auftrag der Europäischen Kommission, Brüssel, available at: http://ec.europa.eu/public_opinion/ archives/ebs/ebs_239_de.pdf (in German) and at: http://ec.europa.eu/ public_opinion/archives/ebs/ebs_239_en.pdf (in English) (accessed 18 October 2015).

German Cancer Research Centre (2005) 'Passivrauchen – ein unterschätztes Gesundheitsrisiko' ['Passive smoking – an underestimated health risk'], *Rote Reihe,* Band 5, Heidelberg.

Grüning, T., Strünck, C. and Gilmore, A. B. (2008) 'Puffing away? Explaining the politics of tobacco control in Germany', *German Politics* 17(2): 140–64.

Herweg, N. (2013) 'Der Multiple-Streams-Ansatz – ein Ansatz, dessen Zeit gekommen ist?', *Zeitschrift für Vergleichende Politikwissenschaft* 7(4): 321–45.

Joossens, L. and Raw, M. (2007) 'Progress in tobacco control in 30 European countries 2005 to 2007', report presented at the 4th European Conference on Tobacco or Health, Basel, Switzerland, 11–13 October.

Kingdon, J. W. 2003[1984] *Agendas, Alternatives, and Public Policies,* Boston, MA: Little, Brown & Co.

Münter, M. (2005) *Verfassungsreform im Einheitsstaat. Die Politik der Dezentralisierung in Großbritannien,* Wiesbaden, DE: VS Verlag für Sozialwissenschaften.

Rahmede, J. (1983) *Passivrauchen und Recht. Gesundheitliche Wirkungen und rechtliche Konsequenzen,* Gelsenkirchen, DE: Mannhold Verlag.

Reus, I. (2014) 'Neue Eigenständigkeit oder Unitarismus wie bisher? Landespolitik nach der Föderalismusreform I am Beispiel der Nichtraucherschutzgesetzgebung', der moderne staat, 7(1): 157–172.

Rüb, F. W. (2009) 'Multiple-Streams-Ansatz: Grundlagen, Probleme und Kritik', in K. Schubert and N. C. Bandelow (eds) *Lehrbuch der Politikfeldanalyse 2.0,* München, DE: Oldenburgverlag, pp. 348–78.

Siekmann, H. (2006) 'Die Zuständigkeit des Bundes zum Erlass umfassender Rauchverbote nach In-Kraft-Treten der ersten Stufe der Föderalismusreform', *Neue Juristische Wochenschrift* 59(47): 3382–5.

Stern, K. and Geerlings, J. (2008) *Nichtraucherschutz in Deutschland. International- und verfassungsrechtliche Vorgaben*, München, DE: Vahlen-Verlag.

Zahariadis, N. (1992) 'To sell or not to sell? Telecommunications policy in Britain and France', *Journal of Public Policy* 12(4): 255–376.

Zahariadis, N. (1995) *Markets, States, and Public Policy: Privatization in Britain and France*, Ann Arbor, MI: University of Michigan Press.

Zahariadis, N. (2003) *Ambiguity and Choice in Public Policy: Political decision making in modern democracies*, Washington, DC: Georgetown University Press.

Zahariadis, N. (2007) 'The multiple streams framework. Structure, limitations, prospects', in P.A. Sabatier (ed.) *Theories of the Policy Process*, Boulder, CO: Westview Press.

Zohlnhöfer, R. and Herweg, N. (2012) 'Explaining paradigmatic change in German labor market policy. A multiple streams perspective', paper prepared for the workshop The Politics of Labour Market Policy in Times of Austerity, ECPR Joint Sessions of Workshops 2012, Antwerp, 11–13 April.

Zohlnhöfer, R. and Huß, C. (2015) 'How Well Does the Multiple-Streams Framework Travel? Evidence from German case studies', in R. Zohlnhöfer and F. Rüb (eds) *Decision-Making under Ambiguity and Time Constraints: Assessing the Multiple-Streams Framework*, Colchester, UK: ECPR Press.

Newspaper and online news articles

Badische Zeitung, 5 December 2006, 'Ob das Antirauchergesetz kommt, ist ungewiss – Der Bund ist für Gesundheitsschutz zuständig, die Länder für die Gaststätten – da tut sich ein neues Streitthema auf'.

Berliner Morgenpost, 20 June 2006, p. 2, 'Bund kann Rauchverbot nicht umsetzen. Auch Länder und Kommunen gefordert.'

Berliner Morgenpost, 16 January 2007, no. 15, p. 1 'Raucher müssen ins Separee'.

Der Spiegel, 26 June 2006, p. 27, 'Koalition der Willigen'.

Die Welt, 27 September 2006, p. 4, 'Rauchverbot in Kneipen vorerst vom Tisch. Fraktionen von Union und SPD streiten um einen besseren Nichtraucherschutz.'

Die Welt, 10 June 2008, 'Deutschlands Rauchverbots-Kämpfer Nr. 1', available at: http://www.welt.de/politik/article2086482/Deutschlands-Rauchverbots-Kaempfer-Nr-1.html (accessed October 20 2015).

Die Zeit, 1 March 2007, p. 2, 'Warum jetzt?'.

Frankfurter Allgemeine Zeitung, 12 June 2006, p. 001, 'Bätzing: Rauchverbot nicht mehr undenkbar'.

Frankfurter Allgemeine Zeitung, 23 February 2007, p. 003, 'Ein langer Atem Martina Pötschke-Langer vom Deutschen Krebsforschungszentrum in Heidelberg streitet für ein rauchfreies Deutschland'.

Frankfurter Rundschau, 22 November 2006, p. 24, 'Grüne machen Rauchern der CDU-Fraktion Vorwürfe. Abgeordnete Schulz-Asche und SPD fordern rauchfreien Landtag. Christdemokraten und FDP plädieren für Freiwilligkeit.'

Frankfurter Rundschau, 5 April 2007, p. 4, 'Niedersachsen. Wulff erwägt Kurswende bei Rauchverbot.'

Neue Westfälische, 12 October 2006, 'Im Visier der Tabak-Lobby. Große Koalition will Anti-Raucher-Gesetz – aber die Industrie macht Druck.'

n-tv, 7 December 2006, 'Föderalismus als Problem. Rauchverbot vom Tisch', available at: http://www.n-tv.de/politik/Rauchverbot-vom-Tisch-article202367.html (accessed October 20 2015).

n-tv, 8 December 2006, 'Bundesregierung "vernebelt". Streit ums Rauchverbot.', available at: http://www.n-tv.de/politik/Streit-ums-Rauchverbot-article202589.html (accessed October 20 2015).

Rhein-Zeitung, 30 May 2008, 'Bürger begrüßen Rauchverbot'.

Schweriner Volkszeitung, 13 July 2007, p. 4, 'Abschied vom Glimmstengel'.

Spiegel Online, 02 March 2005, 'Freiwillige Verpflichtung: Mehr Nichtraucherzonen in Kneipen', available at: http://www.spiegel.de/politik/deutschland/freiwillige-verpflichtung-mehr-nichtraucherzonen-in-kneipen-a-344422.html (accessed October 20 2015).

taz, 3 April 2007, p. 21, 'Proteste gegen "Drogenwulff"'.

taz, 6 March 2008, 'Rauchverbotspionier Binding. Der Schrecken der Tabaklobby', available at: http://www.taz.de/!5185577/ (accessed October 20 2015).

Thüringer Allgemeine, 7 June 2008, 'Bierdurst ist versiegt – Die Kneipiers hatten es befürchtet: Kommt das Rauchverbot'.

Appendix: index-construction and scoring

A general smoking ban can imply a wide range of exemptions. Hence, the first step for analysis is to present the content of the laws in a way suitable for systematic comparison. As shown in the following, I have developed an index to classify the German states' anti-smoking laws according to their restrictiveness. The index is constructed as followed: at first, central aspects of the policy were identified, represented by the eight dimensions of the index (A to H). Subsequently, in each dimension, scores were assigned to the different regulations in the laws. The index is built on empirical variance, which means that both the dimensions and the values are directly obtained from the laws. The dimensions grasp all essential variance in the laws. Similar formulations concerning the different values are treated as equal. Special weight is given to some values, according to their implications for the addressee of the norm. For instance, if restaurants can be declared smoking clubs, the entire restaurant is inaccessible for non-smokers without incurring the dangers of passive smoking; while private functions in restaurants are limited to certain spaces of time and, normally, also to certain rooms.

A = Room for smokers in restaurants and pubs
    0 = no rooms for smokers allowed
    1 = secondary room/access only for adults/exemption only for pubs
    2 = secondary room/access only for adults/exemption for restaurants and pubs
    3 = secondary room/access for everybody
    4 = free choice/access for everybody

B = Room for smokers in discos
    0 = no rooms for smokers allowed
    1 = secondary room/access only for adults
    2 = secondary room/access for everybody

C = Restaurants run by their owners (without employees)
    0 = smoking forbidden
    2 = smoking allowed

D = Smoking clubs
    0 = not allowed
    2 = allowed (access only for members)

E = Private functions
    0 = smoking forbidden
    1 = smoking allowed

F = Food served in temporary marquees
    0 = smoking forbidden
    1 = smoking allowed

G = Occasional (time-limited) traditional events
    0 = smoking forbidden
    1 = smoking allowed

H = Single-room restaurants and pubs
    0 = smoking forbidden
    1 = smoking allowed if < 75 m^2/no prepared meals offered/access only for adults
    2 = smoking allowed if < 75 m^2/only simple dishes offered/access only for adults
    3 = smoking allowed if < 75 m^2

The index is additive, which means that the points for each dimension are summed up to a total score for each law, so that the sixteen laws can be ranked from 'restrictive' (low score) to 'lenient' (high score). The total score shows whether a law is, on the whole, designed to be more or less restrictive, so different arrangements can lead to the same total score.

Table A1: Original state laws

	A	B	C	D	E	F	G	H	Total
North Rhine-Westphalia	3	2	0	2	1	1	1	0	10
Saarland	3	2	2	0	0	1	0	0	8
Hamburg	3	2	0	2	0	1	0	0	8
Schleswig-Holstein	3	2	0	0	1	1	0	0	7
Hesse	3	2	0	0	0	1	0	0	6
Thuringia	3	2	0	0	1	0	0	0	6
Saxony-Anhalt	4	2	0	0	0	0	0	0	6
Rhineland-Palatinate	3	2	0	0	0	1	0	0	6
Bremen	3	2	0	0	0	1	0	0	6
Mecklenburg-West Pomerania	3	2	0	0	0	0	0	0	5
Lower Saxony	3	2	0	0	0	0	0	0	5
Saxony	3	0	0	0	0	1	0	0	4
Baden-Württemberg	3	0	0	0	0	1	0	0	4
Berlin	3	1	0	0	0	0	0	0	4
Brandenburg	3	0	0	0	0	0	0	0	3
Bavaria	0	0	0	2	0	0	0	0	2

Table A2: Amended state laws

	A	B	C	D	E	F	G	H	Total
North Rhine-Westphalia	3	2	0	2	1	1	1	1	11
Saxony	2	1	0	0	1	1	0	3	8
Rhineland-Palatinate	3	2	0	0	1	1	0	2	9
Saarland	2	1	2	0	0	1	0	2	8
Baden-Württemberg	3	1	0	0	0	1	0	2	7
Hesse	2	1	0	0	1	1	0	2	7
Saxony-Anhalt	4	1	0	0	0	0	0	2	7
Lower Saxony	3	2	0	0	0	0	0	1	6
Bavaria	2	1	0	0	0	1	0	2	6
Schleswig-Holstein	2	1	0	0	1	1	0	1	6
Thuringia	2	1	0	0	1	1	0	1	6
Bremen	2	1	0	0	0	1	0	1	5
Berlin	2	1	0	0	0	0	0	2	5
Brandenburg	2	1	0	0	0	0	0	1	4
Mecklenburg-West Pomerania	2	1	0	0	0	0	0	1	4
Hamburg	1	1	0	0	0	0	0	1	3

Chapter Twelve

Crisis Policy-Making: Traceable Processes of Multiple Streams

Dan Hansén

Crisis policy-making

Our societies are disposed to disruptions, some less appreciated than others. Among the disruptions that are less welcome are those that threaten or destroy important values (lives, properties, infrastructure, democratic rule of law, national independence, organisational credibility and so on), such as earthquakes, hurricanes, acts of terrorism and infrastructural breakdowns. Such disruptions are here referred to as crises, regardless of their origin. 'Catastrophe' or 'disaster' are sometimes fitting synonyms, but the defining characteristic of importance here is that they are 'episodic breakdowns of familiar symbolic frameworks that legitimate the pre-existing socio-political order' (Boin, McConnell and Hart 2008: 3). Policy-makers and their policies are then exposed to the critical scrutiny of the public, media and politicians alike.

In the crisis-management literature, the last two decades have witnessed a broadening scope of managerial tasks, from a narrow focus on operative challenges on the disaster scene – which is a very direct form of crisis-management – to a more encompassing approach in which the before- and after-crisis periods are included (Birkland 2006; Boin *et al*. 2005; Boin *et al*. 2008). Managing crises has, in this wider perspective, evolved into a constant process, with different degrees of intensity. The managerial challenges associated with the 'during' phase then represent highly intensive crisis-management; whereas the challenges implied by preparedness, sense-making, termination, accountability and learning are characterised by relatively low-intensity crisis-management, but occasionally and, in reverse, highly intensive politics.

Crisis policy-making is indirect to crisis-management, in the sense that it does not comprise the acute decision-making of the first response. It often takes place in the aftermath of a crisis; but it can also happen simultaneously. Its chief characteristic is that it involves the political and administrative entity that ultimately has authority over legislation, budgets and how to prioritise activities; that is, authoritative leadership is required. Even though operative staff are included in the process, crisis policy-making is not where operative tasks are managed directly. Crisis policy-making is event-related (Birkland 2006) but the objective is, ideally, to foster a more robust society, in which the preconditions for successful direct crisis-management are present; where the risks of disasters happening again are minimised; and where crisis consequences are mitigated. It is also an environment that makes and breaks careers by virtue of accountability. Ideas, ideologies and organisational positioning are on the line, testifying to the high-intensity politics occasionally being brought to bear. Crisis policy-making is, in that sense, just like any policy process marked by 'an extremely complex set of elements that interact over time' (Sabatier 2007: 3). On the other hand, to the extent that ambiguity is a fact of political life (Zahariadis 2003: 1) and policy-making is typically marked by a sense of urgency (Zahariadis 2003: 6), making choices over political alternatives is pretty much like crisis decision-making, which, in addition to ambiguity and urgency, also includes threats to important values (Sundelius, Stern and Bynander 1997; Boin *et al.* 2005).

Policy responses to crises are often serious in their consequences. It is not a matter of course that hopes for increasingly purposeful crisis-management machinery are met during crisis policy-making. Overreaction to terrorism may injuriously affect civil rights and neglect of natural hazards can put inhabitants of coastal zones at unnecessarily high risks. It even seems to be the case that overreaction to certain risks produces blind spots to others. May, Workmann and Jones (2008) argue, for instance, that the Department of Homeland Security's (DHS) one-sided focus on anti-terrorism policies so distracted FEMA (the Federal Emergency Management Agency, an organisation within DHS) from natural disasters (their area of expertise) as to leave that agency unprepared when Hurricane Katrina hit New Orleans. It is therefore important to better understand the forces at play at the top political-administrative level when it is under pressure to react to a crisis situation.

The issue of attention is important in crisis policy-making. How policy-makers attend to different aspects of the ambiguous environment that surrounds the management of crises has important consequences for the ensuing policy-process. This chapter aims to account for how the policy-process unfolds in crisis policy-making; and why. The theoretical insights of the multiple-streams framework (MSF) are valuable tools for such an endeavour. The framework's attentiveness to the importance of time and timing is essential for capturing event-related or crisis-induced policy-processes. The above mentioned aim may signal that the phenomenon of crisis policy-making as such is not yet, or not accurately, accounted for. The claim here is that the phenomenon is underspecified, in particular in relation to its relative importance.

In the following section, eight theoretical propositions derived from the MSF will be presented that describe and explain the process-logic of public policy-making. The propositions help sketch out ideal-typical policy trajectories. Next, these theoretical propositions are confronted with empirical data, in the form of a case study of the murder of Swedish Prime Minister Olof Palme and the subsequent quest to establish a counter-terrorism police unit. The case is fairly old; it was nevertheless chosen because it offers a very clear example of garbage-can policy-making – the prime element of multiple-streams thinking. The subsequent analysis will try to focus on aspects that the case shares with other cases of crisis policy-making.

Multiple-streams processes: attention, search, selection

The MSF is often mentioned with, if not compared to, punctuated-equilibrium theory (PET) (Baumgartner and Jones 1993; Jones and Baumgartner 2005) and the advocacy-coalition framework (ACF) (Sabatier and Jenkins-Smith 1993). In contrast to PET and the ACF, the influence exerted by the MSF has not depended on a coherent scholarship; in fact, the lack of scholarship has been lamented (Zahariadis 2007: 79). This is interesting, and suggests that a framework that makes a point of capturing serendipities and the messiness of political life has an important place in this field of knowledge, even if the MSF is not normally associated with theoretical parsimony. The theoretical generosity of the MSF should not, however, be mistaken for difficulty in generating explanatory propositions. In this section, a number of propositions will be presented, most of which are extracted from Zahariadis' (2007) succinct outline of the MSF. The formulation of theoretical propositions contributes to fostering scholarship by way of allowing empirical observations to build up a body of knowledge. The propositions in this chapter use the building blocks of the MSF to capture processes that begin with the opening of a policy-window and end with the coupling of streams (or not) before the window closes. The opening of the policy-window represents, in a rudimentary sense, the independent variable and the dependent variable then varies between coupling and non-coupling. The propositions detail the intervening variables that provide the actual explanation of each examined case and are therefore eminently suited for a process-tracing research strategy (George and Bennett 2004: 206–7).

As the streams metaphor indicates, the relentless passing of time is essential to understanding policy-making behaviour. For decision-makers, managing time precedes, or constitutes a precondition for, managing issues (Zahariadis 2007: 68): therefore the process-oriented focus of the MSF perspective.

The policy-process contains three distinct elements that affect the probability of successful coupling: attention; search; and selection. For policy-makers, *attention* precedes search and selection, regardless of whether or not the search effort chiefly results in the selection of old ideas. Pet projects developed over long periods need to be brought to the attention of decision-makers in order to bear fruit. For the same policy-makers, the *search* effort is therefore a reactive behaviour, even if they themselves are the policy-entrepreneurs who have been entertaining the policy idea for a long time. Remember that the distinction between policy-maker and policy-entrepreneur is primarily analytical. In reality, makers of policy typically also advocate certain ideas, at least in some issue-areas. Selection, finally, requires there to be a list of solutions or ideas to choose from. If policy-entrepreneurs do a good job, this list appears very short for top-level policy-makers; that would mean that their preferred solution concurred with those of competing entrepreneurs. The attention–search–selection sequence is inescapable but can be very short or very long-drawn-out.

Attention

Nikolaos Zahariadis (1999, 2007) has argued that different kinds of policy-making processes can be expected, depending on whether the policy-window opens in the problem or the politics stream. The assumption is that problems that occur more or less capriciously generate a search for solutions that address those problems; whereas changes pertaining to the politics stream, such as government turnover or drastic fluctuations in the national mood, tend to turn conditions into problems. Hence, the two first descriptive propositions that straightforwardly capture this logic are:

1. *In cases where the window opens in the problem stream, the process is consequential; solutions are developed in response to specific problems.*
2. *In cases where the window opens in the politics stream, the process is doctrinal; solutions are instrumental to the identification of problems.*

Institutions provide more or less fertile soil for bringing issues to the attention of top-level policy-makers because they differ in how they organise attention. May, Workmann and Jones (2008) elaborate *via* the concepts of a centralised versus a delegated mode of organising attention. When in a centralised mode, normal bureaucratic hierarchies tend to be short-circuited and decision-making is controlled from the top, without much consultation from subordinated levels of expertise. As a consequence, signals from above, such as political signals to the bureaucratic leadership, are likely to be magnified. When in a delegated mode, expertise at lower levels take care of such signals, which typically has a dampening effect; the route for an issue to come to the attention of top-level decision-makers gets considerably longer. Hence the third proposition on the organisation of attention:

3. *A centralised institutional mode is likely to result in amplifying of external signals; whereas a delegated mode tends to dampen such signals.*

The boundedly rational individual is prone to attend selectively to external stimuli; individuals are likely to ignore some and overreact to others (Jones 1994, 2001; Jones and Baumgartner 2005; Zahariadis 2007). This tendency, arguably, increases at the top bureaucratic level, including among its political leadership. From that vantage point, there exists just a policy system, or at most a policy sub-system, that is still quite broad in scope. Lower down in the bureaucracy, the outlook naturally becomes more segmented and specified. A consequence of increasingly selective attention at the top, or rather, overreaction to certain attention-grabbing issues, is that policy lines of action may alter quite quickly and drastically. This does not imply, however, that beliefs or preferences have altered. Jones (1994: 13) noted, 'that preferences change only grudgingly but that attentiveness to those preferences can shift rapidly'. This observation is compatible with the MSF in that timing and time-management is essential to this effect and generates the fourth proposition, on attentiveness to issues:

4. *Situations influence attention so as to activate specific preferences without altering core policy beliefs.*

These four propositions on the topic of attention relate to more-or-less hardwired conditions that, foremost, say something about why issues are attended to and the reasons for the likely effects of attentiveness.

Search

Zahariadis uses a helpful descriptive characterisation of how ideas progress, developed by Durant and Diehl (1989, cited in Zahariadis 2007: 76–7). The characterisation deals with the tempo by which ideas develop and their novelty, summarised in Table 12.1.

The evolution of ideas is a direct product of the attention given to any issue. It follows quite logically that the consequential policy process that supposedly follows when the policy-window opens in the problem stream generates novel ideas (quantum or emergent); whereas doctrinal processes that follow when the window opens in the politics stream are likely to propel old ideas to the fore (convergent or gradualist). In accordance, the fifth descriptive proposition on the evolution of ideas:

5. *Consequential policy processes are likely to generate a quantum or emergent development of ideas; whereas a doctrinal process is likely to lead to convergent or gradualist evolution of ideas.*

Selection

It is when ideas have been developed and articulated that the most important job begins for the policy-entrepreneur; generating meaning by way of manipulation. It is true that this process typically begins before, with what Kingdon (1995) referred to as 'softening up', that is, paving the way for a new policy, but it only yields results if manipulative activities are carried out in the selection phase of the policy process. There are circumstances that make it more likely that policy-entrepreneurs will be successful in coupling the three streams.

First, following the insights from Kahneman and Tversky's prospect theory (1979), individuals are risk-averse, which, for policy-makers, means that they are probably cautious about embarking on completely new policy projects. New ideas are also viewed with suspicion in the organisational domain (March 2010).

Table 12.1: Typology of evolution of ideas

		Tempo	
		Rapid	**Gradual**
Content novelty	New	Quantum	Emergent
	Old	Convergent	Gradualist

However, prospect theory also suggests that individuals who experience a big loss are likely to take rather big risks to recuperate. The policy-entrepreneur needs to encourage a sense of operating under crisis conditions: important values are at risk or have been lost; time is short; uncertainty prevails. Hence, the sixth proposition, on manipulative strategies to couple streams:

6. *Coupling is more likely to be successful if the proposed solution is presented as a large deviation from the* status quo *and the problem is presented as a significant loss.*

Zahariadis (2007) has observed that attaching higher-order symbols to policies is likely to be successful in foreign-policy challenges. The idea is to evoke the identity of important segments of the population. It seems as if this strategy is apt for containing policy rather than for suggesting radical change. However, prospect theory applies here, too; if the situation is presented as having the potential to damage the identity of a people, evoking higher-order symbols can push a country's leadership into war. Proposition 7 reads as follows:

7. *The chances of successfully coupling the streams increase when entrepreneurs attach higher-order symbols to their pet proposals.*

What qualities does a policy-entrepreneur need, in order to manipulate policy-makers successfully? And which tactics should she deploy to that effect? Kingdon (1995) captures the obvious in pointing at the 'clout' of the entrepreneur. A person with a lot of clout is likely to be already known and trusted; to have passed the test, since her credibility hinges upon the success of the ideas she has previously advocated. The manipulative strategies of framing and affect-priming (proposition 6), and the use of symbols (proposition 7) have already been mentioned. Zahariadis (2007) singles out the use of 'salami tactics' as a particularly promising way to couple streams. In particular, when risky projects (uncertain political profits) are on the line, it is advantageous to sell the idea little by little, in a way that encourages agreements in stages. Hence the last proposition on the selection of ideas:

8. *Entrepreneurs with a lot of clout and who pursue 'salami tactics' are more likely to be successful at coupling.*

The propositions pertaining to various aspects of the policy-process assume sequential interdependence, so far as the time-logic implied by MSF applies. Therefore, the attention phase affects the rest of the process in various ways. It is the logic of attention that determines the evolution of ideas. There is some, however limited, scope to manipulate the process at this stage. From the evolution of ideas to the selection phase, the process is chiefly a matter of manipulation. In Table 12.2, ideal-typical policy trajectories are depicted that summarise the eight propositions.

The leftmost time arrow is certainly irreversible, which means that the process gradually narrows to dichotomous likelihoods of coupling success or failure. One could argue that the high probability of coupling success that follows quantum and convergent evolutions of ideas is even higher than the corresponding high

Table 12.2: Ideal-typical policy trajectories

Time	Phase	Policy-window opens	In problem stream		In politics stream	
	Attention	Logic of attention	Consequential		Doctrinal	
		Institutional mode	Centralised	Delegated	Centralised	Delegated
		Situations influence attention	Yes	No	Yes	No
	Search	Evolution of ideas	Quantum	Emergent	Convergent	Gradualist
	Selection	Deviation from *status quo* and significant loss	Yes	No	Yes	No
		Entrepreneurial clout	High	Low	High	Low
		Higher-order symbols attached	Yes	No	Yes	No
		Salami tactics	Yes	No	Yes	No
	Coupling	Success probability	High	Low	High	Low

probabilities in the emergent and gradualist trajectories: that is, at best, the latter results in a only a medium-high probability of coupling. The values (high and low) are relative and not absolute, however, which justifies the simpler dichotomy.

Case study: the quest to establish a National Counter-Terrorism Unit (NCTU) after the murder of Olof Palme

An ideal-typical crisis policy-making process would likely follow the leftmost trajectory (as shown in Table 12.2) to produce policy-change. Such an assumption seems to depart from a view of crisis as predominantly threatening and contained within the policy community that experiences the threats. Focusing events (which includes crises as discussed in this chapter), however, tend to attract attention from the previously disinterested, who may be more inclined to explore opportunities (Jones and Baumgartner 2005). Even when crises are contained, policy-makers may see them as opportunities to transform policy programmes in ways that are deemed necessary but are unattractive to the electorate (Boin *et al.* 2005: chapter 4). Some austerity measures in the wake of the financial crisis in Europe may bear such traits. Kingdon's (1995) metaphorical window of opportunity seems to be quite fitting when it comes to crisis policy-making, at least under certain conditions.

It should also be kept in mind that crises are likely to give rise to more than one policy-process. In the short run, a consequential process with rapid propulsion of new ideas may take place, only to be superseded when older ideas emerge after a slower gestation process. A case in point is the Swedish reaction to the radioactive pollution from the 1986 Chernobyl disaster. Initially, the Swedish government considered pursuing legal procedures to make the Soviet Union indemnify Swedish property-owners, which was a confrontational stance alien to Swedish foreign-policy doctrine. After closer consideration, the Swedish government instead decided to suggest co-operative nuclear-energy-security programmes with the Soviet Union, which was entirely in keeping with the non-confrontational Swedish tradition (Sundelius, Stern and Bynander 1997). Obviously, a number of short- and long-term policy-processes instigated by a crisis may take place in parallel, leading to several policy-outputs.

In the following, a case study of the crisis that the murder of Swedish Prime Minister Olof Palme gave rise to will be presented. It will focus on the ensuing efforts to create a National Counter-Terrorism Unit (NCTU). Apart from this policy-process, the crisis also instigated a quest for a permanent terrorist law and, with a vaguer connection to the case, a more independent security service (Hansén 2007). Thus, the case study contains both a (short) case of crisis-management/ response and a (more developed) case of post-crisis policy-selection. In terms of crisis policy-making, no other trajectories are discernible from this crisis.

The Palme murder crisis case

The Swedish Prime Minister Olof Palme was shot and killed on 28 February 1986. The murder took place at around 11.20 p.m., as the unprotected Prime Minister walked with his wife in Stockholm city centre after having been to a movie. Many crucial decision-makers, including the Stockholm and national police commissioners and the Speaker of the Parliament, were out of town on that Friday, it being the school holidays. The police arrived at the crime scene within minutes but failed to secure forensic evidence. The crime-scene was not roped off and scores of shocked people came to lay red roses. Escape routes were not secured and it took several hours before a nationwide alert was sent out. Police patrols searched the surroundings unsystematically and, by the dawn of March 1, the prospects of finding the murderer had been severely damaged. But it would get worse. When the Stockholm police commissioner, Hans Holmér, came back from vacation, he took charge of the murder investigation (normally the job of a prosecutor) and the search operation (normally carried out by an experienced police superintendent), all with the tacit consent of the cabinet. Open conflict between Holmér and the side-lined prosecutor and experienced murder investigators within the police led to a situation in which the investigation hardly moved forward. The Stockholm police commissioner pursued a few leads, which the prosecutor rejected as delusions, such as the idea that the Kurdish Labour Party (PKK) had been involved. Holmér tended to give priority to potential motives for the murder, instead of relying on traditional police investigation techniques. It took almost a year before the cabinet intervened and moved the investigation from the local Stockholm level to the national level. A national investigation team is still working on the case. This crisis, in sum, represented compounded failure: failure to protect the Prime Minister in the first place; failure to secure the crime scene; failure to investigate the murder with due professionalism; and failure to catch the culprit (Hansén 2000; Hansén and Stern 2001; Stern and Hansén 2001).

The policy-making case: the quest for an NCTU[1]

Considering the many apparent problems in the Swedish criminal-justice sector revealed by the Palme crisis case, it is quite astonishing that one of its few policy-outcomes was the creation of a National Counter-Terrorism Unit, with a specialised strike-capacity for entering buildings, freeing hostages and taking dangerous people into safe custody. Such a force may have been needed but would not have prevented the Palme murder from taking place; nor would it have aided the search effort. It is difficult to see a consequential logic of attention spurring such a process. The remainder of this section gives a description of how the process unfolded.

The Stockholm police took the initiative after the Palme murder to produce a report, presented to the National Police Board on 26 November 1986, which concluded that the Stockholm police force was not prepared to meet the challenge of terrorism. Shortcomings in training and equipment were likely to prove disastrous in the event of a terrorist attack (Government report 1988: 177).

---

1.   This description is a slight modification of the account in Hansén 2007: 90–2.

These observations were in keeping with what the National Police Board had pointed out in 1980 and 1982, when the Board scrutinised safety at nuclear-power plants.

In January 1987, a conservative MP raised a motion (1986/87:Ju208) urging that a counter-terrorist police unit be set up. When the Parliament Justice Committee discussed the motion (Parliamentary Standing Committee on the Administration of Justice 1986–7: 20), it was left with an inconclusive reference to the ongoing Jurist Commission – set up to scrutinise the Palme murder – and work that was carried out by the National Police Board. However, the Justice Committee would not sanction a self-contained police counter-terrorism force, as was suggested in the motion.

On 27 April 1987, the Jurist Commission presented its first report dealing with the night of the murder. The commissioners devoted the concluding chapter to the protection of public persons and combating terrorism (Government report 1987: 107–36). More in passing, they called attention to the fact that the existing Special Response Units (belonging to the three largest local police districts in Stockholm, Gothenburg and Malmö) were incapable of handling a severe terrorist assault of the type that had happened at the West German embassy in Stockholm in 1975 (Government report: 131).

The Parliamentary Commission set up after the Palme murder, with a more policy-oriented approach, picked up on the issue of the insufficient assault capacity of the police that the lawyers in the Jurist Commission had left open (Government report 1988: 175–203). They recommended creating an anti-terrorist police unit.

The commission made four main arguments for setting up an NCTU (Government report: 178–80). First, the frequency of terrorist acts perpetrated around the world was continuously increasing, raising the probability of terrorism taking place in Sweden. Nuclear-power plants were mentioned as potential terrorist targets. Second, inadequate training and equipment would put the safety of police officers dealing with a terrorist assault at risk. Third, Sweden's ratification of various international-terrorism-related conventions obliged the country to act effectively against terrorists. Foreign governments might otherwise insist on having their police forces operate inside Sweden. Such situations could cause unnecessary conflict with other states. Fourth, if Sweden was less well prepared than neighbouring countries it would be an incentive for terrorists to choose Swedish targets.

The National Police Board was tasked with analysing issues regarding organisation and costs in August 1989; they delivered a report that October. According to their instructions, they were supposed to use the Parliamentary Commission's suggestions as a point of departure. In terms of organisation, the National Police Board suggested that an anti-terrorist police force be established only in Stockholm, separate from the existing Special Response Units and with a strength of fifty-three officers. While the Parliamentary Commission's policy suggestions were on under consideration in 1988, the National Police Board proposed reinforcing the Special Response Units of Sweden's three largest cities (Stockholm, Gothenburg and Malmö). In the fall of 1989, they instead suggested a special unit be set up in Stockholm, which was in keeping with the Parliamentary Commission's proposal but at odds with statements made by the Parliament Justice Committee in 1987 (Proposition 1989/90:100, appendix 15).

When the Cabinet presented its budget proposition for FY 1990/91 (Proposition 1989/90: 100), the arguments put forward in it for setting up an NCTU were identical to those made by the Parliamentary Commission. The Cabinet suggested that a force of about fifty men be organised in the Stockholm police district but separately from the Special Response Units.

Only two motions in Parliament objected to the Cabinet proposition (Motions 1989/90: Ju211 and Ju233). The former, authored by a faction of the Communist Party, cited negative international experiences with the kind of police force proposed by the cabinet; similar forces in other countries had allegedly been rather counterproductive and caused more violence than necessary. The latter motion, written by a Social-Democratic Party faction, opposed the militarisation of the police. Both motions called for decentralised, but specialised, training of ordinary officers in a number of police districts, especially those encompassing nuclear-power plants. The Parliament Justice Committee did not comply with these motions, instead approving the Cabinet proposition.

On 25 April 1990, Parliament discussed the police budget (Protocol 1989/90:109 §6). The issue of an NCTU was brought up and criticised by only one Communist Party and one Environmental Party MP. The communist wondered why the Cabinet had argued that the proposition was in keeping with what the Parliament Justice Committee had concluded in 1987, when, in fact, they had two different views over the organisation of such a force. The Social-Democratic representative avoided a discussion of the anti-terrorist force by ignoring the questions. The debate was instead between the Social-Democrats and the three non-socialist parties; and focused exclusively on the need to recruit more police officers. When it was time to vote (Protocol 1989/90 §11), the suggestion by the Justice Committee – which was essentially the same as the governmental proposition on the anti-terrorist police force – won by 258 to 38. In June 1990, the Cabinet made the decision to create the National Counter-Terrorism Unit.

As we have said, in the early 1980s the National Police Board had suggested the establishment of a similar force. In fact, the National Police Commissioner had previously tried to promote the idea after the 1972 skyjacking by Croatian separatists in southern Sweden, but his suggestion fell on deaf ears. Police demands for an NCTU got yet louder after the 1975 Red Army Faction seizure of the West German embassy in Stockholm, which came close to ending in a bloodbath, but the idea still failed to catch on among policy-makers in general. Not even the horrifying prospect of a terrorist threat to a nuclear-power plant, evoked by the National Police Board in their above-mentioned 1980 and 1982 reports that came in the wake of the 1979 Three Mile Island meltdown, had much impact (Hansén 2007). But the Palme murder did; previously unavailing ideas quickly started to germinate, even though it took four years before those ideas passed as new policy. In light of this, the evolution of ideas qualifies as convergent, where the selection phase required a good deal of manipulation by policy-entrepreneurs.

Theoretical assumptions revisited

This case description provides values for the descriptive propositions developed within the MSF. It is a rather clear case of a garbage-can process (Cohen, March and Olsen 1972), in that the solution predated the problem; a doctrinal logic of attention enabled the rapid gestation of ideas that had previously failed to attract attention and support from policy-makers. This section will revise the explanatory assumptions with the help of this case, in order to better understand the crisis policy-making process. In overview, the process is presented in Table 12.3.

Attention and selection

The first two descriptive propositions merit some further comment. The threat–opportunity duality of crises was briefly discussed in the previous section, suggesting that the logic of the two propositions is likely to be appropriate if the threat-perspective dominates the process. The Palme case is congruent with such an amendment to the propositions, that is, policy-windows that open in the problem stream are likely to follow a consequential logic, provided that a threat frame overshadows an opportunity frame. In keeping with Kingdon's conclusion (1995: 203), it was in this case a policy-window of *opportunity* to push for pet solutions that opened in the problem stream. What is perhaps more surprising in this case is that, despite the completely botched murder investigation, no policy-process of a more consequential nature ensued. The nature of the crisis may be important in this regard. The Palme case revealed a veritable cascade of failures, which did not point unambiguously to one particular problem. In other words, the way the crisis was managed in itself fragmented the attention of policy-makers, rather than focusing it. This is a tentative explanation that may be relevant for our understanding of the logic of attention when the policy-window opens in the problem stream; in particular, when it comes in the shape of a crisis. Crises are likely to pose a number of different problems and, occasionally, multiple managerial failures are the actual cause of a crisis.

The crisis case caused a centralised institutional mode. The highest priority for the police, other players in the criminal justice system and at the political level was to catch the murderer. The expected pattern of a centralised authority amplifying signals from above and ignoring the expertise of their own rank and file is clearly observable in the search machinery around Stockholm Police Commissioner Holmér. The normal bureaucratic chains of command were repeatedly side-stepped.

In the policy-making case, the institutional mode appears to have been delegated. As the police investigation went on, in May 1986, the Cabinet appointed the so-called Jurist Commission to scrutinise the first 24 hours following the assassination in particular (Government report 1987). The commission worked in a backwater relative to the ongoing and conflict-ridden murder investigation.

Table 12.3: Policy trajectory in Palme murder/quest for NCTU

Time	Phase	Policy-window opens	In problem stream		In politics stream	
			Consequential		Doctrinal	
			Centralised	Delegated	Centralised	Delegated
→	Attention	Logic of attention				
		Institutional mode	Consequential		Doctrinal	
		Situations influence attention	Yes	No	Yes	No
	Search	Evolution of ideas	Quantum	Emergent	Convergent	Gradualist
	Selection	Deviation from *status quo* and significant loss	Yes	Yes	Yes	No
		Entrepreneurial clout	High	High	High	Low
		Higher order symbols attached	Yes	Yes	Yes	No
		Salami tactics	Yes	Yes	Yes	No
	Coupling	Success probability	High	High	High	Low

It chose to conduct interviews with a little less than two hundred people who, in various capacities, had been involved during the night of the murder, or else were relevant experts. Some of these people brought the need for an NCTU to the attention of the commission (Government report 1987). The policy idea was, in this sense, generated in a delegated institutional mode. This observation is, by and large, congruent with the proposition on the role of the institutional mode (proposition 3). The propulsion of an old idea was rather quick but, probably because it went through layers of experts (including the Jurist Commission), it took a few years before the NCTU was set up. It is interesting to observe, though, that this case and, arguably, others marked by a need for redress after a violent outrage to public feeling, created scope for parallel institutional modes, centralised *and* delegated, to operate.

Proposition 4, about the situational influence over attention that does not affect policy core beliefs, is supported by the case evidence presented here. The case, however, rather brings into question what the predominant beliefs in the matter of an NCTU actually were. There had been great opposition to the idea, both in Parliament and in parts of the criminal-justice sector, including the police (Hansén 2007), but the debate was hardly lively by the mid 1980s. Since the crisis in itself did not make the issue of an NCTU topical, there may have been fewer voices mobilised to pronounce opposing beliefs; or maybe the issue had lost salience. Beliefs may have changed gradually enough to allow a comparatively peripheral old idea to gestate quickly.

The fifth proposition relating to the search phase maintains its internal consistency through this case study. The evolution of ideas qualifies as convergent, which is one of the logical consequences of a doctrinal policy process. As discussed above, it is more of a deviation from expectations that a crisis-induced policy process is doctrinal in the first place rather than consequential.

The initiative for an NCTU obviously dated back to the early 1970s. And the arguments against such a force – articulated by the Communist/Left party and, from 1988, also by the Environmental Party and a Social-Democratic faction – were the same as earlier: that militarisation of the police would lead to more violence than necessary; and that the force could be used in situations other than those for which it was originally intended. It could hence be both counterproductive and dangerous. The main difference this time, however, was that arguments for an anti-terrorist force were articulated at all. In the Parliamentary Commission after the Palme murder (Government report 1988: 175–203) as well as in the governmental proposition (Proposition 1989/90: 100), the arguments referred to international solidarity and national sovereignty. But what convinced Parliament, in particular its Justice Committee, to reappraise this policy issue, which heretofore had been politically stalemated? Two arguments were pivotal in this regard, of which only one had been brought up by the Commission and in the governmental proposition: the occupation of the West German embassy in Stockholm in 1975. If such a thing happened again, and if a foreign power insisted on using its own police units to handle the incident due to a lack of Swedish capacity, how would we react? The second argument built on experience from abroad, according to Lars Nylén.[2] Well trained and well equipped police were less likely to resort to unnecessary violence in a stressful situation than were ill-trained and ill-equipped – and therefore insecure – officers. The focus thereby moved from the original concern, regarding the type of situations for which a specially trained and equipped police force would be used (would it also be used against processions of demonstrators?), to how such a force would handle a given and very particular situation compared with how the existing police would cope.

Representatives of the Stockholm police and the National Police Board paid visits to the Parliament Justice Committee and succeeded in convincing the previously indifferent or sceptical of the necessity of the NCTU policy-solution. Committee-members were exposed to a different dimension, or situation, of the problem from previously, which made the solution politically viable. Given that fifteen years had passed since Sweden last experienced a terrorist situation in which a specially trained and equipped anti-terrorist police force was called for (the 1975 West German embassy drama), the alarming statistics presented in the commission reports, together with the prospect of the intervention of foreign countries, arguably, functioned as what Kingdon (1995: 98–100) referred to as 'accompaniment': impressions that reinforce acquired standpoints on a policy.

In terms of manipulative strategies, it is interesting to note how affect-priming and framing were used to portray the Swedish lack of an NCTU as a comparative loss and disadvantage *vis-à-vis* the international community. To do so, policy-entrepreneurs within the police played up an older crisis that had very little to do with the Palme murder. It is as if fear and unpleasantness travel easily from one crisis to another. This observation is in keeping with the sixth proposition.

The national mood in the wake of the murder was a state of shock. The bullets that killed Palme also hit the spinal column of Swedish identity as a peaceful and open society where all could move around freely. The assassination and the subsequent failure to catch the murderer became symbolically loaded with a need for redress. In accordance with proposition 7, on higher-order symbols, the national mood may very well have reduced the room to manoeuvre of those opposing an NCTU. This is, arguably, similar to the national mood in the US after 9/11 and its relation to the subsequent decision to go to war in faraway countries.

The case shows mixed results as far as the importance of entrepreneurial clout is concerned. It matters that the Jurist Commission brought up the need for an NCTU and that the Parliamentary Commission explicitly suggested its creation. But it may have been of greater importance that police officers without much clout paid visits to the Parliament Justice Commission to present their arguments. In the 1970s, the National Police Commissioner, who did have a lot of clout, had strongly advocated the creation of a counter-terrorism unit but it is probable that

---

2. Interview with author about counter-terrorism policy-making, 16 March 2004, in his capacities as Police Chief in a nuclear-power plant municipality in the 1970s and 1980s and later as head of the Criminal Division of the National Police Board.

his entrepreneurship was counterproductive; many in the political-administrative elite liked his ideas but feared his methods, according to Henry Montgomery.[3] In light of this, it was probably a good idea to let credible low-clout expertise deliver the message. To the extent that credibility is on the line, which it often is in crisis situations, clout is important, but better suited is an untainted credibility.

Conclusions

At the outset of this chapter, it was argued that the crisis policy-making process was important enough to merit further clarification. The propositions developed by the multiple-streams framework are useful for describing and explaining sequential movements of the policy process. The phenomenon of crisis, normally conceived of as archetypical of the problem stream, is, however, better described as a particular occurrence in the problem stream. The main conclusion from the empirical evidence presented here is that crises may generate many different problems, or reveal numerous failures of both an individual and systemic nature, which fragments rather than focuses the attention of concerned policy-makers. This, in turn, makes a dogmatic policy process more likely to ensue.

In addition, the evidence from the case study points to a few crisis-related circumstances that may be worth taking into account in further MSF theorising. The crisis is a focusing event, in the sense that it crowds out the agenda for policy-makers; but the focus does not need to be of much policy relevance. In the case presented here, the focus was more a matter of public redress for the slaying of the head of state. The centralised mode that characterised the organisation of attention with regard to the unsolved murder still left room for policy-entrepreneurs to manoeuvre in a more delegated institutional mode. The national mood was likewise marked by a need for redress; a strong symbolic load that limited the room for meaning-making manipulation. Finally, the case study draws attention to the role of entrepreneurs and entrepreneurship. The MS lens has traditionally attributed policy-change to a successful entrepreneur with a lot of clout. The relevant entrepreneur is easily identified when taking the point of policy change as the starting point and tracing the process backwards. The policy-making case here had a long history before the Palme murder but had failed to catch on earlier. This was partly due to counterproductive policy-entrepreneurship. Crises are said to make and break careers; they can also sanction a changes in the roster of those whom top-level policy-makers trust enough to listen to.

The Palme murder case and the policy-process of establishing an NCTU were selected because they epitomise the garbage-can model of decision-making. Further studies of different types of crisis policy-making are needed to assess the theoretical propositions. It is, however, clear that they have been fruitful in explaining the policy process following the Palme murder.

---

3. Interview with author about counter-terrorism policy-making, 22 January 2004, in his capacity as non-partisan Deputy Justice Minister, 1976–9.

References

Baumgartner, F. and Jones, B. (1993) *Agendas and Instability in American Politics*, Chicago and London: University of Chicago Press.

Birkland, T. (2006) *Lessons of Disaster: Policy change after catastrophic events*, Washington, DC: Georgetown University Press.

Boin, A., t'Hart, P., Stern, E. and Sundelius, B. (2005) *The Politics of Crisis Management: Public leadership under pressure*, Cambridge, UK: Cambridge University Press.

Boin, A., McConnell, A. and t'Hart, P. (2008) 'Governing after crisis', in A. Boin, A. McConnell and P. t'Hart (eds) *Governing After Crisis: The politics of investigation, accountability and learning*, Cambridge, UK: Cambridge University Press, pp. 3–30.

Cohen, M., March, J. and Olsen, J. (1972) 'A garbage can model of organizational choice', *Administrative Science Quarterly* 17: 1–25.

George, A. and Bennett, A. (2004) *Case Studies and Theory Development in the Social Sciences*, Cambridge, MA: MIT Press.

Government report (1987) 'SOU 1987:14 Juristkommissionens rapport om händelserna efter mordet på statsminister Olof Palme. Del 1', Stockholm: Justitiedepartementet.

Government report (1988) 'SOU 1988:18 Rapport av Parlamentariska kommissionen med anledning av mordet på Olof Palme', Stockholm: Justitiedepartementet.

Hansén, D. (2000) *The Crisis Management of the Murder of Olof Palme*, Stockholm: Crismart.

Hansén, D. and Stern, E. (2001) 'From crisis to trauma: the Palme assassination case', in A. Boin, L. Comfort and U. Rosenthal (eds) *Managing Crises: Threats, dilemmas, opportunities*, Springfield, IL: Charles C. Thomas, pp. 177–99.

Hansén, D. (2007) *Crisis and Perspectives on Policy Change: Swedish Counter-terrorism Policymaking*, doctoral dissertation, Stockholm and Utrecht, NL: Crismart, vol. 34.

Jones, B. (1994) *Reconceiving Decision-Making in Democratic Politics: Attention, choice, and public policy*, Chicago: University of Chicago Press.

—— (2001) *Politics and the Architecture of Choice: Bounded rationality and governance*, Chicago: University of Chicago Press.

Jones, B. and Baumgartner, F. (2005) *The Politics of Attention: How government prioritizes problems*, Chicago and London: University of Chicago Press.

Kahneman, D. and Tversky, A. (1979) 'Prospect theory: an analysis of decision under risk', *Econometrica* 47(2): 263–91.

Kingdon, J. (1995) *Agendas, Alternatives, and Public Policies*, 2nd edn, New York: Longman.

March, J. (2010) *The Ambiguities of Experience*, Ithaca, NY: Cornell University Press.

May, P., Workman, S. and Jones, B. (2008) 'Organizing attention: responses of the bureaucracy to agenda disruption', *Journal of Public Administration Research & Theory*, 18: 517–41.

Motion 1986/87:Ju208 "Göran Ericsson (m) En specialutbildad polisstyrka", Swedish Riksdag, available at: https://www.riksdagen.se/sv/ Dokument-Lagar/Forslag/Motioner/mot-198687ju208-En-specialut_ GA02ju208/?text=true (accessed October 24, 2015).

Motion 1989/90: Ju211 "av Lars Werner m.fl. (vpk) Bekämpning av terrorism", Swedish Riksdag, available at: http://www.riksdagen.se/ sv/Dokument-Lagar/Forslag/Motioner/Bekampningen-av-terrorism_ GD02Ju211/?text=true (accessed October 24, 2015).

Motion 1989/90: Ju233 "av Hans Göran Franck m.fl. (s) Beredskapsstyrka inom polisen", Swedish Riksdag, available at: https://www.riksdagen.se/sv/ Dokument-Lagar/Forslag/Motioner/mot-198990Ju233-Beredskapsst_ GD02Ju233/?text=true (accessed October 24, 2015).

Parliament Protocol 1989/90:109 §6 "Anslag till polisväsendet", Swedish Riksdag, available at: http://www.riksdagen.se/sv/Dokument-Lagar/Kammaren/ Protokoll/Riksdagens-protokoll-1989901_GD09109/?html=true (accessed October 24, 2015).

Parliament Protocol 1989/90:109 §11 "Beslut", Swedish Riksdag, available at: http://www.riksdagen.se/sv/Dokument-Lagar/Kammaren/Protokoll/ Riksdagens-protokoll-1989901_GD09109/?html=true (accessed October 24, 2015).

Parliamentary Standing Committee on the Administration of Justice (1986–7), JuU 1986/87:23 "Om anslag till polisväsendet m.m.", Swedish Riksdag.

Proposition 1989/90:100 "Statsverkspropositionen", appendix 15, Swedish Riksdag,

Sabatier, P. (2007) 'The need for better theories', in P. Sabatier (ed.) *Theories of the Policy Process*, 2nd edn, Boulder, CO and Oxford, UK: Westview Press, pp. 3–20.

Sabatier, P. and Jenkins-Smith, H. (eds) (1993) *Policy Change and Learning: An advocacy coalition approach*, Boulder, CO: Westview Press.

Stern, E. and Hansén, D. (2001) 'Framing the Palme assassination', in J. Eriksson (ed.) *Threat Politics: New perspectives on security, risk and crisis management*, Aldershot, UK: Ashgate, pp. 164–88.

Sundelius, B., Stern, E. and Bynander, F. (1997) *Krishantering på svenska: teori och praktik*, Stockholm: Nerenius & Santérus Förlag.

Zahariadis, N. (1999) 'Ambiguity, time, and multiple streams', in P. Sabatier (ed.) *Theories of the Policy Process*, Boulder, CO and Oxford, UK: Westview Press, pp. 73–93.

—   (2003) *Ambiguity and Choice in Public Policy: Political decision making in modern democracies*, Washington, DC: Georgetown University Press.

—   (2007) 'The multiple streams framework: structure, limitations, prospects', in P. Sabatier (ed.) *Theories of the Policy Process*, Boulder, CO and Oxford, UK: Westview Press, pp. 65–92.

Chapter Thirteen

Reinterpreting the Multiple-Streams Framework from a Process Approach: Decision-Making and Policy-Shift in Public Health Management in Catalonia, 2003–7

Raquel Gallego, Nicolás Barbieri and Sheila González[1]

Introduction

The multiple-streams framework (MSF) has greatly improved our understanding of decision-making processes. The MSF explains how policies are made, with a particular focus on the processes of agenda-setting and decision-making – for which a temporal order is assumed – and examines policy-choice under conditions of ambiguity. A central question of this approach is why some agenda-items achieve prominence and others are neglected. To answer this, the MSF identifies three streams flowing through the system: the problem, policy and politics streams; each stream is conceptualised as largely independent, with its own internal dynamics. At critical points in time, these streams are 'coupled' by policy-entrepreneurs. Such moments open 'policy-windows', allowing the issue to rise up the agenda of policy-makers and become the object of their consideration (Kingdon 1984, 1995; Zahariadis 1999, 2003).

Under such conceptualisation, the MSF has been extensively discussed, praised and criticised over the past two decades (Durant and Diehl 1989; Mucciaroni 1992; King 1985; Skok 1995; Stone 1988; Weir 1992; Zahariadis 1996, 2005; Barzelay and Gallego 2010a). An open question in this literature is to what extent streams are independent and how to analyse and account for empirical evidence about interrelations among them. Critics also question Kingdon's argument that the generation of specific alternatives in the policy stream remains incremental – ideas are constantly recombined – and point to the need to account for issue-trajectory shift. Another question is about the role played by policy-windows in coupling: Kingdon defined two types of windows, those that open in the problem stream and those that open in the politics stream, but he was unclear on the conditions that structure different relationships between problems and solutions in each of them. A further question is how entrepreneurial position and strategy affects stream-coupling and how to account

1. This paper integrates findings from two research projects, one funded by the Spanish government (*CSO-2011-27547*) and one funded by the Catalan government (*Ordre GRI/6/2012 de gener de 13, Resolució 20 July 2012.*

for potential regularities. The overall argument in this literature is the need to build an integrative explanation of the policy-formation process, linking stages into a causal role.

These open questions derive from the prevailing interpretation of Kingdon's framework. However, over the past decade, an attempt to answer them has relied on reinterpreting the explanatory potential of Kingdon's framework from a different analytical approach that was elaborated under the title of 'institutional processualism' (IP) (Barzelay and Gallego 2006, 2010a). Within this approach, Kingdon's framework is seen as integrating both institutional and process factors into a dynamic explanation of the outcomes of policy-cycles, which would overcome analytical concerns with the independence of the three streams and about the independence of sub-processes –namely, alternative-specification, alternative-selection and decision-making. IP sees Kingdon's framework as strongly processual (authoritative decisions are the result of prior ideational efforts and expressly political activity) and, at least weakly, institutional (actors involved in policy-making inhabit distinct roles within a governmental bureaucratic system). This model examines the causal interrelation between ideational efforts and role differences: politicians and high officials are more sensitive to political-stream dynamics, while experts and bureaucrats are more sensitive to policy- and problem-streams dynamics. Thus, ideation is an interactive, relational and social process between role-specific actors.

As for concerns about sub-processes' independence, IP highlights that although Kingdon identifies component categories of the policy-making process, such as agenda- setting and alternative-specification, and claims that each of them requires its own distinctive analysis, he also points out that the trajectory and outcome of each of them affects those of the others. For example, an explicit causal linkage is identified between issue-status (an outcome of agenda-setting) and the availability of substantive policy-proposals (an outcome of alternative-specification): more effort is expended in developing specific policy-proposals when the issue is high on the agenda (actors respond to the temporal opportunity to bring about a decisive policy-change) (Barzelay and Gallego 2006, 2010a).

IP also addresses the criticism that the MSF more resembles an heuristic device than an empirically falsifiable guide to policy-analysis (King 1985) and the subsequent claim that there should be more emphasis on causal explanations. IP argues that Kingdon's model shows an appreciation both for contingency and for causal regularities. Concepts such as 'focusing event' and 'spillover effect' point to recurring causal processes and lead us to consider the causal relationship between context (fleeting occurrences and ongoing policy histories) and situation (ideation and interactions among participants within the focal policy-making process) (Barzelay and Gallego 2006: 539). Thus, an IP interpretation of Kingdon's framework enables us to focus on the flows of interaction between role-specific actors and between actors and context and *vice versa*; and it bases our analysis on the explanatory potential of event-causation and the role of social mechanisms.

Kingdon's model is geared toward explaining politically visible authoritative decisions made by legislators or political officials. This chapter analyses the case of a shift in public-management policy in the Catalan health sector over the past decade, with a particular focus on a legislative decision of 2007 that changed the public management of healthcare provision – namely, from an administrative law to a public-enterprise framework. Over almost three decades, the Catalan political and managerial elite in the healthcare sector had explicitly considered such a change not worth pursuing, because it was too difficult from both a political and a juridical point of view. These reasons, they argued, derived from structural features of the Catalan health-policy sector that, in principle, could be expected to remain stable over time. So, two questions suggest themselves:

Why was reform finally addressed through the negotiation and passage of a law in 2007? and

Why were those structural factors no longer an obstacle?

The empirical data for this analysis includes semi-structured interviews with over twenty key experts who either were directly involved in the policy-process or have privileged knowledge about it, as well as hard data on the factors relevant for our theoretical approach. We will rely on the analytical dialogue between theory and empirical data to provide a resilient interpretation of these processes.

The chapter first summarises the analytical approach of this study, distinguishing those aspects from the MSF that are useful for the analysis from those that are not and which, therefore, need IP's contribution. The following section narrates the episode – that is, a slice of history (empirical data) comprising analytically defined events – as the empirical case. The next section provides the analytic explanation of the case, following the IP event-causation framework, with a particular emphasis on the role of social mechanisms. The chapter's conclusion provides research arguments on the sources and dynamics of public-management reform that complement those that the MSF would have generated on the basis of this case study.

Institutional processualism: re-interpreting the multiple-streams framework

The institutional processualism (IP) approach used in this case study preserves some useful concepts from the MSF – such as stream, policy-window and policy-entrepreneur – but suggests their reinterpretation to overcome problems of analytical argumentation and empirical applicability. Stream is a useful concept, as long as it points to the interaction between factors of a particular nature and, therefore, might lead to conceptualising them as flows of events. IP complements this interpretation by providing an analytical account of how such flows of events are not independent but interrelated in empirical cases. The policy-window concept is useful for understanding why issues get policy-makers' attention but cannot explain how they open up. Nor does the policy-window concept explain the (feedback) interrelationship between actors and context and between role-specific actors. To do so, IP focuses on how and why policy-entrepreneurs in each stream, acting within different sub-processes of policy-making, interact to help bring about the opening of policy-window at that critical point in time.

In answer to these caveats, the IP approach suggests an interpretation of Kingdon's framework different from that of the MSF (Barzelay 2003; Barzelay and Gallego 2006, 2010a). Kingdon defines the policy-cycle in terms of a flow of events including process components – agenda-setting, and alternative-specification. In tune with the MSF (Zahariadis 2003), IP also adds decision-making to this sequence. Within this overall process, agenda-setting events influence alternative-specification events; both of them influence decision-making events. That is, issue-framing or problem-definition, as well as its assignment to particular actors and venues for elaboration (agenda-setting), may create expectations of policy-change, which may encourage some actors to put effort into it (alternative-specification). The availability of policy alternatives in combination with a sustained or high issue-status on the agenda may facilitate bringing the issue to a decision-point. Thus, from the MSF's policy stream, the concepts of selection-criteria – namely, technical feasibility and value-acceptability – as well as the influence of issue-framing on alternative-specification are used by IP to account for the interrelationship between policy-making sub-processes.

In this flow of events, Kingdon sees decisions as the result of ideational effort and political interaction among numerous actors. Decision-makers, media and policy-entrepreneurs interact to frame issues; experts, bureaucrats and policy-entrepreneurs interact to elaborate policy-alternatives; and decision-makers interact to provide policy-decisions. IP interprets these policy-making actors as inhabiting distinct roles within a governmental-bureaucratic system and acting across different institutional venues. They build different identities depending on the institutionally biased role they play, which conditions how they perceive issues, how they interpret contextual factors and how they respond to the flow of events (Barzelay and Gallego 2006). Thus, from the MSF's politics stream, factors such as legislative or administrative turnovers are relevant for IP as long as they condition role-(re)definition. On the contrary, the MSF's interpretation of the politics stream as party ideology and national mood is not useful because it does not reflect the complexity of the dynamic context of decision-making, particularly in cases of decentralised states. In a multi-level government scenario, the analytical and empirical relevance of party ideology on the regional level depends on its relationship to the party in office at central-government level. Similarly, the definition of national mood and its relevance depends on the territorial correlation of political forces.

Thus, for the MSF, Kingdon's central explanatory heuristic lies in the concepts of problem, policy, and politics streams and the idea of an opportunity-window; for IP, however, the explanatory potential of Kingdon's model lies in the idea of process and the conceptualisation of interactions between agency and situational factors as experience unfolds throughout the episode. This IP interpretation of Kingdon's framework allows us to explain issue-trajectories and case-outcomes of the selected episode of policy-making through the use of analytic narratives (Abell 2004). In this sense, an IP analysis of empirical cases may proceed through the identification of conceptual *schema*, which Barzelay (2003) defines as: sources of policy-entrepreneurs' efforts (such as logic of appropriateness); conceptual entities of the policy-making process (agenda-setting, alternative-specification, decision-making); dynamic relations among such components (changes in issue-status, pace of alternative-specification); stable context factors; dynamic context factors; and mechanisms providing a dynamic linkage between context factors and the trajectory of the policy-making process.

Mechanisms, as theoretical constructs, suggest causal relationships between context and situation – that is, interactions among participants in the policy-making process being analysed. Causal mechanisms are a delimited class of events that alter relations between specified sets of elements in identical or closely similar ways over a variety of situations. Thus, a causal process is a regular sequence of such mechanisms that produce similar (generally more complex and contingent) transformations of those elements – recurrent combinations and sequences of mechanisms (McAdam, Tarrow and Tilly 2001). Following Barzelay's (2003) classification, agency-mechanisms may include attribution of opportunity and actor-certification (McAdam, Tarrow and Tilly 2001); policy-entrepreneurship (Kingdon 1995); or performance-feedback (Levitt and March 1988). Mechanisms pointing to recurring causal processes among process and context may include focusing events and spillover effects (Kingdon 1995); interference effects; or policy-diffusion (McAdam, Tarrow and Tilly 2001). For example, the MSF's concept of focusing event, from the problem stream, is useful for IP as it helps explain the origin of an issue-trajectory on the basis of interrelations between streams: an event in the problem stream activates efforts in the political and policy streams; or, in IP terminology, focusing events are linkages (causal mechanisms) between occurrences in the dynamic context and the agenda-setting process. IP interprets policy spillover effects as linkages between agenda-setting and alternative-specification processes, on the one hand, and the trajectory of neighbouring public-policy areas, on the other hand. Similarly, actor-certification would show how situational conditions influence actors' properties, such as the ways their identities are framed. On this line, attribution of opportunity would show how actors use each other's responses to a situation to interpret the opportunities they face (Barzelay and Gallego 2006, 2010a).

To apply this analytical framework to a case study, we first need to organise the empirical data of the episode into a narration, following the sequence of sub-processes within a policy cycle. Narration should pay attention to actors' activities that are analytically relevant within each sub-process; to their beliefs and their interactions with other actors; and to the arguments and reasoning they use to make sense of their decisions. In the analysis and interpretation, empirical observations about an episode are then explained by causal processes and mechanisms affecting the policy-making process. Explanation of the policy cycle outcome will be based on the IP *schemas* above, which combine institutional and processual elements within a dynamic analytic interpretation of episodes (Barzelay and Gallego

2006). Emphasis on process will involve focusing on the flows of interactions among actors, the interrelation between their beliefs and actions and their connection with the temporal context (Abbott 2001; Elster 1989). Emphasis on institutions will involve being attentive to how situated interaction (human agency within particular circumstances) is influenced by stable context factors (Thelen and Steinmo 1992). By integrating both focuses, this approach also asks how such situated interactions feed back into context (Tendler 1997). The resulting explanation requires appreciating contingency and causal regularities (Skocpol 1984; McAdam, Tarrow and Tilly 2001).

As shown in the analysis of the case presented here, the IP explanation of the case tries to overcome the MSF's analytical problems of the independence of streams and of sub-processes, as well as the role of policy-windows and policy-entrepreneurship within a policy-cycle. The conclusions of this case study aim to contribute to the pool of limited historical generalisations that the comparative research on public management policy under this approach has generated so far.

Narrating the episode: reforming public management in the Catalan health sector

The trajectory of health policy in Catalonia over the last two decades of the twentieth century has been frequently analysed (Gallego 2000, 2001, 2003b; Gallego, Gomà and Subirats 2005; Gallego and Subirats 2011, 2012). Catalonia was the first Autonomous Community to receive health-policy competence in 1981, at the onset of the devolution process. The public-health providers transferred by the Spanish government to the Catalan government were all integrated into a single organisation – the Catalan Health Institute (ICS) – replicating the Spanish direct public-provision model. These providers included over 90 per cent of primary-care provision in Catalonia but only a third of the hospital beds at that time, which left scope for contracts with external providers to play a prominent role. In this scenario, the Catalan government gradually consolidated a contract-based health-provision system that built on pre-existing private (both for-profit and non-profit) and public providers. Meanwhile, the ICS remained an isolated exemplar of direct, public provision: a large provider of health services, with a single legal personality, operating under administrative-law regulations. As a result, it was persistently seen as an isle of obsolete privilege by the contracted providers, particularly in relation to the different regulation of labour relations (largely civil service) and financing mechanisms (budget allocations).

The need to reformulate the ICS's legal nature, the criticisms of its inefficiency, and the insistence on the need to modernise its management tools had been permanent issues in the discourse of a large number of the actors in the Catalan health-policy sector (politicians, managers and professionals), attracting varying degrees of attention throughout that time. However, the studies mentioned previously also highlight that these same actors considered that such changes had not been addressed over those years because: a) from a legal point of view, it was very difficult to change the institution from a social-security management body form to a publicly-owned enterprise or to an autonomous body; b) the Ministry of Economy and Finance of the Catalan government, and particularly its Intervention Unit, due to the institutional bias derived from its control role, opposed a management model that might involve *ex-post* economic and financial control; and c) unions would probably mobilise strong professional opposition if that proposal involved a change in labour conditions and regulations. Some arguments also pointed out that a legal redefinition of the ICS required an injection of economic resources (to balance budgets) that was not affordable given the budget of the Catalan government. Taking into account that these arguments are based on structural factors that, in principle, could be expected to remain stable over time, the question is:

Why were these factors not an obstacle to the passage of the 2007 ICS Law that transformed the ICS into a public enterprise?

Elections and government transition

The Catalan regional elections of November 2003 brought the first ideological changeover in the Catalan government since the Spanish democratic transition of the late 1970s. The nationalist, centre-right party coalition Convergència i Unió (CiU) had formed the Catalan government for twenty-three consecutive years, since the first regional election in 1980; it had an absolute majority between 1984 and 1995. As a result of the 2003 Catalan elections, a post-electoral centre-left coalition that commanded an absolute majority in parliament took office. Ordered from highest to lowest number of seats, the coalition included the Party of the Socialists of Catalonia (PSC); the pro-Catalan-independence Republican Left of Catalonia (ERC); and the eco-socialist coalition Initiative of Catalonia-Green (ICV), each of them representing different intensities of Catalan nationalist and leftist leanings.

The post-electoral agreement reached by the three parties that would form the Catalan government at the end of 2003 drew up the framework for a government that defined itself as 'Catalanist'[2] and leftist. On the 'Catalanist' side, the overarching political priority embraced by PSC Catalan Prime Minister, Pasqual Maragall, included the formulation of a new Statute of Autonomy that would enhance Catalan political and economic autonomy *vis-à-vis* the Spanish government. On the leftist dimension of the tripartite government agreement, the text made an explicit political option of strengthening social policy in general, and health policy in particular, with strong support for the modernisation and sustainability of public services. At the end of 2001, a new regional financing system had been approved that increased the budgets available to regional governments and established that economic transfers for health would no longer be ring-fenced but merged with

---

2.   'Catalanist' is not equivalent to 'nationalist': the former implies a weaker claim for a differentiated status as a political community. The use of the term 'Catalanist' points to the need to accommodate different preference-intensities within the political parties signing the agreement.

the rest of the regional budget. This change meant that regional governments' decisions on health budgets would more clearly reflect their own policy priorities.

Setting the agenda: modernising the Catalan Health Institute

The PSC Minister for Health of the Catalan government, Marina Geli, made her first address to the Catalan Parliament one month after being appointed. She did not question the defining features of the Catalan health model built over the previous twenty-five years, which had enjoyed wide political support, but pointed to potential lines of what she termed 'modernisation'. Concerning the ICS, she highlighted the need to modernise the management of all its services and to increase investment in areas that had long needed the increase. She expressed the need to truly understand the ICS and the non-ICS providers as parts of the same system (a provision-network under public responsibility) and to address a redefinition of ICS's organisational features and management practices, in order to reinforce its provider-role and ensure its sustainability. This management-modernisation strategy would also require, according to her, decentralisation of structures and provision-processes. She called for 'autonomy in management and decentralisation in decision-making'. Also, having been an active voice in the 'municipalist'[3] discourse in Catalonia, Marina Geli explicitly clarified her choice for how to improve public health and providers' management by getting local governments more involved in health policy and opening new channels for citizens' participation.

Only in answer to a question from a Popular Party (PP) member of the opposition in parliament, did the possibility of legislating on reforming the ICS come to the fore. The question explicitly asked whether Geli's ministry intended to pass a law for the ICS. Without having apparently considered it, Geli answered:

> We have to give it more autonomy and, obviously, probably, therefore, through a new, let's say, legislative framework. There are 31,000 [approximately] workers that work at the Catalan Health Institute. It seems to me that it would be a mistake to revise the civil service [regulation] through the Health [sector]. By contrast, we do have to provide enough tools for [management] autonomy (Parlament de Catalunya 2004).

Geli also insisted that her ministry would respect the agreements signed by CiU and the majority of unions on the different regulations for ICS and non-ICS providers, but that she would search for compliance with the legal obligation to reach a minimum common labour regulation for the whole health system (ICS and non-ICS).

Geli's commitments were translated into effort priorities: the Decree of Health Territorial Governments was passed at the beginning of 2006 and the Law

---

3. Political ideology that advocates the strengthening of local governments through the devolution of a wider range of functions and resources to local municipalities.

on Public Health in 2009, during the following legislative term. However, the unplanned, ambiguous commitment to legislate on the ICS met an also unplanned, quick translation into a specific effort. At the outset of her mandate, Marina Geli appointed a new managing-director for the ICS, Raimon Belenes. As a doctor and previous top executive of the health services of the Autonomous Community of Andalusia, Belenes had a reputation as an experienced, pragmatic and strict manager, who was committed to the sustainability of the public sector through the development of quality, efficiency and management-modernisation strategies. He received a mandate to draw up a project for the modernisation of ICS's management – to pass a specific law on this was a political mandate from the outset and he accepted it. According to numerous political and executive officials interviewed, several previous ICS's managing-director had tried to address this issue both with and without legal changes but, over two decades, they had not received political support. A common interpretation of this lack of support is that CiU identified ICS as an example of Spanish centralist politics (the ICS was an institution from the Franco era transferred to the Catalan government in 1981, after the democratic transition), on the one hand, and of bureaucratic and obsolete management model, on the other.[4]

The tripartite government promoted a different view of the ICS. Knowing she had the support of Catalan Prime Minister Maragall, Geli made her intention explicit to address the ICS's modernisation through a change in its legal nature and the improvement of its management tools and autonomy, with the aim of making it closer to the way contracted providers operated, to ensure its sustainability. She was aware that in order to take this path, she had to gain the support of the Minister of Economy. Most of the political and managerial officials interviewed for this study argued that one of the key reasons for the lack of political support for ICS reform up to that point was opposition from the Ministry of Economy and Finance of the Catalan government – and its Intervention Unit – to any loss of *ex-ante* financial control. The ICS had a differentiated budget within the government's budget, a unitary structure and strict *ex-ante* control routines, which were considered to facilitate expenditure- and deficit-control by the Intervention Unit. The options of decentralisation or *ex-post* controls would weaken this supervision capacity. The Ministry of Economy's top officials commonly thought that this possibility should be avoided, as the health budget was, for structural reasons (technology costs, age-structure of the population and so on), potentially unstoppable.

Geli was determined to have the Ministry of Economy as a collaborator instead of as an opponent and to do so she needed to gain credibility. According to top officials interviewed from both departments, their political bosses perceived that the recent budget increase, both in the general regional budget and in the health

---

4. The ICS was seen as a huge unmanageable structure, on top of which a managing-director was appointed by the Catalan government, but which had fragmented and, therefore, weak political bosses: the ministries of Economy and Finance (budget allocation and control), Interior (labour-relations and civil service), Health (activity and services portfolio), Universities and Research (medical research).

budget, facilitated collaboration. Since the beginning of their mandates and, at Geli's initiative, both Geli and the Minister of Economy and Finance, Antoni Castells, agreed that their highest political officials would meet monthly, so that the Ministry of Economy could monitor and closely follow how the ICS improved its management objectives. They also reached an agreement to clear the public debt in the area of health, meaning that a substantial part of the projected growth of the health budget would go for clearing the deferred spending – that is, spending incurred in the previous years, but on the basis of a deferred payment. Moreover, Geli and Castells jointly set up a Commission for the Reform of the Financing of Health in 2005, composed of experts with explicitly different stances, and gave it the mandate to come up with specific proposals for guaranteeing the sustainability of the health system.[5]

Specifying alternatives: transforming the Catalan Health Institute into a public company

On the ICS's side, Belenes knew that most reports and studies carried out by previous ICS top directive teams had been elaborated without the participation of the Ministry of Economy. For this reason, Belenes met on two occasions with the Ministry of Economy and with the head of the Intervention Unit to explain the project to them. Belenes specifically committed to providing evidence that ICS management could be efficient and would reduce the deficit over the following years. He prepared a first draft of the law project and got approval from Geli. Then, over two years, Belenes himself discussed the different options about legal forms available for framing the new ICS with other government departments, with political parties and with the trade unions.

The negotiations centred on four issues: legal personality; degree of financial autonomy; (non-)civil service status of health professionals; and degree of organisational unity or disaggregation. The negotiations concerning the ICS's future legal personality progressed relatively quickly. Minister Geli and the ICS team supported the option of maintaining the ICS's public ownership and suggested transforming it into a public company. Other alternatives were discarded for different reasons. For example, the idea of a public firm or state-owned enterprise was dismissed because it would require links to state legislation. The alternative of creating an SA corporation (in civil-law jurisdictions, this is roughly equivalent to a public limited company in common-law jurisdictions) using public capital was rejected, in order to limit the debate on the issue of privatisation. For most of the agents interviewed, it was a debate on a technical aspect on which there was consensus.

Negotiation on the degree of the future ICS's financial autonomy was conditioned by the historical opposition of the Intervention Unit of the Catalan Ministry of Economy and Finance. The ICS operated with *ex-ante* financial

---

5. The report by this Commission (Working Group for the Rationalisation and Financing of Health Expenditure 2005) is available at: http://www.metgesdecatalunya.cat/uploaded/File/Documentacio/Informes/General/document_savis_sanitat.pdf (accessed 22 February 2013).

intervention (a lower level of autonomy) but had gradually incorporated (in certain aspects) permanent financial auditing (a medium level of autonomy) with monthly or quarterly auditing. There was a third possibility: *ex-post* control (the highest degree of autonomy), usual in a public company. According to the officials involved, the collaboration set up between the ministries of Health and Economy on the basis of their monthly monitoring meetings had built some degree of trust on the ICS's capacity for efficient management. The position of the heads of the Ministry of Economy and of its Intervention Unit was to favour greater autonomy while demanding direct responsibility: permanent auditing was preferred to *ex-post* auditing, even though the latter was more flexible. Trade unions preferred the ICS to remain within the previous administrative framework of control: 'It's a question of ideology' (interview with a former trade union representative). According to some ICS management-team members, some within ICS itself also preferred the existing model, as it placed responsibility on the controller (Inspection Unit within the Ministry of Economy). The result of the negotiation led to the choice of the alternative of quarterly permanent auditing, which meant an increase in the existing ICS's financial and accounting autonomy, but still not to the autonomy level that is usually enjoyed by public companies.

While the negotiation process was relatively fast for the two issues described, the negotiation with respect to the staff-employment regimes and the degree of organisational unity or disaggregation of the future ICS was slower and more complex. This process involved not only the Department of Economy and Finance and the trade unions, but also the Department of Interior (responsible for regulation of public employees), which was in the hands of another of the governing coalition parties: ERC. Top political officials interviewed agreed that this negotiation was marked by ideological positioning and a turbulent context among the medical profession. In fact, nine days before the bill was sent to parliament, the Union of Doctors of Catalonia, the largest Catalan union of the medical profession, announced a five-day strike – which they held at the end of March 2006; two months later they called for a new strike that was eventually cancelled. The strikes were to protest against what the union considered to be unreasonable working conditions for medical professionals and also against the differences between working conditions in the contracted providers and in the ICS.

With this background, the bill went to parliament at the beginning of April 2006. Even though the initial agreements progressed well, such as the preservation of the workers' civil-service status the bill lost in July 2006, as a result of the anticipated call for new elections. The reason came from the macro-political scenario: after the new Statute of Autonomy was passed in September 2005 by the Catalan Parliament, it went to the Spanish Parliament, which considerably reduced its nationalist and financing claims and passed it in March 2006. ERC considered that revision unacceptable and called for a 'No' vote in the coming referendum in Catalonia on the Statute. Prime Minister Maragall expelled the ERC from the coalition government and called for elections after the referendum. The elections held in November gave a victory to CiU, both in the percentage of votes and the number of seats;[6] but the three parties of the previous government (PSC, ERC and IC-V) agreed the re-formation of a centre-left government (*Govern de Entesa*).

Decision-making: passing the 2007 Catalan Health Institute law

The new PSC Prime Minister, José Montilla, supported the continuity of the ICS law-negotiation process and reappointed Geli and Castells as ministers of Health and Economy and Finance, respectively. However, a significant change was the replacement of Raimon Belenes by Francesc José María as managing-director of the ICS. José María was a lawyer and the secretary of the Hospital Consortium of Catalonia, an association which had represented the interests of local governments in the health sector over the previous twenty years (Gallego 2001). His profile was associated with decentralised, public corporate health management. His explicit desire was to introduce significant changes in the ICS, such as its disaggregation into different units across the territory and the progressive incorporation of non-civil-service staff. So, with the consent of Geli, the bill was quickly sent to parliament again; José María took on the task of negotiating with the political parties and trade unions and the process speeded up.[7]

With the issues of legal personality and the degree of financial autonomy of the future ICS more or less defined during the previous legislative period, negotiations now centred on the degree of organisational unity or disaggregation of the future ICS and on the (non-)civil-service-status of its staff. Concerning the latter issue, there were two alternatives. CiU and the PP wanted a progressive reduction in the number of civil-service staff. The trade unions, together with the ERC and ICV, supported the continuation of the civil-service employment regime. Within the PSC there were mixed opinions. Finally, an agreement was reached with the trade unions in which the government would not change the civil-service employment status of ICS's staff. There would be the possibility of contracting new staff with non-civil-service status but only in particular and exceptional circumstances.

There were several options for addressing the issue of organisational unity *versus* disaggregation of the future ICS: disaggregating the ICS into different public companies; creating a public holding company (organisations with different legal statuses); or maintaining the existing legal unity. Within the tripartite government, and even within the PSC, there were different opinions. Some of the leaders (including the ICS's managing-director José Maria) preferred disaggregation; whereas others (such as Minister Geli) favoured decentralisation (territorial and in terms of decision-making) and were less in favour of the creation of a holding company. The heads of the Department of Economy and Finance (and of its Intervention Unit) did not trust the disaggregation option since they saw the possibility of increased public spending without prior control as a danger.

---

6. CiU obtained 31.5 per cent (with 48 members) and the PSC 26.8 per cent (37).

7. 'It was necessary to pass the law quickly because when you get into the second half of the term of office everyone starts to think about the elections and then you can't get it through.' (interview with a former senior politician of the Catalan government).

The Department of Interior (under ERC) also opposed disaggregation but, in their case, it was because of the ideological position of the party (and its main advisors on health matters) in favour of maintaining legal unity and a clearly public, direct provision of health services.

Within the parliamentary opposition, CiU also expressed mixed opinions with respect to this issue. A significant sector defended the disaggregation option, a position that was shared with the College of Physicians of Barcelona, which encouraged the establishment of companies managed by health-service professionals themselves. Even the alternative of formally introducing public–private collaboration in order to allow the use of unused capacity of the ICS by private companies was contemplated.[8] However, another significant sector of CiU opposed such proposals, interpreting them as a possible scenario for competition between the public and private sectors, in which it was not clear which would benefit. Paradoxically, and for different ideological reasons, IC-V and ERC were in agreement with this last sector of CiU in their opposition to the disaggregation and use of the unused capacity of the ICS. Thus, the policy chosen was transforming the ICS into a unitary public company; its provider units (hospitals and primary-care centres) would not have independent legal personality and the use of the ICS's premises and services for private health-care would be prohibited.

The Law for the Creation of the Public Company Catalan Health Institute was passed by consensus in July 2007, with a vote in favour by the main opposition party (CiU), among others. The agents interviewed agreed that it would have been difficult for CiU to pass a similar law if they had been in power and in a context of economic recession. The characteristics of the law did not satisfy CiU, which wanted to see the introduction of non-civil-service status for staff and organisational disaggregation. But the party heads (and also their health advisors) saw the law as an opportunity and a first step that would open the door to further reforming the ICS – a reform that could continue in what they saw as a near future, with CiU once again ruling the Catalan government, if opinion polls were right.[9]

The passing of the law by consensus was also interpreted from an opposite view – as a lock-in against deeper changes. For the great majority of agents interviewed, the law had a limited impact on the specific management of ICS's activity. It was seen more as a formalisation of change pressures that came from the organisation itself. The law would demonstrate that it is possible to halt some of the inertia opposed to reform through gradual improvements and, above all, it legitimised the place of the ICS in the Catalan health model.

Explaining public management policy-reform in the Catalan health sector

How can we explain the inclusion on the agenda of the ICS's reform? As we have seen, there was an apparent consensus on the structural reasons that had

---

8.   For example, establishing agreements for the use of ICS's health resources. This alternative was considered by the director of the ICS.

9.   See CEO 2013.

hindered its inclusion on the agenda over the previous two and a half decades. The lack of CiU governments' political support for successive ICS's directive teams' initiatives for modernising management had been justified on the basis of *stable contextual factors*: juridical complexity; unions' opposition to changes in workers' civil-service status; opposition from the Catalan Ministry of Economy and Finance to *ex-post* auditing; and lack of resources for clearing debt before relaunching ICS as a public company. In CiU's political discourse, those factors were explicitly related to the *issue-image* that the ICS was an obsolete, unmanageable organisation, which represented the opposite provision model from the one that had developed and consolidated over the previous two decades in Catalonia. CiU was convinced that efforts to reform or modernise the ICS were doomed to failure. Moreover, in their discourse, the ICS's management and organisation model were considered reminiscent of Francoist centralist politics across the territory. CiU's preference was for disaggregating the ICS into a contracted network of autonomous-provider units, with a diversity of juridical regimes. In sum, ICS's reform *issue-image* was defined within the public-management policy-domain and within a potential contentious politics arena because it was explicitly linked to controversy about the territorial organisation of power in Spain.

With the change of government at the end of 2003, which brought the PSC-ERC-ICV coalition to power in Catalonia, the MSF would argue that a policy-window opened up as a result of events in the politics stream. From an IP view, we can add that the ideological shift of 2003 helped activate the mechanism of *attribution of opportunity* on several fronts, leading numerous actors to believe that their efforts might eventuate in policy-change. The impact of that mechanism was strongly reinforced by several factors. First, an event in the political stream – namely, the legislative turnover that brought the Spanish Workers' Socialist Party to office at the central government level in early March 2004 – created positive expectations about Spain–Catalonia relationships. This was particularly relevant for the coming negotiation of the new Statute of Autonomy and the related financing system, which were both supposed to enhance self-government across all policy-sectors. Second, a sensible increase in the regional budget since 2002 also created expectations for policy-survival in many policy domains, including health-policy. That budget increase had resulted from a change in the macro-economic policy domain, with the passage of the 2001 new territorial financing system, and the upward economic cycle. IP interprets this type of cross-streams influences on the bases of a *spillover effect* mechanism. That is, this spillover effect does not necessarily originate from feedback from previous programmes and solutions, as in the majority of cases the MSF has been used to explore but from events taking place in the political stream – high-profile negotiations concerning the territorial organisation of power in Spain had positive effects on public-management reform in the Catalan health sector. From an MSF view, when a policy-window opens as a result of events in the political stream, attention tends to focus on solutions first, before problems can clearly be defined. This case study shows that this may not be so. IP has prompted us to focus on policy-entrepreneurship to understand how role-specific actors make explicit links between events taking place in the politics stream and events taking place in the policy stream, with a clear reference, in this case, to controversy about the state territorial organisation.

As a leftist leader of the 'municipalist' movement, and with a prospective generous budget, Catalan Health Minister Marina Geli's priorities may be interpreted under the *logic of appropriateness*: she could be expected to promote the modernisation and sustainability of public health-care, but through enhancing the political role of local governments in health policy-making and management. She explicitly defined non-contentious policy aims at the outset of her mandate: consolidating the structural features of the Catalan health-provision system; promoting better public-health regulation; promoting service quality; and modernising ICS's management, all under the general umbrella of the reorganisation of ICS health provision on the bases of a closer involvement of local governments in its organisation.

By appointing Belenes as managing-director of the ICS, Geli *certified* him as an *actor*, on the basis of his managerial reputation – from an IP view, this is a mechanism activated by an actor in the political stream and which helped him to emerge as a policy-entrepreneur in the policy stream. In contrast to previous ministers, Geli's political support for a legal-managerial reform was made explicit when she commissioned Belenes to undertake the project. The message was clear and involved a redefinition of the *issue-image*: legal changes could be defined and promoted from within the ICS itself and modernisation was necessary – and viable – to ensure the ICS's sustainability within the Catalan health system. From an MSF view, this issue image met both selection-criteria for a policy-alternative to get serious consideration in the political stream: technical feasibility and value-acceptability. IP would add that issue-framing affects not only alternative-selection and problem-representation but also inclusion on the agenda.

Both Geli and Belenes defined the ICS modernisation as a public-management *issue*, conceptually and processually distinct from other issues and initiatives promoted by the Catalan Health Ministry that fell under other policy domains. Thus, the elaboration and passage of the 2006 Decree on Health Territorial Governments in the territorial-policy domain, and the elaboration and passage of the 2009 Public Health Law in the health-policy domain, would have, if any, positive *spillover effects* on the public-management policy-cycle of the ICS law. If the ICS law was eventually passed, it would be conceived as a piece of legislation that reinforced the government programme; but its development would not be expected to interfere with the other two main pieces of regulation.

How can we explain why the alternative-specification process involved the consideration of options that had been until then disregarded as unviable and too complex? Both Health Minister Geli and ICS's managing-director Belenes were aware that the health public-management policy subsystem was highly fragmented between the Departments of Health; Economy and Finance and its Intervention Unit; Interior; and the ICS itself. The *policy-learning* mechanism made them interpret such a fragmentation as one of the main obstacles for negotiation over the previous years. Thus, both Geli and Belenes consciously took actions to build bridges and promote co-operation in order to build trust – for example, through regular control and report meetings between top officials of the ministries of Health and Economy, including an agreement to gradually clear the health-budget debt. A positive *interference-effect* to allow this agreement came from the increase in the regional budget.

The effort to provide evidence of management improvement was initially decoupled from the law-drafting efforts of the ICS's directive team, in order to show political will to pursue real change – rather than just the symbolic act of passing a law. Such efforts allowed regular *performance feedback* on the improvement of ICS's financial management, which helped the Ministry of Economy and Finance accept the alternative of an increase in the degree of financial autonomy. At this point, the *logic of appropriateness* did not lead to the persistent institutional bias of previous years that had led the Ministry of Economy to oppose any decrease in *ex-ante* control.

The *pace* of specifying alternatives was fast, partly because of the professional commitment of the *actor certified* for specifying alternatives – namely, the ICS's managing-director – and by the frequent contact between the Minister of Health and the ICS's managing-director, which provided a sense of political support to the *actors certified* for specifying alternatives. This helps to explain why even though legislating on the ICS was not a priority for the Minister of Health, the *issue-status* of that initiative boosted its position on her agenda and the policy subsystem built momentum for a decision.

From an MSF perspective, the search for solutions and their availability is heavily influenced by the structure of the policy communities involved in this process, particularly by their degree of integration. However, IP focuses on how those community features may vary throughout their policy-making activities due to the actions of policy-entrepreneurs, because such features are not invariable.

How can we explain why a decision was passed by consensus in parliament after a relatively rapid process, when over two and a half decades it had been considered not worth pursuing because of its inherent complexity? The bill had been lost as a result of the premature end of the legislative session in 2006, therefore, the mechanism of *actor-certification* by which the ministers of Economy and Health were ratified in their posts in the new government involved approval of their previous initiatives and helped speed up the process. The appointment by Geli of a new ICS's managing-director, with a more pro-municipalist and pro-private-management profile, also activated the mechanism of *actor-certification*: the change signalled a clearer political commitment to passing the reform.

However, the new Prime Minister's overarching mandate to preserve social peace called for concessions and negotiation. The MSF provides here a suitable 'salami tactic' explanation of the process of alternative-selection and decision-making by policy-entrepreneurs. Geli and the new ICS's managing-director, as entrepreneurs at a high level in government, cut the process into distinct stages, which were presented sequentially to policy-makers. Doing so promoted agreement in steps. This 'salami tactic' led in this case to a *sui generis* solution of a public company legal personality and a single unitary structure, which gathered consensus on the bases of providing legal exceptions: avoiding links to central government legislation; avoiding a potentially controversial debate on privatisation; and protecting workers' civil-service status. IP would argue that the mechanism activated here was *attribution of opportunity* by all actors involved: some interpreted this design as the protection and consolidation of the ICS's strength within the Catalan health system; others considered this effort as a first step towards further changes.

Conclusions

This case study shows how an MSF interpretation of Kingdon's approach includes concepts such as streams, policy-windows and policy-entrepreneurs that are analytically useful for the interpretation of empirical data on policy-making episodes. However, it also shows that an IP interpretation of Kingdon's approach increases the explanatory potential of these concepts. Within this framework, this study reinforces some research arguments already formulated by comparative research on the politics of public-management policy-making (Barzelay 2003; Barzelay and Gallego 2010b).

First, in a decentralised state such as Spain, public-management reform may be intertwined with political controversy about public governance – that is, about the territorial organisation of political authority and the consequent relation between central and regional governments. Thus, while the MSF would suggest that the political-stream factors influencing the politics of public-management reform are the national mood, partisan competition and change of government after the end of one legislative session, IP also includes political contention about characteristics of the country's political and governmental systems. Second, such an influence may be channelled into the framing of public-management issues and into the alternatives they consider for negotiation and eventual choice. As the case analysed here shows, actors' perceptions of multi-level governance-dynamics led them to make explicit arguments for or against reform in general, or specific alternatives, on the basis of potential links to Spanish politics and authority structures. That is, in contrast to the MSF, IP highlights the connection between the politics and the policy streams and between policy-making sub-processes – namely, issue-framing and alternative-specification activities.

Third, agenda-setters tend to be within the executive and their political will and actions are of pivotal influence in determining which issues are included on the agenda. However, this study shows that when public-management reform is circumscribed to a particular policy-sector, such as health, the agenda-setter is most probably within the top political level of the corresponding ministry. The successful inclusion of the issue on the general government agenda depends on how the issue-framing reflects governmental discourse on multi-level governance. Thus, IP links the policy and political streams through the activity of policy-entrepreneurs. Fourth, as in cases of government-wide public-management policy, the agenda-setting and alternative-specification processes in sector-specific public-management reform appear to be closely coupled, which shortens the length of pre-decisional phases of the policy cycle. Thus, IP visualises the relationship between policy-making sub-processes.

Fifth, as shown in other studies, alternative-specification is influenced by the prerogatives of institutional actors in the policy subsystem, their background profile, and inherited conditions in the policy stream. Sixth, the politics of public-management policy-making in a specific sector, such as health, is influenced by how actors in the policy subsystem interpret past and future events in their relations with actors affected by the policy-alternatives under consideration. Therefore, IP integrates both institutional and process aspects.

Last, an IP interpretation of this case study shows that the politics of sector-specific public management is highly sensitive to spillover and interference effects coming from conditions and occurrences in neighbouring policy-domains. However, while comparative research has provided a wide range of evidence that economic crisis has tended to prompt public-management reform, this study shows how upward economic cycles may also pave the way for reform. The question persistently posed by the literature has been why, in answer to an economic crisis, many countries dived into public-management reform over the 1980s, the 1990s, and beyond, while others did not (Ongaro 2008, 2010). However, there are still unexplored issues, such as how upward economic cycles influence public-management policy-making and how, in decentralised states, such influence differs between central and regional governments.

References

Abbot, A. (2001) *Time Matters: On theory and method*, Chicago: University of Chicago Press.

Abell, P. (2004) 'Narrative explanation: an alternative to variable-centered explanation?', *Annual Review of Sociology* 30: 287–310.

Barzelay, M. (2003) 'The process dynamics of public management policy change', *International Public Management Journal* 6(3): 251–402.

Barzelay, M. and Gallego, R. (2006) 'From new institutionalism to institutional processualism: advancing knowledge about public management policy change', *Governance* 19(4): 531–57.

— (2010a) 'The comparative historical analysis of public management policy cycles in France, Italy and Spain: symposium introduction', *Governance* 23(2): 209–24.

— (2010b) 'The comparative historical analysis of public management policy cycles in France, Italy and Spain: symposium conclusion', *Governance* 23(2): 297–308.

CEO (Centre d'Estudis d'Opinió) (2013) *Intenció de vot autonòmiques*, available at: http://www.einesceo.cat/evolutius/intencio-de-vot-autonomiques/32 (accessed 22 February 2013).

Durant, R. F. and Diehl, P. F. (1989) 'Agendas, alternatives, public policy: lessons from the U.S. foreign policy arena', *Journal of Public Policy* 9(2): 179–205.

Elster, J. (1989) *Nuts and Bolts for the Social Sciences*, Cambridge, UK: Cambridge University Press.

Gallego, R. (2000) 'Introducing purchaser/provider separation in the Catalan health administration: a budget analysis', *Public Administration* 78(2): 423–42.

— (2001) 'La política sanitària Catalana: la construcció d'un sistema de provisió pluralista', in R. Gomà and J. Subirats (eds) *Govern i Polítiques Públiques a Catalunya (1980–2000)*, Barcelona: Edicions Universitat de Barcelona-Servei de Publicacions Universitat Autònoma de Barcelona.

— (2003b) 'Las políticas sanitarias de las Comunidades Autónomas', in R. Gallego, R. Gomà. and J. Subirats (eds) *Estado de Bienestar y Comunidades Autónomas*, Madrid: Tecnos-UPF.

Gallego, R. and Subirats, J. (2011) 'Regional welfare regimes and multilevel governance', in A. M. Guillén and M. León (eds) *The Spanish Welfare State in the European Context*, London: Routledge.

— (2012) 'Spanish regional and welfare systems: policy innovation and multi-level governance', *Regional and Federal Studies* 22(3): 269–88.

Gallego, R., Gomà, R. and Subirats, J. (2005) 'Spain, from state welfare to regional welfare', in N. McEwen and L. Moreno (eds) *The Territorial Politics of Welfare*, London: Routledge.

King, A. (1985) 'John W. Kingdon, *Agendas, Alternatives, and Public Policies*, Boston: Little, Brown, 1984, xi+ 240 pp., $9.95', book review, *Journal of Public Policy* 5: 281–283.

Kingdon, J. (1984) *Agendas, Alternatives, and Public Policies*, New York: Harper Collins.

— (1995) *Agendas, Alternatives and Public Policies*, 2nd edn, Boston: Little, Brown & Co.

Levitt, B. and March, J. G. (1988) 'Organizational learning', *Annual Review of Sociology* 14: 319–40.

McAdam, D., Tarrow, S. and Tilly, C. (2001) *Dynamics of Contention*, Cambridge, UK: Cambridge University Press.

McEwen, N. and Moreno, L. (eds) (2005) *The Territorial Politics of Welfare*, London: Routledge.

Mucciaroni, G. (1992) 'The garbage can model and the study of policy making: a critique', *Polity* 24(3): 459–82.

Ongaro, E. (2008) 'The reform of public management in France, Greece, Italy, Portugal, and Spain', *International Journal of Public Sector Management* 21: 101–17.

— (2010) *Public Management Reform and Modernization: Trajectories of administrative change in Italy, France, Greece, Portugal and Spain*, Cheltenham, UK: Edward Elgar.

Parlament de Catalunya (2004) *Diari de Sessions* (30/1/2004, Sèrie C, núm. 4:30), Parlament de Catalunya, available at: http://www.parlament.cat/document/dspcc/54515.pdf (last accessed 16 October 2015).

Stone, D. (1988) *Policy Paradox and Political Reason*, Boston: Little, Brown & Co.

Skocpol, T. (1984) *Vision and Method in Historical Sociology*, Cambridge, UK: Cambridge University Press.

Skok, J. E. (1995) 'Policy issue networks and the public policy cycle: a structural functional framework for public administration', *Public Administration Review* 55(4): 325–32.

Tendler, J. (1997) *Good Government in the Tropics*, Baltimore, MD: Johns Hopkins University Press.

Thelen, K. and Steinmo, S. (1992) 'Historical institutionalism in comparative politics', in S. Steinmo, K. Thelen and F. Longstreth (eds) *Structuring Politics: Historical institutionalism in comparative analysis*, Cambridge, UK: Cambridge University Press.

Weir, M. (1992) 'Ideas and the politics of bounded innovation', in S. Steinmo, K. Thelen and F. Longstreth (eds) *Structuring Politics: Historical institutionalism in comparative analysis*, Cambridge, UK: Cambridge University Press.

Zahariadis, N. (1996) 'Selling British Rail: an idea whose time has come?', *Comparative Political Studies*, 29(4): 400–22.

— (1999) 'Ambiguity, time, and multiple streams', in P. A. Sabatier (ed.) *Theories of the Policy Process*, Oxford, UK: Westview Press.

— (2003) *Ambiguity and Choice in Public Policy*, Washington, DC: Georgetown University Press.

— (2005) *Essence of Political Manipulation: Emotion, institutions, and Greek foreign policy*, New York: Peter Lang.

Chapter Fourteen

Path-Departing Labour-Market Reforms in the United Kingdom and Sweden: An Analysis Combining the Multiple-Streams Framework and Historical Institutionalism

Florian Spohr

Introduction

Labour-market and employment policies are characterised by a large degree of path-dependence. This implies that certain courses of political development are hard to reverse, due to initial choices that, once institutionalised, increase the cost of adopting once-possible alternatives. Furthermore, institutional systems, composed of both formal rules (labour laws, social laws) and informal rules (social norms), shape constellations of actors and their goals (Pierson 2001: 414–15; Erhel and Zajdela 2004: 132, 135). Accordingly, studies in this policy-area tend to stress the difficulty of accomplishing significant change (see Barbier and Ludwig-Mayerhofer 2004; Peck and Theodore 2001; Berkel and Hornemann Møller 2002). This expectation, however, is contradicted by a number of far-reaching and path-departing 'activating' labour-market reforms that took place, for example, in the Netherlands, the United Kingdom, Ireland, Germany, Denmark and Sweden; and these suggest that labour-markets in Europe 'may be much more malleable than previously thought' (Boyle and Schünemann 2009: 1). Although path-dependence theory appears to be highly significant in understanding the dynamics of national regimes, it can hardly explain fundamental change and paradigm shifts.

A possible model that is appropriate to explain such a far-reaching policy change could be the multiple-streams framework (MSF), which regards decisions as the result of the coupling of three relatively independent streams – problems, policies and politics – during windows of opportunities (Kingdon 2003[1984]). Conversely, capturing path-dependency with the MSF is problematic, due to its insufficient incorporation of institutions. The MSF is grounded in the behavioural tradition of political science (Schlager 1999: 247) and has been developed in the pluralistic American setting of policy-making, where institutions do little to reduce contingency and ambiguity. The framework focuses on individual behaviour and pays little attention to the institutional context of decision-making. Institutions, however, channel and shape participants' behaviour, which helps to determine which solutions reach the agenda (Mucciarioni 1992: 466).

This chapter aims to introduce the effect of path-dependence in the MSF by combining it with insights from historical institutionalism (HI). HI explains the maintenance of contingent institutional decisions by examining conditions under which a particular trajectory was followed: large set-up or fixed costs; learning effects; co-ordination effects; and adaptive expectations all encourage actors to focus on a single alternative (Pierson 2001: 414–15). The MSF and HI have contrary assumptions, which, however, are not mutually exclusive. While the MSF highlights the contingency and ambiguity of processes and issues, HI suggests that institutionalisation reduces uncertainty. The argument in this chapter is that a combination of these contrasting views can provide a framework for the analysis of both path-dependent and path-departing processes. This argument is introduced in the next section and afterwards illustrated in two case studies that deal with labour-market reforms: in the United Kingdom (UK) under the Labour government from 1997 onwards and under the conservative Alliance for Sweden government, starting from 2006. The last section concludes.

Multiple-streams framework and historical institutionalism

In the following, the MSF is combined with historical institutionalism to introduce the impact of institutions on the three streams as well as mechanisms for path-departing change.

In the *problem stream* changing indicators, focusing events or feedback from existing programmes may highlight problems and occupy the attention of governments. However, conditions come to be defined as problems only when actors believe in the necessity of changing them. While in the MSF the violation of prevailing values transforms conditions into problems (Kingdon 2003[1984]: 198–9), the path-dependence hypothesis suggests that institutions act as a filter, transforming an initial shock into a political outcome (Erhel and Zajelda 2004: 128). As institutions shape values, they also affect interpretations and the definition of problems.

In the *policy stream,* ideas have to fulfil the criteria of technical feasibility and value-acceptability to win acceptance in policy-networks. Technical feasibility means that policies have to be implementable to be chosen, which involves compatibility with existing institutional or organisational structures (Kingdon 2003[1984]: 131–2; Rüb 2009: 355). Thus, the institutional setting is important for the criterion of technical feasibility. Put simply, proposals that are difficult to implement have a lower chance of surviving the selection process (Kingdon 2003[1984]: 72). Independent of their feasibility, ideas that do not conform to the values of policy-makers are less likely to be considered for adoption. Since the perceptions and preferences of actors are strongly influenced by the current institutional context (Scharpf 2000), institutions shape the common understanding of equity. HI theorists argue that institutions are reproduced because actors believe they are morally just or appropriate (Mahoney 2000: 517). Furthermore policy-makers evaluate the efficiency of alternatives (Kingdon 2003[1984]: 136–7) and may choose to reproduce even sub-optimal institutions. They may choose this through rational cost–benefit assessments, because any potential benefits of transformations may be outweighed by their costs (Mahoney 2000: 517). In sum, as long as established institutions fulfil the criteria of equity and efficiency, they have a self-reinforcing effect and decisions on policies are path-dependent.

Moreover, whether an idea will float to the top of the policy stream depends on its network's degree of integration and the mode of exchange (Kingdon 2003[1984]). In integrated networks, participants are supposed to be consensus-seekers. Because of a search for unanimity, ideas tend to be worked out internally, before they are aired in public. Slow entry into the stream and a long softening-up process[1] is expected. Less integrated networks with a competitive mode are more open for new actors and ideas, which are likely to enter the policy stream quite abruptly without regard for continuity with pre-existing policies (Zahariadis and Allen 1995). Thus, ideas which are path-changing have a greater chance of popping up in the policy stream in less integrated networks.

The *politics stream* is most likely to encompass institutions as part of the explanation, but even the refinement of Zahariadis does not capture institutional arrangements (Schlager 1999: 247). The MSF only refers to the fluid, changeable aspects of politics, such as shifts in public mood, changes in the preferences of policy-makers, governing-party turnover and the emergence of new interest-groups (Mucciaroni 1992: 466). However, institutions influence variables that determine the dynamic in the politics stream. First, political institutions constitute part of the national mood, which is a core variable in Kingdon's explanation of agenda-setting. Second, institutions empower and shape constellations of actors. Even unpopular institutions are reproduced, if they are supported by elite groups that benefit from existing arrangements (Mahoney 2000: 521). Third, formal and informal 'veto-points' tend to lock existing policy arrangements into place and push reform-agendas in the direction of incremental adjustments to existing arrangements (Pierson 2001: 414).

Since HI views institutions in configurative turns, emphasising their path-dependent qualities (Cox 2001: 474), it tends to overestimate resistance to change. Due to the general stability of institutions, it is argued that change in well institutionalised polities is likely to be both incremental and bounded. Nonetheless, Mahoney (2000: 517–18) points out mechanisms for reversing self-reinforcing processes, which can be applied in the MSF. An increased competitive pressure can trigger change in the policy stream, when it is no longer efficient to follow a distinct path. Learning processes, which help rational actors to anticipate negative consequences and encourage them to absorb short-term costs, have a comparable effect. A weakening of elites and strengthening of subordinated groups can induce change either in policy-networks or in the politics stream, where organised interests are an important indicator for governments. Similarly, changes in the values or beliefs of actors affect the selection-criteria for ideas in the policy stream, as well as the national mood in the politics stream.

---

1. The term 'softening-up' refers to the process of getting policy communities and larger publics used to new ideas and building acceptance for proposals (Kingdon 2003[1984]: 128).

It is argued here that these mechanisms are necessary, but not sufficient, for a path-departure. In addition to changes in the three streams, other elements are needed: *windows of opportunity* as critical moments when change is possible; and *policy entrepreneurs*, who strategically exploit the ambivalence of institutions, values and problems. The assumption that actors can manipulate the context of decision-making links the two approaches. A strategy is captured in the MSF by the manipulating the skills of policy entrepreneurs, who couple problems, policies and politics into a single package (Zahariadis 2007: 77): HI takes into account institutional ambiguity by noticing that ideational repertoires may have different meanings to different actors (Borrás and Radaelli 2011: 474). In particular, Pierson (1996, 2001) introduced the strategic use of ambiguity by politicians to institutional theory.

Therefore, HI and the MSF are well suited to connect ambiguity and political manipulation (Borrás and Radaelli 2011: 474). In both approaches, two strategic skills of political actors are crucial for the successful enacting of path-departing policies.

First, advocates of a reform need to employ strategies to overcome the scepticism of others. Such *path-shaping* can cause policy reform when actors change the discourse in an area of policy, establishing new grounds for evaluating the legitimacy of policy-proposals (Cox 2001: 474–5). Political actors frame alternatives in ways that could increase their popular support. Frames constitute a discourse that helps political actors to sell policy choices to the public. Policy-makers can also frame policy alternatives in a manner that hides their actual departure from a well accepted paradigm (Béland 2005: 2, 11). Similarly, problem-representation makes a difference in what people perceive to be losses or gains and helps entrepreneurs to establish their interpretation in ambiguous situations (Zahariadis 2007: 77; Rüb 2009: 362).

Second, *blame-avoidance* for unpopular policies is important (Weaver 1986, Pierson 1996). The success of entrepreneurs will vary with the chances of lowering the visibility of reforms, either by obscuring the impact of reforms on voters or diminishing their own accountability. With regard to the former, the prospects of changing institutions may be of great significance, if advocates can restructure the way in which the trade-offs between taxes, spending and deficits are presented (Pierson 1996: 177–8); or when 'salami tactics' cut the process into small stages which are presented sequentially to reach the desired solution (Zahariadis 2007: 78). If a blame-generating decision has to be made, policy-makers are likely to delegate it to someone else, for example, to another level of government or a commission. Another tactic is to find a scapegoat by claiming that the action was made necessary by someone else (Weaver 1986: 386–7). Additionally, unpopular decisions may be facilitated when governments have significant electoral slack, that is, when they believe that their support is strong enough to absorb the electoral consequences (Pierson 1996: 176).

In sum, the argument here is that a successful path-departure needs to fulfil three criteria. First, a change in the policy stream, due to competitive pressure or learning effects that challenge the reproduction of institutions and the path-dependent evolution of ideas. The structure of policy-networks is an intervening factor, since the development of path-departing options is more likely in less integrated networks. Second, a window of opportunity, which opens either in the problem stream, as an exogenous shock, or in the politics stream, due to a weakening of elites or changes in values or beliefs. Third, policy entrepreneurs need to apply techniques of path-shaping and blame-avoidance.

This argument will be tested in two case studies dealing with activating labour-market reforms. Activating policies combine two elements that are expected to reconcile individual expectations with vacancies on the labour market. *Workfare* policies aim towards rapid integration of the jobless into the labour market, by making benefits conditional upon job-search activities, stricter availability-criteria and sanctions for non-compliance. *Enabling* policies enhance individual employability by qualification and training measures, to make job-searchers more attractive to potential employers. Appropriate measures for this purpose are active labour-market policies like job-search assistance, training schemes and subsidised employment. Active labour-market policies aim at a better matching of labour-supply and -demand, that is, an improvement of labour-market structures. In contrast, an activating approach promotes an improvement of individuals' employability, including a modification of work attitudes and personal behaviour. Following the principle of benefit-conditionality in an activating approach, participation in training schemes is made mandatory by being a prerequisite for further benefit-receipt. In addition, measures to make work pay, like earnings-disregard clauses or wage supplements (in-work benefits), serve as incentives to take up low-paid jobs (Eichhorst and Konle-Seidl 2008: 4–5; Lodemel and Trickey 2000: 6; Serrano Pascual 2007). Due to their explicit focus on integration into the labour market, activating policies cause an enhancement of the re-commodification of labour,[2] the conditionality of social rights and the flexibility of labour markets (Dingeldey 2007).

Two activating reforms cases were selected, exhibiting two different path-departures. The Labour government's employability reforms intervened in the liberal British welfare state by combining tax credits and a minimum wage; while labour-market reforms had traditionally focused on re-commodification and cost-containment. In contrast, the workfare reforms made by the Alliance for Sweden took the form of a deviation from the universalistic, de-commodifying Swedish welfare state.

Labour-market reform in the United Kingdom

The Labour government under Prime Minister Tony Blair implemented a fundamental reform of labour-market policies in 1997 and 1998. The diverse New Deal schemes were the first noteworthy active employment policies in the

---

2. De-commodification is the degree to which social rights permit people to make their living standards independent of pure market forces (Esping-Andersen 1990: 3). Accordingly, re-commodification is the weakening of social rights.

UK. Recipients of benefits now had to undertake training and take up subsidised jobs. In combination with the introduction of negative taxes (tax-credits) and a minimum wage, this marked a significant change in British employment policies, which were traditionally characterised by only limited state interventionism (Lindsay 2007: 39).

The policy stream and mechanisms of change

Workfare policies were largely feasible within British institutions, since improving work incentives is common in liberal welfare regimes. Labour-market- and wage-flexibility is treated as a buffer against high unemployment, which implies a hardening of conditions for income-support by tightening eligibility rules and reducing benefit levels significantly (Pierson 2001: 434–5). This is backed by the British understanding of equity, including the promotion of self-regulation and scepticism towards social-welfare policies (Sturm 2009: 292). Differentiation between the 'deserving' and 'undeserving' poor legitimates the enhancement of work incentives by cutting welfare rights, and reducing the reservation wages of unemployed people. In contrast, expenses for enabling policies were less acceptable, because of British scepticism towards the welfare state. Until the middle of the 1990s, virtually no active labour-market policies were present in the UK. The absence of intermediate labour markets for the most vulnerable is an essential characteristic of the Anglo-American model (Daguerre and Taylor-Gooby 2002: 27). Furthermore, Britain has only a poorly institutionalised system of vocational training as a result of pluralistic labour-relations and weak unions (Schmid and Picot 2001: 235–6). That a large proportion of the UK's workforce had only low qualifications had two consequences. On the one hand, technological change hit the UK severely (Hills 1998: 16). It resulted in a significant mismatch between the unemployed and job vacancies. On the other hand, jobs obtained by former unemployed were mostly in the low-pay sector. This served business interests in the sense that it created a cheap labour force at an employer's disposal, the 'working poor'. Therefore, conservative governments under Thatcher and Major followed the usual British path of labour-market de-regulation and low workforce-qualification level. However, by the early 1990s, even the Confederation of British Industry (CBI) was putting increasing stress on the need to train the labour force and acknowledged that more money should be spent for this purpose (Daguerre, Larsen and Taylor-Gooby 2003: 110).

Another factor that hampered the evolution of enabling policies was the structure of the policy-network. The policies of the British welfare state were mainly developed by the politically neutral and permanent civil service ('Whitehall'). Whitehall, due to its expertise in the implementation of social and labour-market policies, is responsible for working out the alternatives upon which the minister decides. Although networks within Whitehall tend to be messy, the absolute number of participants in the policy-network is relatively small (Kavanagh *et al.* 2006: 221–3). Furthermore, the British policy-network had been department-centred and little effort had gone into making sure that policies were devised across institutional boundaries. This hampered the development of policies that stretched over a variety of areas, like enabling policies.

Meanwhile, the opposition Labour party formed a parallel policy-network by consulting with a range of actors, including interest-groups, think-tanks and academics, on the issues and policy areas that would enable the party to adjust its policies to appeal to a changing electorate with more swing voters (Hay and Richards 2000: 6). A Commission on Social Justice was initiated to meld economic competitiveness and social-democratic goals in a supply-side-oriented agenda of the left. The commission suggested continuing 'Tory policies for affordable social security which actively encourages participation in work, including low paid and relatively insecure work' (Commission on Social Justice 1994: 221). The commission's argumentation that voluntary programmes were not effective and would not solve problems of behaviour became widely accepted by Labour's policy-specialists. Nonetheless, the Commission on Social Justice also suggested policies to enhance employability, by fostering lifelong learning and a making-work-pay approach using tax-credits and a minimum wage. Viewing education and training investments as legitimate public spending, these policies differed from the dominating ideas of de-regulation and state restraint.

Agenda-setting and political manipulation

Tony Blair and the Chancellor of the Exchequer, Gordon Brown, as agents of strategic change (Kavanagh *et al.* 2006: 233), promoted the ideas of the Commission on Social Justice but they placed a greater emphasis on compulsion. Blair and Brown wanted to take tough stances on issues like fiscal conservatism and welfare, to reassure middle-class voters about the limits to the party's egalitarian aspirations (King and Wickham-Jones 1999: 67). To free the Labour Party from its tax-and-spend image, Brown and Blair promoted activating and supply-side-oriented policies, which combined social-democratic goals with competitiveness and budgetary discipline.

The opportunity to put these policies on the agenda came up in the context of the 1997 elections. As early as in September 1995, the criticism had been made that the Labour Party was weakly positioned in some policy areas. A confidential paper by Philip Gould, the party's campaigns and strategy consultant, warned that the party lacked the political ideas to sustain a Labour government in power and urged Blair to draw up a definitive statement of his New Labour message (Wood 1995). While the conservatives had clear positions on labour-market and social policies, Labour's positions remained vague. Brown took this opportunity to announce a 'welfare-to-work programme' to combat youth unemployment, consisting of in-work benefits, education and work training, but also sanctions in case of non-compliance; this later became the New Deal for Young People (King and Wickham-Jones 1999: 69). In its election manifesto, Labour focused on getting the young and long-term unemployed back to work, by encouraging employment and work incentives with a welfare-to-work programme and a making-work-pay approach, in order to guarantee a significantly higher income from working compared to social benefits, by means of employment subsidies and a (moderate) minimum wage. 'The best way to tackle poverty is to help people into jobs – real jobs. The unemployed have the responsibility to take up the opportunity of training places or work, but these must be real opportunities' (Labour Party 1997). If windows open in the politics stream, attention is focused on solutions first before problems can be clearly defined. In such cases, the process is ideological. 'What matters more is the solution to be adopted rather than the problem to be solved.' (Zahariadis 2007: 75–6).

Unemployment was not a pressing problem at that time. The interventions of the former conservative government contributed to a marked fall in unemployment that the Labour government inherited (Finn 2001: 75–6). Paradoxically, this unburdened the agenda-setting of the reforms, since enabling policies are more costly and stricter benefit conditionality is more difficult to legitimate when availability of jobs is diminishing (Clasen 2000: 107). Singling out young people to participate in activation policies acted as additional legitimisation, because persuading the public to agree that the principle of compulsion should be applied to this relatively unpopular group was unlikely to be difficult (Clasen 2000: 100–1).

However, expenditure on employability policies was unpopular in the UK. The support-group for the welfare state is relatively small and the median voter is likely to be comparatively far to the right. Means-testing divides the recipients of benefits from most taxpayers and the institutionalisation of market alternatives weakens middle-class attachment to public provision (Pierson 2001). After eighteen years of Thatcherism, the UK's middle class had become increasingly resistant to providing resources to the unemployed. At the same time, the progressive electorate has been galvanised in defence of social rights (Clasen and Clegg 2004: 95). This divided national mood posed a twofold problem for activating policies. On the one hand, the financial outlay for costly New Deal policies needed to be justified; on the other hand, the coercive approach ran counter to previous Labour positions (King and Wickham-Jones 1999: 69–70). To persuade new voters without alienating the old ones, Blair shaped the path for the scheduled reform by establishing grounds for its legitimacy: activation policies were announced in accordance with the principle of reciprocity, which means that social-rights imply corresponding duties. 'We will design a modern welfare state based on rights and duties' (Labour Party 1997: 4). This dualism is connected to the differentiation between 'deserving' and 'undeserving' poor and served to legitimate the coercive workfare approach in the labour party, as well as to appease the welfare-sceptical median voter.

> Citizenship gives rights but demands obligations, shows respect but wants it back, grants opportunities but insists on responsibilities. So the purpose of economic and social policy should be to extend opportunity, to remove the underlying causes of social alienation. But it should also take tough measures to ensure that the chances that are given are taken up (Blair 1996: 218–19).

The party's welfare-to-work programme became a flagship policy in the election campaign. Its tough stance on welfare issues helped the Labour Party to win over middle-class voters (King and Wickham-Jones 1999: 73). After Labour won the 1997 general election, the new government reorganised the department-centred and sealed-off structures of policy-making, to pursue a cross-policy approach (Cabinet Office 1999). Led by Gordon Brown, HM Treasury took on a special role, co-ordinating the other departments by a Comprehensive Spending Review (Kavanagh *et al.* 2006: 201). Furthermore, stakeholders and experts were increasingly involved in diverse councils and commissions. This restructuring of policy-networks significantly reduced the influence of Whitehall and aimed to introduce new actors and ideas and to legitimise and depoliticise controversial issues. For example, in July 1997, the Low Pay Commission was established, in which representatives of unions and employers' associations among others produced recommendations to the government on the level at which a national minimum wage should be set. At that time, the introduction of a minimum wage was a highly contentious issue. However, the Labour Party tended to listen more to employers than employees and, in general, emphasised inclusive methods only when they were unable to control powerful stakeholders (Daguerre, Larsen and Taylor-Gooby 2003: 91; Larsen, Taylor-Gooby and Kananen 2006: 643–4).

Instead of avoiding blame for spending cuts, the Blair government rather followed a strategy of credit-avoidance for the expansion of the welfare state (Zohlnhöfer 2007: 1127). Labour lowered the visibility of the redistributive character of the reforms by restructuring the way in which trade-offs between taxes and spending were presented. The costly New Deals were met by a windfall tax on the profits on newly privatised utilities (Labour Party 1997: 12) and therefore were not perceived as expenditure falling on regular taxpayers. The other employability policies were supported by financial incentives, securing income-protection with a minimum wage and tax credits with the intention of increasing differentials between incomes in and out of work. The new Working Families Tax Credit was a 'rebranding' of the old Family Credit, which had the presentational advantage that part of the costs appeared in the public accounts as lower taxation rather than as higher public spending (Hills 1998: 27–8). This restructuring was inspired by the US Earned Income Tax Credit (EITC).

> It would ensure greater acceptability to both the claimants and taxpayers. It is noticeable that the US Administration has secured widespread political support for the EITC at a time when the US welfare budget more generally has been under remorseless attack (HM Treasury 1998: 20).

In a 'salami tactic' activation policies were cut up into small stages. In 1997, the New Deal was initially introduced as a New Deal *for Young People.* The fact that the New Deals initially focused on the young helped to justify activation policies. An improved labour-market situation, with a decreasing number of young, long-term unemployed, made policies less expensive and appear more successful (Clasen 2000: 100). After the Employment Department evaluated the New Deal for Young People positively, and the revenue from the windfall tax was higher than expected, cabinet members demanded the extension of the New Deals to other target groups. Accordingly, in 1998 and 1999 the Government successively introduced New Deals for long-term unemployed, for disabled people, for lone parents, for partners of the unemployed and for the over-50s (Spohr 2016: 115–31).

Labour-market reform in Sweden

The reforms adopted in 2007 by the Alliance for Sweden, a coalition of four centre-right parties, focused on the activation of the unemployed by the retrenchment of benefits and the use of stronger compulsion, combined with a making-work-pay strategy operating *via* a negative income tax. The impact of the reform has been a strong re-commodification, which meant a path-departure in the Swedish context. In social-democratic regimes, restructuring of the welfare state usually focuses on cost-containment and the recalibration of programmes; retrenchment and re-commodification are not common alternatives (Pierson 2001).

The policy stream and mechanisms of change

The concept of activation was not in itself a new idea in the Swedish policy stream. Social-democratic regimes focus on the development of human capital (Pierson 2001: 442). Skills-enhancement and pushing people into work has always been at the centre of Swedish labour-market policies. Universalism and equality are pursued by the inclusion of the whole population in work. As a consequence of the goal of full employment, the priority of employment over benefits – the work-first principle – is institutionalised (Jochem 2009: 8). However, full employment is not only a normative goal, it is also necessary to finance the universal welfare state, since both social expenditure and the total tax-burden in Sweden are among the highest in the world (Kangas and Palme 2009: 70). Because the high level of de-commodification was reached by producing a high rate of employment, active employment policies had a priority over transfer payments. Accordingly, activating policies were technically feasible in the Swedish welfare state. However, as long as full employment remained, the workfare element attracted hardly any attention. This changed due to the recession in the 1990s (Schwarze 2012: 241–2; Wadensjö 2007: 140–2). Two mechanisms of change promoted activating and re-commodifying policies.

First, competitive pressures had implications for the acceptability and feasibility of policies in Sweden. By the mid–late 1970s, affected by global recession, Sweden's economic performance began to drop below the OECD average. In the context of currency devaluations, rising inflation and declining economic growth, neo-liberal norms successfully permeated Swedish policy-networks. Economic debates were dominated by the idea of 'Swedosclerosis', which means that the welfare state undermined Sweden's international competitiveness and was causing Sweden's economic growth to lag behind comparable countries. By the end of the 1980s, this argument had become widely accepted. Indeed, both social expenditure and the total tax-burden in Sweden are among the highest in the world and, in the 1990s, Sweden experienced a severe economic recession, which put heavy pressure on public finances (Agius 2007: 590–1; Kangas and Palme 2009: 68–70).

At the same time, the convergence criteria for entry in the European Monetary Union (EMU) demanded budget consolidation. Thus, pursuing a traditional full-employment policy was no longer possible (Eichhorst and Wintermann 2005: 23).

Second, a weakening of elites supported change in the policy stream, which was interrelated with changes in the policy-networks. The decline of Swedish corporatism started in the 1980s and was present in all policy sectors, including the labour market (Christiansen *et al.* 2010: 32). Particularly in the 1990s, the most important welfare-state reforms were not designed in co-operation with social partners but mainly pushed through by governments in a unilateral way. Instead, government-financed commissions played a significant role in the development of social and employment policies. These commissions act as forums for parliamentarians, representatives of the bureaucracy, research institutes and (occasionally) interest-groups. The Swedish commissions form the nucleus of a policy-making process that produces generally acceptable policy-decisions. Their work is issue-oriented and deliberative, with a pragmatic approach to social problems and their potential solutions (Bergh and Erlingsson 2009; Eichhorst and Wintermann 2005: 23). Because the commissions are usually temporary and installed *ad hoc*, participation is fluid and relatively open to new actors. In Swedish policy-networks, path-departing ideas could enter the policy stream due to its competitive mode: various commissions produce different options that compete with each other.

In sum, as a result of increasing competitive pressure and the erosion of corporatism, a change from active and demand-side-oriented to activating and supply-side-oriented ideas could be observed in the Swedish policy stream. While activating concepts were predominant in the policy stream, a stronger commodification, by lowering wages and social benefits, proved to be politically difficult to pursue. The Swedish government's policy discretion is narrowed since social provision by a universal, income-based unemployment insurance scheme enjoys strong popular support. Working for a wage under the poverty line and the creation of excessive flexibility in the labour market were unacceptable to the middle class (Timonen 2003: 41). Furthermore, although the trade unions' importance had declined in policy-making, they remained a strong actor in the politics stream. Trade unions are both possible partners in dialogue and formidable political opponents in cases where dialogue fails (Pierson 2001). This was proven when the social-democratic government withdrew the plan to tighten the public unemployed insurance in 1996 and 1997, when trade unions demonstrated against a social-democratic government for the first time (Clasen and Viebrock 2005: 47). And the Activity Guarantee in 2001, the largest scheme of active labour-market policies, was weakened because the unions rejected the idea of exerting pressure on the unemployed to seek work by reducing their benefits.

Agenda-setting and political manipulation

Fredrik Reinfeldt, chairman of the liberal-conservative Moderate Party and subsequent Prime Minister, along with his Finance Minister, Anders Borg, were entrepreneurs of a supply-side-oriented agenda consisting of lowering taxes and benefits and establishing a low-pay sector.

Borg's priority was sound public finances. He advocated the making-work-pay idea and a strict commodification in labour-market policy. To pursue tax cuts and commodification, these policies were coupled with the problem of unemployment in a package of activating labour-market reforms. Thus, the logic of attention was ideological: policies were made in search of a rationale (Zahariadis 2007: 75–6). The Moderate Party emphasised unemployment in the election campaign for two reasons. On the one hand, due to robust public finances in 2006, unemployment filled the 'something-to-complain-about gap' (Toynbee 2006). On the other hand, despite strong economic growth, the SAP failed to reach its target of 4 per cent unemployment. Prime Minister Persson, however, maintained that his policy on unemployment would not change, making it seem that the SAP had little to offer apart from extending benefits. Led by the Moderate Party, the Alliance for Sweden made unemployment its key election issue in 2006; it campaigned to preserve the welfare state while making some relatively minor adjustments (Agius 2007: 586, 593). Concerning the pro-welfare Swedish national mood, Reinfeldt dropped the Moderates' former radical neo-liberal programme and adjusted the Moderate Party 'to what is considered the best possible option in the existing context' (Lindbom 2008: 544). He did it by transforming the party into the 'new workers' party', 'Nya Moderaterna', which claimed to defend the 'Swedish model' and the welfare state by making it competitive and viable and emphasising individualism (Agius 2007: 587, 592; Jochem 2012: 88). Reinfeldt drew on a social-democratic narrative incorporating terms like 'the Swedish model', 'the work-first principle', and 'exclusion' (Bengtsson 2010). By use of these positive, but ambiguous, terms, Reinfeldt shaped the path for the later reforms by altering the national discourse.

> We want our work to stand for clear values, which have been shown to enjoy broad support among the Swedish people. Values that are about people's control over their daily lives, about the work-first principle and the goal of full employment. About effective and tax-financed welfare services. ... The basis of our Government's policy is, and will remain, the fight for full employment. By reasserting the work-first principle and the value of work, more people will have the opportunity to take part in building Sweden. It is a policy that provides resources for good welfare, and hence security, for all of us when we need it. It is a policy that in the long term reduces the gaps and combats exclusion (Reinfeldt 2007: 14–15).

A strategy of path-shaping was the representation of unemployment as a problem of structural exclusion from the labour market. Reinfeldt argued that the social democratic government figures on unemployment masked the real extent of the number of jobless. According to his statements, a quarter of the workforce was unemployed, on extended sick leave or had taken early retirement; immigrants and youth, especially, were 'excluded' from the labour market. Sweden lacked a 'business climate', fostering dependence on the welfare state (Agius 2007: 586). Furthermore, he blamed the welfare state for eroding the Swedish work ethic and the system of high taxes and generous welfare for punishing hard work. Reinfeldt employed this problem-definition to bring the Moderate Party's policies into accordance not only with the problem of unemployment but also with the Swedish national mood. His rhetoric drew on the Swedish ambivalence between the goals of de-commodification and full employment. 'The way for the future is increasing the incentive to work, to get better value for money and better results in tax-paid welfare' (*Daily Mail* 2006: 12).

The election of the conservative Alliance for Sweden and Prime Minister Reinfeldt in 2006 opened a window of opportunity for the agenda-setting of these policies. For the first time in 25 years, the Swedish government had a majority in parliament, which allowed the coalition to implement controversial policies without taking into account the Swedish imperative of consensus and negotiation. Although the Swedish political system contains few checks on parliamentary majorities, the frequency of coalition or minority governments makes political authority less concentrated than in Westminster settings (Pierson 2001: 440). Therefore, reforms usually tend to be negotiated, consensual and incremental.

In December 2006, shortly after the new majority government took office, the Swedish parliament approved the labour-market reform. It consisted of three tiers. First, a making-work-pay approach, including an in-work tax-credit for low- and medium-income wage earners, 'which makes it more worthwhile to work' (Swedish Government 2008: 17) and reductions in social contributions to make it cheaper to take on employees (Finansdepartementet 2007: 19). Second, a change from active to activating labour-market policies, by curtailing active labour-market programmes and imposing stricter rules for the receipt of benefits. Insufficient job-search efforts could be sanctioned and the replacement rate of the previous income was lowered. Third, highlighting the work-first principle in unemployment insurance by reductions in benefit-levels and rights to benefit, which enhanced commodification and the pressure to take up low-wage jobs.

The short time-period for preparing and adopting these policies was unusual for consensus-oriented Swedish policy-making. Normally, such a big change would have been referred for long consideration and inquiry. The Minister of Employment, Sven-Otto Littorin, admitted that the goal of the government was to implement these unpopular reforms as fast as possible (Gamilscheg 2007: 6). 'But this is smart politics – get the unpopular policies out of the way early so that they are distant memory by the time the election comes around, especially if these decisions are translated into economic benefits in the long term' (Gregory 2007). Since the party needed its proposals to be implemented very soon in order to have a chance of winning the election in 2010 (Lindbom 2008: 557), the window of opportunity was open only for a short time.

Conclusion

The case studies of labour-market reforms in the UK and Sweden have proved institutions to be important in all streams. In the problem stream, institutions shape values that resonate in society and therefore affect interpretations and definitions of problems. Similarly, the institutional setting influences the selection-criteria for ideas in the policy stream, which biases path-dependent evolution of policies. Lastly, institutions influence the national mood, which determines the dynamic in the politics stream and empowers and shapes constellations of actors.

How does the inclusion of institutions affect the MSF? Since the same institutions filter problems, structure policies and influence politics, institutionalisation obviously reduces contingency and bring into question the independence of streams, the basic assumption of the framework. However, combined with institutionalism, the MSF still seems to be suitable for explaining contingency and change in policy-areas that are characterised by a high degree of institutionalisation. Historical institutionalism not only provides explanations for path-dependence but also mechanisms for permitting path-departing change. The case studies have shown that the path-dependent evolution of policies is challenged mainly by competitive pressures; but also by policy-learning. In addition, change in the policy stream is interrelated with changes in policy-networks. In both countries, a weakening of traditional elites (the civil service in the UK and the social partners in Sweden) enabled the advance of new ideas.

The argument put forward in this chapter is that a change in the policy stream is a necessary, but not sufficient, condition for a path-departure. Windows of opportunity – as critical moments at which change is possible – are a further condition for change. In both case studies, the window of opportunity for agenda-setting opened in the politics stream and the logic of attention was ideological; the solutions to be adopted mattered more than the problems to be solved. A moderate problem-pressure proved to be advantageous for implementing the path-departing reforms.

However, the opportunities of open windows need to be used by policy entrepreneurs. Particularly, two strategic skills of policy entrepreneurs are crucial for the successful enacting of path-departing policies. On the one hand, advocates of a reform need to employ strategies to overcome the scepticism of others. Such path-shaping involves creating a discourse that changes the collective understanding of the welfare state in both cases. British Prime Minister Tony Blair announced activating policies in accordance with the principle of reciprocity, which means that social rights imply duties. In comparison, Swedish Prime Minister Fredrik Reinfeldt represented unemployment as a problem of structural exclusion and used positive loaded but ambiguous terms to shape the path for his reforms. On the other hand, it is important to avoid the blame for unpopular policies. Labour used a 'salami tactic' by cutting the reform into small stages, established commissions to legitimise and depoliticise controversial policies and lowered the visibility of reforms by restructuring the way in which trade-offs between taxes and spending were presented. The Alliance for Sweden used its electoral slack, by implementing the reforms very soon in order to absorb the electoral consequences for the next election.

Nonetheless, this argument must evidently be subject to further research on other policy areas to test its viability. A particularly interesting case would certainly be pension policies, which are characterised by particularly strong path-dependence.

References

Agius, C. (2007) 'Sweden's 2006 parliamentary election and after: contesting or consolidating the Swedish model?', *Parliamentary Affairs* 60(4): 585–600.

Barbier, J.-C. and Ludwig-Mayerhofer, W. (2004) 'The many worlds of activation', *European Societies* 6(4): 423–36.

Bengtsson, H. A. (2010) 'Die schwedische Sozialdemokratie nach der Wahl 2010. Hintergründe, Strategie und Ergebnisse', Friedrich Ebert Stiftung, available at: http://library.fes.de/pdf-files/id/ipa/07503.pdf (accessed 10 October 2014).

Béland, D. (2005) 'Ideas and social policy: an institutionalist perspective', *Social Policy & Administration* 39(1): 1–18.

Bergh, A. and Erlingsson, G. Ö. (2009) 'Liberalization without retrenchment: understanding the consensus on Swedish welfare state reforms', *Scandinavian Political Studies* 32(1): 71–93.

Berkel, R. van and Hornemann Møller, I. (eds) (2002) *Active Social Policies in the EU: Inclusion through participation?*, Bristol, UK: Policy Press.

Blair, T. (1996) *New Britain: My vision of a young country*, London: Macmillan.

Borrás, S. and Radaelli, C. M. (2011) 'The politics of governance architectures: creation, change and effects of the EU Lisbon Strategy', *Journal of European Public Policy* 18(4): 463–84.

Boyle, N. and Schünemann, W. (2009) 'The malleable politics of activation reform: the "Hartz" reforms in comparative perspective', paper presented at the EUSA Biennial Conference, Los Angeles, April 2009.

Cabinet Office (1999) *Modernising Government, Presented to Parliament by the Prime Minister and the Minister for the Cabinet Office, by Command of Her Majesty*, London: HM Stationery Office.

Christiansen, P. M., Nørgaard, A., Rommetvedt, H., Svensson, T., Thesen, G. and Öberg, P. (2010) 'Varieties of democracy: interest groups and corporatist committees in Scandinavian policy making', *Voluntas* 21(1): 22–40.

Clasen, J. (2000) 'Motives, means and opportunities: reforming unemployment compensation in the 1990s', *West European Politics*, 23(2): 89–112.

Clasen, J. and Clegg, D. (2004) 'Does the Third Way work? The Left and labour market policy reform in Britain, France and Germany', in J. Lewis and R. Surender (eds) *Welfare State Change: Towards a third way?*, Oxford, UK: Oxford University Press, pp. 89–110.

Clasen, J. and Viebrock, E. (2006) 'Das Genter System der Arbeitslosenversicherung – immer noch gewerkschaftliches Rekrutierungsinstrument oder sozialpolitisches Auslaufmodell? Dänemark und Schweden im Vergleich', *Zeitschrift für Sozialreform* 52(3): 351–71.

Commission on Social Justice (1994) *Social Justice: Strategy for national renewal*, London: Vintage/IPPR.

Cox, R. H. (2001) 'The social construction of an imperative. Why welfare reform happened in Denmark and the Netherlands but not in Germany', *World Politics* 53(3): 463–98.

Daguerre, A. and Taylor-Gooby, P. (2002) 'Welfare reform in the UK, 1985–2002', working paper, University of Kent, available at: http://s3.amazonaws.com/zanran_storage/www.kent.ac.uk/ContentPages/3151974.pdf (accessed 6 October 2015).

Daguerre A., Larsen, T.P. and Taylor-Gooby, P. (2003) 'The UK: policy maps on employment, social assistance, long-term care, women and the labour market and pensions', working paper, University of Kent, available at: http://www.sociology.ku.dk/research/research_groups/welfare-inequality-and-mobility/?pure=en%2Fpublications%2Fthe-uk(1c386460-b4f1-11df-825b-000ea68e967b)%2Fexport.html (accessed 6 October 2015).

Daily Mail (2006) 'Swedish voters turn to the conservatives', 18 September, p. 12.

Dingeldey, I. (2007) 'Wohlfahrtsstaatlicher Wandel zwischen "Arbeitszwang" und "Befähigung". Eine vergleichende Analyse aktivierender Arbeitsmarktpolitik in Deutschland, Dänemark und Großbritannien', *Berliner Journal für Soziologie* 17(2): 189–209.

Esping-Andersen, G. (1990) *The Three Worlds of Welfare Capitalism*, Princeton, NJ: Princeton University Press.

Eichhorst, W. and Konle-Seidl, R. (2008) 'Contingent convergence: a comparative analysis of activation policies', IZA Discussion Paper No. 3905, available at: http:/ftp.iza.org/dp3905.pdf (accessed 15 October 2015).

Eichhorst, W. and Wintermann, O. (2005) 'Generating legitimacy for labor market and welfare state reforms: the role of policy advice in Germany, the Netherlands and Sweden', IZA Discussion Paper No. 1845, available at: http://ftp.iza.org/dp1845.pdf (accessed 6 October 2015).

Erhel, C. and Zajelda, H. (2004) 'The dynamics of social and labour market policies in France and the United Kingdom: between path dependency and convergence', *Journal of European Social Policy* 14(2): 125–42.

Finansdepartementet (2007) 'Budget Statement: economic and budget policy guidelines', Ministry of Finance, Sweden, Prop. 2006/07:1.

Finn, D. (2001) 'Welfare to work? New Labour and the unemployed', in S. P. Savage and R. Atkinson (eds) *Public Policy under Blair*, Basingstoke, UK: Palgrave, pp. 72–85.

Gamillscheg, H. (2007) 'Premier Reinfeldt hat die Schweden gründlich enttäuscht', *Frankfurter Rundschau*, 23 January, p. 6.

Gregory, N. (2007) 'Don't write off the government yet', available at: www.thelocal.se/8246/20070821 (accessed 10 October 2014).

Hay, C. and Richards, D. (2000) 'The tangled webs of Westminster and Whitehall: the discourse, strategy and practice of networking within the British core executive', *Public Administration* 78(1): 1–28.

Hills, J. (1998) 'Thatcherism, New Labour and the welfare state', Centre for Analysis of Social Exclusion discussion paper 13, available at: http://eprints.lse.ac.uk/5553/1/Thatcherism_New_Labour_and_the_Welfare_State.pdf (accessed 6 October 2015).

HM Treasury (1998) *The Modernisation of Britain's Tax and Benefit System (Number Two) – Work incentives: a report by Martin Taylor*, London: HM Treasury.

Jochem, S. (2009) 'Skandinavische Beschäftigungspolitik – Stärken und Schwächen im internationalen Vergleich', *WSI Mitteilungen*, 1/2009: 3–9.

Jochem, S. (2012) *Die politischen Systeme Skandinaviens*, Wiesbaden: VS.

Kangas, O. and Palme, J. (2009) 'Making social policy work for economic development: the Nordic experience', *International Journal of Social Welfare* 189(S1): S62–S72.

Kavanagh, D., Richards, D., Smith, M. and Geddes, A. (2006) *British Politics*, 5th edn, Oxford, UK: Oxford University Press.

King, D. and Wickham-Jones, M. (1999) 'From Clinton to Blair: the Democratic (Party) origins of welfare to work', *Political Quarterly* 70(1): 62–74.

Kingdon, J. W. (2003[1984]) *Agendas, Alternatives, and Public Policies*, 2nd edn, Boston, MA and Toronto: Longman.

Labour Party (1997) *New Labour Because Britain Deserves Better*, Labour Party Manifesto, General Election 1997, available at: http://www.politicsresources.net/area/uk/man/lab97.htm (accessed 7 October 2015).

Larsen, T. P., Taylor-Gooby, P. and Kananen, J. (2006) 'New Labour's policy style: a mix of policy approaches', *Journal of Social Policy* 35(4): 629–49.

Lindbom, A. (2008) 'The Swedish Conservative Party and the welfare state: institutional change and adapting preferences', *Government and Opposition* 43(4): 539–60.

Lindsay, C. (2007) 'The United Kingdom's "work first" welfare state and activation regimes in Europe', in A. Serrano Pascual and L. Magnusson (eds) *Reshaping Welfare States and Activation Regimes in Europe*, Brussels: P.I.E., pp. 35–70.

Lodemel, I. and Trickey, H. (2000) 'A new contract for social assistance', in I. Lodemel and H. Trickey (eds) *'An Offer You Can't Refuse'. Workfare in international perspective*, Bristol, UK: Policy Press, pp. 1–40.

Mahoney, J. (2000) 'Path dependency in historical sociology', *Theory & Society* 29(4): 508–48.

Mucciaroni, G. (1992) 'The garbage can model & the study of policy making: a critique', *Polity* 24(3): 459–82.

Peck, J. and Theodore, N. (2001) 'Exporting workfare/importing welfare-to-work: exploring the politics of Third Way policy transfer', *Political Geography* 20(4): 427–60.

Pierson, P. (1996) 'The new politics of the welfare state', *World Politics* 48(2): 143–79.

— (2001) 'Coping with permanent austerity. Welfare state restructuring in affluent democracies', in P. Pierson (ed.) *The New Politics of the Welfare State*, Oxford, UK: Oxford University Press.

Reinfeldt, F. (2007) 'Statement of Government Policy 18 September 2007', available at: http://www.government.se/contentassets/6b5aa5d6eefa48a

aa2faa1f6f4ca9fdd/statement-of-government-policy-18-september-2007 (accessed 15 October 2015).

Rüb, F. W. (2009) 'Multiple-Streams-Ansatz: Grundlagen, Probleme und Kritik', in K. Schubert and N. C. Bandelow (eds) *Lehrbuch der Politikfeldanalyse 2.0*, München: Oldenbourg.

Scharpf, F. W. (2000) *Interaktionsformen. Akteurzentrierter Institutionalismus in der Politikforschung*, Opladen: Leske+Budrich.

Schlager, E. (1999) 'A comparison of frameworks, theories, and models of policy processes', in Sabatier, P. A. (ed.): *Theories of the Policy Process*, Boulder, CO: Westview Press, pp. 233–60.

Schmid, J. and Picot, G. (2001) ' "Welfare to work" bei Blair und Schröder – eine Idee, zwei Realitäten?', in G. Hirscher and R. Sturm (eds) *Die Strategie des "Dritten Weges": Legitimation und Praxis sozialdemokratischer Regierungspolitik*, München, DE: Olzog.

Schwarze, U. (2012) *Sozialhilfe in Schweden und Deutschland. Lebenslaufpolitik zwischen modernisierter Kommunalverwaltung und aktivierendem Wohlfahrtsstaat*, Wiesbaden, DE: VS.

Serrano Pascual, A. (2007) 'Reshaping welfare states: activating regimes in Europe', in A. Pascual Serrano and L. Magnusson (eds) *Reshaping Welfare States and Activation Regimes in Europe*, Brussels, Bern, Berlin, Frankfurt, New York, Oxford and Vienna: Peter Lang, pp. 11–34.

Spohr, F. (2015) *Pfadwechsel in der Arbeitsmarktpolitik. Eine Analyse aktivierender Reformen in Großbritannien, Deutschland und Schweden anhand des Multiple Streams Ansatzes*, Baden-Baden, DE: Nomos.

Sturm, R. (2009) 'Das politische System Großbritanniens', in W. Ismayr (ed.) *Die politischen Systeme Westeuropas*, 4th edn, Wiesbaden, DE: VS.

Swedish Government (2008) *The Swedish Reform Programme for Growth and Jobs 2008–2010*, available at: http://www.government.se/contentassets/ 47d9ce7a43bc4229a3ee7c330984e2bf/the-swedish-reform-programme-for-growth-and-employment-2008-2010 (accessed 15 October 2015).

Timonen, V. (2003) *Policy Maps – Finland and Sweden*, working paper, University of Kent, available at: www.kent.ac.uk/wramsoc/workingpapers/index. htm (accessed 5 September 2012).

Toynbee, P. (2006) 'Brown must beware the human hunger for the shock of the new: the Chancellor must use the plight of the Swedish social democrats as a spur to make a radical break with the past', *Guardian*, 25 August, available at: http://www.theguardian.com/commentisfree/2006/aug/25/ comment.politics (accessed 13 October 2015).

Wadensjö, E. (2007) 'Activation policy in Sweden', in A. Serrano Pascual and L. Magnusson (eds) *Reshaping Welfare States and Activation Regimes in Europe*, Brussels: P.I.E., pp. 127–44.

Weaver, K. R. (1986) 'The politics of blame avoidance', *Journal of Public Policy* 6(4): 371–98.

Wood, N. (1995) 'Leaked memo says Labour "not ready to govern"', *Times*, 12 September.

Zahariadis, N. (2007) 'The multiple streams framework: structure, limitations, prospects', in P. A. Sabatier (ed.) *Theories of the Policy Process*, 2nd edn, Boulder, CO: Westview Press, pp. 69–92.

Zahariadis, N. and Allen, C. S. (1995) 'Ideas, networks, and policy streams: privatization in Britain and Germany', *Policy Studies Review* 14(1/2): 71–98.

Zohlnhöfer, R. (2007) 'The politics of budget consolidation in Britain and Germany: the impact of blame avoidance opportunities', *West European Politics* 30(5): 1120–38.

Index

Note: Locators followed by '*f*' and '*t*' refer to figures and tables respectively

www.ingramcontent.com/pod-product-compliance
Lightning Source LLC
Chambersburg PA
CBHW072055020426

42334CB00017B/1523